INDIA'S ECONOMIC DEVELOPMENT

INDIA'S ECONOMIC DEVELOPMENT

Falendra K. Sudan

SERIALS PUBLICATIONS
NEW DELHI

First Published - 2006

ISBN : 81-8387-043-0

Published by

SERIALS PUBLICATIONS
4830/24, Ansari Road, Darya Ganj
New Delhi-110002 (India)
Phone : 91-11-23245225
Fax : 91-11-23272135
E-mail: serials@satyam.net.in,
serialspublications@vsnl.net
Website : www.seriealspub.com

CONTENTS

PREFACE

The state and pace of India's development show many troubling signs. In the 1990s, there was a dream, which seems to be tantalizingly within reach- the dream of becoming a fast growing economy, so that poverty could be wiped out. However, this dreams remains elusive. The excitement and optimism generated by the economic reforms have abated. The ability of policy makers to obtain radical changes greatly diminished and the progress of reforms have been blocked. Industrial growth has decelerated. Export growth fell. Infrastructure bottlenecks persist. Poverty, illiteracy and ill-health still remain major problems. The political instability has not provided atmosphere conducive to domestic and foreign investment. However, there are many positive signs. The rate of economic growth is quite significant. The performance of agriculture is remarkable. Inflation is well under control for most of the years. Exports are keeping up. The financial sector reforms have resulted in radical institutional development in securities markets. The level of food security has improved. There is remarkable success in information technology. Overall, there are dramatic changes in India's economic development. With this backdrop, it is intended to look into Indian development experiences covering macroeconomic aspects; regional perspectives, state specific analysis and micro level studies, and twenty-two papers are included in this volume.

The paper titled "Industrial Sector Growth Accounting–A Data Envelopment Analysis (Experiences of Some Indian States and Union Territories) by Somesh K. Mathur and Sahid Ahmed decomposes net value added per worker growth into components attributable to technological changes (shifts in the overall production frontier), technological catch up (movement towards or away from the frontier), capital accumulation (movement along the frontier) and human capital accumulation (proxied by life expectancy). The overall production frontier is constructed using data envelopment analysis, requiring no specification of functional form for neither the technology nor any assumption about market structure or the absence of market imperfections. They analyzed the evolution of cross states net value added distribution for the 22 Indian states and union territories from 1980-81 to 1997-98 using Kernel densities. The results seems to suggest that there are other factors suggested in the literature like barriers to exit, a maze of rules and regulations, government import policies, high concentration, among others, rather than the ones that are included for the growth accounting exercise, which are primarily responsible for the existence of multi-modal net value added per worker distribution for the 22 states. These latter factors also seem to explain reasons for the regional variations of net value added per worker across states. Also, they found that the efficiency levels for the Indian states have gone down from what it was in 1980s to what it were in 1997-98. However, the smaller states have out performed the larger states in terms of their efficiency levels.

R. Albert Christopher Dhas and M. Helen Mary Jacqueline in their paper titled "Trends in Non-Agricultural Enterprises in India: Its Implications" emphasized that the trends in the non-agricultural enterprises and the labour market reveal the deplorable conditions of the labour. This situation would affect not only the social and economic conditions of the present working population, but also the further additions to it. Therefore, it can be argued that the policies towards de-linking budgetary support to the working population, reducing labour absorption in public sector as part of the globalization strategy and relying on the market forces to absorb labour and fix their wages would adverse affect the employment situation in India. Hence, efforts should be initiated towards the development of non-agricultural enterprises, and thereby, problems of production and unemployment could be minimized. Moreover, the welfare of the workforce population in terms of real wages and their income should be at least maintained, so that they would also benefit in that process and contribute towards the growth of Indian economy. Badar Alam Iqbal in his paper titled "Agro-Industries: Key to Economic Development", emphasized that agro-industrial development implies the growth and development of industries in rural areas through interdependence with agriculture under a system of mutual and complementary output relation. It is a process of joint growth and development of industry and agriculture in which the output of agriculture serves as the input to industry and vice versa. It must function either as an input acceptor or as an output donator to bring about an integration i.e. interdependence between industry and agriculture. Thus, an integrated agro-industrial development is dynamic and self–generating process.

In the paper titled "Handicrafts and Socio-Economic Development of Rural Tribals in District Surguja", Dalip Kumar highlights the socio-economic status among the handicraft artisans in rural India especially handicraft artisans of Surguja District. According to this study, there is a big paradox in the handicraft sector in Surguja district having a huge potential and traditional skill handed down through generations. But it needs to be tapped and oriented towards gainful employment. With the rapid growth of population, production of these handicrafts could be an important source of employment and income in rural areas. However the development of this sector has been limited because there is no formal organization to support the marketing of handicrafts produced in rural areas. Individual production and selling of products is still the common practice followed. Lack of infrastructure facilities, credit facilities, lack of raw material and insufficient market facilities are quite noticeable in Surguja district. The problem of non- availability of rural technology could possibly have been solved to a great extent by installation of handicraft industries based on locally available raw material in this district. The status of rural development is linked with the poverty among the handicraft artisans. It is noticed that the large gap in economic status in rural area in Surguja could be due to differential level of productive resources and their productivity. From the policy point of view there is a clear need for diversification of employment in productive resources to reduce the artisan's migration from the rural to urban sectors. The main challenge is to adopt relevant policies and regulations on industry, technology transfer, and small and cottage industries. This would include developing specific policies with respect to rural industries, which is labour-intensive, and most importantly which uses local resources (such as cane, bamboo, straw grass, fiber, stone, skills, and raw materials). Subsequently, it will be necessary to transfer these policies into appropriate legislation and co-ordination and monitor implementation. It is a high time that all relevant steps be taken to patronize the handicraft industries which has big potential for employment It should be done sooner the better otherwise the already languishing sector will be completely wiped out by the mighty storms of globalization and influx of giant multinational companies. For this, the handicraft sector and household artisans must get supports like subsidies and credit facilities, better marketing facilities and linkage to the global market.

In the paper titled "Globalization and Indian Agriculture", S. N. Yogesh emphasized that the last decade has witnessed much talk about globalization, economic liberalization and economic integration of the Indian economy with the world economy. Specially, after the completion of Uruguay Round of Trade Negotiations in April 1994 and the establishment of the World Trade Organization in January 1995 many issues have been raised regarding India's participation in World Trade in future, its integration with the world economy and the likely costs and benefits from the integration. From a review of decade of performance after the introduction of globalization, it became evident that policies of globalization related to agricultural sector had not been able to deliver the intended benefits. In another paper titled "Agricultural Policy and Land Reforms Measures" S. N. Yogesh highlighted that the National Agricultural Policy, which was presented in the parliament on July 28, 2000 has been necessitated due to the relatively poor growth of agriculture during the 1990s. The policy document stated: "capital inadequacy, lack of infrastructural support and demand-side constraints such as controls on movement, storage, and sale of agricultural products etc., have continued to affect the economic viability of agricultural sector, consequently growth has also tended to slacken during 1990s." The establishment of an agrarian economy which ensures food and nutrition to India's billion people, raw-materials for its expanding industrial base and surplus for exports and a fast and equitable reward system for the farming community for the services they provide to the society will be the mainstay of reforms in the agricultural sector. Further, he found that the land reforms in India have failed miserably and the process of implementation of land reforms was wrought with serious defects. The speedy and successful implementation of land reforms requires not only strong political will on the part of government but also awareness of lights on the parts of peasants.

Aroon Sharma his paper titled "Transformation of Agriculture in Jammu and Kashmir: Programmes and Performance" has examined the role of agriculture in the economy of Jammu and Kashmir and has also studied the role of government intervention through institutional reforms. According to his study, land distribution is less skewed in Jammu and Kashmir, which could be attributed to the agrarian reforms undertaken since early 1950s. Though the land concentration has marginally increased in the recent years yet the absolute values of inequality indices continue to be reasonably low. The experience in land distribution highlights the significance of land reforms in reducing asset inequalities in the rural areas where land occupies a key position in asset structure. The analysis also shows a high degree of proliferation of marginal and tiny holdings, studies have shown that given the state of technology and cropping pattern net returns from these holdings are low and most of these holdings are non-visible. This is a disturbing phenomenon of far reaching consequences. Changes in the techniques of production and cropping pattern can go a long way in making these holdings viable.

The paper titled "Food security in India: Issues and Challenges" by Jayasheela and Vishwanatha concluded that even though Indian agricultural production systems have undergone dramatic changes over the last 30 years, much work remains to be completed, to ensure that the grains already achieved are extended to vast numbers who remain food insecure. Indian policy makers currently face the difficult challenge of dismantling a heavily state centered food production system that has historically involved heavy input and consumption subsidies, as well as import and export controls. Beyond the wastefulness and inefficiencies associated with such policies, a record of slow per capita consumption growth and persistent food insecurity on a massive scale speaks for itself. Given the realities of local production capacity, Indian policy makers must acknowledge the fact that food self-sufficiency is not a viable option if the nation wishes to achieve true food security in the foreseeable future. Democratic accountability renders the process of gradual liberalization inevitable over the long run, but the resistance of those who benefit from wasteful and expensive policies, as well as the reluctance among much of the leadership to return to high levels of cereal imports has rendered reforms difficult in the short run. Taking advantage of the opportunities available and working to ensure a more food-secure world in 2020 will remain the primary challenge for policy makers at all levels over the next 20 years and decline in food insecurity also requires above all reduction in population and sustainable agricultural development. In the paper titled "Agricultural Environment and Its Impact on Nutrition Supply in Rural Andhra Pradesh" K. Dasaratha Ramaiah, Y.V Ramanaiah and N. Sreedhara Naidu emphasized that the man and environment relationship has been remained an important paradigm in geographical study for a long time. Man has always been dependent on healthy and productive natural environment. By and large, the major relationship between man and arable land resource is the quantity and quality of food production and consumption. The type and the amount of food availability for human consumption are dependent to a great extent on geographic conditions. Food habits and factors are, therefore, the product of man's environment and history. However, demographic structure is the most depending factor of the nutritional standards and intake of food.

S. Vaidehi and K. Raja Mohan Rao in their paper titled "Bamboo Cultivation for Livelihood Security" emphasized that the bamboo is an important resource in the Indian socio-economic, cultural, ecological, climatic and functional context with more than 1,500-recorded uses. It has multiple economic possibilities, important ecological value and enormous potential to meet the needs of the people. However, bamboo has always been considered as the poor man's timber. It contributes significantly to the subsistence needs of over two billion people living in the tropical and sub-tropical belts of Asia Latin America, and Africa. Recent research in China has resulted in production of an excellent alcoholic beverage from bamboo leaves. Research in Japan has shown that bamboo based charcoal may be a major source for chemical substances for exotic application of very high value. Recognizing the urgent need for an appropriate and cost-effective roofing technology for disaster prone areas, a technology for manufacture of laminated bamboo mat corrugated roofing technology for manufacture of laminated bamboo mat corrugated roofing sheets has been developed at the Indian Plywood Industries Research and Training Institute, Bangalore, in collaboration with the Building Materials and Technology Promotion Council, New Delhi. In another paper titled "Export of NTFPs: With Special Reference to Medicinal Plants from India, they emphasized that the medicinal plants are one of the important products of the non-timber forest products (NTFPs). In India, medicinal plants are widely used by all sections of the population, and over 7,500 species of plants are alone estimated to be used by the Eco-system people" that belong to some of ethnic communities. Today this rich biodiversity of medicinal plants are facing serious resource threat because of the rapid loss of natural habitats, and overexploitation of medicinal plants from the wild. To meet the demands of the Indian herbal industry, which has annual turnover of about US \$300 million, tons of medicinal plants are being harvested every year from some of

165,000 ha of forests. India is one exception and has banned export of several threatened wild species in the form of raw materials although the export of finished products containing the material is selectively allowed.

Shrinivas P. Dandin and Manoj Raj Saxen in their paper titled "Declining Forest Concentration and Its Impact on Land Use: A Case study of Uttar Kannada District, Karnataka, pointed out that the forests precede civilizations and deserts follow them. Many great empires of the past (Egyptians, Babylonians, Persian, Greek) were situated in lands that were fertile, had plenty of rivers, lakes and forests. Today they lie within semi-arid desert belts with their forests gone. Even Socrates warned the Greeks against cutting down the forests for timber. But all such warnings about deforestation were ignored by selfish, thoughtless people and these lands inevitably underwent changing land use and barren wastes. In the paper titled "Role of Forests in Tribal Development", S. Nirmala Mary highlighted that the evolution of the tribal society took place within the forest and they had the birth right for their survival, livelihood, occupation, recreation, belief and act. But it is the tribals who bear the brunt of most big, industrial, mining and development projects. Due to the interference of the colonial government in their rights. They were deprived of their rights and robbed of their dignity. So, the government decided to develop tribal co-operatives societies, to prevent exploitation of tribals. Various types of tribals co-operative societies have been formed to help the cause of tribals in different stages. Still, tribals have been exploited by middlemen while purchasing the NTFPs collected by the tribals, therefore if the government wants to develop tribal economy, there is a need to protect their benefits by providing them strong marketing network. Tribal societies may also be formed to safeguard the benefits of the tribals. Thus, along with other developmental approaches the community forest management has been recognized as an effective developmental approach to alleviate the tribal people from their poverty and promote their cultural traditions of biodiversity conservation to their sustainable livelihoods. In her another paper titled "Role of Women in Forestry: An Overview", she pointed out that the forest Department programmes by and large had not been planned to meet the needs of women. Though grass is available and often free of cost, it has not reduced the time women spend collecting fuel and fodder. Also closing of open grazing lands has produced additional hardships. Income generation based on forestry or non-forestry activities may stimulate women's involvement in afforestation programmes as they tend to meet their basic needs. It is essential to involve women in the micro- planning stages to obtain their constant involvement in the needs and concerns of women will have to take primary importance.

In the paper titled "Gender and Development Debate in India, Vibhuti Patel highlighted that the states in which women's studies and women's movement are influential and articulate in including women's needs, aspirations and demands on the decision-making agenda, we find effective engendering of state policies. The

United Nation Development Programme (UNDP) has also taken lead in evolution of Gender Equity Policy of Gujarat state. Maharashtra, Kerala, West Bengal, Madhya Pradesh, Karnataka, Andhra Pradesh and Tamil Nadu have been pro-active states with regard to engendering their policy documents. Inter-state comparison in the women empowerment discourse through Human Development Reports and in the publications of Department of Women and Child Development, Government of India have created urge among sensitive administrators, politicians and non-government organizations (NGOs) to make concerted efforts to improve women's profile in the economic, social-cultural and political spheres.

In the paper titled "Utilization of Public Health Facilities in India with Special Reference to Maternal Health Care Services", Amlan Majumder pointed out that poor health care infrastructure and poor status of health India is on the mid-way to the desired level of development. It is well understood that public health care system which has a nation-wide network of delivering health and family welfare related services, has the crucial role to achieve that desired level of development. However, acceptability or utilization of public health care across culture and societies in India is very poor. As the Southern region is the most demographically advanced in India, we will see whether we can take any lesson from its experience. We have seen that odds ratios of high 'health problems', high 'birth order', 'scheduled caste' and 'scheduled tribe', and 'availability of health facilities' (or place of residence) indicate chances of higher utilization of public health facilities. On the other hand, odds ratios of large 'family size', medium and higher 'education of the respondent', 'husband's literacy', 'other religion', 'having toilet facility', and medium and high 'affordability' point towards utilization of private health facilities. In such a situation (relaxing necessary econometric technicalities), if we assume that in the process of development health problems during pregnancy reduces, birth order comes down, and urban growth tends to stop in the upper asymptotes of its logistic pattern of growth, the credibility of the public health care system in the Southern region will be deemed to some ethnic groups only. The system may face severe crisis if the light of education touches more and more people and cultural values get worthy gradually. A careful revision of the results would confirm that situation is almost same in other regions also and in India as whole. However, if other things remain the same, prospects of public health care system is better in the Eastern region as compared to the Southern one. If things change as above, future of the system is very uncertain in the Eastern region also. In such a situation, the only instrument in the hands of Government is to raise quality of care in the public health facilities through quantitative development in infrastructure. Failure to achieve this goal may cause serious set back of the system again in future pushing back the goal of 'Health For All' further.

Rajesh Jaiswal in his paper titled "Economic Analysis of Nutrition Programme in India emphasized that increasing interest in rural poverty alleviation has resulted in a new focus on the 'nutrition dependent poor' especially women and children and the actual and potential contribution of nutrition to women and children. Nutrition-deficient areas are frequently associated with rural poverty. Remote locations, rugged terrain, low population densities, limited communication and transportation infrastructure, infertile soils, and difficult climates act as constraints that limit nutrition intake by the most vulnerable segment of the society i.e. women and children. The same factors limit economic opportunities of people living in rural areas. Development in the field of nutrition rapidly changes both the physical and the economic landscapes and the corresponding opportunities for local people. Analysis of the relationship between such development and rural development and social change is needed to better understand its impact and to target interventions aimed at improving livelihoods of rural people. The study has put forward two complementary types of approach. Both these need support and better calculation of resource needs. Local programs through community organizations must be massively expanded, with input from facility-based resources. Micronutrient deficiency control programs, usually linked to the local programs, must be sustained and new approaches (notably multiple micro-nutrient fortification and supplementation) researched and adopted.

In the paper titled "Dynamics of Development and Demography: An Empirical Study from Uttar Pradesh, Manju K. Johari and Anjani Koomar pointed out that Lot of investigations are focused on the effect of rapid population growth on development goals lately. All development programmes can affect fertility but not through the same channels. United Nations has suggested a very comprehensive framework for analyzing population variables including fertility; 15 development variables (per capita income etc.) 14 economic variables (capital stock etc), 15 socio cultural and exogenous variables and & instrument variables (Family Planning Programmes etc.) This research is limited to socio–economic variables related to the psychological affect on demography of a developing state of India where family planning exists at low levels. Factor analysis, correlations, and regressions are carried out on variables such as type of house, water source, religion, caste, education of the couple, age at first stable cohabitation (marriage), number of children born, contraceptive practices and infant mortality etc. The characteristics of women with less than two children were compared with those of women who have more than two children. The results along with personal interviews with the respondents revealed that "autonomy" or decision making power of women of second group were generally very low due to low status in the families. Development programmes, which could provide legal support (through NGO's) to such women and empower them to make their own fertility choices by using traditional methods, family planning, or simply by abstaining, the population goals could be attainable.

A.N. Sadhu and Falendra K. Sudan in their paper titled "Experiences of Jammu and Kashmir Economy and Its Lessons for North-East" have highlighted that Jammu and Kashmir has realized the importance of floricultural and medicinal herbs. Floriculture, with improved packaging and fast transportation, has become a highly remunerative enterprise internationally. The hill economies are ideally suited for the purpose and want to realize its full potential. The state of J&K also failed in so far as tourism diversification is concerned. Neither was tourism was not diversified geographically nor was it diversified category wise. Adventure tourism, pilgrimage tourism, business tourism and sports tourism is opening out new avenues for the state and hold a promising prospect in this regard. The hill economies in the North-East need to identify their sectors and activities where they have a comparative advantage and should develop the same as priority sector. It is hoped that the lessons drawn will be of use for the planners and policy makers to plan logically for the overall development of the North-Eastern hill economies. The North-East states could shift its agricultural development strategy from food security mode to the value addition mode. The states should grow certain products like high-valued fruits, vegetables and some cash crops, which could give adequate monetary returns to the cultivators. For optimum utilization of the productive potential of the primary sector, diversification should be the main focus. In order to develop the handloom and handicrafts sector, a multi-pronged strategy should be pursued. In the tourism sector, there is urgent need to take drastic steps to revive the tourism activities in the North-East India. Last but not the least, the good governance is vital for accountability and transparency in decision-making and programme implementation by the various public agencies. The concept of people's participation should be operationalized in effective way to make the administrative system more accountable and transparent.

In the paper titled "Striking Harmony Between Environmental considerations and Developmental Needs Through the Use of Hydropower", Anu Singh pointed out that India is facing an acute power shortage with an energy shortage of 7.5 % and a peaking shortage of around 12.6%, this continue to plague the economy in almost all the states of the country on the one hand In recent years explosive growth of population, has increased the demand for energy, this has resulted in the environmental damage all over the world on the other. India is also concerned about climate change because of its potential adverse impact. Traditionally; India's energy is based on coal, its most abundant resource. Major share of power generation till date, is carried out by coal-fired power plants. With the threat of climate change, India is being called upon to change this and use alternative oil, gas, renewable and Nuclear energy. This paper discusses the role of hydro power in removing the problems of power shortage as well as how it is helpful in constraining the environmental damage due to increasing use of coal in the generation of electricity. The objective of this article is to review critically the present status and environmental concerns for Hydro-Power Development in India while making suggestions for accelerating the Hydro-generation.

Md. Abdus Salam in his paper titled "Magnitude of Waste Management Problems in India: A Review" highlighted that there is no Indian policy document which examines waste as part of a cycle of production-consumption-recovery or perceives waste through a prism of overall sustainability. Until now, the problem of waste has been seen as one of cleaning and disposing as rubbish. But a closer look at the current and future scenario reveals that waste needs to be treated holistically, recognizing its natural resource roots as well as health impacts. In India, over a million people find livelihood opportunities in the area of waste; they are engaged in waste collection (popularly known as rag picking) and recycling through well-organized systems. Waste can be wealth, which has tremendous potential not only for generating livelihoods for the urban poor but can also enrich the earth through composting and recycling rather than spreading pollution as has been the case. Increasing urban migration and a high density of population will make waste management a difficult issue to handle in the near future. The wastes generated by various sectors need to be assessed and evaluated for their energy potential or reuse in any other form.

In the paper titled "Environmental Accounting and Reporting for Sustainable Development", Siddhartha Sarkar highlighted that the challenge of environmental accounting is to deliver meaningful disclosure within accounting practices and standards. Further challenge of environmental accounting is to extend practices to include new accounting procedures for costing out and investigating possible recycling alternatives. Introducing environmental accounting and reporting the organization need to ascertain all environmental impacts from a cost benefit point of view and to measure eco-assets and liabilities for the organization. An accounting standard devoted for the purpose of measurement and reporting of environment must be pronounced. Although a global environmental accounting standard is under consideration by the International Accounting Standards Committee, there is an urgent necessity of a generally accepted environmental accounting standard to keep pace with the sustainability.

Falendra K. Sudan

LIST OF CONTRIBUTORS

Somesh K. Mathur, Senior Lecturer, Department of Economics, Jamia Millia Islamia (JMI), New Delhi-25.

Sahid Ahmed, Senior Lecturer, Department of Economics, Jamia Millia Islamia (JMI), New Delhi-25.

R. Albert Christopher Dhas, Faculty Member, The American College, Madurai-2.

M. Helen Mary Jacqueline, Faculty Member, Lady Doak College, Madurai-2.

Badar Alam Iqbal, Professor and Fulbright Scholar in Residence, Business School, Claflin University, Orangeburg, South Calorina, USA.

Dalip Kumar, Manager (Projects), National Council of Applied Economic Research, Parisila Bhawan, 11, I.P. Estate, New Delhi-110002.

S.N. Yogesh, Faculty member, Department of Studies in Economics, Kuvempu University, Shankaraghatta, Shimoga District, Karnataka-577451.

Aroon Sharma, Reader, Department of Economics, University of Jammu, Jammu, Jammu and Kashmir–180006.

Jayasheela, Reader, Department of Economics, Mangalore University, Mangalagangothri-574199.

Vishwanatha, Professor and Chairman, Department of Economics, Mangalore University, Mangalagangothri-574199.

K. Dasaratha Ramaiah, Associate Professor, Department of Economics and Applied Economics, S.K. University, Anantapur, A.P.-515003.

Y.V Ramanaiah, Professor, Department of Geography, S.K. University, Anantapur, A.P.-515003.

N. Sreedhara Naidu, Research Fellow, Department of Geography, S.K. University, Anantapur, A.P.-515003.

S. Vaidehi, Research Scholar, Department of Economics, Gandhigram Rural Institute, Gandhigram, Dindigul, Tamilnadu.

K. Raja Mohan Rao, Reader, Department of Economics, Gandhigram Rural Institute, Gandhigram, Dindigul, Tamilnadu.

Shrinivas P. Dandin, Research Scholar, Department of Geography, Karnatak University, Dharwad-3.

Manoj Raj Saxen, Scientist–E, Landuse and Urban Studies Group, National Remote Sensing Agency, Balanagar, Hyderbad–37.

S. Nirmala Mary, Research Scholar, Department of Economics, Gandhigram Rural Institute, Gandhigram, Dindigul, Tamil Nadu.

Vibhuti Patel, Professor and Head, Department of Economics, SNDT Women's University, Smt. Nathibai Thakersey Road, Chuchgate, Mumbai-400020.

Amlan Majumder, Lecturer in Economics, Dinhata College, P. O. Dinhata, Dt. Cooch Behar, West Bengal-736 135.

Rajesh Jaiswal, Associate Fellow, National Council of Applied Economic Research, Parisila Bhawan, 11, I.P. Estate, New Delhi-110002.

Manju K. Johari, Research Scholar (Demography), Department of Statistics, Lucknow University U.P. 226013.

Anjani Koomar, Professor (Human Resource) Indian Institute of Management, Prabandh Nagar, off Sitapur Road, Lucknow, U.P.-226013.

A.N. Sadhu, Professor (Retd.), Department of Economics, University of Jammu, Jammu, Jammu and Kashmir–180006.

Falendra K. Sudan, Reader, Department of Economics, University of Jammu, Jammu, Jammu and Kashmir–180 006.

Anu Singh, ICSSR Doctoral Fellow, Giri Institute of Development Studies, Lucknow.

Md. Abdus Salam, Reader, Department of Economics, Aligarh Muslim University, Aligarh.

Siddhartha Sarkar, Department of Commerce, Dinhata College, Dinhata, Cooch Behar, West Bengal.

1

STRIKING HARMONY BETWEEN ENVIRONMENTAL CONSIDERATIONS AND DEVELOPMENTAL NEEDS THROUGH THE USE OF HYDROPOWER

Anu Singh

INTRODUCTION

"The pace of Power Development in the country has not moved rapidly enough and chronic power shortages continue to plague the economy in almost all the states of the country."[1] by the end of Ninth Plan the country was facing an energy shortage of 7.5% and a peaking shortage of around 12.6%. It is a matter of great concern that the annual Per Capita Consumption in India, which stands at about 350 Kwh, is among the lowest in the world. Even today many households in a large number of villages have no access to electricity. The end users of electricity like households, farmers, commercial establishments, industries etc. are confronted with frequent power cuts, erratic voltage levels and wide fluctuations in the frequency of supply, have added to the 'power woos' of the consumer. This situation may worsen in the coming years because of the following factors:

1. Deteriorating financial condition of SEBs;
2. Inadequate resource availability of fuels transportation;
3. Growing gap between Demand-Supply;
4. Operational and Technical inefficiencies in system; and
5. Low Hydro Thermal mix.

The decline in the proportion of Hydro capacity, which started in the early seventies, has continued over the period. The share of Hydropower projects in the total installed capacity, which stood at 51% during 1962-63, slipped to 33% in 1985-86 and further to 25% at present. It is therefore necessary that the government must address these problems for the Power situation to improve in tune with the demand from different sectors. Only 15% of the total hydro electric potential (84000 MW at 60% load factor) has been developed. Maximum unexploitable potential lies in the northeast and the northern region it has adversely affected the capacity utilization of thermal power plants. A large programme of hydro capacity addition needs to be taken up on a priority basis. Presently more than 70% of power generation is based on coal combustion in India. Since the supply of Indian coal for Power generation is not of good quality, therefore, the use of coal leads to increase in the generation of fly ash.

To save the environment many environmental laws and rules have been framed and implemented and are being revised as the need arise. This is in the line Constitution of India, under part IV A on Fundamental Duties, Article 51 A (9) states "it shall be the duty of every citizen of India to protect and improve the natural environment including forests lakes, rivers and wild life, and to have compassion for living creatures." In this paper, an attempt has been made to discuss the relative significance of the advantages of the Hydropower generation, keeping in the mind Environmental issues. The main objective of this article is to review the present status and environmental concerns for Hydro Power Development in India while making suggestions for accelerating the Hydro generation.

In recent years explosive growth of population, has increased the demand for energy. Although this has increased the standard of living, particularly since the Industrial revolution we have been using up the wealth of earth's natural resources at an ever-increasing pace, and this has resulted in the environmental damage all over the world. This can be viewed as: global warming, ozone layer destruction and acid rain, besides, endangerment of animal and plant species, desertification, deforestation, marine pollution, Transboundary movement of hazardous waste. Among these the first three are of special concern, while the issue of global warming deserves our most critical attention.

The threat of climatic change due to accumulation of green house gases (GHG) is well known. A number of gases can cause the green house effect. Accumulated green house gases in the atmosphere let in solar radiation but trap infrared radiation from the earth. Among the gases emitted from burning of fossil fuels like coal and oil etc, carbon dioxide alone accounts for nearly 65% of the green house gas. Unlike other green house emitting activities of limited nature, such as refrigeration, air conditioning, fires fighting and so on, fossil fuels are used in almost every sector of the economy directly or indirectly. According to UN estimates, an average of 4 per cent of GDP is lost due to environmental degradation caused by the industrialization and development process carried out in developing countries.

In the areas, like energy sector, the problem has become more complicated. Major share of power generation till date, is carried out by coal-fired power plants. The thermal power demand, thus accumulated over the last five decades, has been leading to increasing coal-mining activities. Life cycle analyses of coal mining and power production on the one hand, and cost of land reclamation, mitigating of coal-dust pollution, disposal on the other hand, could never be rationally balanced. It led to the Frame Work Convention on Climate Change (FCCC) at Rio de Janeiro. Different countries perceive the seriousness of the threat and its implications differently. India is also concerned about climate change because of its potential adverse impact. Traditionally, India's energy has been based on coal, its most abundant resource. With the threat of climate change, India is being called upon to change this and use alternative oil, gas, renewable and nuclear energy as the inputs for Power generation.

The figure given below shows emissions by sectors and one can see that power sector accounts for 48%of emissions. This gives an idea about sectors, which offer possibilities for large reduction in emissions, if modernized. Energy efficiency and conservation is gradually taking an important place in the energy and industrial sector plan in India. Improving the efficiency of coal and electricity use could significantly reduce emissions from these sectors. But for the increasing demand of energy especially in developing countries these steps are not enough. Framework convention on climate change implies that renewed attention should now be given to the development and utilization of renewable source of energy, because if energy demand is to be met with fossil fuels, to any significant degree, carbon dioxide emissions will increase and considerably and not decrease. For example, CO2 emissions are projected to grow by 93% in the high-growth scenario of the World Energy Council Commission (1993).

Figure1: Carbon Emissions by Top Six Contributing Sectors

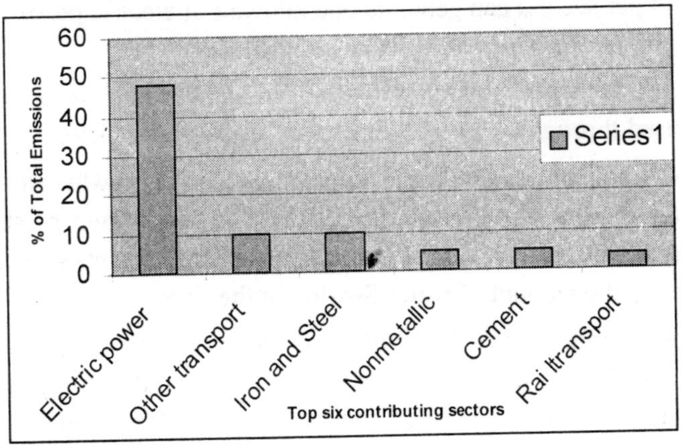

Source: India Development Report, 2002

"The flow of renewable energy to the earths land surface is thousands of times greater than mankind's present rate of total energy use. Utilizing a small fraction of this resource would provide clean alternative and environmentally sound path towards meeting future energy needs."[2] A study done by Johansson et al., 1993 concluded that given adequate support, renewable energy technologies could meet much of the growing demand at prices lower than those usually forecast for conventional energy. Moreover, making a transition to a renewable-intensive energy economy would provide environmental and other benefits not measured in standard economic accounts. For e.g. by 2050 global CO2 emissions would be reduced to 75% of their 1985 levels provided that energy efficiency and use of renewable sources of energy are both pursued aggressively. And because renewable energy is expected to be competitive with conventional energy, such benefits could be achieved at no additional cost.

HYDRO ELECTRIC POWER: AN ALTERNATIVE SOURCE

While recent shortages of electricity supplies have spurred calls for increased generation, no one believes that new generation should come at the expense of cleaner air. One strategy to reduce emissions while increasing generating capacity is to emphasize the development of non-carbon electricity generation alternatives like hydropower. Hydropower is an abundant, renewable, reliable, and low -cost source of power with potential for growth. Hydroelectric power is electricity produced by the movement of fresh water from rivers and lakes. "Hydro" comes from the Greek word hydra, meaning water. Gravity causes water to flow downwards and this downwards motion of water contains kinetic energy, and then from mechanical energy into electrical energy in hydro-electric power stations. At a good site hydro electricity can generate very cost effective electricity. As a rule of thumb, one gallon of water falling at the rate of one hundred feet per second can generate one kilowatt of electric power.

There are several types of hydropower facilities:

1. "Storage" projects impound water behind a dam, forming a reservoir. Water is released through turbine-generators to produce electricity.
2. "Run-of-river" projects typically use relatively low dams where the amount of water running through the powerhouse is determined by the water flowing in the river. Electricity generation from these plants will vary with changes in the amount of water flowing in the river.
3. "Pumped-storage" projects use off-peak electricity to pump water from a lower reservoir to an upper reservoir. During periods of high electrical demand, the water is released back to the lower reservoir to generate electricity.

The first hydroelectric plant was built in 1882 in the United States. This plant made use of a fast flowing river as its source. Some years later, dams were constructed to create artificial water storage areas at the most convenient location. These dams also controlled the water flow rate to the power station turbines. Originally, hydroelectric power stations were of a small size and were set up at waterfalls in the vicinity of towns because it was not possible at that time, to transmit electrical energy over great distances. The main reason why there has been large-scale use of hydroelectric power is because it can now be transmitted over hundreds of kilometers to where it is required. The electricity can be transmitted as either AC or DC.

Unlike conventional coal-fired power stations, which take hours to start up, hydroelectric power stations can begin generating electricity very quickly. This makes them particularly useful for responding to sudden increases in demand for electricity by customers ("peak demand"). Hydro-stations need only a small staff to operate and maintain them, and as no fuel is needed, fuel prices are not a problem. However, the construction of dams to enable hydroelectric generation may cause significant environmental damage and involve a substantial investment.

HOW HYDROELECTRIC POWER STATIONS OPERATE

The amount of electricity, which can be generated at a hydroelectric plant, is dependant upon two factors. These factors are (1) the vertical distance through which the water falls, called the "head", and (2) the flow rate, measured as volume per unit time. The electricity produced is proportional to the product of the head and the rate of flow. The following is an equation, which may be used to roughly determine the amount of electricity, which can be generated, by a potential hydroelectric power site:

POWER (KW) = 5.9 X FLOW X HEAD

In this equation, FLOW is measured in cubic meters per second and HEAD is measured in meters.

A hydroelectric generating unit is simpler and consists of a water turbine to convert the energy of flowing water into mechanical energy, and an electric generator to convert mechanical energy into electrical energy. The amount of energy available from water depends on both the quantity of water available and its pressure at the turbine. The greater the height (or head) of the water above the turbine, the more energy each cubic meter of water can impart to spin a turbine (which in turn drives a generator). The greater the quantity of water, the greater the number and size of turbines that may be spun, and the greater the power output of the generators, determines the amount of energy which can be generated.

Hydropower can play a critical in the development process as well as in meeting carbon reduction commitments to address climate change goals. It will also be a key resource fostering sustainable development in a developing the economy. A study of NHA (National Hydro Association) in USA estimates that hydroelectric generation avoided 77 million metric tons of carbon from being emitted from fossil fuel generation in 1999. That is equivalent to burning an additional 121 million barrels of oil, and 741 billion cubic feet of natural gas combined. By generating carbon free electricity the carbon emissions avoided by hydroelectric generation is equivalent to removing 62.2 million passenger cars-nearly 50%- from the road way in a year in U.S.A.

Other pollutants avoided by the generation of hydropower in 1999 included 1.6millions tons of sulfur dioxide (SO2) and 1 million tons of nitrogen oxides, both key ingredients in acid rain.

ADVANTAGES OF HYDROPOWER

Some points, which are advocated in support of the hydropower, are as follows:

1. Hydropower is a clean, renewable and reliable source of energy like wind solar, geothermal and biomass that serves national environmental and energy policy objectives. Water its "fuel" is essentially infinite, replenished by the hydrologic cycle, which is powered by the sun i.e., continually renewable source that is not consumed.
2. Hydropower's operational flexibility is unique, its ability to change output quickly is highly valued, and will become even more so in a competitive market. Its unique voltage control, load following and peaking capabilities help maintain the stability of the electric grid ensuring economic growth and a high quality of life.
3. Hydroelectric installations have long life; because the machinery operates at low temperature and at slow speed and the shut down periods are of short duration
4. Apart from large scale Hydro Power projects output can be made by greater use of small plants i.e., mini power plants with capacities ranging from 100 KW to 2000KW located in succession at suitable places on a river system. Such plants are called the run of river plants, which are cheaper with no rehabilitation and other environmental problems.
5. A road head at the proposed dam site will in most cases open up remote regions that are backward only because they lack access. Dams can therefore trigger social and market opportunity, for a section of society which have hitherto been deprived both economically as well as socially.
6. The most important reason or factoring favour of using water, as the "fuel" for electricity generation is that, it does not release carbon dioxide, sulphur

oxide and other polluting gases and therefore helps in reducing global warming. "*Coal power plants are responsible for 93 per cent of the sulfur dioxide and 80 per cent of the nitrogen oxide emissions generated by the electric utility industry*"[3].

7. Hydropower projects provide a dependable source of drinking water people from the irrigated areas may therefore enjoy better health and sanitation facilities, thus reducing the incidence of disease. The improved economic status also makes people health conscious and capable of availing of requisite health care. The development of area due to these projects make available health care units in villages, along-with other facilities like electricity, roads, irrigation, drinking water and communication services.
8. The water bodies in controlled form offer opportunities for recreational activities, the gardens developed in water resource projects like Brindavan, Ukai, Ramganga, Kalindi Kunj, Matatila and Bhakra dam are great source of tourist attractions in India.
9. A case study done by R.S. Goel (Director Central Water Commission, GOI, New Delhi) for Ramganga dam project (U.P.) clearly shows that there has been a substantial increase in the numbers of tigers and other wild lives in the National Corbett park due to availability of clean water through out the year and environmental security after the construction of Ramganga Multipurpose Dam Project.
10. Seismic impacts-in discussing this much debated issue one must not forget the basic conclusion drawn at the international symposium on earthquake and dams in china may 1987 it was pointed out that dams designed by modern techniques and built according to the latest specifications have considerable reserve strength to withstand severe earthquakes. Because of the application of the application of such advanced techniques in both the design and execution, large dams have larger earthquake resistance capability.

STATUS OF HYDRO POWER WORLD WIDE

In 1994, hydroelectric power represented 2% of the world's primary energy consumption. There was in 1998 about 700GW of installed hydro capacity worldwide generating about, 2600twh (2.6 x 1012 kWh) of electricity per year, and producing 19% of the world's electricity. It is estimated that only 32 % of the economically feasible hydro power potential worldwide has been developed so far. In 1997, Asia had an installed hydroelectric capacity of about 100 GW. Asia is the continent with many countries stating that hydropower is the main focus for the development of their power sectors. China currently has the highest level of hydropower development activity in the world. The United

States is one of the largest producers of hydropower in the world, second only to Canada. It contributes between 8 and 12% of total electrical generation in the USA. Through out the world, about one-fifth of the electricity is generated from hydropower.

HYDRO POWER POTENTIAL IN INDIA

India celebrated 100 years of hydro power development in 1997. Around that time there were about 225 hydro electric power stations (excluding mini hydro) in the country, with an installed capacity of about 25,000 MW. This was about 25% of the total installed capacity from all sources. The first two five year plan rested heavily on hydro power development through a series of multipurpose projects. The Thermal-Hydro ratio was then around 60:40.however, with increasing power shortage, it was felt expedient to favour short-gestation thermal projects. Hydropower, therefore, went into decline. Today the thermal-hydro ratio is about 75:25. Only 17% of vast hydel potential of 1,50,000 MW has been tapped so far. The overall responsibility of planning, promotion and organization of an integrated development of hydroelectric power in India has been assigned to national hydroelectric power corporation (NHPC) which was incorporated in 1975.Now let us look at the physiographic features of India.

Looking at the physiographic features of India the country can be dived in three major divisions namely Himalayas and their associated young fold ancient blocks of peninsular India and the Indo-Gangetic plains lying between the two. Out of these three divisions, the Himalayan range comprising greater lesser or middle Himalayas and the Shivalik range posses vast hydro potential. Greater Himalaya being inaccessible, do not provide an opportunity to harness hydro potential but they do act as reservoirs of water for all the rivers of this range. This leaves the left ranges viz. Lesser Himalaya and Shivalik as potential source for development of hydroelectric power. The country has been classified into six major river system for hydro electric potential survey namely, Indus basin, Brahamputra Ganga, central Indian river system east flowing rivers and west flowing rivers. These have been further divided into 49 basins.

With the help of the table 1, we can see that, the hydroelectric schemes in operations accounts for only 17% of potential capacity. As compared to this the figures for Norway and Canada are 58 and 41 per cent respectively. Even in a country like Brazil this percentage is as high as 31. it is not essential that this entire potential has to be exploited because that itself will have its problems but at least we can exploit it to the optimal level.

In addition to potential of medium and major hydro schemes, a sizable potential also exists for development of small hydro schemes on rivulets and canal drops. A systematic study for the development of small hydro potential was done during 1987 and completed during June 1996.as per this assessment, 1512 small hydro electric schemes having the capacity of above 6782 MW on canal falls /rivers have been identified.

Table 1
Hydroelectric Potential in India

Basin/Rivers	*Exploitable Potential (MW)*
Indus	33832
Ganga	20711
Central Indian rivers	4152
West Flowing rivers	9430
East Flowing rivers	14511
Brahamputra	66065
Total (India)	148701 (17%)

Source: www.cea.nic.in/hydro.

Table 2
Small Hydro Potential Identified in India

State	*No. of Sites*	*Capacity (MW)*
Arunachal Pradesh	190	111
Bihar	110	134
Gujarat	197	157
Himachal Pradesh	298	1393
Jammu and Kashmir	131	859
Kerala	216	561
Madhya Pradesh	80	238
Maharashtra	122	68
Meghalaya	36	8
Orissa	48	28
Punjab	198	196
Uttar Pradesh	328	1128
West Bengal	69	69
Total	2023	4950

Source: Water Power and Dam Construction, 1995.

At present the major hydro electric projects (above 750 MW Capacity) are: Bhakra, Dehar, Koyna, Nagarunasagar,Srisalam,Shravasthy,Kalinadi and Idukki. By giving the data of Hydro Power potential of India our intention here is just to give an idea about the efforts taken up by government in exploiting its resources for generating pollution free electricity since independence. In spite of the vast Hydro Power potential in the country it has explored only 17% so far. Some projects are under construction, thus the bulk of the potential (77%) remains unexploited.

POLICY MEASURES BY GOVERNMENT

The Union ministry of power has taken several steps to accelerate the pace of hydroelectric Power generation and these include:

(a) Higher budgetary allocation for the hydel sector,

(b) Investment approval of new hydro electric projects,

(c) Identification of new projects in central sector for advance action,

(d) Improving tariff dispensation for hydel projects, and

(e) Promoting state sector projects, which were languishing or could, not progress due to interstates disputes.

So far we have discussed the need to emphasize on the system of Hydropower generation in comparison to Thermal power as a cleaner source of energy. We have also seen that the world and the government of India are engaged in the formulation of hydropower policies for the maximum utilization of the resource available.

But we should not ignore some of the disadvantages of hydropower, which results due to the construction of large dams, and lead to some serious environmental and human costs some of these are being outlined below.

1. Valuable agriculture and forestlands are lost because of the storage of large volume of water and this disrupts the hydrological cycle and causes water logging in the vicinity as well as salinisation of soil.
2. In the periods of drought power production is disrupted, because a minimum water level is required to ensure regular generation according to the capacity of the plant, which may adversely affect the growth process.
3. Large population are displaced, their rehabilitation involves serious economic and social problems Population displacement, the drowning of arable land archeological sites and danger to downstream population must be included on the debit side of river development schemes.
4. The eco system in the dam area is adversely affected. Changes in the river conditions and the land and vegetation boarding caused by the dams and powerhouse turbines may impact fish populations and wildlife significantly. Dams slow down the flow of the river, which directly effects the migration of many species, by disorienting them, and significantly increase the duration of their migration. These can also become bruised, stressed or mortally injured from contact with turbines or other parts of the generation plant.

The impeded sediments collect on the river and reservoir bottoms where it affects the habitat for fish spawning. This deposited sediment may contain chemical or industrial residues from upstream sources.

1. Oxygen is necessary to sustain aquatic biota and provides a self -purification capacity for the water. If the river is heavily loaded with organic material, the amount of oxygen consumed to degrade it may be more than can be absorbed through the water/air interface, so that the oxygen content quickly falls. Once the oxygen has been removed in this way, the river reaches and advanced stage of malodorous pollution with a scum over the surface, and all aquatic life ceases
2. A hydroelectric facility disrupts natural flow of the river by withholding and then releasing water to generate power for peak demand periods, which erode soil and vegetation and flood or strand wildlife, these irregular releases destroy natural seasonal flow variation that trigger natural growth and reproduction cycles in many species.
3. Peaking power operations can also cause dramatic changes in reservoir water levels up to 40feet that can degrade shorelines and disturb fisheries, waterfowl and bottom dwelling organisms.
4. Impoundment can cause changes and variation in temperature or the amount of dissolved gases in the river. This affects the habitat growth rate, or even the survival of fish and other species.

The last two limitations (points 3 & 4) are of great concern to environmentalist and socialist therefore in this connection some anti dam campaigns have been launched.

SOME EXAMPLES OF ANTI DAM CAMPAIGNS

1. Chandi Prasad Bhatt has started a campaign against the Vishnuprayag hydroelectric projects because of the dangers it poses to the unique ecosystem of the valley of flowers and the general geological havoc it could create.
2. Another instance of intervention at the highest level resulting of a large dam in Lalpur in Gujarat, Harivallabh Parikh raised two issues destruction of forest and displacement of tribal problems. These very issues are cited by Baba Amte, while mobilizing protest against Sardar Sarovar-with the continuing work on the project more than 20 villages have been submerged this year and acres of standing crops lost while the new reservoir is filling up.
3. The years of protest by the local people who have yet to be adequately rehabilitated remain unheard, Bhopal Patnam and Inchampali Dams.
4. The protest against the Tehri dam in Garhwal is another, where along with the rehabilitation; environmental issues relating to large dams have also been highlighted. The 'Bandh Virodhi Sangarsh Samiti' led by advocate

V.D. Saklani has underlined the threat to the ecological balance of this sensitive mountain region through rallies, seminars and even wall writings. The movement has gained momentum and local support because of the strident protest by citizens of Tehri town, which is submerged by the hydro projects.

In the wake of such controversies, the international funding agencies are becoming more responsive to the concern of environmentalists and project affected population.

SUGGESTIONS

As it is clear, the government's national hydropower policy is taking keen interest in exploiting the hydropower potential to generate pollution free clean electricity. But "how so ever strong be the case for hydro power, prejudices lingered on accounts of long gestation and environmental and social costs"[3] discussed above. Though often exaggerated and torn out of context these criticisms must be answered.

With a view to balancing the environmental considerations and development needs in the case of hydroelectric projects adequate precautions are also available in India. To ensure sustainable Power supply from water resources, following acts of government of India are of relevance:

1. Environmental Protection Act, 1986
2. Water (prevention and control) of Pollution Act, 1974 (amended in 1983)
3. Forest Conservation Act, 1980
4. EIA Notification of 1994.

Besides, a multi-disciplinary Environmental Monitoring Committee has also been constituted by Ministry of Water Resources so as to oversee that the implementation of Environmental safeguards as stipulated.

The acts passed above are not acting accordingly which may satisfy the feelings of the people concerned, therefore government should look out for some measures to tackle these problems and include these in its Hydropower policies, the remedies which can up to some extent reduce the adverse environmental impact caused by hydroelectric projects are as follows:

1. Many impacts like slow down of river and long migration of fish can be reduced up to some extent by technological and operational enhancements to the hydro project like converting a dam from peaking to 'run of river' operation, minimum flow turbines, regulating weirs, and pulsed operation at peak efficiency.
2. We can also install fish passage (Bypass) system like fish ladders, fish locks, fish lifts or other special means, which give positive results.

3. Plantation of the upper surface of a reservoir with a flora similar to that existing outwards nearby at the same elevation can help in preserving population of fish. In case of barrages, weirs and small diversion dams, under water stone revetments can be made which can create conditions of suitable flora and fauna so vital for the life and growth of fish.
4. For draining of sediments the Government should make use of dredgers although it is costly. Various flushing and piping techniques are also available for moving non-contaminated sediments downstream.
5. Like in USA recently the Low Impact Hydropower Institute has created a Low Impact Hydropower Certification Program to identify and reward efforts by dam owners to minimize the impacts of hydropower dams. Government of India should also establish such type of institute or agency, which will have an eye on the construction of hydropower projects.
6. The erosions can be corrected (or reduced to some degree) by constructing the slope of the channel and/or by changing the discharge from the dam.
7. B.S. Bhavanishankar, President, Sahayoga proposed for the Diversion of Brahmaputra at selected locations along the course connecting the sources of the tributaries of Ganga by tunnels across Himalayas bored through Tunnel Boring Machines for the better utilization of water to generate large hydro-electric power as run of the river system. According to him the traditional strategy of conventional surface irrigation in the Gangetic plains should be completely stopped and we should resort only to ground water irrigation exploiting the aquifer characteristic of the huge Gangetic plains in future. The surface irrigation in Gangetic plains needs to be gradually eliminated out giving way to ground water exploitation fully. This will avoid water logging and prevent salinity of lands. Further it will reclaim lost areas. Recharging by means of reverse tube wells recharge the Gangetic aquifer to maintain the water table at reasonable depths by diverting the tributaries flow including the Brahmaputra waters. At the same time Ganga will be cleaned automatically with fresh water in large quantities even in lean seasons.
8. Small hydropower system allow achieving self-sufficiency by using as best as possible the natural resource that is the water, as a decentralized and low cost of production, since they are in forefront of many developing countries. Small hydropower have a lesser adverse effect on the environment, in particular in water quality, comparing with others power system. Small hydropower schemes do not contribute for green house effect or atmospheric pollution and for resentment, as happen with large dams, offering a decentralized electrification at low running cost and long life. This is preferable from an environmental point of view as seasonal river

flow patterns downstream are not affected and there is no flooding of valleys upstream of the system.

9. India has one of the world's largest irrigation canal networks with thousands of dams. It has monsoon-fed; double monsoon-fed as well as snow-fed rivers and streams with perennial flows. An estimated potential of 10000 MW of small hydro exists in India. However, nearly 5000 MW have been actually identified through more than 2000 sites in 13 states of India.

10. A New National Water Policy shifted the priorities of public investment towards small irrigation projects. Here the most important consideration is that decentralized rehabilitation of small groups of people with in their local area is much less likely to result in the destruction of the entire existence of people as happens in the case of large dams, Financially also minor irrigation costs per hectare only one-tenth of those of major irrigation.

In the case of social and human cost the best way to handle the situation is to ensure that environmental, economic and social issues are adequately addressed right at the conceptualization stage, in consultation and association with all stakeholders, the local community and PAFs, NGOs activists, and the local government. This process of consultations and dialogue between all constituents should be maintained through out the life of the project.

Apart from an initial environmental cost in terms of submergence and displacement, which can and must be appropriately compensated, hydro-electricity is about the cleanest form of power there is.

CONCLUSION

Finally it may be said that the country has a vast potential for developing hydropower and although generation of power through this technique does have some limitations, the positives, which arise, outweigh the shortcomings. Thus we may say that with an eye toward the environment as well as the growing demand of energy for the development and other requirements this is the best option at our disposal.

Government should follow the measures cited above which may not wholly but partially solve the problem of environmental impact. Hydropower development is not and need not be the enemy of the environment. Along with this other alternatives such as solar and wind energy for Power generation may also prove to be economically viable as a result of other on going research and ultimately we may be able to do away completely with thermal Power generation in the long run.

If we are serious about developing new sources of energy while protecting the atmosphere, the obstacle to hydropower development must be overcome. Today, the hydropower industry stands at a crossroads: we can do nothing and lose the many benefits of this emission free and renewable source of power, or we can create appropriate incentives, and let the power of water meet both environmental and energy needs of our nation.

NOTES

1. Pant K.C. (2003), *India Development Scenario,* Academic Foundation, New Delhi
2. Yoichi Kaya (1999), 'Environment, Economy, Energy and Sustainable Development', In Yoichi Kaya and Keichi, Eds, *Environment, Energy and Economy.* United Nations University Press.
3. *www.powerscorecard.org/tech-detail.cfm* 'Electricity From Hydro'.
4. Varghese B.G. (2002), 'Hydel: The Energy Multiplier', *The Economics Times,* July 24,2002.

REFERENCES

Abbasi, A.S. (1991), *Environmental Impact of Water Resource Projects,* Discovery Publishing House, New Delhi.

Ghosh Asish (2000), *Environment and Development*, APH Publishing Corporation, New Delhi.

Jhadhav, H.V. (1997), *Energy and Environment*, Himalaya Publishing House, Bangalore.

Brower, Michael (1998), *Cool Energy-Renewable Solution to Environmental Problems,* MIT Press, London.

Venkatraman, K. (1971), *Power Development in India,* Wiley Eastern: New Delhi.

Pant K.C. (2003), *India Development Scenario,* Academic Foundation, New Delhi.

Lodha R.M. (1991), *Environmental Essays,* Ashish Publishing House, New Delhi.

Jain Deepak (2002), Preventive Environment Management, In Jauhari, B.M, Eds., *India's Development after Independence*, Gyan Publishing House, New Delhi.

Kumar Raj (2002), Development of Power Sector after Independence, In Jauhari, B.M, Eds., *India's Development after Independence*, Gyan Publishing House, New Delhi.

Veltrop A.J. (1993), Importance of Dams for Water Supply and Hydro Power, In Biswas.K. Asit et. al., Eds., *Water for Sustainable Development in the 21st Century,* Oxford University Press: New Delhi.

Falkenmark Malin (1993), Environment and Development: Urgent Need for a Water Perspective, In Biswas K. Asit et. al., Eds., *Water for Sustainable Development in the 21st Century,* Oxford University Press: New Delhi.

Yoichi Kaya (1999), Environment, Economy, Energy and Sustainable Development, In Yoichi Kaya and Keichi, Eds., *Environment, Energy and Economy*, United Nations University Press.

Johansson T.B. (1999), Global Warming and Renewable Energy: Potential and Policy Approaches, In Yoichi Kaya and Keichi, Eds, *Environment, Energy and Economy*, United Nations University Press.

Rehman Hifzur & Ziauddin Khairoowala (1999), Management of Energy Resources: Issues and Challenges in 21st Century, In Khan, Farooq, Eds., *Energy Management*, Anmol Publication, New Delhi.

Gopalakrishnan M. (2003), The Role of Large Dams in India, In Prasad Kamta Eds., *Water Resources and Sustainable Development*, Shipra Publications, New Delhi.

Goel R.S and Srivastava, R.N. (1997), Environmental Concerns and Prospects of Hydropower Development India, In Chowdhary Pradeep Eds., *Sustainable Energy Supply in Asia,* Volume I, World Energy Council, Concept Publishing Company, New Delhi.

Parikh Jyoti K, *'et al'*, 'Energy System Need for New Momentum', *India Development Report 1997*, Oxford University Press.

Parikh Jyoti K. and Parikh K.S. (2002), Climate Change: India's Perceptions, Positions, Politics and Possibilities, *India Development Report 2002*, Oxford University Press: New Delhi.

Varghese B.G. (2002), Hydel: The Energy Multiplier, *The Economics Times,* July 24, 2002.

2

TRANSFORMATION OF AGRICULTURE IN JAMMU AND KASHMIR: PROGRAMMES AND PERFORMANCE

Aroon Sharma

INTRODUCTION

Despite the urge of industrialization, under developing countries continue to be heavily dependent on agriculture. The urge for the developing agriculture is a prime necessity for large overpopulated country. Hence, the role of agriculture is self-evident. The economist favouring industrial sector for the economic development of the country confers that the problem of development is a problem of industrialization and the industrial sector is the main hope for most of poor countries trying to improve the economic well being of their people. Today, this illusionary phenomenon has changed. The lesson from the economic development of some developed countries confirms that industrial development without agriculture development cannot deliver the goods in densely populated under developing country. A slowly growing agriculture sector can drag on the economic development even if the growth of industrial sector is at higher level. Thus, due emphasis should be laid upon the agriculture sector for its own development, to increase the aggregate rate of economic growth.

During the course of economic development, the development of agriculture and industrial sector plays an important role as, industrial or agriculture sector on its own cannot generate rapid economic growth, and thus, some criterion of balance is unavoidable. Hence, the balance-growth is considered essential for the under developing country. The effort for the development for agriculture must be associated with the rapid expansion of non-farm rural and urban sector, so as to eradicate poverty and lay stronger foundation for the establishment of a dynamic rural society. Thus, the rise in agriculture production and income across a wide spectrum of agriculture sector is essential for the general well being of the people living in the state of Jammu and Kashmir. However, it must be pointed out that increasing the efficiency and productivity is not enough for speedy economic development. It must be supported by the proper infrastructure and agriculture allied pursuits in the rural areas. Thus, an efficient agriculture made up of farm families with a high standard of living and a high buying power per person contributes much towards a high national income and the economic well-being of the nation, but the same can be said for each of the other groups. It is impossible to say which is most important is modern economic society. It is our feeling that the choice between sectors cannot be revealed until the economy has succeeded in achieving and sustaining a reliable food surplus.

The state of Jammu and Kashmir is the northern most state of India. It is located between latitudes 32° 17" north and 36° 58" north, longitudes 73° 28" east and 80° 30" east. Its boundaries touch the neighbouring country of China in the northeast, Afghanistan in the northwest and in the west by Pakistan. The geographical set up of the state has made it one of the most strategic tracts of land in the world. The state of Jammu and Kashmir with sealed international boarders is accessible only through south. In the south, it embraces the state of Punjab and Himachal Pradesh (states of India). Major portion of the state is hilly and height from the mean sea level varies between 1000 to 28,500 feet, except on southwest, there are mountains all over the state. On the southern side, the state has a strip of plains, which is just adjacent to the great plains of Punjab. Hence, a variation in its atmosphere, vegetation and climate can be experienced.

On geographical bias, the area of the state of Jammu and Kashmir is 2,22,236 sq. kms in which, Pakistan illegally occupies 78,114 sq. kms, 5180 sq. kms of area was illegally handed over by Pakistan to China and China illegally occupies 37,555 sq. kms, leaving 1,01,387 sq. kms on the Indian side. The state of Jammu and Kashmir with an area of about 1,01,387 sq. kms, constituting 3.2 per cent of the total area of the country, is the 11th largest state of the Indian Union in terms of physical size. However, in terms of population, with 100.70 lakh inhabitants in 2001, constitutes 0.98 per cent of the countries population. It ranks 19th in the country. The growth rate of population per annum is 2.9 per cent, which is alarming for the state's economic development. On employment front, the agriculture sector is providing jobs to sustain the state working force and agriculture labour productivity, which is 53 per cent as compared with the non-agriculture sector. The share of agriculture in the state economy is 33.2 per cent, which has decreased with an absolute rise in numbers. Thus, with 99 persons per sq. km., the state has one of the lowest densities of population and hence more availability of natural resources in relation to other state's of the country. The per-capita income at current price is estimated at Rs.

7,296 (93-94 price) during '001, it is less than the all India average of Rs. 9,733 (93-94 price).

Despite of having such adverse condition in the state agriculture, the role played by the state agriculture is significant. It reduces unemployment, contributes one-third of the state income, provides food for the labour engaged in non-agriculture sector and secures labours for future expansion of non-agriculture sector.

According to the state supplement, the total area covered by the village papers is 24.16 lakh hec, out of which, 6.58 lakh hec of area is under forest, 5.82 lakh hec of area is under the category of not available for cultivable land, 4.28 lakh hec is under uncultivable land and 7.48 lakh hec, which is 30.96 per cent of the reported area (village paper's) is under the net sown area. The per centage of net area sown is comparatively less than the per centage net area sown of the neighboring states and the country. This low per centage of net area sown can be attributed to the typical geographical condition prevailing in the state. The area covered by the forest is 42 per cent of the state's area, is also less than the standard prescribed by the Agro-Climatic-Regional Planning for the hilly regions of the state's in the country.

The state of J & K having such low per centage of area under net area sown is a major concern for the ongoing development of the state agriculture. Especially, with the absolute rise in the state population, increasing the absolute number of holdings, resulting a smaller holding size for an average peasant. The national study, on land size and productivity reveals that there is an inverse relationship between land size and productivity. However, it is also observed that too small or marginal holding is uneconomic from the personal-; commercial relationship. Hence, 1-2 hectares of land holding is considered most economic land for the intensive cultivation. The problem of uneconomic holding is more severe in the Kashmir division. The study of the tenurial status suggests that three-fourth of the holdings and two-fifth of the net area sown is considered as uneconomic. This has crippled the development of the stated culture. Hence, the holdings that are considered uneconomic should be either consolidated or co-operative farming should be encouraged so that the transformation of uneconomic land to economic land can be made possible.

Some of the over whelming aspects that are designed for the speedy transformation of agriculture sector is:-the proportion of individual holding is 80 per cent (approx) is more conducive for better management and higher returns. Moreover, major portions of tillers in all size class are the; owners of the land in which they practice cultivation. This can be attributed to the adoption of land reforms in the state. After the dawn of independence, land reforms were adopted and implemented for the development of the state agriculture.

The land reforms not only made the tillers the owner of the cultivated land but n as also compensated to the mediator's (land lords). Hence, the vested interest of both the mediator's and peasants were taken care off in the land reforms act. Attempts to revitalize the agrarian structure by eliminating the parasitic elements through land reforms and efforts to infuse development have not helped to pull out a break through in state agriculture. However, there is no doubt that due to the adoption and implementation on various land reforms act, the state agriculture is facing a transformation.

Due to the introduction of the land reforms and modern inputs, cropping pattern have tilted towards the wheat, maize, oil seeds, fruits and vegetable crops. The reason behind this tilt over can be attributed to the significant increase in its productivity. Despite, the inability to experience a break through in the agriculture can be attributed to the cropping intensity. Only 48 per cent of the total net area sown is cultivated more than once. Hence, due to improper infrastructure, the major portion of area is cultivated once a year. Provisions of irrigation facility will not increase the food grain production but it will also uplift the availability of cultivable land that will support the agriculture-allied activities in the state.

The forgoing discussion amply suggests that in the present stage of economic construction and in distant future, among most economic problems are the acceleration of the rate of development of agriculture by raising its effectiveness and the creation of agricultural potential that is necessary for the realization of full and uninterrupted growth rate of the state economy. The agrarian structure of Jammu and Kashmir economy is due to the prepondence of many kinds of "built in depressants" that has thwarted the limited efforts of the rural areas. To achieve sustained growth, it is essential to secure the participation of the weaker section of the rural population in the process of growth. This is the only way to transform the economic and social conditions of small and marginal farmers and land less agricultural labourers, rural artisans and other engaged in traditionally disadvantage occupation.

Precisely, the future prospective of agricultural development depends upon the rising investment by providing credits and building proper infrastructure. Hence, by raising the investment, the objective of agriculture development can be achieved. Therefore, the present study covers detailed explanation of the above-mentioned variable and draw important interference out of the available data.

OBJECTI VES AND METHODOLOGY

The present study has the following objectives:

1. To find out the role of agriculture in the states economy, and
2. To study the role of government intervention through institutional reforms.

In order to provide empirical support to the arguments and objectives, the statistical data on various cause and indicator variables will be presented. The statistical data and information which will be presented in the report will be collected from different records, books and journals scanned in various booklets published by the state government, state digest of statistics and documents etc. Despite the statistical information collected from various sources, the information was of haphazard nature and very often incomplete. For this purpose, the difficulty has been overcome by compiling the data in a single unit for the purpose of comparison. Where the comparison was possible, the statistical information has been left in their original form.

Productivity in agriculture essentially depends on two sets of factors-institutional and technological. The institutional set up deals with the relationship between decision-makers and actual producers. It is concerned with some of the basic decisions regarding production: what will be produced, why will it be produced, who will produce it and how the production will be distributed between the producer and decision-makers. In contrast to this, technological factors emphasize the relationship between inputs and outputs. The technological relationship analysis suggests various method of producing a particular commodity. It refers to the question; how can and does actual production take place? The emphasis here is on the alternative forms of combining the different inputs. (In the present study, we have taken only the institutional reforms and not the technological factors due to scarcity of space and paucity of time.)

Some opine that the institutional framework on agriculture in the developing economies dominates as it is by the feudal or semi-feudal-relations is the real cause of backwardness and poverty in rural communities. Thus, they argue that the emancipation of the peasantry from the bondage of institutional depressors will unleash forces, which shall raise levels of production in agriculture. Some other emphasizes that agricultural productivity is purely a technological phenomenon and thus it can only be raised by the application of superior agriculture methods. Amidst these constraining opinions, it must be stressed that these factors are not independent of each other. Land reforms and technological changes are not mutually exclusive factors but are complementary in the process of agricultural transformation. It is believed that technological changes can be assimilated more affectivity in a congenial agrarian structure. The government of Jammu and Kashmir immediately after the dawn of independence in 1947 embarked upon a program of action enshrined in the document entitled 'Naya Kashmir'.

INSTITUTIONAL REFORMS

Farming was the most uncertain, ugly and painful occupation in the pre-independence period. Whatever the tiller has produced, the landlords snatched away, leaving the tillers helpless and to fight with starvation at all times.

Therefore, to remove the mediators from these dreadful structures, high priority was placed by the govt. of Jammu a Kashmir under the able leadership of 'Sheikh Mohammed Abdullah'. The state govt. came up with a bold scheme to redesign and formulate land reform. Late Sheikh Mohammed Abdullah in April 1948 abolished as many as 3910 Jagirs and Maufis. Due to the execution of mediators, annually Rs. 7 lakh vas saved and the peasantry were relieved by the great burden of tax payments. These burden of tax over peasant's were approximately of Rs. 3.25 lakh, and nearly 2.5 lakh people were freed from subjection and medieval autocracy. About 4250 acres of land granted as a privilege to jagirdars for residential to the cultivator of the land.

By another act, tenancy rights of the tenants were protected in respect to land not exceeding 17 kanals (irrigated) or 33 kanals (unirrigated) in the Kashmir province. In the Jammu province, the rights were limited to 33 kanals (irrigated) and 65 kanals (unirrigated). This act was named as "The Act of Protected Tenancy Right".

PROTECTION FROM EJECTION AND RENTAL FIXATION ACT-1948

In October 1948, the state government amended the old law known as "The State Tenancy Act, 1924". In the amendment, it was proposed that the tenant holding not more than 2.12 acres of wetland or 4.12 acres of dry land in Kashmir province would have to pay a predetermined per centage of rent. In case of wetland, maximum rent of 25 per cent was charged on its annual produce, in case of dry land, 33 per cent of its annual produce was charged on the annual produce. In case of Jammu province, the tenant holding must not be more than 4.25 acres of wet land or 8.25 acres of dry land and the per centage of tax payable in both the land were equal.

The amended law also provides a chance to the rehabilitation of the tenants, who had ejected after April 1947. This was done to simplify the procedure for the partition of co-operative land holding. These allowed the weaker section of the cultivating peasantry for rehabilitation and share; appropriate shares of land piece, allotted to the peasants.

DISTRESSED DEBTOR'S RELIEF ACT, 2006 SAMVAT

This act was brought to distress the debtor. The debtor who had heavy burden of debt was provided a loophole, by which the debtor can bring the burden of debit down. For this purpose, Debt Conciliation Board (D.C.B.) was formed with voluntary conciliation between the debtor and creditors. This act also provides the mortgage property back to its owner (debtor), which included all properties including pawned boat. The D.C.B. conciliated in-between and claims made up to Rs. 175 lakh were scaled down to Rs. 85 lakhs. Moreover, the D.C. Board liquidated 14.59 lakhs values of mortgage property.

BIG LANDED ESTATE (ABOLITION) ACT, 1950

The big landed estate abolition act (BLEAA) was brought on 17th October 1950. The BLEAA brought a new revolutionary change in man and relationship. This act brought pace in the direction of achieving the objective of setting up a new society. A ceiling of 22.75 acres on all property holdings was put under the act.

The main features on this legislation were:

1. The proprietor will retain only 22.75 acres of land.
2. The proprietor's holding of ceiling were fixed, with 22.75 acres (182 kanal). Orchard, fuel and fodder reserves and uncultivable wasteland were excluded from the holdings.
3. Expropriation of proprietor's from areas exceeding the ceiling.
4. Transfer's of area from which owner's were expropriated to the tillers in cultivating possession of the area without compensation.
5. Fixation of ceilings at 160 kanals or 20 acres including land already held by them in ownership rights in respect of lands transferred to tillers in proprietorship.
6. Such land's from which proprietor's were expropriated and were nor in cultivating possession of any person, went to the state and were made available for the settlement of land less peasant's and field labourers.
7. No tiller's who owns more than 20 acres of land in ownership right should be with the land.
8. The law also applied to the lands owned by the evacuees and to those, which belonged to the enemy agents and had since been forfeited to the state.
9. All rights, title and interests of the proprietors in land (including trees, wells, tanks, ponds, water channels and pathways) from which he was expropriated, vested in the tillers.
10. If any proprietor or tiller- owner dies or transfer's his land or any interest there in without due permission or a tiller-owner sub-lets his land continuously for two harvests, the right of ownership was liable to be extinguished and the land would lapse to the state.

The benefits of Big Landed Estate (Abolition) Act, 1950 was considered beneficial by the Planning Commission Publication, according to them, about 9 thousand proprietors were expropriated from 4.5 lakh acres of land held in excess of such a ceiling. Out of this, 2.3 acres of land were transmitted to the tillers, who hold the ownership rights. Remaining land got vested in the state. This part of land was to be distributed from time to time, among landless agricultural labourers. The Act however was carried out with care but certain clauses made it truly unfair. For example, the ceiling was fixed at a uniform rate-throughout the state but no weightage was given to the fertility of soil, geographical conditions etc. Secondly, no limits were placed to restrict the protected tenant who violated the sprit of law by sub-letting their land. All these were removed by introducing several legislations in later years.

A land commission was set up in the year 1963 fôr detailed examination of the existing land laws. They proposed certain basic changes in laws to fine-tune with broad objectives to increase agriculture produce and social justice. After examining the problem at the grass root level. The commission recommended in the report of the land commission to the govt. of Jammu and Kashmir that if maximum production is to be secured, the tiller should be made the owner of the land in which he tills, and guaranteed that he would get the full benefits, enhancing interest in the cultivation. The cultivator's full participation in the economy is to be assured, then only maximum produce could be secured. The state govt. desired to make a direct relationship between the state and the tiller. So, the state govt. abolished all the intermediaries' interests in land. The state government came up with a bold legislation in the year 1972, which was latter known as "The Jammu and Kashmir Agrarian Reforms Act 1972".

JAMMU AND KASHMIR AGRARIAN REFORMS ACT, 1972

The Jammu and Kashmir Agrarian Reforms bill was presented in state legislative assembly in March 1972. Important provisions of Jammu and Kashmir Agrarian Reforms Act were:

1. Vesting of ownership rights of land (excluding orchards) held by the owners and intermediaries who are not in its personal cultivation to those who held such land in personal cultivation on 1-9-1971;
2. Imposition of a ceiling (excluding orchards) of 100 standard kanals (12.5 acres) and vesting of all land in excess of this ceiling in the state;
3. Compensation in exchange to all land vested in the state as a result of (1) and (2) above at rates specified by the government;
4. Provision for resumption of land by any intermediaries or absentee land lord on certain specified conditions;
5. Full compensation for evacuee lands; and
6. Standard acres have been defined with reference to various kind of soil in irrigated and unirrigated areas.

The introduction of this act resulted in a breakdown of relationship between a landlord and tenant. The ceiling of land was curtailed to 12.5 acres and considerably the act curtailed the exempted categories of land. Areas known as

Kah-I-Kreshan Bedzars, and other fuel and fodder growing areas were included in the ceiling area, which was restricted to 12.5 standard acres of ownership rights.

The objectives of the new act of the land reforms appear to be;

1. To abolish the absentee land lord including the allied forms of intermediaries;
2. To make the tiller the owner of the cultivated land; and
3. To fix a ceiling on land holding.

The new government of Sheikh Mohammad Abdullah suspended this bill. Main reason of its suspension was that many representative and counter representative made by both landlords and tenants. Many difficulties were observed in practical operation of the act. The government constituted a committee of experts consisting of officials and non-officials to examine the whole situation and to report to the government. Then, a revised form of bill was introduced in the state legislative assembly on 1st March 1976. With some amendments made by both the houses, the bill was finally passed by the two houses of states legislative and called as "The Jammu and Kashmir Agrarian Reforms Act, 1976", which received the accent of governor.

JAMMU AND KASHMIR AGRARIAN REFORMS ACT; 1976

As stated above, this act was formed with great difficulty. This act came into existence in the year 1976. The main objectives of this act is stated briefly as under:

1. The tiller was the sole individual to get the basic principle of land;
2. The right of all owners or intermediatories not cultivating the land personally in the kharif 1971 will shift their owners right to an ex-owner provided that he (ex-owner) wants to cultivate land personally and will have the right to resume a part of such land subjected to certain condition;
3. According to the class of soil and availability or otherwise of irrigation, the ceiling area of 12.5 standard acres (varies between 9 to 25 ordinary acres). The act provides that this ceilings area is related to a family consisting of a person, his and her spouse and their children excluding a married daughter and a major son, separated from his parents on or before 1st Sept. 1971 and holding land in his own name.
4. To ensure that with a few exceptions which are in general public interest ownership follows personal cultivation.
5. Providing rehabilitation facilities for parties expropriated from a land by permitting resumption in certain cases and requiring payment of levy in full lumpsum except in case of indigenous tillers; and

6. Providing secured land to the landless and poor persons.

The salient features of this act are stated as under:

1. To abolish absentee land lords;
2. To provide land to land less;
3. To make provision for the resumption;
4. To make provision for the selection of land, subjected to the exceeding ceiling area;
5. To impose ceiling on agricultural land and orchards;
6. To provide adequate compensation to the parties;
7. To allow cultivation of land in genuine cases;
8. To protect the interests of mortgagor and mortgage;
9. To recognize the private agreement between landlords and tenants with regard to the appointment of land;
10. To prohibit the creation of new tenancy and extinguish the existing tenancy except in certain cases;
11. To protect alienation of land by way of sale, gift, mortgage with possession, bequest, and exchange;
12. To make provision for the attachments by the collector of the orchard or a plantation of trees on state land or land reserves for grazing purpose; and
13. To create new administrative machinery to implementation of the provision of the act.

This bill was passed with minor amendments and it took a form of an act on 8th April 1979 and came into force on 12th July 1979. The main amendment of the Jammu & Kashmir Reforms (amendment) Act, 1979 were,

1. The orchard was kept out of the operation.
2. The land cultivated by the tenants personally (subjected to the evacuated land) will be liable to pay rent equal to the amount of land revenue and ceases assessed there on.
3. No person (personally or family members), holding orchards exceeding 199 kanals or 24.87 acres can resume land for personal cultivation.
4. An ex-serviceman who has served in the defense services can hold 1 acre over and above the ceiling fixed in the sub-section 7.

The Jammu & Kashmir Reforms (amendment) Act 1978 has provided a great support not only to our older generation but will provide assistance to our future generation too. The amendment made under this act has equipped the act to achieve a huge milestone in the Land Reforms.

LAND USE PATTERN IN THE STATE OF JAMMU AND KASHMIR

An analysis of the land use pattern in the state of Jammu and Kashmir based on the data in table 1 reveals that 77.97 per cent of the holding are in the size category of below 1 hectare and hence can be characterized as sub marginal holdings. The small and semi-medium holding that is the holdings belonging to the category of 1 to 4 hectares constitutes only 20.6 per cent of the total holdings in the division while medium and large sized holdings accounts for only 1.13 per cent. The holding in the size category of below 1 hectares accounts for 39.71 per cent area while small and semi-medium farms cover 48.86 per cent of the area and medium and large farms accounts for 11.43 per cent of the total area. It can also be observed from the table that net area sown at the marginal and sub-marginal holding is 77.13 per cent of area in that size category and is the highest in relation to the small, semi-medium and large sized holdings. Similarly, the net cultivated area at the marginal and sub-marginal holding constitutes 83.27 per cent of area in the size categories. These trends are consistent with the logic that agricultural activity is carried out more intensively at smaller farms than the area under larger ones. Another important point to be observed is that the area under current fallows in the size category of below 4 hectares constitutes 85.04 per cent of the total area in the state and this demands the introduction of suitable cropping pattern, with the increase in the use of fertilizers, to avoid the necessity of keeping the land untilled for one or two cropping season.

SIZE AND STRUCTURE OF HOLDINGS

Size of operational holding is a critical factor in determination of pace and shape of agriculture transformation. Whatever may be the pretension of the

Table 1
Size and Structure of Holding (in 000's) (1995-1996)

Sl. No.	*Size category (hec)*	*No. of holding*	*% age*	*Area*	*% age*	*Average size*
1.	Below–0.5	696.15	52.12	165.37	16.33	0.24
2.	0.5–1.0	345.34	25.85	236.72	23.38	0.68
3.	1–2	186.59	13.97	257.65	25.45	1.38
4.	2–3	64.15	4.80	153.95	15.20	2.40
5.	3–4	24.40	1.83	83.12	8.21	3.40
6.	4–5	10.69	0.80	45.32	4.67	4.42
7.	5–7.5	5.84	0.44	35.16	3.47	6.02
8.	7.5–10	1.65	0.12	14.47	1.43	8.77
9.	10–20	0.75	0.06	9.98	0.99	13.30
10.	20–above	0.13	0.01	8.79	0.87	67.61
	Total	1335.69	100	1012.33	100	

Source: State Agriculture Census 1995-96, and State Digest of Statistics, 2001-02, Table-4.01, page 40.

protagonists of large sized farming and small-sized farming, there is at least a convergence of opinion on the need to identify/quantify the size of holdings below which continuation of agriculture activity is uneconomical. Estimation of such a size of holding for the economy as a whole is an extremely difficult proposition as many economic, social, cultural, institutional and technical factors are involved in it. The variability of these factors in the complex regional setting of an economy further aggravates the problem of estimation.

On the basis of the data made available by the agriculture census 1995-96, the agricultural holdings in India and also in the state of Jammu and Kashmir appear to suffer from two main defects viz.;

1. Concentration of holdings in the size category classified as sub marginal and marginal holdings, and
2. Wide dispersal of smallholdings due to sub-division and fragmentation.

A depressing observation about the agrarian economy of Jammu and Kashmir is an increase in the number of holdings in 1995 was 13.36 lakh in correspondence to 7.9 lakh and 10.35 lakh in 1970-71 and 1980-81 respectively (refer table). It can be observed that while the land holding increased by 31 per cent in the decade 1970-80, the per centage increase in the following decade viz. 1980-90 was as much as 14.5 per cent. This per centage of increase in the number of holdings may be attributed to high growth rate of population, rigorous implementation of laws of inheritance, spurious method adopted by the land lords to evade the provisions of various land Reform Acts and under development of non-agriculture activity in the state, necessitating the growing population to depend on agriculture for its livelihood.

The growing number of agriculture holdings and the marginal decrease in area under operational holdings estimated at 10.12 lakh hectares in 1995-96 is responsible for an exceeding small size of holding in the state. A vivid picture of structure of holdings in the state can be viewed from the data condensed in the table 1.

The information contained in the table 1 reveals that 52.12 per cent holdings are in the size category of less than 0.5 hectares and accounts its for 16.33 per cent of the area with an average size of holding estimated at 0.24 hectares. Another depressing aspect of the structure of holding is that 77.97 per cent of the holdings are in the size category of less than 1 hectare and accounts for 39.71 per cent of the area with an average size of holdings estimated as 0.39 hectares. A further look on the data provided in the table shows that 91.94 per cent holdings are in the size category of less than 2 hectares and accounts for 65.16 per cent of the area. In contrast to this, 6.63 per cent of the total holding in the size category of 2-4 hectares accounts for 23.41 per cent of the area while as 1.49 per cent of the holdings in the size category of 4 hectares and above accounts for 11.43 per cent of the total area.

These observations inevitably lead to the conclusion:

1. That is uneven distribution of area in the different size category of holdings.
2. That the magnitude of proletariation is very high in the state. If this phenomenon is viewed temporally, it is observed that the per centage of holdings in the size category has been of below 2 hectares has increased from 88.6 per cent in 1970 to 89.7 per cent in 1985-86 and 91.9 per cent in 1995-96.

The size and structure of holdings are analyzed with division and districts, which can be observed by the table 2. The table 2 indicates that the average size of holdings in the 7 districts of Kashmir division (all districts except Leh) is less than the average size of holdings in all the districts of Jammu Division. Moreover, not only the average size of holdings is greater than Kashmir Division but also but also the extent of proliterisation is less pronounced, as the per centage of holdings in the category of 'less than 1 hectare' is 66.94 per cent in comparison to 86.66 per cent in the Kashmir Division. Further, in the Jammu division, 55.62 per cent of area is commanded by 30.33 per cent of holding in this category of 1 to 4hec where as in Kashmir division 38.99 per cent of area is commanded by 12.92 per cent of the holding in this category.

These observations indicates that in Jammu region, the thrust of agricultural development program which should be towards the creation of more irrigation facilities, and propagation of high yielding seeds, chemical fertilizers and other

Table 2
Holding Size-District Wise (2001-02)

District	*No.of Holdings*	*Area (in000's hec)*	*Average size (in hec)*	*Ranking*
Srinagar	87.99	32.39	0.37	14
Anantnag	166.39	81.33	0.49	13
Baramulla	165.32	95.76	0 .58	10
Budgam	107.36	57.92	0.54	12
Pulwama	103.61	66.28	0.64	9
Kupwara	87.51	48.30	0.55	11
Leh	12.04	16.58	1.38	1
Kargil	16.63	12.94	0.78	8
Jammu	65.20	159.16	0.96	5
Udhampur	113.56	125.56	1.11	4
Kathua	82.94	96.57	1.16	3
Rajouri	66.39	79.10	1.19	2
Poonch	51.88	49.01	0.94	6
Doda	I 108.95	91.48	0.84	7

Source: State Agriculture Census 1995-96, and Digest of Statistics, 2001-02, Directorate of Economics and Statistics, Department of Planning and Development, Govt. of Jammu and Kashmir, Table-4.02, page-81.

improved agriculture practices. Where as in Kashmir division, the necessary concomitant of these development programs has got to be an organizational reform such as co-operative farming with the view to increase the average size of the operational-holding and make the farming activity mare fruitful and purposeful.

INDIVIDUAL AND JOINT HOLDING

Yet another feature of state agriculture is the predominance of joint holding over individual holding as can be observed from the table 3. The proportion of joint holdings for the state is 21.69 per cent of total holdings. The inter district study based on table 3 indicates joint ownership status of the holding except the district of Jammu, Udhampur, Kathua, Rajouri, Poonch, Srinagar and Leh is minorly spread in the state. Such an ownership is hardly conducive to better management and higher returns from the land. A further study of the ownership pattern of holdings based on different size a category indicates that the per centage of joint holding varies from 42 per cent to 62 per cent is in the size category of more than 3 hectares.

This increase to 61.11 per cent is the highest in the size class of 7.5 to 10 hectares and in the lowest that is 18 per cent in the size catagory of less than 0.5 hectare. The reason for the greater proportion of joint holdings in the size class of 10 to 20 hectares can be traced to the methods adopted by the land lords to evade the provision of abolish land lord in the Jammu and Kashmir Agrarian Reform Act 1976 where, the tiller was the owner of the cultivated land.

Table 3
Per centage of Joint Holdings to the Total Holdings in 1995-96(%)

Districts of J & K	*Per centage*
State	21.69
Srinagar	29.95
Anantnag	6.50
Baramulla	17.13
Budgam	11.08
Pulwama	7.32
Kupwara	20.03
Leh	28.80
Kargil	4.83
Jammu	24.99
Udhampur	30.95
Kathua	50.03
Rajouri	39.83
Poonch	28.87
Doda	21.64

Source: State Agriculture Census, 1995-96.

TENURIAL STATUS OF HOLDINGS

The tenurial status of holdings has a commanding influence on the capacity of the farmers to save and invest in agriculture and also to enjoy the fruits of their labour. It helps in the estimation of the magnitude of parasitism in the rural economy and identification of depressants in institutional setting of agriculture. Despite the adoption of highly progressive measure of land reforms the state agriculture has experienced that out of 13.35 lakh holdings in the state, only 81.53 per cent holdings and 80.88 per cent of the area accounts for wholly owned and self operated, as against 18.47 per cent holdings in partly owned and partly rented and wholly rented accounting for 19.12 per cent of area. More comprehensive information about the tenurial status of holding is obtained in table 4.

The table depicts that all types of tenurial holdings are concentrated in the size category of less than 1 hectare. For instance, the wholly owned and self operated category holds 78.56 per cent of the holding accounting for 39.89 per cent of the area, and in the size category of below 1 hectare, 13.54 per cent of the holding accounting for 25.11 per cent of the area in the size class of 1 to 2 hectares. In the size class of 10 hectares and above, there are 0.82 thousand holdings accounting for 16.28 thousand hectares of area. Similarly, of the partly owned and partly rented holdings, 75.69 per cent accounting for 38.06 per cent of the area in the size class of below 1 hectare. The concentration of the holdings wholly rented from others in the size category of below 1 hectare is also similar to the above categories 74.37 per cent holdings in the wholly rented from others accounting for 41.77 per cent of the area.

Table 4
Tenurial Status of Holdings (1995-96) (000's)

TenurialStatus	*Size Category*					*Total*
	Below 1 hec	*1 to 2 hec*	*2 to 4 hec*	*4 to10 hec*	*Above 10 hec*	
1. Wholly owned and self operated						
(a) Numbers	855.59	147.48	69.98	15.25	0.82	1089.12
(b) Area	326.73	205.69	188.52	81.77	16.28	819.00
2. Partly owned and Partly rented						
(a) Numbers	140.61	28.29	13.93	2.80	0.13	185.77
(b) Area	56.24	37.93	36.54	14.58	2.48	147.78
3. Wholly rented from others						
(a) Numbers	45.28	10.81	4.65	0.13	-	60.88
(b) Area	19.11	14.02	12.01	0.6	-	45.75

Source: State Agriculture Census 1995-96, Collected from State Financial Commissioners Office, Government of J & K.

ACHIEVEMENTS

The land reforms has provided a great support to make productive changes in the rural sector, which has a crucial role to play in Jammu & Kashmir's economy, the following achievements were made a result of implementation of land reforms in the state.

1. Out of 6652 villages in the state of Jammu & Kashmir, work has been carried out in all the villages. Out of it, the work under 4, 5 and 6 of the agrarian Reforms Act has been completed in 5944 villages;
2. In respect to displace person, 6046 person or individual families were benefited when occupancy right has been vested to them 156569 kanals or 19571.12 acres of evacuees land were recovered from excess personal holding cultivators;
3. The state took the vest of 2344251 kanals or 294406.37 acres of land from those who have not cultivated their personal land in kharif, 1971. There ownership right of land had submerged;
4. 437912 tillers were recorded prospective owner's in respect to the land measuring 2304251 kanals or 288031.37 acres held for the personal cultivation;
5. Under the section 15 of the Agrarian Reform Act, 14000 kanals or 5125 acres of surplus land were to be distributed to the referred person;
6. Under the section 15 of the Agrarian Reform Act, 5.2 lakh kanals or 65 thousand acres of land was vested absolute ownership right to 63,822 prospective owners; and
7. An amount of Rs. 14022302 was recovered from the prospective owner's in the form of levy out. Out of these Rs. 4002721 were distributed to the ex owner in support to leave their ownership right on land.

The land reform has brought an end to the age-old system. This abolished the intermediators who were obstacles for the development of land. The state with the functional status of this act had made the tiller, the owner of the land. This acquired proprietorship has boosted the development of agrarian structure. The land in which the tillers tills with heavy sweat and physical pain, with absentee tenants claims healthy, encouraging environment between the tillers (proprietor ownership) and petty landowners. This encourages self-cultivation.

Owing to land reform measures, the government has succeeded in eliminating considerably the elements of exploitation from the agranian system. It has abolished Zamindari system, protected the tenancy rights, and regulated the rents, distribution of the surplus land among the land less and marginal and sub marginal tillers of the soil. These measures undoubtedly have strengthened peasant proprietorship in the state, which is considered by all standards conducive to the speedy transformation of agriculture. However, the agrarian structure still continues to be dominated by marginal and sub marginal holdings, the tenancy holdings and by inequalities in the distribution of land which definitely do not augur well for the prosperity of agriculture.

With the influx in absolute size of state-population, the land has been fragmented and passed on to the next generation in accordance with the tenancy right. This phenomenon has increased the absolute number of holdings in the below one hectare category. The study of Taiwan and Japan reveals that there is an inverse relationship between productivity and operational holdings until its size becomes economic for cultivation. From here, we can infer that this fragmentation should be with held in order to stop degradation of economic land.

CONCLUSION

From the analysis of the Land Distribution data it is obvious that compared to the rest of the country. Land distribution is less skewed in Jammu & Kashmir. This could be safely attributed to the agrarian reforms undertaken in the state right from early fifties. Though the land concentration has marginally increased in the recent years yet the absolute values of inequality indices continue to be reasonably low.

The states experience in land distribution highlights the significance of land reforms in reducing asset inequalities in the rural areas where land occupies a key position in asset structure. The analysis also shows a high degree of proliferation of marginal and tiny holdings, studies have shown that given the state of technology and cropping pattern net returns from these holdings are low and most of these holdings are non-visible. This is a disturbing phenomenon of far reaching consequences. Changes in the techniques of production and cropping pattern can go a long way in making these holdings viable.

REFERENCES

Aggarwal, A.N. and Singh S.P. (1969), The Economics of Underdevelopment, Oxford University Press, New York.

Desai, R.G. (1998), Agricultural Economics: Models, Problems and Policy Issues, Himalaya Publishing House, Mumbai.

Gupta, N.S. and Sing, A. (1998), Agriculture Development of States in India, Vol. 1, Jammu and Kashmir Seema Publications, New Delhi.

Singh, Jasbir (2004), The Economy of Jammu and Kashmir, Radha Krishan and Annual Co. Jammu.

Subramanya, S. and Sundaram, I.S. (1987), Recent Trends in Size of Land Holding in Andhra Pradesh, Deep and Deep Publications, New Delhi.

Viner, J. (1953), International Trade and Economic Development, Oxford University Press, London.

3

AGRO-INDUSTRIES: KEY TO ECONOMIC DEVELOPMENT

Badar Alam Iqbal

INTRODUCTION

Agro-Industries are the backbone of developing economies. The role and contribution of agro-industries have been of paramount significance. These industries have been contributing positively and constructively in the process of economic development of developing economies. Their share in employment generation, earning foreign exchange is of vital nature. These industries served a better cause of helping the domestic economies by creating regional balances and minimizing regional disparities. These industries can also preserve ecological balances. These industries may serve a better cause in hilly regions. They establish meaningful linkages between input and output. One of the most vital aspects of agro-industries has been their backward and forward linkages between agriculture and industry which sine-quo-none for accelerating the pace of economic progress and economic emancipation whoich is the distant dream for developing economies.

Agro-industries have become pre-requisite for speeding industrialization in developing nations. These industries may enter into cooperative sector to serve the rural masses and may serve as springboards for brining the needed economic progress and emancipation in rural areas. These industries may protect and preserve environment in rural areas. They are the need of the hour.

AGRO-INDUSTRIES: KEY TO ECONOMIC DEVELOPMENT

Basic to an objective study of the role and contribution of agro-industries in the economic progress of an economy is an understanding of the term 'agro-industries'. Unless the connotation of the term is clear, it would not be possible whether to appreciate the true purpose, potential and opportunities and opportunities associated with agro-industries or assess their relevance to economic progress of an economy. Moreover, when a progarmme for the growth and development of agro-industries seeks recognition and acceptance as an integral part of a progarmme national economic progress with emphasis on the growth and development of modern large scale industries, the need for such clarity becomes manifest, as only against such clear idea can the nature, range and duration of aids, specially oriented to serve the needs of agro-industries be understood, examined and assessed in relation to the nation's resources in men, material, money and market.

AN INVALUABLE WEAPON

Industries manufacturing 'input' for agriculture or processing agricultural 'output' or those industries, which are supported by agriculture goods, are classified as agro-industries. In the first instance, agro-industries provide the essential input and in the second phase they function as an outlet for the agricultural produce.

Still in the present economic scenario, the agro-industries constitute the backbone or corner stone of an economy. These industries have become an invaluable weapon in bringing out harmoniously balanced and integrated socio-economic order in global economy in general and developing countries economy in particular like that of India. The role and the contribution of agro-industries is significant both in respect of employment and value added by manufacture, not only in the developing economies, but also in the highly developed economies of the world.

Economic progress or prosperity of a developing economy like India is dependent on effective and meaningful integration of its agriculture with industry. Rural India, the real India wherein rural people form bulk of our population and their emancipation from evils arising out of economic imbalances would depend upon how best we diversify rural economy of India. Taking away a few millions of the people from villages to industrial areas could not remove the fundamental constraints of increasing pressure of population on agriculture, lack of employment opportunities in the rural areas, and the resultant limitations on equitable distribution of national income. Hence, the strategy of economic progress and emancipation has to be such that it integrates rural and urban economies by eliminating regional imbalances. Only introducing or injecting industry in the rural areas in a big way could attain this. In this process, agro-industries' development would then signify a pattern of deliberate planned development that accords with the need of rural areas in different parts of the Indian economy, i.e. while basic approach to, and objective of development would remain the same for the Indian economy as a whole, the choice, the range of operations in any given area, would be determined wholly by the resources of that area in men, their skills, aptitudes and adoptability on the one hand, and on the other the material's market and the state of other essential infrastructure in relation to felt needs. Development would not therefore, be so much prescribed as in an elective pattern.

A PREREQUISITE

Industrialization feeds upon agricultural surpluses. Unless the farmers produce more their needs, they will have nothing to sell and hence, nothing to buy. Increase in agricultural output furnishes increase in purchasing power. Industrialization thus cannot precede, but will only follow increased agricultural output. Increase in productivity of land in thus, a vital prerequisite for diversification of rural economy. Rise in productivity of land in its turn depends upon structural land and technological changes in agriculture. Agro-industries are considered the most vital, strategic and most suitable agencies for achieving this. Experiences have shown that rural areas wherein agro-industries have come up in a big way, they have set in motion forces that have changed the socio-economic structure of the areas. It means development of agro-industries on the one hand and on the other, of the entire group of industries to cater to the needs of the masses in as decentralized a fashion as possible. This is not merely to raise the level of material living but also to promote the basic and essential values of social cohesion, unity and inner strength in the rural economy.

Imperfections in the system of processing, marketing of agricultural produce constitute a significant restraint on agricultural output. There is therefore, immediate need for developing an efficient, effective and orderly processing and marketing system. Such a system has to render services efficiently, effectively and ensure incentives to the farmers for better quality and more output. Hence, while formulating arrangements for processing of agricultural produce and inducting agro-industries in the rural Indian economy, care should be taken to see that they not only offer services but at the same time involve the farmers too. In this respect, the conclusion that processing of agricultural commodities will have to be undertaken in the cooperative sector on an increasing scale is inescapable.

Growth and development of agro-industries in the cooperative sector is vital and strategic from one more point of view. Agro-industries help to strengthen other cooperative services namely-supply of agricultural credit, marketing and storing etc. In a subsistence economy like India, integration of cooperative societies with agro-industries is of paramount significance, if the former have to grow vigorously and steadily. Because of their vital interest in increasing the productivity of land, they are considered as most suitable agencies to take up agricultural functions. The agriculturist and the processing units, both have mutual interest in bettering the production of agricultural produce. For the former, it means wealth and for the later, a steady supply of raw materials of requisite quality and quantity for fuller utilization of their installed capacity. Tying up of functions relating to agricultural extension services with agro-industries is thus, an important arrangement that needs to be encouraged fro-modernizing agriculture through industry.

Establishment of agro-industries in Indian economy has one more dimension. Excessive dependence on agriculture is never considered desirable for an all-round and balanced growth and development or economic progress and emancipation in Indian economy. Excessive dependence on agriculture forms a vicious circle and leads to unemployment, low productivity, low income and consequently low savings and low investment i.e. burden of providing capital for economic progress and emancipation, falls heavily on agriculture alone. Therefore, to bear in mind the fact that there cannot be prosperity and progress in agriculture without prosperity and progress in industry. Interlinking of these two factors or variables has one more angle. Continuous investment in land and adoption of improved techniques would lead to decrease in the demand for labor working on farmlands. Absorption of surplus labor released is possible only if simultaneously industries are inducted or injected in rural economy of India. In this regard, the role of agro-industries is pivotal and strategic.

Agro-industries set up in rural India has to be designed in such a way that they operate more as catalytic agents fro development of infrastructure that would bridge the gap between rural and urban India. These industries need to be looked upon primarily as an agency to pave the way for occupational shifts and for creating new social groupings, which would form the basis for creation necessary social, cultural and psychological premises for modern industrial India. One the other hand, agro-industries if functioning in a cooperative framework, inject industries in the rural India in a democratic and decentralized form involving bulk of rural population in the process of peaceful and concurrent socio-economic development of all the classes. Added to this, these industries create not only economic opportunity but also the much-needed self-confidence among the farmers. This is utmost importance in building up new industrial and business leadership from the villages. The result would be that as the farmers as a class feel confident of themselves, it would be easier to carry out the goals set for the national economy.

COOPERATIVES: A MUST

Efficacy of the cooperative agro-industries as a sector would depend upon their percentage coverage in the total arrangements made for processing and marketing of agricultural produce of the rural India. The strength of the cooperative agro-industries would help the economy not only for rural industrialization but also for implementing effectively agricultural progarmme. It is not lack of proper strategy stands in the way of integration of rural and urban economies of India. It is considered that cooperative set up would be more advantageous for rural industrialization in Indian economy.

Industries recline on agriculture, and the future will witness greater fusion of industry and agriculture, and one of the instruments for brining their fusion will be agro-industries. In this process of integration the agro-industries could render a yeomen service by exporting the rural population gradually to present-day culture, thus, reducing tension and friction to a minimum which would lead in removing regional and sect oral imbalances which is also prerequisite of economic progress and emancipation as well as for attaining the goal of establishing a modern industrial society.

Apart from providing additional work in the villages these industries together with other cottage industries facilitate the expansion of creative skill and maintain the traditional arts, skills and efficiency of the artisans. Depending on the potentialities of utilizing science and modern technology these industries promote input-output relations.

CONCLUSION

It emerges from the foregoing discussion that agro-industries are still vital for economic progress and emancipation. These industries provide true basis for a pattern of socio-economic progress and emancipation that would contribute for the growth of the economy in all respects. These industries are not only labor intensive but also hold out promise of relatively high propensity to save as compared to the large scale industries which is very important from the point of view of economic progress and prosperity. These industries may preserve and protect environment especially in the rural areas.

4

NON-AGRICULTURAL ENTERPRISES IN INDIA: ITS IMPLICATIONS

R. Albert Christopher Dhas and
M. Helen Mary Jacqueline

INTRODUCTION

The Indian economy has been undergoing significant changes in all the sectors in recent years. While certain changes are visible and that are quantifiable, the others are invisible that could be realized. Similarly, certain changes are already felt and realized, while the rest could be visualized. Needless to state that "globalization[1]" which refers to cross-national flows of goods and services, investment, production and technology, and people (James Petras and Henry Veltmeyer, 2001) contributes towards the transitions in both the rural and urban economies. As Indian economy is agriculture-based, its development has been also agri and agro-oriented. In both rural and urban sectors, the developments in the non-agricultural enterprises provide a fillip to the growth in agriculture and for its efficient forward and backward linkages. It also absorbs the additional labour forces that are added to the total work force every year and the workers pushed into the unorganized sector from the organized sector. The overall objective of this paper is to examine the trends in non-farm enterprises. However, the specific objectives are (a) to highlight the major characteristics of non-agricultural enterprises in India and (b) to examine the trends in the non-agricultural enterprises and its implications in Indian economy.

CHARACTERISTICS OF AGRICULTURAL AND NON-AGRICULTURAL ENTERPRISES IN INDIA

Data on non-agricultural enterprises are systematically collected by Central Statistical Organization and published in its Economic Census. It also provides information on various dimensions of non-agricultural enterprises and their changes over time. As per the Economic Census, an enterprise is defined as an undertaking engaged in production and/or distribution of goods and/or services not for the sole purpose of own consumption. More over, these enterprises do not cover those enterprises engaged in agricultural production and plantation. Thus, an enterprise as per the Economic Census refers to a commercial unit, which includes both agricultural and non-agricultural enterprises, but excludes agricultural production and plantation.[2]

Table 1
Number of Enterprises by Type, Location and Employment in India (1998)

	Agricultural Enterprises		*Non-Agricultural Enterprises*		*Total Enterprises*	
	Numbers	*%*	*Numbers*	*%*	*Numbers*	*%*
Number of Enterprises (in ' 00)						
Rural	32006	92.11	145068	53.98	177074	58.35
	(18.07)		(81.93)		(100.00)	
Urban	2742	7.89	123672	46.02	126414	41.65
	(2.17)		(97.83)		(100.00)	
Total	34748	100.00	268740	100.00	303488	100.00
	(11.45)		(88.55)		(100.00)	
Number of Own Account Enterprises (in' 00)						
Rural	28862	93.02	107145	58.64	136007	63.63
	(21.22)		(78.78)		(100.00)	
Urban	2167	6.98	75583	41.36	77750	36.37
	(2.79)		(97.21)		(100.00)	
Total	31029	100.00	182728	100.00	213757	100.00
	(14.52)		(85.48)		(100.00)	
Percentage Share of Own Account Enterprises to the Respective Region's Total Enterprises						
Rural	90.18		73.86		76.81	
Urban	79.03		61.12		61.50	
Total	89.30		67.99		70.43	
Number of Persons Employed (in ' 00)						
Adult Male	41036	60.80	600890	78.50	641926	77.06
	(6.39)		(93.61)		(100.00)	
Adult Female	22472	33.30	121425	15.86	143897	17.27
	(15.62)		(84.38)		(100.00)	
Children	3981	5.90	43191	5.64	47172	5.66
	(8.44)		(91.56)		(100.00)	
Total	67489	100.00	765506	100.00	832995	100.00
	(8.10)		(91.90)		(100.00)	
Employment Per Enterprise						
Adult Male	1.18		2.24		2.12	
Adult Female	0.65		0.45		0.47	
Children	0.11		0.16		0.16	
Total	1.94		2.85		2.74	

Note: Figures in brackets show percentages to the respective totals.
Source: Government of India (2001): Economic Census 1998: All India Report, Central Statistical Organization, Ministry of Statistics and Programme Implementation, New Delhi.

The comparison of agricultural and non-agricultural enterprises highlights the features of non-agricultural enterprises sharply. It can be seen that there exists a vast difference in the distribution of enterprises across rural and urban areas. While agricultural enterprises are distributed in an uneven manner (92 per cent in rural areas and the rest 8 per cent only in urban), non-agricultural enterprises are spread almost evenly (54 per cent in rural and the rest 46 per cent in urban) across regions. Though Own Account Enterprises[3] (OAEs) account for a major share (70.43 per cent) of the total enterprises, and its dominance is on both agricultural and non-agricultural enterprises, there are striking patterns across areas. Of the 21 million OAEs, 85 per cent are of non-agricultural enterprises. More over, among the total OAEs, 64 per cent are located in rural areas and the rest in urban areas. The share of OAEs to the respective region's Total Enterprises have shown that they are relatively more among the agricultural enterprises, compared to that of non-agricultural enterprises. This indicates an important aspect of the higher dependency on hired workers by non-agricultural enterprises. The share of OAEs is of very high in rural areas compared to that of urban areas.

As far as the employment generation is concerned, the total number of persons working in all enterprises is of the order of 83 million, of which 48 per cent working in rural areas and the rest in urban areas. Interestingly, it is observed that the employment of workers in the non-agricultural enterprises is very high, indicated by the 92 per cent of persons employed in it. It also revealed the existence of child labour up to 6 per cent in both agricultural and non-agricultural enterprises. In fact, the extent of child labour is relatively higher in non-agricultural enterprises as compared to that of agricultural enterprises. The ratio of employment per enterprise revealed that non-agricultural enterprises absorb higher amount of workers per enterprise relatively.

With the above understanding on the basic features of non-agricultural enterprises, as revealed by the Economic Census, we shall examine the broad trends in it for the period between 1980 and 1998.

TRENDS IN NON-AGRICULTURAL ENTERPRISES IN INDIA

The first Economic Census was conducted in 1977, covering non-agricultural establishments (employing at least one hired worker on a fairly regular basis). However, a fairly comparable data is available from the second Census (1980) onwards as it is covered both agricultural and non-agricultural enterprises of Own Account and establishments. Hence, in order to understand the changing dimensions of non-agricultural enterprises, the data from the Economic Censuses 1980, 1990 and 1988 are analyzed (see Table 2).

In terms of absolute numbers, there has been a steady increase in the total number of Non-Agricultural Enterprises and the total employment in it. The number of NAEs has increased from 167 lakhs to 291 lakhs between the years1980 and 1998, recording an increase of about 75 per cent. The total number of employment in the NAEs also showed an increase from503 lakhs to 738 lakhs during the same period, recording an increase of 47 per cent. It could be seen that the increase in employment is much lower than that of the number of enterprises, indicating the low labour absorption capacity of NAEs.

Table 2
Trends in Non-Agricultural Enterprises (NAEs) in India (1980-98)

Particulars	*Numbers/Percentages*			*Growth Rates (%)*	
	1980	*1990*	*1998*	*1980-90*	*1990-98*
Total Number of Non-Agricultural Enterprises (in lakhs)	167.2	221.9	290.9	3.27	2.20
Total Employment in Non-Agri-cultural Enterprises (in Lakhs)	503.1	656.8	738.3	3.05	1.55
Share of NAEs to the Total Enterprises (in %)	92.03	90.55	88.32		
Share of Rural NAEs to the Total NAEs (in %)	58.27	55.37	53.70		
Share of NAEs workers to the Total Workers in Enterprises (in %)	94.62	93.32	91.57		
Number of Workers per NAEs	3.01	2.96	2.83		

Source: Economic Census, 1998.

In terms of growth rates, a differential pattern of change could be observed between the eighties and the nineties. Both the number of NAEs and employment are at the higher order of growth during the eighties compared to that of nineties, indicating a deceleration of NAEs in India, in recent years. While the number of NAEs recorded an annual growth rate of 3.27 per cent during the eighties, it declined to 2.2 per cent during the nineties. The similar decline in the growth rate of employment from 3.05 per cent to 1.55 per cent during the respective periods is also observed.

The relative role played by the Non-Agricultural Enterprises compared to that of Agricultural Enterprises and its changes are revealed by the trends in the share of NAEs to the Total Enterprises, share of employment and the workers per enterprise. The share of NAEs to the Total Enterprises has declined from 92 per cent to 88 per cent between 1980 and 1998. Almost similar decline in the share of workers of NAEs to the total employment (95 to 92 per cent) is also observed during the period under reference. In fact, the share of Rural NAEs to the total NAEs have also shown a marginal decline (from 58 per cent to 54 per cent). Above all, the number of workers per enterprise has shown a steady decline from 3.01 persons to 2.96 persons between 1980 and 1990 and further to 2.83 by 1998. This trend revealed the falling trend in the labour absorption of non-agricultural enterprises. Altogether, the above discussion revealed that the role of NAEs have been declining in the recent past.

IMPLICATIONS FOR INDIAN ECONOMY

The deceleration in the non-agricultural enterprises, in terms of the growth rates in the number of enterprises and the employment indicate the deplorable situation of our economy. The critical situation is felt on the unorganized sector of the economy as a whole. While the above analysis do not indicate anything on production, its implications on the labour market could be traced systematically as below.

As per the 2001 census, the total work force in our country is 402 million, of which 313 million are main workers and 89 million are marginal workers. Out of the 313 million main workers, only about 28 million (9 per cent) are employed in the organized sector[4] and the remaining about 285 million (91 per cent) are in the unorganized sector[5] (Economic Survey, 2003-04).

The extent of workforce in the organized and unorganized sectors, and their changes over time could be understood by the information provided by the Alternative Survey Group. Accordingly, the share of organized workforce was about 8.33.per cent by 1983, which declined to 7.65 per cent by 1999-2000. The corresponding share of unorganized workforce was about 91.67 per cent by 1983, which increased to 92.65 per cent by 1999-2000 (Table 3).

Table 3
Trends in Employment in India (in lakhs)

Year	*Organized*	*Unorganized*	*Total Workforce*
1983	240.10 (8.33)	2640.00 (91.67)	2880.00
1987-88	257.00 (8.75)	2680.00 (91.25)	2937.00
1991-92	267.33 (8.27)	2966.22 (91.73)	3233.55
1992-93	270.56 (8.20)	3027.42 (91.80)	3297.98
1993-94	271.77 (8.09)	3089.14 (91.91)	3360.91
1994-95	273.75 (7.98)	3157.21 (92.02)	3430.96
1995-96	275.25 (7.97)	3224.26 (92.03)	3499.51
1999-2000	277.89 (7.65)	3355.41(92.35)	3633.30

Source: Alternative Economic Survey: 1991-1998 and 2000.
Note: Figures in brackets are percentages to the respective totals.

The growth of employment (overall and organized sector) from the Seventies is given in Table 4.

It can be seen that the growth rate of organized sector employment maintained its declining trend from the period 1977-88 to 1983-84. The growth rate of public sector employment declined sharply and this trend continues up to the present. From 1997, the public sector employment grew negatively

(Economic Survey, 2002-2003). The situation of declining labour absorption capacity in the organized sector gets worsen if pruning or retrenchment activities by the public sector as initiated under reforms are taken into consideration. Taking into account the backlog of unemployment and overall magnitude of additional employment to be generated, there lies a major gap between demand and supply of labour in India.

Table 4
Growth of Employment in India

Period	*Growth rate of overall employment*	*Growth rate of employment in the organized sector (%)*		
		Public	*Private*	*Total*
1972-73 to 77-78	2.75	—	—	2.45
1977-78 to 1983	2.36	2.99	1.41	2.48
1983 to 1987-88	1.77	2.17	0.43	1.38
1987-88 to 1993-94	2.37	1.00	1.18	1.05
1993-94 to 1999-2000	1.07	(-) 0.03	1.87	0.53

Source: Economic Survey 1998-99 and Planning Commission, 10th Five year Plan, Vol.1.

In the context of declining growth rate in employment generation in organized sector and no scope for creating additional jobs, the additional labour force have to find work on self-employed activities of both agricultural and non-agricultural enterprises or remain casual workers. In other words, when the labour absorption in the organized sector declines, it would naturally push the additional labour force to the unorganized sector leading to further swelling of unorganized workers. If we assume the total workforce as the supply of labour, the total employment could be considered as the total demand for labour. But, in a real sense, all those employed under the organized and unorganized sectors could not be treated as the demand for labour. This is because of the fact that high level of disguised employment is found in the unorganized sectors and those who are not demanded or absorbed by the organized sectors are invariably pushed into the unorganized one. If one accepts the above argument, the study of labour market becomes more complex.

As large number of labourers are pushed into the unorganized category of workers, the excess labour supply creates disequilibrium or imbalance in the labour market that leads to several adjustments in the unorganized labour economy. The surplus or excess labour supply into the unorganized category leads to partial or casual employment at low wages and with out job or social security of any kind (Rao and Rao, 1994). Unni (2001), based on the study conducted in Ahemedabad highlighted the differential benefit between a regular and casual employee. It revealed that the casual labourers are highly exploited in terms of assurance of employment, contract procedures, paid leave, PF/ pension, medical and other benefit and notice for termination. Hence, as per this argument, the disturbance in the labour market would be disadvantages to the unorganized workers.

The disturbances in the labour market causing disequilibrium between the demand and supply of labourers is further aggravated by the jobless growth promoted by the new technological changes and structural shifts in the global economy in favour of the so-called new economy. Though a country like India needs a labour intensive technology to accommodate the job-seeking labour force, the process of globalization and liberalization sets on a shift towards capital-intensive technology. Needless to say that in order to meet competition and to increase productive efficiency, firms are forced to modernize their operations involving machineries, capital and high technologies, setting aside the labour intensive technologies. The choice of labour intensive technology becomes obsolete.

The immediate and direct consequence of the shift in the industrial technology is the replacement of unskilled personnel with skilled people (Rao and Rao:1994, Wood:1997). Under the new production environment, the nature of work changes and that warrants skilled workers. Taking into account the basic qualifications and nature of an Indian worker, it is difficult to visualize the effort and time needed to shift an unskilled person into a skilled worker. Till then, the inefficiency would continue even in the new production environment and the labour market would be in the state of disequilibrium.

CONCLUSION

The foregoing analysis revealed the major features and trends in the non-agricultural enterprises in India and its implications on the labour market. The main findings of the study are:

1. There were 30.35 million enterprises in India during 1998 engaged in different economic activities other than crop production and plantation. Of these, 26.87 million (88.6 per cent) were of non-agricultural enterprises while the rest 3.47 million (11.4 per cent) were engaged in agricultural activities.
2. Agricultural and non-agricultural enterprises were found to be in the ratio of 1:8, indicating the dominance of non-agricultural enterprises.
3. Non-agricultural enterprises are spread almost evenly (54 per cent in rural and the rest 46 per cent in urban) across regions.
4. Own Account Enterprises (OAEs) account for a major share of the non-agricultural enterprises. Among the total OAEs, about 60 per cent are located in rural areas and the rest in urban areas.
5. There is higher dependency on hired workers by non-agricultural enterprises.

6. The employment of workers in the non-agricultural enterprises is very high, indicated by the 92 per cent of persons employed in it. The existence of child labour about 6 per cent in non-agricultural enterprises is observed. In fact, the extent of child labour is relatively higher in non-agricultural enterprises as compared to that of agricultural enterprises.
7. The ratio of employment per enterprise revealed that non-agricultural enterprises absorb higher amount of workers per enterprise compared to that of agricultural enterprises.
8. In absolute numbers, there has been a steady increase in the total number of Non-Agricultural Enterprises and the total employment in it. However, the increase in employment is much lower than that of the number of enterprises, indicating the low labour absorption capacity of NAEs.
9. Both the number of NAEs and employment are at the higher order of growth during the 80's compared to that of 90's, indicating a deceleration of NAEs in India, in recent years.
10. The share of NAEs to the Total Enterprises has declined from 92 per cent to 88 per cent between 1980 and 1998. Almost similar decline in the share of workers of NAEs to the total employment (95 to 92 per cent) is also observed during the period under reference.
11. The number of workers per enterprise has shown a steady decline from 3.01 persons to 2.96 persons between 1980 and 1990 and further to 2.83 by 1998, revealing the falling trend in the labour absorption of non-agricultural enterprises. Altogether, it revealed that the role of NAEs has been declining in the recent past.

With the understanding of the declining role of non-agricultural enterprises in recent years, its implications on the labour market are analyzed. The supply of labour to the organized and unorganized sectors would expand further in the present context of new economic reforms. But, the demand for labour would decline further. This would lead to an imbalance in the labour market, due to excess supply of labour and low demand for labour.

To conclude, the trends in the non-agricultural enterprises and the labour market reveal the deplorable conditions of the labour. This situation would affect not only the social and economic conditions of the present working population, but also the further additions to it. Therefore, it can be argued that the policies towards de-linking budgetary support to the working population, reducing labour absorption in public sector as part of the globalization strategy and relying on the market forces to absorb labour and fix their wages would adverse affect the employment situation in India. Hence, efforts should be initiated towards the development of non-agricultural enterprises, and there by, problems of production and unemployment could be minimized. More over, the welfare of the workforce population in terms of real wages and their income should be at least maintained, so that they would also benefit in that process and contribute towards the growth of our economy.

NOTES

1. Globalization involves liberalization, privatization, minimizing economic regulations, reducing expenditures on public goods, tightening fiscal discipline, favouring free flows of capital, strict controls on organized labour, tax reductions and unrestricted currency repatriation.
2. An agricultural enterprise was defined as one engaged in livestock production and agricultural services including hunting, trapping and game propagation, forestry logging and fishing. Enterprises engaged in activities pertaining to agricultural production and plantation was not covered under agricultural enterprises. Enterprises engaged in all other activities were termed as non-agricultural enterprises.
3. The enterprises operated with the help of household labour only were termed as Own Account Enterprises.
4. The organized sector included both under public and private sector employment.
5. Ministry of Labour has categorized this unorganized labour force under four groups in terms of occupation, nature of employment, specially distressed categories and service categories.

REFERENCES

Alternative Survey Group (1998), *Alternative Economic Survey, 1991-1998*, Rainbow Publishers Limited, Delhi.

——(2000), *Alternative Economic Survey, 1998-2000*, Rainbow Publishers Limited, Delhi.

Dalip S. Swamy (1997), The World Bank and Globalization of the Indian Economy, In George K.K., Sankaran Nair, V. and Jose Jacob (Eds.) *Economics, Development and the Quest for Alternatives*, Concept Publishing Company, New Delhi.

Government of India, *Economic Survey, Various* Years.

Government of India, *Economic Census, 1980, 1990, 1998.*

Government of India, Ministry of Labour, *Annual Report, 2000-2001.*

James Petras and Henry Veltmeyer (2001), *Globalization Unmasked*, Madhyam Books, Delhi.

Rao K.V. and Rao M.K. (1994), *Restructuring Indian Economy and Its Impact on Labour,* In Rao M.K. (Eds.), *Growth of Urban Informal Sector and Economic Development*, Volume 1, (Edited) Kanishka Publishers Distributors, Delhi.

Unni, Jeemol (2001), *Gender and Informality in Labour Market in South Asia*, Economic and Political Weekly, Vol. 36 (26).

Wood, Adrian (1997), How Trade Hurt Unskilled Workers, In Borkakoti J. and Milner C. (Eds.), *International Trade and Labour Markets*, Macmillan Press: London.

5

HANDICRAFT AND SOCIO-ECONOMIC DEVELOPMENT OF RURAL TRIBALS ARTISANS IN DISTRICT SURGUJA

Dalip Kumar

INTRODUCTION

The handicrafts sector is a home-based industry, which requires minimum expenditure, infrastructure or training to set up. It uses existing skills and locally available materials. Inputs required can easily be provided and these are more in terms of product adaptation than expensive investment in energy, machinery or technology. Also, income generation through craft does not (and this is important in a rural society) disturb the cultural and social balance of either the home or the community (Dastkar, 1995). Many agricultural and pastoral communities depend on their traditional craft skills as a secondary source of income in times of drought, lean harvests, floods or famine. Their skills in embroidery, weaving, and basket making are a natural means to social and financial independence.

Official concerns for handicrafts can be traced to the late 19th century and early 20th century, and the ideals of Swadeshi (self-reliance, home industry) put forward by nationalist intellectuals to counter the perceived demise of indigenous industry in the face of cheap European imported goods (Sarkar, 1973). Many scholars regard the Swadeshi movement of 1905-1908 as both a cultural and political watershed in the history of the Indian Independence movement. Despite its shortcomings and failures, the movement awakened an interest in handicrafts, folk craft, and lifestyles in direct contrast to those associated with industrialization and urbanity.

What is referred to as handicraft to day used to be categorized under 'art manufactures' (Mukharji, 1974) or 'industrial arts' (Birdwood, 1880) in the colonial period. In the post-Independence era, handicraft has been portrayed as any product made under the so-called traditional relationship of patronage of the court or the village (Chattopadhyaya, 1963), or as any object in which some work has been done by hand particularly, purely decorative portions. While broadly similar to any kind of production that is localized, informal, and small scale, handicrafts are distinct from village or small-scale industries because handicraft products and processes differ widely from region to region, and handicraft producers differ in their organization, numbers, and ability to retain skills in the midst of social change.

Till today there is no clear and scientific definition of handicrafts. According to Task Force on Handicrafts for the VIII Five-year plans (1990-91 to 1995-1996) says:, it is difficult to give a cut-and-dried definition of handicrafts. Yet it is felt necessary, for the purpose of planning, to a general description of what constitutes handicrafts. Handicrafts are items made by hand, often with the use of simple tools, and are generally artistic and /or traditional in nature. They include objects of utility and objects of decoration (Saraf, 1991).

Handicrafts are hand-made manufactured produced with the application of mainly human energy and skills with or without the aid of mechanical devices for various types of end uses. These are items of:

(a) Utility, for everyday functional requirements

(b) Decoration, for ornamentation

(c) Wear, for donning as apparel and accessories

(d) Collection, for acquiring as possessions

According to UNCTAD, "the term 'hand-made' should be taken to include those articles produced with or without the use of tools, simple instruments, or implements operated directly by the craftsmen mainly by hand or by foot'.

At times, handicrafts may have additional attributes such as traditional or artistic features derived from the geographical region of production, or production by craftsmen working at cottage scale. Some goods may be partly machine-made and partly hand-made. For example, hand embroidered tablecloth will have a machine-made fabric for ground and exquisite hand embroidery to enhance its appeal. It can be ultimately classified as a hand-made product.

In India the Supreme Court has laid down the following tests for an article to be recognized as a handicraft:

- it must be predominantly made by hand; it does not matter if some machinery is used in the process, and
- it must be graced with visual appeal in the nature of ornamentation or ivory work or some similar work lending it an element of artistic

improvement. Such ornamentation must be of a substantial nature and not a mere pretence.

STATUS OF HANDICRAFT ARTISANS IN INDIA

In India handicraft sector contributes significantly to employment and export earning. The estimates based on NSSO for the unorganized cottage industry sector, reveal that the annual growth rate of employment in the handicrafts sector is around 2.5 per cent. It is presumed that during the Ninth plan, employment in the handicrafts sectors increased from 52.92 lakh in 1997-98 to 58.41 lakh in 2001-02. By the end of the Tenth Five plan, it is presumed that 9.29 lakh more artisans will be employed. The employment increased from 60.16 lakh in 2002-03 to 61.96 lakh in 2003-04.

Despite the vast prevalence of the handicrafts industries in India, precise statistics on its extent and production were until very recently not available. It was claimed by the Office of the Development Commissioner for Handicrafts that the country accounted for over 80 lakh artisans in various branches of handicrafts and the total value of their production in 1999 was estimated to be Rs. 31,000 crores. However, under the sponsorship of the Development Commissioner for Handicrafts, a national census of the handicrafts sector was undertaken by the National Council of Applied Economic Research, New Delhi in 1995-96. The results of the census, finalized in 1999 are reported below.

Table 1 presents key data for the aforesaid year 1995-96 for all states. In the 24 states, the total units of handicraft production were 12.66 lakhs. The artisans working in these units were 41.03 lakh. The table indicates the estimated value of production to be Rs. 26, 213 crores. The average scale of a unit in these 24 states was 3.24 artisans. Uttar Pradesh, by itself, accounted for a share of 22.41 per cent of units and 28.79 per cent of artisans; the average scale per unit in U.P was 4.14 artisans. Among the remaining states the ones that accounted for impressive shares of the aggregate were, in descending order, West Bengal, Rajasthan, Manipur, Tripura, Madhya Pradesh, Andhra Pradesh, and Maharashtra. Among themselves, these states accounted for a share of 57.02 per cent of the aggregate units and 49.75 per cent of the number of artisans.

Table 2 depicts craft-wise numbers of units and artisans in India . Textiles accounted for a big share of the handicrafts sector; 50.57 per cent of units and 54.35 per cent of artisans belonged to this group of crafts. The next largest group was cane and bamboo crafts followed by straw grass/fibres group, clay and ceramics and the wood group. Together with these 4 other major groups made up 36.20 per cent of units and 32.15 per cent of artisans. Other important groups were metal, leather and glass.

Table 1
State-wise Status of Handicrafts Units and Artisans in India

States	*No. of Units*	*No. of Artisans*	*Value of Production (Rs. Crores)*
Andhra Pradesh	76,283 (6.02)	1,21,88, (2.98)	379.41 (1.44)
Assam	30,360 (2.39)	1,00,482 (2.45)	7,820.94 (29.72)
Bihar	70,533 (5.57)	2,13,115 (5.21)	91.51 (0.34)
Delhi	17,021 (1.34)	44,904 (1.09)	74.65 (0.28)
Goa	572 (0.04)	1,122 (0.02)	107.20 (0.40)
Gujarat	32,697 (2.58)	1,31,970 (2.81)	72.25 (0.27)
Himachal Pradesh	26,058 (2.05)	49,015 (1.19)	45.60 (0.17)
Haryana	16,222 (1.28)	1,17,933 (2.88)	776.58 (2.95)
Karnataka	12,383 (0.97)	21,779 (0.53)	41.37 (0.15)
Kerala	7,395 (0.58)	15,258 (0.37)	1,748.26 (6.64)
Madhya Pradesh	21,954 (1.73)	51,123 (1.25)	65.46 (0.24)
Maharashtra	52,449 (4.14)	1,12,816 (2.76)	139.62 (0.53)
Mizoram	2,213 (0.17)	5,260 (0.12)	5.93 (0.02)
Manipur	98,051 (7.74)	3,79,988 (9.29)	147.600 (0.56)
Meghalaya	11,512 (0.90)	53,564 (1.31)	2,580.67 (9.80)
Nagaland	17,603 (1.39)	79,878 (1.95)	9,463.99 (35.98)
Orissa	25,968 (2.05)	69,396 (1.69)	56.71 (0.21)
Rajasthan	1,28,871 (10.17)	4,07,700 (9.97)	278.40 (1.05)
Sikkim	2,198 (0.17)	9,768 (0.23)	5.59 (0.02)
Tamil Nadu	31,749 (2.50)	1,25,342 (3.06)	63.10 (0.23)
Tripura	77,375 (6.11)	2,44,495 (5.98)	60.10 (0.23)
Uttar Pradesh	2,83,804 (22.41)	11,76,529 (28.79)	1,004.50 (3.81)
West Bengal	2,18,697 (17.27)	5,54,281 (13.56)	426.42 (1.62)
Total of Above	12,66,009	41,03,293	26,312.13

Note: Figures in parentheses are percentages to total.
Source: Census Survey of Handicrafts Sector (state-wise reports), National Council of Applied Economic Research, New Delhi, 1999.

Table 2
Craft-Wise Status of Handicrafts Units and Artisans In India

Craft Group	*Number of Units*	*Number of Artisans*	*Est. Production (Rs. Crore)*
Textiles	6,40,247 (50.57)	22,30,343 (54.35)	12,832.41 (48.76)
Cane and Bamboo	1,76,556 (13.94)	4,94,844 (12.05)	6,287,13 (23,89)
Wood	86,474 (6.83)	2,61,387 (6.37)	4,161.90 (15.81)
Metal	54,507 (4.30)	1,79,996 (4.38)	1,323,95 (5.03)
Stone	11,553 (0.91)	35,593 (0.86)	106~06 (0.40)
Straw, Grass, Fibre & Leaf	1,21,529 (9.59)	3,05,876 (7.45)	541.76 (2.05)
Leather	36,246 (2.86)	1,22,704 (2.99)	152.73 (0.58)
Glass	12,136 (0.96)	65,619 (1.59)	48.14 (0~18)
Clay & Ceramics	73,966 (5.84)	2,57,714 (6.28)	498.86 (1.89)
Ivory, Bone, Horn and Shells	8,797 (0.69)	28,123 (0.68)	91.39 (0.34)
Miscellaneous	43,998 (3.47)	1,21,094 (2.95)	267,8 (1,01)
Total of Above	12,66,009 (100.00)	41,03,293 (100.00)	26312.13 (100.00)

Note: Figures in parentheses are percentages to total.
Source: As Table 1.

The handicraft artisans of India enjoy the dual benefits. It imparts to the economy through substantial foreign exchange earning and high level of employment generation in international trade, Ho and Huddle (1976) and, Robinson, (1979). In handicrafts, as compared to the rest of the economy, capital is no less efficiently employed in terms of output and—on limited evidence—considerably more so in terms of value-addition. This sector provides productive employment to the underemployed and to the unemployed, they earn foreign exchange for the economy, they help to redistribute the income among the poor, and also create employment opportunities for disadvantaged groups. They also add to preservation of traditional skills and cultural heritage. Handicraft production can help in the realization of plan objectives, especially those relating to the creation of employment and poverty alleviation. As argued by Minhas "inspire of a number of references to the employment problem, the creation of employment opportunities was seen more or less as an adjunct to or a by-product of the development strategy (Minhas, 1994). Chaudhari, analyzing Indian planning strategy between 1950 and 74, wrote in a similar vein that the "treatment of employment as a side issue, so to speech, had particular implications on the question of removal of inequality and poverty. (Chaudhuri 1978)".

DATA SOURCE

In this paper, the secondary data is used, which is obtained from the State Series of the Census of Handicrafts Artisans 1995-99. This study was conducted by the National Council of Applied Economic Research in 1998-99 covering 1335 Villages of Madhya Pradesh. In the covered villages, they contacted 21954 units of handicrafts wherein 51123 artisans are employed.

In Surguja district 603 units are selected where approximately 1177 artisans are involved in this study. This district is known as special crafts concentration pocket. During this study investigators covered only major handicraft groups like Woolen & Silk carpets, other floor coverings, other textiles, cane & bamboo, wood ware, Art metal ware, stone ware, Straw, Grass & Leaf, Leather ware, glass ware, clay & ceramics, and miscellaneous. The details of handicrafts units, artisans and its location as per specific crafts along with the physical perspective of Surguja District are presented in the following section.

PHYSICAL PROFILE OF DISTRICT SURGUJA IN CHHATTISGARH

On November 1, 2000, India gave birth to a new state-Chhattisgarh. The new state is carved out of India's largest state of Madhya Pradesh with an area of 443,000 square kilometers. Though Chhattisgarh with an area of 135,194 square kilometers accounts for only 30 per cent of the total area of Chhattisgarh, it is still of a considerable size, which is equivalent to almost sixteen times the size of Kerala.This state has 16 Districts, 978 Tahsils,146 Community Development Blocks, 97 towns and 20308 villages in 2001 Census. (Census, 2001).

(a) Profile of Scheduled Tribes Population in State

The proportion of Scheduled Tribes population to total population in the state is 31.8 per cent in 2001 Census as compared to 32.5 per cent in 1991. This proportion is four times higher than the national average of 8.2 percent. This state holds eighth position among all the states and UTs so far as proportion of STs population is concerned. The Scheduled tribe's population has recorded 15.7 per cent growth in the state during 1991-2001, while this was 23.2 per cent during the decades 1981-91. In Surguja district the proportion of STs to total population of district is 54.6 per cent. The sex ratio of STs population in the state shows preponderance of female at 1013 in the 2001 Census against 1009 recorded in 1991 Census. Scheduled Tribes population has recorded a literacy rate of 52.1 per cent at state level in 2001 against 26.7 per cent in 1991

Census. The literacy rate of Surguja is 54.8 per cent as a total but the STs rate is only 48.3 percent.

The total work participation rate in the state is 46.5 per cent against 39.1 per cent recorded at the national level in the 2001 Census. This rate among the state level of STs population is 53.4 per cent in 2001 against 54.1 per cent in 1991. This rate in the Surguja district is 49.8 as a total and 53.1 per cent among the STs as a whole. Male work participation rate at the state level has decreased from 54.3 per cent in 1991 to 52.8 per cent in 2001 Census. This rate has also declined from 58.8 per cent in 1991 to 56.7 per cent in 2001 Census in case of STs population. Female work participation rate has a slightly declined from 41.0 per cent in 1991 to 40.0 per cent in 2001 Census. In case of Female Scheduled Tribes workers which increased from 49.4 per cent in 1991 to 50.5 per cent in 2001 Census.

(b) Profile of Surguja District

The growth rate of population in the new state of Chhattisgrah is 18.06 per cent over the population of 1991. In 1991, the growth rate was 25.73 per cent. The population of Chhattisgarh in the last decade has increased but at a lower rate. Chhattisgrah is one of the states where population has registered a growth rate less than 20 per cent. The population growth rate of Chhattisgrah is less than national average growth rate of 21.34 per cent and two of 16 district namely, Surguja (24.58 per cent) and Korba have got greater growth rate than the national average. Population growth trends can be seen on box-1 & chart-1

Box 1
Population Growth Rate 1961-2001

Years	*India*	*Chhattisgarh*	*Surguja*
1951-61	21.51	22.77	12.17
1961-71	24.8	27.12	28.61
1971-81	24.66	20.39	20.61
1981-91	23.82	25.73	26.68
1991-2001	21.34	18.06	24.5

Source: Census of India 2001, Chhattisgrah, Series -23, Provisional Population Totals , Paper 1 of 2001.

The population density of Chhattisgrah has increased to 154 person per sq .km. from 130 person per sq. km. in 1991. The density of this state is much below the national average of 324 persons per sq. km. The density of Surguja has increased to 125 person per sq. km. from 101 persons per sq. km. in 1991. The density of this district is less than half of the national average.

Chart - 1

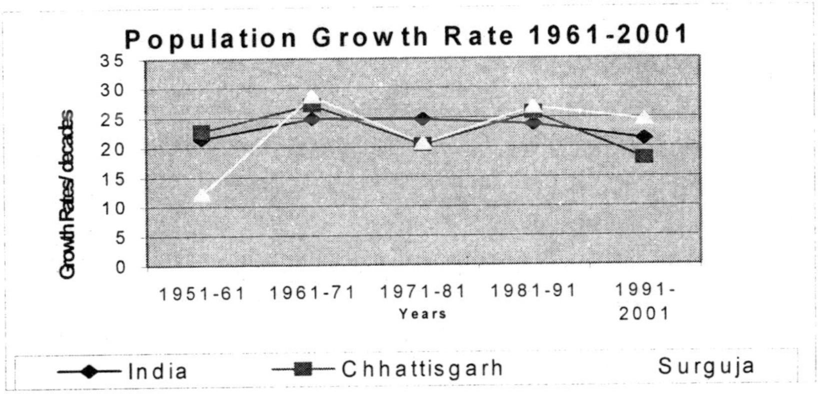

The Chhattisgarh has the highest sex ratio in the country except Kerala and Pondicherry. India's sex ratio has gone up from 927 in 1991 to 933 in 2001 where as Chhattisgrah ratio has increased from 958 to 990 in 2001. Surguja district trends is more or less the same as Chhattisgrah. When the sex ratio of Chhattisgrah is compared with the sex ratio of neighboring state, it is the highest.

(c) Scheduled Tribes in Chhattisgrah

The scheduled tribes, with a population of over 57 lakhs constitute 32.5 per cent of the state population as per 1991 census. About 98 per cent of this population lived in rural areas and only 2 per cent in urban Chhattisgarh. This state has the highest percentage of STs population. The STs are concentrated in the southern, northern and northeast parts of this State. The highest concentration is in the Baster District. The new district of Dantewara has 79 per cent tribal followed by Baster (67 per cent) Jashpur (65 per cent) Surguja (57 per cent) and Kanker (56 per cent).

The Gonds at 55.1 per cent from the largest proportion within the tribal population. The *Oraons, the Kawars, the Halbis, the Bharias or Bhumiars, the Bhattras and the Napesias* also from a substantial portion of the tribal population. Thirty other STs have small population residing in a various pockets across the State. The *Gonds* are concentrated in the hilly parts of the Southern Chhattisgarh but are also spread across most districts whereas the *Baigas, Bharias, Korwas and Napesias* occupy only specific pockets. The *Bhattras, Kolams* and *Rasjas* largely live in Baster and the Kamras in Raipur. The *Halba* tribe inhabits parts of Baster, Raipur and Rajnandgaon. The *Oraons* live in Surguja and Raigarh districts. There are a total of 42 tribes in Chhattisgrah, principal among then being the Gond tribe. Beside, a large population of *Kanwar, Brinjhwar, Bhaina, Bharta, Oraon, Munda, Kamar, Halba, Baiga,*

Sanwra,Korwa, Bharia, Nageshia, Manghwar, Kharia and Dhanwar tribe are also found in the State.

(d) Rich in Natural Resources

The newly formed state is richly endowed with natural resources. Its forest revenue which alone accounts for 44 per cent of the total states forest revenue has been the main source of income of Madhya Pradesh. In addition, teak, bamboo, saja, sarai, haldi etc. are also grown at large scale. Tendu leaf , which is used in *beedi* making, is a principal forest produce of the state. It has rich deposits of limestone, iron-ore, copper-ore, rock phosphate, manganese ore, bauxite, coal, asbestos and mica that contribute to around 48% of Madhya Pradesh's revenue from minerals.

(f) Agriculture, the Mainstay

Agriculture is the main activity for the population of 1,76,00,000 of this landlocked state enveloped by Maharashtra, Andhra Pradesh, Orissa, Madhya Pradesh, and Uttar Pradesh and of course Madhya Pradesh. 80 per cent of the population is engaged in agriculture, which is one crop a year. Known as the Rice Bowl of India, the region of Chhattisgarh supplies food grain to 600 rice mills.

(g) The Paradox

However, in spite of its abundant natural resources and manpower pool, Chhattisgarh remains a poverty stricken and socially backward region. A cursory look at some parameters will reveal this fact. Take literacy rate, as high as 81.3 per cent of the population above 19 years of the district of Bastar is illiterate. The rest of the state is slightly better in this respect. 49 per cent of the households do not have drinking water. 68per cent of the households do not have an electricity connection (though it produces more power than it consumes; Chhattisgarh contributes 35.66 per cent of total power generated in Madhya Pradesh). Infant mortality is high: 84 deaths per thousand live births against the national average of 71 per cent. 41per cent of the women work as labourers in the grueling activities (the national average is just 22.3). About half of its female population gets married between the ages of 15 and 19. Now with a new government in place for Chhattisgarh, there are valid reasons to hope that the general condition of the state will improve, if not dramatically at least the substantially.

(h) Economy of the State

The mineral rich State is economically very poor. It will have to depend on the neighboring states of Orissa and Andhra Pradesh. Agriculturally it is a very productive area. Called the country's Rice Bowl, it supplies foodgrains to almost 600 rice mills. With substantial deposits of limestone, iron-ore, copper ore, rock phosphate, manganese ore, bauxite, coal, asbestos and mica, Chhattisgarh is one of the mineral rich States of India. Chhattisgarh contains about 525 million tones of dolomite reserves, accounting for 24 per cent of the country's share. It has healthy bauxite reserves of an estimated 73 million tones, an impressive reserves of iron ore at about 2,000 million tones and coal at 29,000 million tones. Tin ore reserves exceed 27,000 million tones.

The mineral revenue that will accrue to Chhattisgarh will exceed Rs. 600 crore annually. Deobogh in Raipur district contains deposits of diamonds. Prospecting of diamonds has begun here and when extraction starts in about two years' time, it is expected to generate an additional Rs. 2,000 crore a year for the state. Chhattisgarh also accounts for more than 70 per cent of India's total production of tendu leaves that are used for making bidis. But despite the high levels of productivity with natural and mineral resources, Chhattisgarh has remained backward because the money earned is not ploughed back into the region. Poverty pervades the 16 districts comprising the region. As a result, the region has for long nursed a grudge against the rest of Madhya Pradesh, which had, treated Chhattisgarh like a colony.

ANALYSIS OF DATA: SURGUJA DISTRICT

(a) Location of Units and Artisans

Table 3 indicates that more than 91 per cent handicrafts units and artisans in Surguja district are located in rural areas. Only a few Metal works, embroidery work by hand and Ceramics crafts units and artisans are in urban areas. Rest at the village level units are several types of cottage industries such as basket making, cotton and silk weaving, mat making and hand tools and making of toys. The location wise situation of MP differs from Surguja. Approximately more than 50 per cent of handicrafts units and more than 53 per cent of handicrafts artisans are located in urban areas. Details of handicrafts units and locations are available on Table 3.

(b) Religion- Wise Distribution of Handicraft Artisans

In the Surguja district, more than 85 per cent handicrafts artisans belong to Hindu communities, more than 6 per cent are from Muslim communities and the percentage of Sikh, Christians and others is less than 8 per cent. In MP, more of handicraft artisans are more or less the same as Surguja districts. 16 per cent of Muslim artisans are noticed in all over the State. Details are available on Table 4.

Table 3
Location &Types by Number of Units & Artisans in Surguja District

Type	*Rural*		*Urban*		*Total*	
	Units	*Artisans*	*Units*	*Artisans*	*Units*	*Artisans*
Woolen Carpet By hand	318	687	1	1	319	688
Silk Carpets by hand	36	36	0	0	36	36
Cotton Carper by hand	40	127	0	0	40	127
Embroidery Work by Hand	3	3	3	14	6	17
Zari work by Hand	0	0	1	7	1	7
Crocheted Textile Product	3	4	0	0	3	4
All Textiles	406	867	18	45	424	912
Cane & Bamboo	8	38	1	5	9	43
Wood	59	64	1	1	60	65
Metal	6	12	11	17	17	29
Straw, Grass, Fiber & Leaf	2	4	0	0	2	4
Leather	0	0	1	4	1	4
Clay & Ceramics	55	67	7	13	62	80
Miscellaneous	15	16	9	18	24	34
Total(Surguja Dist)	554	1072	49	105	603	1177
Percentage of Surguja	91.87	91.08	8.13	8.92	100.00	100.00
Total Madhya Pradesh	10828	23664	11126	27459	21954	51123
Percentage of MP	49.32	46.29	50.68	53.71	100.00	100.00

Source: Same as Table 1.

Table 4
Religion by Handicrafts Artisans (%)

District	*Hindu*	*Muslim*	*Others*	*Total*
Surguja	85.24	6.80	7.96	100
MP	83.69	15.89	0.42	100

Source: Same as Table 1.

(c) Handicraft Artisans Classified By Social Groups

In terms of social group, almost all the caste groups are involved in handicraft activities. In Surguja district approximately 10 per cent of total artisans belong to SC, one fourth (25%) OBC and more than 48 per cent are STs. ST's proportion is more because Surguja district is highly Tribal populated district. STs shares are more in handicraft artisans. Only Tribal Artisans are more than 8 per cent and the OBC are more than 58 per cent found in MP. The share of SCs also noticed more than 24 per cent. Details are given on Table 5.

Table 5
Handicraft Artisans Classified By Social Groups (%)

District	SC	ST	OBC	Others	Total
Surguja	10.12	48.76	24.88	16.25	100
MP	24.19	8.94	58.03	8.84	100

Source: Same as Table 1.

(d) Handicraft Artisans Classified by Sex and Age Group

Distribution of handicraft artisans by broad sex group in district Surguja shows that nearly 40 per cent females are engaged in Handicrafts sector. Situation of Madhya Pradesh is also more or less the same. Only 37 per cent female artisans are engaged in handicraft activity. As per Table 6 we can say that men artisans, not only in Surguja district but even in Madhya Pradesh and India dominate the handicrafts sector also.

Distribution of handicrafts artisans by age groups in Surguja district shows that nearly very less percent of male and female falls in the age group of 0-14 years. Approximately 50 and 62 per cent are youth (age group 15-25 years) respectively male and female noticed in this age group in Surguja District. In Madhya Pradesh this percent just differs from Surguja District. In MP as a whole in youth group of artisans found only 36 and 40 per cent male and female respectively. Slightly more than one third of both sex are in the adult age group of 26-40 years noticed in the District and State both. Only 3 and 8 per cent of artisans are in 41-60 years age group in Surguja district. Only 18 per cent male and 13 per cent female artisans found in at State. Less than 2 per cent female artisans are in the older age group of 60 years and above. (Table 6).

Table 6
Handicrafts Artisans Classified by Sex and Age Group

	up to 14 yrs	*15-25*	*26-40*	*41-60*	*60+*	*All*	*Percentage*
			District Surguja (In Number)				
Male	4	353	282	62	9	710	60.22
(Percentage)	(0.56)	(49.72)	(39.72)	(8.73)	(1.27)	(100)	
Female	4	289	158	15	1	469	39.78
(Percentage)	(0.85)	(61.62)	(33.69)	(3.20)	(0.21)	(100)	
			Madhya Pradesh				
Male	1229	11555	12520	5896	868	32068	62.73
(Percentage)	(3.83)	(36.03)	(39.04)	(18.39)	(2.71)	(100)	
Female	1557	7666	6996	6996	275	19055	37.27
(Percentage)	(8.17)	(40.23)	(36.71)	(13.44)	(1.44)	(100)	

Source: Same as Table 1.

(e) Employment Situation in Handicrafts Units

Handicraft sector generate gainful employment for family labour. This industry can help alleviate the seasonal unemployment and under employment problem of the rural people. Most of the handicrafts industry employs labour-intensive technique and to absorb labour is found to be quite significant.

The history of Surguja handicrafts shows that the artisan work is related to textile hand printing, bell metal work, stone ware, Zari embroidery, woodwork as old as the development of land itself. Table 7 discusses about the artisans, who are partly and fully employed in handicraft sectors. It is clear that the Surguja district had 603 units of handicrafts with 1177 artisans. The total share of handicrafts units in Surguja of Madhya Pradesh was approximately 3 per cent, while the employment in handicrafts sectors was only 2.46 per cent, while Madhya Pradesh percentage share of all India is very low, it is only. 1.72 per cent handicrafts units and 1.17 per cent employment (Artisans). In other words, Surguja has only 2 per cent artisans of entire Madhya Pradesh.

CRAFT WISE EMPLOYMENT OF ARTISANS

(a) Textiles

We would like to discuss about the different types of textile activities. This section also covers woolen carpet by hand, handloom Weaving, Hand printed Textiles, printing of cloth by hand, crocheted textile product, embroidery work by hand, zari work by hand etc. Madhya Pradesh is famous for its delicate weaving in its well known Chandler and Maheshwari saries. In Chenderi, craftsmen now use silk as warm and fine cotton for the weft in subtle shades. The saris generally have a rich gold boarder and two gold bands on the *pallu*. The more expensive saris have gold checks with lotus roundels all over. In Maheshwari, fine cotton and silk and cotton *saries* are *woven*, its specialty being the variety of fine checks in its weave. Handloomed *tassa*r silk fabrics are another specialty in MP.

Hand printing is one of the most important crafts of MP. The handprints of this state are vigorous in design, particularly those done with vegetable dyes, for example, the Jawad prints. The important printing centres in the state are Bhairongarh, Mandsaur, Jawad, Tarapur, Umedpura, Indore, Gotampura, Bhopal, Burhanpur, Sohagpur, Sohawal and Jaisingnagar. Nandana prints and tie and the *chunaries* are the main hand printed textiles. Nandana prints are traditional prints in fast colors that were earlier used by villager and tribals of the Nimar areas., but now being used on bedspreads, tablecloths and garments.

As shown in Table 7, more than 5 per cent units and 5 per cent artisans of Madhya Pradesh are located in the Surguja district while the position of Madhya Pradesh to all India, shows only 1.21 per cent units and less than 1 per cent artisans are located in the state. Unit by situation of Surguja district is available on table 8. As per this table this is very interesting to note that more than 75 per cent units of Woolen carpet by hand are located in district where more than 75 per cent artisans of MP are involved in Woolen carpet works in this district. This district has monopoly in the field of woolen & cotton carpet and more than 75 per cent units and artisans are available only in Surguja district.

Table 7
Handicrafts units & Artisans by Specific Crafts (Textiles)

India	*Units*	*Artisans*	*% share of Surguja*		*% share of Surguja, to MP*	*MP to*
			Units	*Artisans*	*Units*	*Artisans*
Surguja	424	912	5.49	4.72	0.07	0.04
MP	7730	19302	100	100	1.21	0.87
All India	640247	2230343			100	100

Source: Same as Table 1.

Table 8
Percentage Share of Units & Artisans (Textiles) in Surguja District to MP

Textile	*Surguja*		*MP*		*% Share of Surguja to MP*		*% Share of MP to total textile*	
	Unit	*Artisan*	*Units*	*Artisans*	*% Units*	*% Artisans*	*% Units*	*% Artisans*
Woolen Carpet By Hand	319	688	1358	3050	75.24	75.44	17.57	15.80
Silk Carpet by hand	36	36	102	272	8.49	3.95	1.32	1.41
Cotton Carpet by hand	40	127	1670	4504	9.43	13.93	21.60	23.33
Painting of cloth by Hand	8	10	255	690	1.89	1.10	3.30	3.57
Crocheted Textile Product	3	4	184	426	0.71	0.44	2.38	2.21
Embroidery Work by Hand	6	17	267	595	1.42	1.86	3.45	3.08
Zari work by Hand	1	7	1243	3493	0.24	0.77	16.08	18.10
Total Textile	424	912	7730	19302	100	100	100	100

Source: Same as Table 1.

The onslaught from urban markets, lack of competitive skills and inaccessibility coupled with financial shortages has pushed the tribal textiles of Madhya Pradesh on the verge of oblivion. Hand printing is scattered over a number of other areas in the state as well, and prints with tribal motifs are being well received in the sophisticated markets of Bombay, Calcutta, Delhi as well as abroad.

The Zari products of MP have always been noted for their aesthetic beauty. The crafts are concentrated mainly at Bhopal, famous for its splendid craftsmanship. Handbags, purses, pouches, brocade and saris are produced in addition to wall hangings, which are also popular. The 'Judli' (Embroidered Jacket), 'Paga' (Turban), 'Ghughri Vadi Para Ki Hed' (Woven Girdle), among others, have been overlapped by the modern urban dress ethics. The tribal sensibility, which at its best revealed a flair for geometric stylization that was wholly compatible with its intuitive feel for symbolic motif and fabric textures, today seems to be at a standstill. The range and strength of its output, which was enough to prove a "rare and mystic" understanding of design language and aesthetic sense, also seems to be losing colour.

Despite the fact that the prowess and skills of a weaver from tribal Bastar region can match with other part of the country, the former today is groping for survival. According to tribal related studies, Bagh is the last surviving producer of a range of printed textiles that were woven in many villages of Dhar and Jhabua districts.

"The textile has survived because of its relative isolation from urban influences and its easy accessibility to the tribal market," concedes a weaver. Even within the limited colour ranges, the Bagh textile gives the spectrum of colours a rare depth and vibrancy, he says. Bhairongarh, near Ujjain, the other great rival to Bagh, was known not only for its range of block prints but also skill and expertise. Catering both to the tribal market and the urban demands, it had a unique grace and finesse in layouts.

The textile was enticed away from its tribal links into a bigger national market leading to a boom in production and eventually a deteriorating quality. The same have unfortunately stumbled to the cheapest semblance of what it once was, the study notes. The traditional tie-dyed saris and veils, primarily made for the Bhils and Bhilalas in the vicinity of Bhairongarh, Mandsaur, Ummedpura and Guatampura, have also lost identity to the mill prints with only a few "Lugda", odhnis and veils being printed in the local market today. The tribal communities of Jhabua and Khargone districts were primarily printed cloth users as far as women were concerned but, there were some items such as the upper shawl-like drape, loin cloths and shoulder cloths which were ornnamented at either end with elaborate extra weft patterning. However, the original dress code today has been taken over by the power loom rayon saris with plain stark oranges and reds in the ground with which the women embroider themselves. The men have also taken to wearing shirts above their loincloths.

In some parts of Sarguja district, the Oraon tribals are however able to spin and weave all the clothes required for their household needs even today. Likewise, Javad is the only place in the state, which has the traditional art of wax-resist block printing. Notwithstanding a limited motif range, the same has been used consistently in the tribal market. 'Nandana-lugda', a head veil or half sari cotton dyed and hand block wax resists printed, were worn by the bhils, bhitals and mina tribes. Nandana, a textile very popular among the tribals, is the name of the print, which represents the mango form in various ways. The striking usage of single maroon red, sometimes darkened to brown, is what distinguishes Bastar from every other tribal region of the state. The 'pata', 'sari' and 'pichori', mens' lower garnments and turban cloths are enlivened with a graceful blend of colours.

Apart from these fabrics, the single most outstanding textile of the Bastar region is the 'bagh chowdah bandhi pata' of the Dhruva tribe. During marriages or certain other festivals, the bhils and the bhilalas instead of wearing the regular lugda, wear chuneri or the peeriya lugda.

(b) Cane and Bamboo

Cane and bamboo works are one of the most important craftwork for tribals of Surguja in Madhya Pradesh. Bamboo is available in plenty throughout MP and bamboo work is done in most villages, particularly in the tribal areas. Treble's products such as baskets, handbags, lamp stands and furniture are easily available in rural areas of Surguja District. They also make varieties of baskets and other containers for storing and carrying paddy and other crops. Details of handicrafts units and artisans involved in particular craft can be seen in Table 9. District Surguja has less than 1 per cent of units and artisan of Madhya Pradesh, who are involved in the cane and bamboo activities. In this crafts Madhya Pradesh's share was only 1.60 per cent in the field of handicrafts units and 1.45 per cent artisans to all India. The share of Surguja to all India is very negligible.

Table 9
Handicraft Units and Artisans by Specific Crafts (Cane and Bamboo)

District	*Units*	*Artisans*	*M P*		*India*	
			% units	*% Artisans*	*% units*	*% Artisans*
Surguja	9	43	0.32	0.60	0.01	0.01
M P	2818	7181	100.00	100.00	1.60	1.45
All India	176556	494844			100.00	100.00

Source: Same as Table 1.

(c) Wood and Woodwork

Evidence of Madhya Pradesh's great woodcrafts can be found in old building , on ledges, chairs, doors, windows and panels. Present day woodwork mostly consists of decorative items like bowls, tray, boxes, lamp stands, cupboards, cabinets, tables and chairs etc. Carved chair, door carvings, ratha carvings are the traditional wooden crafts from Surguja districts. Tribal Villages erected funeral pillars, and those particularly in Baster district are eloquent examples of carvers. In addition to carving some wooden images and panels fore- wall decoration, and furniture in traditional designs. Details of handicrafts units and artisans of Surguja district, can be seen in table-10. Only 2.30 per cent of handicrafts unit in Surguja district and 1.42 per cent of artisans are involved in wood related crafts of Madhya Pradesh. The share of Madhya Pradesh to all India is very negligible, it is only 3 per cent and 1 per cent both in terms of units and artisans respectively.

Table 10
Number of Handicraft Units & Artisans by Specific Craft (wood)

District	Units	Artisans	M P		India	
			% units	% Artisans	% units	% Artisans
Surguja	60	65	2.30	1.42	0.07	0.02
M P	2613	4570	100.00	100.00	3.02	1.75
All India	86478	261387			100.00	100.00

Source: Same as Table 1.

(d) Metals Crafts

Metal casting is one of the oldest and traditional handicrafts of Madhya Pradesh. Local skills of casting, ornamenting and engraving revel great delicacy and taste. Although designs are mostly traditional, the ornaments made these days are lighter and more practical. Sonar or goldsmiths throughout the district manufacture jewelry of various designs in gold and silver and studded with precious stones. Apart from these articles of gold used by richer section of society, Madhya Pradesh also makes a large variety of costume jewelry in base metals and in semi-precious stones. Bell metal casting in MP is essentially a tribal craft, practiced by non-tribals in Baster, Pranpur, Datia and Sagar. Details of unit and artisans can be seen in Table 11. The position of units and artisans of Surguja district is very low in this particular crafts. The share of this district in terms of units and artisans are only less than 1 per cent of totals of Madhya Pradesh. The position of Madhya Pradesh to all India is only 5 per cent and 3 per cent respectively in units and artisans.

Table 11
Number of Handicraft Units &Artisans by Specific Craft (Metal)

District	Units	Artisans	M P		India	
			% units	% Artisans	% units	% Artisans
Surguja	17	29	0.7	0.6	0.03	0.02
M P	2549	5029	100.00	100.00	4.68	2.79
All India	54507	179996			100.00	100.00

Source: Same as Table 1.

(e) Straw, Grass, Fiber & Leaf Crafts

The artisans of Madhya Pradesh have been very skilled in creating articles from local materials like straw, grass and plant leaves. Grass dyed in red, blue, black and gold is imaginatively wrought into a variety of articles, such as baskets and boxes, human figures, replicas of gods and goddesses, toys, animals, birds and models of chariots and temples. Employment status of artisans in this particular units can be seen in table 12. In this table the total no. of units and artisans available are 1 per cent of Madhya Pradesh. Percentage share of Madhya Pradesh to all India is insignificant.

Table 12
Handicraft Units and Artisans by Specific Craft (Straw, Grass, Fiber & Leaf)

District	*Units*	*Artisans*	*M P*		*India*	
			% units	*% Artisans*	*% units*	*% Artisans*
Surguja	2	4	0.44	0.36	0.00	0.00
MP	450	1100	100.00	100.00	0.37	0.36
All India	121529	305876			100.00	100.00

Source: Same as Table 1.

(f) Leather Crafts

The manufacturing of leather articles is carried out all over in rural Madhya Pradesh. Shoes made for rural use have a robust strength, with bold pattern executed in very bright colours and heavy stitches. These shoes are known as the *chamarua Juta.* MP is known for its stuffed leather miniature figures, depicting various aspect of wild life. The product range covers a variety of handbags, wallets and key holder, purses etc. Details of handicrafts units and artisans in leather crafts are available in Table 13. The contribution of leather crafts is very less in Surguja district. It is only 2 per cent of units and 3 per cent of workforce engaged in this crafts of Madhya Pradesh. The percentage share of Madhya Pradesh to all India is also very less, it is only nearer to 1 per cent.

Table 13
Handicraft Units and Artisans by Specific Craft (Leather)

District	*Units*	*Artisans*	*M P*		*India*	
			% units	*% Artisans*	*% units*	*% Artisans*
Surguja	1	4	0.07	0.10	0.00	0.00
MP	1514	3856	100.00	100.00	4.18	3.14
All India	36246	122704			100.00	100.00

Source: Same as Table 1.

(g) Clay and Ceramics Crafts

This craft is basically made in clay by village porters. They generally make dynamic horses, bulls and some times even human figures in various sizes, statues of different gods and goddesses on occasions of festivals like Durgapuja, Saraswatipuja and Laxmipuja. The making of clay toys and images is a seasonal crafts. The terracottas of Baster are especially noteworthy. On the *amavasya* of *Bhadrapad Masa*- the all tribals of state offer terracotta bulls, tigers, elephants and horses—sometimes with one or a pair of *matas* as rider—to the goddess whom they worship for wealth, health and prosperity, and protection from evil spirits.

Details of units and artisans are available on Table 14. In this table we can say that the percentage share of Surguja district to Madhya Pradesh was 2 per cent and 1 per cent handicrafts units and artisans respectively. The percentage share of Madhya Pradesh to all India in particular crafts is just inverse. Here we see that only 4 per cent handicraft units and 3 per cent of workforce are engaged in this crafts.

Table 14

Handicraft Units and Artisans by Specific Craft (Clay and Ceramics)

District	*Units*	*Artisans*	*MP % units*	*MP % Artisans*	*India % units*	*India % Artisans*
Surguja	62	80	2.17	1.15	0.08	0.03
All Madhya Pradesh	2858	6941	100.00	100.00	3.86	2.69
All India	73966	257714			100.00	100.00

Source: Same as Table 1.

(h) Miscellaneous Crafts

In this section we are covering other crafts, which are not discussed in previous sections, like as Agarbati, Glass made crafts, Hand made paper, Miniature painting, Ivory, Bone, Horn & Shells crafts etc. Among the other tribal crafts of MP mention may be made of the textile items: cotton coats, sleeveless jackets, skirts, cholis, decorated with corwires and generally used by the Maria and Muria women, veils, caps, bags and so on . Bajubands (armbands) decorated with cowries and used during tribal dances in Baster, are also common. Other festival items are painted masks and the *chikara,* a stringed musical items, used by the village *Pradhan.* In Table 15 we can see that the number of miscellaneous group of crafts units of total Madhya Pradesh was 546 units and number of artisans was 1336. The share of Surguja districts was 4.40 per cent of handicrafts units and 2.54 per cent of handicraft artisans. The share of Madhya Pradesh to all India is very less, it is only 1 per cent.

Table 15

Handicraft Units and Artisans by Specific Craft (Miscellaneous)

District	*Units*	*Artisans*	*MP % units*	*MP % Artisans*	*India % units*	*India % Artisans*
Surguja	24	34	4.40	2.54	0.05	0.03
MP	546	1336	100.00	100.00	1.24	1.10
All India	43998	121094			100.00	100.00

Source: Same as Table 1.

(i) Average Size of Work Force in the Handicraft Sector in Surguja

Table 16 shows the average size of workforce in selected crafts. Most of the crafts have 2-3 per unit size of work force in Surguja district. Cane & bamboo, Leather these two craft sectors keep more than 3 person's average per unit of crafts. In Madhya Pradesh most of the crafts in this state have 2 persons per unit average work- fore engaged in all crafts.

Table 16
Average Size of Work Force in Handicraft Sector in Surguja
(Artisans Per unit)

Types	*Surguja*	*MP*
Woolen Carpet By hand	2.0	2.3
Other Textile	2.1	2.5
All Textiles	2.2	2.5
Cane & Bamboo	4.8	2.5
Wood	1.1	1.7
Metal	1.7	2.0
Straw , Grass, Fiber & Leaf	2.0	2.4
Leather	4.0	2.5
Clay & Ceramics	1.3	2.4
Miscellaneous	1.4	2.4
All Crafts	2.0	2.3

Source: Same as Table 1.

(j) Requirement and Availability of Credit in Handicraft Sector

It is quite well known that rural handicraft artisans belong to low-income group, residing in rural areas. They generally face financial problems to purchase raw materials for making the crafts. For this purpose they borrow/purchase from local traders and work in place of other artisans. We also know that every state haves co-operative credit societies. They provide credit facilities not only at state level but also at village level. These are Co-operative banks at state level, central co-operative banks at the district level, and primary agricultural societies at the village level. But handicraft artisans generally do not getting such type of facilities in rural areas.

Table 17
Per Unit Requirement and Availability of Credit in Handicraft Sector
(In Rs. Per Unit)

Types	*Surguja*		*MP*	
	Cr. Required	*Cr. Received*	*Cr. Required*	*Cr. Received*
Woolen Carpet By hand	24639	138	31919	1229
Other Textile	29483	0	22003	1185
All Textiles	22646	116	22212	103
Cane & Bamboo	2556	56	13650	233
Wood	14167	67	30439	1188
Metal	74147	14118	45482	1442
Straw, Grass, Fiber & Leaf	12500	0	10020	11
Leather	40000	0	36310	107
Clay & Ceramics	4211	161	14757	692
Miscellaneous	3708	83	20539	505
All Major crafts	20374	507	24381	898

Source: Same as Table 1.

Per unit requirement and availability of credit in handicraft sector is shown in Table 17. In Surguja district, artisans had received credit only in woolen textile, and metal crafts but this is very less than requirement. On an average all major crafts received credit of only 507 rupees per unit, while requirement was Rs. 20374 per unit. Same trends can be noticed in Madhya Pradesh as a whole.

(k) Daily Hours of Work Distribution

In Surguja district more than 45 per cent artisan's daily engagement 3-4 hours in handicraft activities. Female contribution in this field is about 51 per cent. Only 12 per cent artisans work up to 2 hours like part time jobs. 41 per cent of total artisans work full time job, which is in between 5-8 hours. Only 2 percent artisan are engaged for more than 9-12 hours. More or less same trends can be noticed in Madhya Pradesh as a whole. In this state 72 per cent artisans are working full time like as 5-8 hours per day. Details are as under in Table 18.

Table 18
Daily Hours Of Work Distribution Of Handicraft Artisans

(percent)

	Daily Working Hour Group				
	Up to 2 hours	*3-4 hours*	*5-8 hours*	*9-12 hours*	*More than 13 hours*
Surguja					
Male	11.20	41.64	44.48	2.68	00
Female	13.48	51.06	35.11	0.35	00
Total	11.93	44.66	41.48	1.93	00
Madhya Pradesh					
Male	2.63	8.00	72.98	15.93	0.47
Female	3.24	21.50	69.74	5.40	0.12
Total	2.86	13.14	71.75	11.92	0.33

Source: Same as Table 1.

(l) Household Income in Handicraft Sector

Handicraft sector forms a major component of household income. From metal craft alone, a household's income in Surguja district is Rs. 42565 annually where as it is only Rs. 16880 in MP as a whole. Cane & bamboo, wood, straw grass, leaf, leather, clay and ceramics works are very considerable source of income generation in Surguja as well as MP. The share of total income of handicraft artisans is approximately 49 per cent in Surguja and 63 per cent in MP from the crafts side. Details can be seen in Table 19.

Table 19
Household Income in Handicraft Sector By Specific Crafts
(Rupees per Annum)

Types	*Surguja Income (Rs.)*			*Craft Income/ Artisans*	*MP Income (Rs.)*			*Craft Income/ Artisans*
	Craft	*Other*	*Total*		*Craft*	*Other*	*Total*	
All Textiles	12262	12997	25259	7774	10607	6341	16947	4676
(Per cent)	(48.55)	(51.45)	(100.00)		(62.59)	(37.42)	(100.00)	
Cane & Bamboo	9917	5250	!5167	3967	9933	2707	12640	3953
(Per cent)	(65.39)	(34.61)	(100.00)		(78.58)	(21.42)	(100.00)	
Wood	4217	6128	10345	3953	13599	2485	16085	8558
(Per cent)	(40.76)	(59.24)	(100.00)		(84.54)	(15.45)	(100.00)	
Metal	42565	11129	53694	24952	16880	2356	19236	8839
(Per cent)	(79.27)	(20.73)	(100.00)		(87.75)	(12.25)	(100.00)	
Straw, Grass,	3250	4500	7750	1625	8168	4780	12948	3341
Fiber & Leaf	(41.94)	(58.06)	(100.00)		(63.08)	(36.92)	(100.00)	
(Per cent)								
Leather	40000	10000	50000	40000	13850	4237	18087	5994
(Per cent)	(80.00)	(20.00)	(100.00)		(76.57)	(23.43)	(100.00)	
Clay & Ceramics	7005	9511	16516	5791	11558	2989	14547	4798
(Per cent)	(42.41)	(57.59)	(100.00)		(79.45)	(20.55)	(100.00)	
Miscellaneous	12292	27250	39542	939	10651	7472	18123	4720
(Per cent)	(31.09)	(68.91)	(100.00)		(58.77)	(41.23)	(100.00)	
All Major Crafts	11738	12332	24070	7870	12001	4185	16185	5473
(Per cent)	(48.77)	(51.23)	(100.00)		(74.15)	(25.86)	(100.00)	

Source: Same as Table 1.

Handicraft contributes its major share to the household income both in Surguja and MP. Leather works contributes up to 80 per cent of the household income where as contribution of metal, cane and bamboo are 79.3 percent and 65.4 per cent respectively.

TRENDS OF HANDICRAFTS EXPORT IN INDIA

Export in handicraft items take place typically from the developing countries to developed countries. Basic two reasons behind this are that: labour costs in developed countries rise faster than in the developing countries and second, the demand for culture types goods is stimulated as incomes in the developed countries rise. The domestic market of handicrafts is basically very small and so international demand become very important factor. Supply of handicrafts from other countries also becomes an important factor in influencing India's exports.

During 2003-04 the export of handicrafts including hand knitted carpets was to the tune of Rs. 12765.18 crore registering an increase by 16.75 per cent compared to the corresponding figure in 2002-03. The main items, which exhibit increase in exports during 2003-04, are zari and zari goods (32.02%), art metal ware (22.04%), wood ware (19.11 %) and embroidered and crocheted goods (32.62 %). During 2004-05 (April-January 2005) handicrafts exports, including carpets exhibited a growth of 23.11 per cent as compared to the corresponding period of 2003-04. Export growth can be seen in Table 20 and Chart 2. This table reflects a very welcome trend in the export of handicraft items in India. It is a very heartening to know that even in the age of globalization, the export of carpet and other floor- coverings as well as other handicrafts items is on the rise. The total export has increased from Rs. 7157.64 Crores in 1998-99 to 12123.44 Crores up to January 2005.

Table 20
Exports of Handicrafts During1998-2005 (Rs. in Crores)

Year	*Carpet and other floor covering(A)*	*Other Handicrafts (B)*	*Total (A+B)*
1998-99	2013.94	5143.70	7157.64
1999-00	2136.03	5969.60	8105.63
2000-01	2315.15	6955.35	9270.50
2001-02	2436.13	6769.50	9205.63
2002-03	2590.26	8343.41	10933.67
2003-04	2300.04	10465.14	12765.18
2004-05 (Upto Jan,2005)	1819.56	10303.88	12.123.44

Source: Ministry of Textile, Government of India, Annual Rrport,2004-05.
(A) Woolen, Silk and Synthetic.
(B) Art metal were, Wood ware, Textile Scarves, Embroidered and crochet goods, Shawls as art ware, Zari and Zari goods, Imitation Jewelry and Misc. handicrafts.

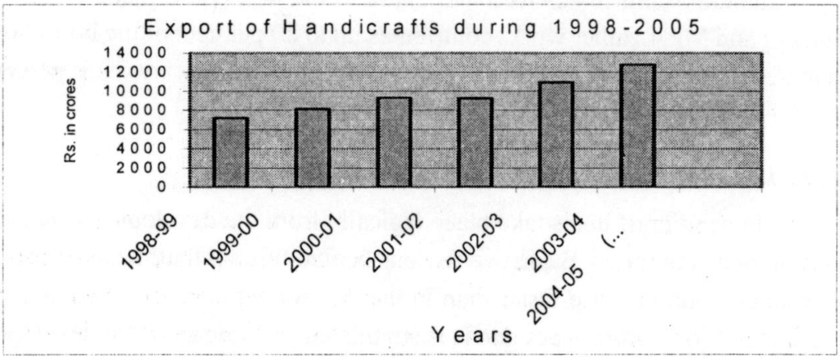

OBSTACLES TO GROWTH OF RURAL HANDICRAFTS SECTOR

Handicrafts and traditional crops (farm produce) could not get this kind of promotional support due to various reasons such as ignorance of local farm & non-farm produce with planners; lack of policy support to promote non-farm produce; dependency of marketing of non-farm sectors (NFS) produce on Government Agencies; dependency on funds and funding agencies; lack of any inventory of farm, non-farm produce and handicrafts with any agency; introduction of alternatives from outside, mass production as a result of use of modern technology, globalization and changing taste of the people under the influence of Western culture. The obstacles are more specially discussed in these following paragraphs.

(a) Raw Material Supplies

All the major crafts are facing problems of procurement of raw materials. Shortage of Certain raw materials such as wood, ivory, wool etc. have been taken up in the past but only partly. Scheme of raw material deports set up by government agencies has not been successful. There is a bottleneck in the supply of raw materials, which can put constraint in the growth and employment generation capacity of the handicraft activities. This source of constraint is not only important for handicraft activity dependent on inputs obtained from the outside region but also for those using indigenous raw materials. Presently private traders are the only sources of procuring raw materials for the crafts persons.

The artisans who need Bamboo, Grass and other forest products are also facing problem of supply of adequate raw material in proper quantity, timely and at reasonable rates. Due to restrictions imposed by Department of Forest under their forest conservation programmes it has made supply of raw material to artisans difficult and time consuming. There is certainly a need of an effective and efficient raw material distribution system, which can protect craft communities from exploitations and artificial shortages.

(b) Working Capital & Rural Credit Facilities

India has a wide network of rural finance institutions (RFIs). But many rural poor remain undeserved left outs in formal financial system. Effective rural financial markets play a key role in promoting rural development and its effect on overall quality of life of rural artisans. Last rural household survey found that only about a six of rural household borrowed from formal RFIs. Various estimates suggest that India's rural poor rely almost entirely on informal sources (Money lender, traders, commission agents) to meet their credit needs at annual interest rates ranging from 36 per cent to 120 per cent a year. (World Bank, 2003). The artisans of the area are poor with little resources or working capital to purchase raw material, tools etc. They depend exclusively on the moneylender or middleman who would lend money or make advance on terms not in the interest of craftsmen. They borrow/purchase from local traders and work in place/tools etc. of other artisans. Most of them are in multiple debts and borrow money from various sources. A major part of their earnings goes on repayment of borrowed money/interest.

Craftsmen need easy credit to free themselves from moneylenders. Earlier, a few of them could get small loan from state government , under the State Aid to Industry Acts. Then came liberalized credit schemes, after the nationalization of banks, which also helped the craftsman only marginally. There are several schemes of NABARD, for providing financial assistance to handicraft artisans and promotional agencies. But the problem persists mostly in case of illiterate poor craftsmen, who still cannot avail many of the schemes because of either lack of knowledge or difficulties actually faced in availing of the credit facilities.

(c) Lack of Awareness and Infrastructure Gaps, Communication, Transport, etc.

The craftsmen and craft places are scattered in the region from cities to villages and to remote areas. India's rural road network faces two major problems. First, about 40 per cent of the rural villages are not yet connected by roads to market or main road connection. Second, much of the rural road network is poorly maintained, thus severely damaged. Due to poor maintenance of bridges and culverts, many rural roads become impassable in the rainy season. The geographical status of areas makes it difficult to approach these places. In some places it takes 2-3 days journey on foot to reach these craft pockets. As a result schemes of Govt. reach these places late. Further the crafts persons face difficulty in popularizing their crafts. They cannot arrange the supply of their products as transportation charges are very high. Due to lack of finance the artisans cannot afford the hauling charges and goods are kept at their own places.

(d) Marketing Facilities with Standardization Quality Control

Meanwhile, the lack of regular and assured market support by private and government sectors for such hidden craft and local produce has also been responsible for their extinction. Nevertheless, it may also be considered in this context that the market-oriented economy has opened the new avenues for producers at micro and macro level. Two important aspects affecting the market are : first, keeping in touch with market trends and second, finding out what is being bought, where and, at what price. The increasing opportunities of marketing of various produce in this region is due to increasing tourism activities and comparatively higher purchasing power of local residents in urban and semi-urban areas as compared to earlier days.

The importance of quality control for the development of handicrafts cannot be over-emphasized. In addition the innovations and researches by scientists, NGOs, individuals and government departments in technology transfer, developing appropriate technology, skills and market would be the additional factors for reviving handicraft and local produce in the region.

(e) Awareness of Consumer Demands

A number of rural handicrafts i.e., wooden toys and artifacts have lost their overseas markets as a result of widespread concern over the use of chemical (toxic?) dyes and paints. Helping the artisans develop vegetable coloring alternatives and labeling these as safe can help rebuild a market for these traditional products. Schemes initiated to promote biotechnology in rural areas should have a marketing perspective at the conceptual stage. The lack of such an approach has led to the failure of several programmes initiated by the government to train rural persons as artisans in products that have a sizeable export market.

A few years ago the All India Handicraft Board initiated a program for training rural people in the art of weaving carpets. Despite the fact that a substantial demand for hand-knitted carpets from India exists, those produced under this program could not be sold even in the local market since the products lacked the finish or the colors that the market demanded. Programs of assistance should take into account the fact that the beneficiaries require inputs based on prevailing market conditions, regarding colors, sizes, shelf life, non-toxic materials, etc. The products are traditional and prepared with old tools with typed design and pattern, hence, a limited demand is there.

Generally, the path of technological development has not catered to the needs of women. New innovations have not matched local needs. As a result women have remained indifferent to emerging technologies. The major reasons have been that local technologies were never innovated upon. Technology for local needs was largely neglected, especially those affecting women. Technologies thrust upon women were not relevant to their needs.

GOVERNMENT INITIATIVES

Since 10th Plan, the office of the Development Commissioner (Handicrafts) is implementing some schemes for the development of the status of the handicrafts artisans. The six schemes are continued- Babasaheb Ambedkar Hastshilp Vikas Yojana (HAVY); Design and Technology Upgradation; Export Promotion, Marketing Support and Services, Research and Development; Training and Extension; and financial assistance to State Handicraft Corporation.

Following initiatives have been taken by the Government during Tenth Five Plan: (GOI, 2005):

- Special Handicrafts Training Projects (SHTP) to benefit 10,000 artisan/ weavers (Out of which 2200 would be trained for carpet weaving and 7800 would be trained in crafts other than carpet through existing components of the Guru Sisya Parampara under the Design and Technology

Upgradation Scheme and training for carpets and crafts other than carpets under AHVY).

- Work shed for Handicraft Artisan, which provide improved working condition for handicraft artisans. This is expected to improve productivity.
- Bima Yojana for Handicraft Artisans, which is to cover 200000 weavers/ artisans under insurance cover during Tenth Plan period. This scheme is being implemented in association with LIC of India and total 62070 artisans were covered. The main objective of this Yojana is to provide life insurance protection to the Handicraft Artisans, whether male or female, between the age group of 18-60 years. Life insurance cover towards natural death shall be a sum of Rs. 20,000/- per member. For accidental death or permanent disability, the coverage shall be maximum up to Rs. 50,000/- per member. All artisans, of either sex, covered under thrift & credit societies and Self-Help Groups (SHGs) would be eligible to be covered under the Bima Yojana for Handicrafts Artisans. During 2004-05, Rs. 270 lakh has been allotted under this Yojana of, which Rs. 60 lakh has been incurred up to January 2005.
- Artisans' Credit Card (ACC) Scheme, is meant to provide adequate any time assistance to artisan in order to fulfill their working capital needs. A target of 200000 cards was set for 2003-04 but only 16500 cards were issued till last March, 2004.
- Urban Haats, which were to provide permanent marketing outlets to the artisans' community from rural as well as urban areas.

PROMOTING RURAL HANDICRAFT ENTERPRISES: THE ROLE OF GOVERNMENT

In the light of foregoing discussion following measures should be undertake for promoting the handicraft sectors in Surguja District.

- Provide raw material on the subsidized rate.
- Increase flow of working capital and fixed capital for new firms.
- Provide banking facilities on low interest rate.
- Provide protection in the national and international markets.
- Organize craft exhibition on International market through Trade Fair Authority.
- Make publicity and promotion through pamphlets, folders and posters.
- Give importance to quality control for development of handicrafts.
- Provide apprenticeship training for craftsmen.
- Provide training centres for regional crafts.

- Establish district level crafts museum.
- Promote cooperative activities in handicrafts sectors.

CONCLUSION

To sum up the above discussion, there is a big paradox in the handicraft sector in Surguja district having a huge potential and traditional skill handed down through generations. But it needs to be tapped and oriented towards gainful employment. With the rapid growth of population, production of these handicrafts could be an important source of employment and income in rural areas. However the development of this sector has been limited because there is no formal organization to support the marketing of handicrafts produced in rural areas. Individual production and selling of products is still the common practice followed. Lack of infrastructure facilities, credit facilities, lack of raw material and insufficient market facilities are quite noticeable in Surguja district. The problem of non-availability of rural technology could possibly have been solved to a great extent by installation of handicraft industries based on locally available raw material in this district. The status of rural development is linked with the poverty among the handicraft artisans. It is noticed that the large gap in economic status in rural area in Surguja could be due to differential level of productive resources and their productivity. From the policy point of view there is a clear need for diversification of employment in productive resources to reduce the artisan's migration from the rural to urban sectors.

The main challenge is to adopt relevant policies and regulations on industry, technology transfer, and small and cottage industries. This would include developing specific policies with respect to rural industries, which is labour-intensive, and most importantly which uses local resources (such as cane, bamboo, straw grass, fiber, stone, skills, and raw materials). Subsequently, it will be necessary to transfer these policies into appropriate legislation and co-ordination and monitor implementation. After the bifurcation of Madhya Pradesh, most of major industries went to MP. It is a high time that all relevant steps be taken to patronize the handicraft industries which has big potential for employment It should be done sooner the better otherwise the already languishing sector will be completely wiped out by the mighty storms of globalization and influx of giant multinational companies. For this, the handicraft sector and household artisans must get supports like subsidies and credit facilities, better marketing facilities and linkage to the global market.

REFERENCES

Birdwood, G.C.M. (1880), *The Industrial Arts of India*, Chapman & Hall: London.

Cable, V., A.Weston and L.C. Jain (1986), The Commerce of Culture-The Experience of Indian Handicrafts, Lancer International for Indian Council for Research on International Economic Relation, New Delhi.

Census of India (2001), Census of India, Provisional Population Totals, Series-23 Chhattisgrah, pp. XI-VII.

Chattopadhyaya, K. (1963), *Indian Handicrafts*, Allied Publishing: New Delhi.

Chaudhary, Paramit (1978), *The Indian Economy-Poverty and Development*, Indian Edition, Vikas Publishing House: New Delhi.

Dastkar (1995), A Society For Crafts And Craftspeople [http://www.coop4coop.org/highlight/dastkar/].

Government of India (GOI) (2005), *Annual Report 2004-05*, Ministry of Textiles: New Delhi.

Government of India (GOI) (2005), *Mid Term Appraisal of 10th Five Year Plan (2002-07)*, Planning Commission: New Delhi.

Ho, Y.M. and Huddle (1976), Traditional and Small Scale Cultural Goods in International Trade and Employment, *Journal of Development Studies*, January.

Minhas, B.S. (1974), *Planning in the Poor*, S. Chand & Co.: New Delhi.

Mukharji, T.N. (1974), *Art- Manufactures of India*, Navrang: New Delhi.

NCAER (1999), Census of Handicrafts Artisans 1995-96, State Series, Vol. 12, Madhya Pradesh, Sponsored by Development Commissioner (Handicrafts) Ministry of Textiles, Government of India.

National Council of Applied Economic Research (1999), Census Survey of Handicrafts Sector (State-Wise Reports), New Delhi.

Robinson, Austin (ed) (1979), *Appropriate Technologies for Third World Development*, International Economics Association, Macmillan: London.

Saraf, D.N. (1991), *In the Journey of Craft Development 1941-1991*, Sampark: Delhi.

Sarkar, S. (1973), *The Swadeshi Movement in Bengal, 1903-1908*, People's Publishing House: New Delhi.

Sood, Anubha (2002), *Crafts as Sustainable Livelihood Option in Rural India*, London School of Economics and Political Science, University of London: London.

Tuong. H.D. and A. Yeats (1980), On Factor Proportions as a Guide to the Future Composition of Developing Country Exports, *Journal of Development Studies*, Vol. 7, pp. 531-539.

Wilkinson-Weber, C.M. (1999), *Embroidering Lives: Women's Work and Skill in the Lucknow Embroidery Industry*, State University of New York: New York.

World Bank (2003), India Sustaining Reform, Reducing Poverty: A World Development Policy Review, Oxford University Press: Washington, DC.

6

DECLINING FOREST CONCENTRATION AND ITS IMPACT ON LAND USE: A CASE STUDY OF UTTAR KANNADA DISTRICT, KARNATAKA

Shrinivas. P. Dandin and Manoj Raj Saxen

INTRODUCTION

The tropical evergreen forests of the Sahyadris or the Malnad region of Karnataka (a case study of the Uttar Kannada district analyzed here) is one of the richest plant areas ("hot spots") on earth and crucial to the oxygen supply of the world. More than 30,000 varieties of wild life and plants and over 8,000 said to unique are reported to lie here. Unless reckless deforestation is halted soon, some scientists fear that within the next 100 years this virgin forest could become an arid wilderness. Forests are renewable resource and have contributed sustainable to the economic development of the country providing goods and services to the people and industry. They also generate substantial volume of employment. In addition forests have a very major and vital role in enhancing the quality of environment, by influencing the life support system and also interwoven with the culture of the people residing in forest areas. Due to rapid industrialization, urbanization and increasing growth of population and subsequent demand for agricultural land has led to augmentation of the process of deforestation and declining forest density. The highest forest concentration is noticed in Uttar Kannada District of Karnataka State. In this paper an attempt has been made to analysis the impact of declining of forest concentration on land use in Uttar Kannada District.

OBJECTIVES AND STUDY AREA

The study aims to analyze the decreasing trend in forest area in the district of Uttar Kannada from 1971 to 2001 and its impact on the land use of the district with well-established statistical techniques. Uttar Kannada District is one of the 27 districts of Karnataka state. Geographically it is located in the north western part of Karnataka state between 13° 55' to 15° 31' North parallels and 74° 9' to 75° 10' east meridians. It accounts for 5.34% area or 10,25,880 sq. km. of Karnataka (1,91,791 sq. kms.). For administrative purpose, the district has been divided into eleven talukas with its headquarters at Karwar. Five of its talukas are in the coastal belt, four in the Sahyadris or Western Ghats (Malnad) and two in the transitional zone (Semi-Malnad). There are 14 urban centres and 1,282 inhabited villages and 55 uninhabited villages in the district. The district is a long and narrow strip of land and seems to be of irregular shape, bulging at the central part (east to west) and tapering gently towards north and south. As per Gibb's method the shape index of Uttar Kannada district is 40.31%. The economy of the district depends on local agricultural produce like arecanut, coconut, betel, cardamom, cashew, rice, sea and forest produce, like fish, shells, salts, honey, timber, fuel wood, etc., since antiquity. It is worth mentioning that local wood handicrafts have been great demand for centuries not only from other states but also from foreign countries. The district is one of the famous coconut and arecanut producers in the state. It has prime place in the production of pineapple in the state which has high demand from Bombay and Bangalore markets.

CHANGES IN LAND USE

The most dominant land use in Uttar Kannada district is forest with 81.85% (8,32,669 hect.) during 1971, 8,15,040 hect (79.54%) during 2001. The highest forest concentration is noticed in Supa and Yellapur talukas and medium concentration is found in Ankola, Siddapur and Sirsi talukas. The remaining talukas namely, Bhatkal, Halyal, Honnavar, Karwar, Kumta and Mundgod show low concentration.

Forest Area

Uttar Kannada district possesses 81.45% of land under forest out of total geographical area during 1971. It has been reduced to 79.54% during 2001, showing 1.81% reduction of land under forest (17628 hectares) (Table No.1 and 2). As per location quotient method the high concentration of forest is found in Supa and Yellapur talukas. The medium concentration of land under forest is noticed in Sirsi, Siddapur and Ankola taluks during 1971, while Ankola has shown low concentration of land under forest during 2001. During 1971 and 2001 Bhatakal, Honnavar, Haliyal, Karwar, Kumta, and Mundgod talukas have shown low concentration of land under forest. Due to growing urbanization expanding land under agriculture and encroachment of land for public utility and settlement the area under forest is being reduced in these taluks where

Table 1

Land Use Pattern in Uttar Kannada District – 1971 (Area in Hectares)

Taluk	Population and their percentage	Geographical Area(in Sq. Km)	Forest	Arable Land	Area not available for cultivation	Uncultivated land (excluding fallow land)	Cultivable waste	Total percentage-
Ankola	67,871 (7.99)	91,870 (9.15)	76,200 (82.94)* (9.15)**	11,175 (12.16)* (9.59)**	3,274 (3.56)* (8.93)**	N.A N.A	1,221 (1.32)* (8.64)**	100
Bhatkal	71,656 (8.44)	34,890 (3.07)	25,565 (73.27)* (3.07)**	5,598 (16.04)* (4.80)**	1,135 (3.25)* (3.09)**	2,117 (6.06)* (9.46)**	475 (1.36)* (3.36)**	100
Haliyal	85,107 (10.02)	84,740 (6.95)	57,887 (68.31)* (6.95)**	18,839 (22.23)* (16.18)**	5,710 (6.73)* (15.57)**	1,349 (1.59)* (6.03)**	955 (1.12)* (6.75)**	100
Honnavar	1,06,537 (12.55)	75,480 (6.91)	57,587 (76.29)* (6.91)**	10,063 (13.33)* (8.64)**	3,993 (5.29)* (10.89)**	2,124 (2.81)* (9.49)**	1,713 (2.26)* (12.12)**	100
Karwar	1,04,477 (12.30)	73,290 (6.69)	55,763 (76.16)* (6.69)**	11,418 (15.59)* (9.81)**	4,012 (5.48)* (10.94)**	28 (0.04)* (0.13)**	1,989 (2.72)* (14.07)**	100
Kumta	1,00,743 (11.86)	58,200 (4.87)	40,099 (68.90)* (4.87)**	9,635 (16.55)* (8.29)**	4,663 (8.01)* (12.72)**	2,623 (4.50)* (11.72)**	1,180 (2.03)* (8.36)**	100
Mundgod	44,464 (5.24)	66,810 (6.24)	51,929 (77.73)* (6.24)**	7,840 (11.73)* (6.73)**	3,761 (6.98)* (10.25)**	1,778 (2.66)* (7.95)**	1,502 (1.77)* (10.63)**	100
Siddapur	73,802 (8.69)	85,930 (8.25)	68,721 (79.97)* (8.25)**	11,054 (12.86)* (9.49)**	1,673 (1.94)* (4.56)**	3,729 (4.33)* (16.69)**	753 (0.88)* (5.33)**	100
Sirsi	1,14,230 (13.45)	1,32,010 (12.28)	1,03,933 (78.73)* (12.28)**	15,111 (11.44)* (12.98)**	3,573 (2.71)* (9.74)**	7,315 (5.54)* (32.71)**	2,078 (1.57)* (14.70)**	100
Supa	35,762 (4.21)	1,89,030 (21.14)	1,75,991 (93.10)* (21.14)**	8,370 (4.42)* (7.18)**	3,113 (1.64)* (8.49)**	137 (0.07)* (0.61)**	1,419 (0.75)* (10.04)**	100
Yellapur	44,456 (5.23)	1,30,110 (14.29)	1,18,994 (91.46)* (14.29)**	7,337 (5.64)* (6.30)**	1,765 (1.35)* (4.81)**	1,166 (0.89)* (5.21)**	848 (0.65)* (6.00)**	100
Total	8,49,105 100	10,22,280 100	8,32,669 (81.45) 100	1,16,440 (11.39) 100	36,672 (3.59) 100	22,366 (2.18) 100	14,133 (1.38) 100	100

Source: Uttar Kannada District at a Glance, 2001.

* Figures in brackets indicate percentage out of district total.

** Figures in brackets indicate percentage out of total geographical area of respective talukas.

Table 2

Land Use Pattern in Uttar Kannada District – 2001 (Area in Hectares)

Taluk	Population and their percentage	Geographical Area(in Sq. Km)	Forest	Arable Land	Area not available for cultivation	Uncultivated land (excluding fallow land)	Cultivable waste	Total percentage
Ankola	91,310 (7.48)	91,872 (8.92)	75,374 (82.04)* (9.24)**	9,326 (10.15)* (7.37)**	2,138 (2.33)* (5.94)**	2,388 (2.60)* (8.67)**	2,186 (2.37)* (11.31)**	100
Bhatkal	1,29,017 (10.57)	34,892 (3.41)	25,433 (72.89)* (3.12)**	7,295 (20.90)* (5.76)**	1,636 (0.85)* (4.54)**	1,303 (3.73)* (4.73)**	567 (1.63)* (2.88)**	100
Haliyal	1,47,064 (12.05)	84,745 (8.27)	57,819 (68.27)* (7.09)**	24,377 (19.28)* (19.27)**	3,176 (8.32)* (8.82)**	634 (3.67)* (2.30)**	952 (1.23)* (4.85)**	100
Honnavar	1,45,842 (11.95)	75,480 (7.37)	57,632 (76.35)* (7.07)**	9,745 (12.91)* (7.71)**	5,870 (6.51)* (16.30)**	2,774 (3.67)* (10.07)**	423 (0.56)* (2.16)**	100
Karwar	1,40,282 (11.49)	73,510 (7.17)	55,427 (75.35)* (6.80)**	7,094 (9.65)* (5.61)**	772 (1.05)* (2.14)**	787 (1.07)* (2.85)**	4,066 (5.53)* (20.71)**	100
Kumta	1,34,144 (10.99)	58,331 (5.69)	39,641 (67.95)* (4.86)**	9,943 (17.04)* (7.86)**	3,878 (6.64)* (10.77)**	3,361 (5.76)* (12.20)**	2,247 (3.85)* (11.45)**	100
Mundgod	75,046 (6.15)	66,809 (6.52)	49,456 (74.02)* (6.07)**	14,732 (22.05)* (11.64)**	643 (0.96)* (1.79)**	1,120 (1.16)* (4.06)**	1,490 (2.23)* (7.59)**	100
Siddapur	91,646 (7.51)	85,928 (8.39)	68,130 (72.28)* (8.35)**	12,356 (14.37)* (9.77)**	851 (0.99)* (2.36)**	3,836 (4.46)* (13.92)**	1,335 (1.55)* (6.80)**	100
Sirsi	1,52,935 (12.53)	1,32,233 (12.90)	1,03,270 (78.09)* (12.67)**	16,877 (12.76)* (13.55)**	1,400 (1.05)* (3.89)**	8,415 (6.36)* (30.55)**	3,651 (2.76)* (18.60)**	100
Supa	46,818 (3.84)	1,91,069 (18.47)	1,65,873 (86.81)* (20.35)**	6,616 (3.22)* (4.87)**	13,976 (7.31)* (38.81)**	1,463 (0.76)* (5.35)**	1,789 (0.93)* (9.11)**	100
Yellapur	66,156 (5.84)	1,30,110 (12.69)	1,16,986 (89.91)* (14.35)**	8,559 (6.58)* (6.76)**	1,664 (1.28)* (4.62)**	1,462 (1.12)* (5.30)**	920 (0.70)* (4.69)**	100
Total	12,20,260 100	10,24,679 100	8,15,041 (79.54) 100	1,26,465 (12.34) 100	36,004 (3.51) 100	27,543 (2.68) 100	19,626 (1.92) 100	100

Source: Uttar Kannada District at a Glance, 2001.

* Figures in brackets indicate percentage out of district total

** Figures in brackets indicate percentage out of total geographical area of respective talukas.

land under forest is of low concentration (Figure No.1). Considering land under forest as an independent variable and six variables as dependent variables, the correlation is worked out. The relationship between taluka wise forest land and geographical area shows positive correlation (+0.11) Similarly remaining 5 dependent variables viz., arable land, area under uncultivated land (excluding fallow land), area not available for cultivation, waste land, and population of the talukas show positive correlation with forest land. The plain topography has easily attracted the farmers to bring more land under cultivation in the taluka of Haliyal where 28.76% of taluk's geographical area is under cultivation. Similarly in coastal taluka non-forest land use is increasing due to plain topography. Consequently urbanization, industrial growth and transport are expanding. Thus these have posed threat to forest land and ecology of forest, including coastal forest and aquatic ecology. Although mining is very much restricted to (manganese) Supa taluka but construction of hydro power dams in Supa taluka and Kaiga nuclear project in Karwar taluka have swalloed considerable area of ever green forest. The forest ecology and bio-diversity have been very much disturbed in the talukas of Supa and Karwar, due to developmental work, while in coastal talukas and in Sirsi, Haliyal and Mundgod talukas (forest area) ecological disturbance has occurred due to grabbing of forest land for agriculture and settlement purposes.

Arable Land

The Uttar Karnataka district has 11.39% (1,16,440 hect) of arable land during 1971, and 12.3% (1,26,465 hect) during 2001. The plain topography of Haliyal taluk has attracted the farmers to extend agricultural activities, where arable land was 17,839 hect. during 1971 while 24,377 hect. during 2001. The talukas of Supa and Yellapur are not suitable for agriculture due to undulating hill ranges and hence are covered by dense and evergreen forests. The undulating topography of the semi-Malnad and river plain beds of the coastal talukas constitute major share (26.46%) of the arable land in Uttar Kannada District.

Land not Available for Cultivation

This category of land constitutes 3.59% (36,672 hect) during 1971 and 3.51% (36,004 hect) during 2001, of the total geographical area of the district. The percentage of land not available for cultivation in different taluks varies between 1.79 and 38.81 per cent in the year 2001. Supa (38.81%) and Honnavar (16.30%) taluks have highest land under "not available for cultivation, while lowest is noticed in Mundgod (1.79%) and Siddapur (2.36%) during 2001. This is mainly due to submergence of land under Kali hydro project. The land under this category has been increasing at a faster rate due to the rapid growth of population, which require more land for residential, commercial establishments, educational houses, commercial establishments, and other institutions, industries, roads, railways and other developmental projects which are taking place in the district.

Uncultivated Land (Excluding Fallow)

This land is suitable for agriculture but not used for agriculture due to undulating nature of topography. Out of total geographical area of the district 2.18% (22,366 hect) of land during 1971 was under "Uncultivated land "while it increased to 2.68% (27,543 hect) during 2001, which shows an increase of 0.49% (5177 hect) of the total geographical area of the district. Among the 11 talukas the Sirsi taluka represent highest uncultivated land of 32.71% (7315 hect.) during 1971, and also during 2001 i.e. 30.55% (8,450 hect.). The taluka-wise comparison of data of uncultivated land from 1971 to 2001 shows decrease in the talukas of Bhatkal, Mundgod, Siddapur and Wallpaper mainly because of cultivation of pineapple, pepper, cotton and coconut plantation in the uncultivated land.

Cultivable Waste Land

The cultivable waste land in Uttar Kannada Dist was 1.38% (14,133 hect.) during 1971 while it increased to 1.92 (19,626 hect) during 2001. Out of the total area of the district, the Karwar taluka reported high proportion of 14.07% (1,989 hect) land under cultivated waste during 1971, while 20.71% (4,066 hect) during 2001. In coastal region due to saline ingression, encroachment by sea water, marshy land, silting in the agricultural land due to flooding, tidal effect, water logging, erosion etc. the uncultivable waste land is increased. In Sirsi taluk highest land under cultivable waste was 14.70% (2,078 hect) during 1971 while it increased to 18.60% (3,651 hect) during 2001. The in accessibility, difficulties to irrigate undulating topography salinity and alkalinity of the soil, marshy land, erosion and fall of debris are the causes for the formation of cultivable waste land in the Uttar Kannada District.

CONCLUSION

The coastal region has recorded a decline of 6173 hect (5.30%) of arable land. Such a decline was due to transfer of arable land to many developmental activities. The pressure of population is so intense by which nearly every available patch of land is cultivated. Though there is increase in the arable land, there is a gradual conversion of agricultural land into built up area in the vicinity of settlements. The proposed and ongoing "Hydro-electric projects", Conan railway work in the coastal region, 'Naval Base' near Karwar and other developmental projects have been engulfing thousands of hectares of arable and rest land in the recent days. As mentioned earlier, it is interesting to note that the arable land varies from the coastal to the Malnad and the semi-Malnad. The distinction between these three could be made from the geographical point of view. The former occupies the fertile flat coastal flood and estuarine plain but the latter occupies the valley gaps and gentle hill slopes and the third one in an open country and are undulating plain. But the geographical condition of the district is almost similar with a marginal change in the eastern edge. While isolated patches of agricultural land in the thick jungle of the Malnad region are the main causes for such uncultivated land, inaccessibility and controlled attack on crop by wild animals kept the land fallow. The diversified cropping system is the main reason for less fallow land in the semi-Malnad region. These fallow lands are good grazing grounds for the cattle in the Uttar Kannada district.

REFERENCES

Oldham R.M. (1993), *Environmental Rain: The Crises of Survival*, India Publishing Company, New Delhi.

Shari Mohammed and Raze Medic (1994), *Geography of Environment*, Rawat Publications, Jaipur.

Thrived P.R. (1999), *Encyclopedia of Environment, Pollution, Planning and Conservation*, Vol. 3, A.V.H. Publications, New Delhi.

7

EXPERIENCES OF JAMMU AND KASHMIR ECONOMY AND ITS LESSONS FOR NORTH-EAST

A.N. Sadhu and Falendra K. Sudan

INTRODUCTION

The development of hill areas has progressively assumed considerable importance. If we look at the relief map of India, except for the Indo-Gangetic plain and the coastal strips on the eastern and western coasts, the rest of the country comprises of the hills and dales. Though about 4 per cent of the world population lives in hilly areas, which constitutes 10 per cent of the global landmass, they decide the destinies of at least 40 per cent of the people living in the foothills and basins of the rivers. The hilly areas have attained a special significance due to their mineral deposits and hydroelectric potential of snow-fed rivers. It is the economic dimension of the hill development without changing the eco-system of the life style of the aboriginal people that has become more important.

There are numerous reasons for placing the issue of development of hill areas high on the agenda of development issues. In the context of Indian economy, one could refer to the Sino-Indian border war of 1962, which underlined the strategic importance of the hill areas of the North and North-East. "It come to be realized that the backwardness of these areas could be potentially damaging to the security interests of the nation as the situation could lead to feelings of frustration and helplessness among the people– sentiments which the nation could ill afford in a sensitive border region" (Joshi, 1983, p. 1). Besides this another factor responsible for the recent stress on development of hill areas has been the realization, especially after the Third Five Year Plan that they have not benefited much from past development plans and programmes. A part of the problem of slow pace of development in the hill areas lies in the fact that the policies pursued so far have tended to favour the already developed and well-endowed regions of the country. The Sixth Plan has highlighted this fact. "It is now recognized that the pathways of development adopted in the past have resulted in an uneven distribution of the benefits of economic growth as between the socio-economic groups" (GOI, 1980, p. 413).

The development programmes for the hill areas have generally failed to take into account the peculiar problems and constraints, which they have to face and which sets them apart from the other backward regions of the country. The most important of these are geographical, ecological, agro-climatic and socio-cultural features, which are specific to them. Besides, any destabilization in the hill ecology, either through deforestation or due to indiscriminate blasting of the hill sides for mining, quarrying, road construction or dam building can lead to rapid soil erosion and siltation of water courses, river beds and reservoirs. Therefore, unless adequate programmes are evolved for the conservation and proper utilization of the resources of the hill areas, not only the problems of these areas will continue to remain unsolved but would also seriously obstruct the economy of the plains.

Among the hill areas of the country, there exists wide diversity and variation in respect of resource endowment and development potential as well as specific problems and constraints, which they face. No two-hill areas are alike and the difference between one hill area and the other is just as much as the difference between plains and hills. Obviously the problems of the hill economy of Jammu and Kashmir are different than those of the North-Eastern states. However, still numerous similarities can be traced. Keeping the above in view, in the present paper an attempt has been made to examine the experiences of the hill economy of Jammu and Kashmir and its lessons for North-East India. It is hoped that the lessons drawn will be of use for the planners and policy makers to plan logically for the overall development of the North-Eastern hill economies.

HILL ECONOMY OF JAMMU AND KASHMIR

(i) Physical Features

The state of Jammu and Kashmir is situated between 32.17 degree and 36.58 degree north latitude and 37.26 degree and 80.30 degree east longitude, the total area of the state is 22,22,236 sq. kms including 78114 sq kms under the illegal occupation of Pakistan and 42,685 sq kms under that of China, of which Pakistan illegally handed over 5130 sq kms to China. The state is bounded by Pakistan, Afghanistan and China from the West to the East. The state of Jammu and Kashmir is the northern most state of India comprising three distinct Climatic regions viz. Arctic cold desert areas of Ladakh, temperate Kashmir valley and sub-tropical region of Jammu. There is a sharp rise of altitude from 1000 feet to 28250 feet above the sea level within state's four degree of latitude. The climate varies from tropical in Jammu plains to semi-arctic cold in Ladakh with Kashmir and Jammu mountainous tracts having temperate climatic conditions. The annual rainfall also varies from region to region with 92.6 mm in Leh, 650.5 mm in Srinagar and 1115.9 mm in Jammu (http://jammukashmir.nic.in). A large part of the state forms part of the Himalayan Mountains. The state is geologically constituted of rocks varying from the oldest period of the earth's history to the youngest present day river and lake deposits.

It has four geographical zones, which are as under:

(a) Sub-mountain and semi-mountain plain known as kandi or dry belt;

(b) The Shivalak ranges;

(c) The high mountain zone constituting the Kashmir valley, Pir Panchal range and its off-shoots including Doda, Poonch and Rajouri districts and part of Kathua and Udhampur districts; and

(d) The middle runs of the Indus River comprising Leh and Kargil.

(ii) Flora & Fauna

The state is rich in flora and fauna. In Jammu, the flora ranges from the thorn bush type of the arid plain to the temperate and alpine flora of the higher altitudes. Of the broad leaf trees there are maple, horse chestnuts, silver fir etc. At the higher altitudes there are birch, rhododendron, Berbers and a large number of herbal plants. In the hilly regions of Doda, Udhampur, Poonch and Rajouri there is a large and varied fauna including leopard, cheetah and deer, wild sheep, bear, brown musk shrew, muskrat. Varieties of snakes, bats, lizards and frogs are also found in the region. The game birds in Jammu include chakor, snow partridge, pheasants, and peacock. Kashmir abounds in rich flora. The Valley, which has been described as the 'Paradise' on Earth, is full of many hues of wood and game. The most magnificent of the Kashmir trees is the Chinar found throughout the valley. It grows to giant size and girth. The trees presents itself in various enchanting colours through the cycle of the seasons among which its autumnal look is breath-taking. Mountain ranges in the valley have dense deodar, pine and fir. Walnut, willow, almond and cider also add to the rich flora of Kashmir. The dense forests of Kashmir are a delight to the sport-lovers and adventures for whom there are Ibex, Snow Leopard, Musk deer, wolf, Markhor, Red bear, Black bear and Leopard. The winged game include ducks, goose, partridge, chakor, pheasant, wagtails, herons, water pigeons, warblers, and doves.In otherwise arid desert of Ladakh some 240 species of local and migratory birds have been identified including black-necked crane. The Ladakh fauna includes yak, Himalayan Ibex, Tibetan antelope, snow leopard, wild ass, red bear and gazelle (http://jammukashmir.nic.in).

(iii) Demographic Features

The state ranks 6th in area and 17th in population among the states and Union Territories of India. The state consists of 14 districts, 59 tehsils, 119 blocks, 3 municipalities, 54 towns and notified area committee, 6477 inhabited villages and 281 uninhabited villages. The total population of Jammu and Kashmir was 10.07 million in 2001 with a sex ratio of 900 females per 1000 males. The infant mortality rate (IMR) is estimated at 108 per thousand. About 54 per cent of the population in the state is literate, as against the national literacy rate of 65.38 per cent (http://jammukashmir.nic.in). In the state of Jammu and Kashmir, there are wide inter-district variations in the population growth. Six districts of the state recorded decadal growth rate of population higher than the state average of 29.04 per cent in 2001 and all of these districts are lying outside the Jammu region, i.e. in the Valley of Kashmir and Ladakh region. The nine districts of the state have recorded sex ratio higher than the state average of 900 females per 1000 males. Five districts of the State have recorded unfavorable sex ratio in 2001 compared with 1991 and all are lying in the Jammu region except Leh in the Ladakh region and Srinagar in the Valley of Kashmir, which may be attributed to male out-migration and prevailing socio-economic and cultural factors (GOI, 2002).

Except the districts of Ladakh region and Doda, all other districts of the state of Jammu and Kashmir have recorded a significantly higher density of population than the State average of 77 and 99 persons per sq. km. in 1991 and 2001 respectively. As against one third in Maharashtra and West Bengal and one fourth in Karantaka, only one fifth of the population in the state resides in urban areas. 23.83 per cent population has been recorded as urban in the state against the National Average of 25.72 per cent. Jammu city has recorded very rapid growth and presently ranks as the 48th biggest city in the country (GOI, 2002). Besides the cities of Jammu and Srinagar, other important towns are the district headquarters. The remaining towns continue to have many rural features and pursuits reflecting the state's predominant agro-pastoral economy.

(iv) Economic and Social infrastructure

The Net State Domestic Product (NSDP) at current prices was 12.45 per cent during 1980-81 to 1999-2000. The average annual growth of Per Capita Net Domestic Product at current prices during 1980-2000 was estimated as 9.63 per cent. The state ranks 17th in terms of per capita Net State Domestic Product. In terms of industries per lakh population, the state ranks 19th. In terms of Net Sown Area irrigated, it ranks 16th (GOI, 2003). Both social and economic development and demographic situation are actually multi-dimensional processes and each dimension of development as well as demographic change has its own specific determinants.

In spite of a large natural and human resource base, the state lags behind in industrial development. However, due to environmental factors and its geographical location, setting up of large manufacturing industries with a huge capital base is not possible, although many small and medium-scale industries have come up. In 2000-01, there were 42,808 medium and small industrial units with an employment of 1,87,399 (GOJ&K, 2003). The main industries are hosiery, basic metal products, wood and food product industries, which contribute a large proportion of total industrial output in the registered manufacturing sector.

The economic infrastructure, which includes power sector, roads and transport and telecommunication, plays a very important role in economic and social development. The state of Jammu and Kashmir possesses immense potential for development of the power sector (based on hydel and solar), but the performance has not been on a scale commensurate with the possibilities. In 1998, the total installed capacity was 374.13 MW, with 190.19 MW in hydel plants and 183.94 MW in thermal plants. Jammu and Kashmir stood at 12th position in terms of per capita consumption of electricity (KwH) in 1998-99. The generating capacity of the hydel plants increased to 232.7 MW in 2001 with no addition to capacity in thermal plants (GOI, 2003). In terms of road length per 1000 sq. Km, Jammu and Kashmir is the lowest (127/1000 sq km) as compared to Himachal Pradesh (542/1000sq km) and Assam (872/1000sq km) in 1996-97. The total road length is 13660 sq. km. under state PWD, 20,332 sq. km. under other departments (including BRO) (GOJ&K, 2002a). The state also has the lowest figure (0.40/1000 sq. km.) for railways.

Road development in Jammu and Kashmir is important, given the terrain of the state and limited development of alternate means of transportation. A well-developed network of roads is necessary not only for the economic development of the state but also for its social, political and cultural development. It is required to exploit the rich natural wealth of the state, to develop indigenous industries, to explore new markets for its products and to promote tourism. The state government has been paying required attention to build new roads, maintain and upgrade existing roads, construct new bridges and culverts and connect villages with a network of roads.

There were 13539 km of roads in the state in 2000, of which 11.260 km were surfaced and 2279 km were un-surfaced, which also excludes the length of National Highways and other roads not maintained by the state P.W.D. Besides, other departments such as forest, irrigation and flood control and C.D. & N.E.S. maintain a total of 16,090 km of roads. The Boarder Road Organization (BRO) has taken up the maintenance of National Highways in the sate. The total road length maintained by BRO was 3715 km in 2000, of which 2954 km were surfaced and 761 km un-surfaced roads (GOJ&K, 2001a).

Due to difficult terrain, the ongoing insurgency has contributed to poor accessibility. The inter-district variations in accessibility of roads are very sharp. For example, in terms of road length per 100 sq. km., Budgam district has the highest road density of 81.84 km. and the districts of Leh, Kargil and Doda have poor accessibility to the tune of 2.58, 4.82 and 5.24 km respectively (GOJ&K, 2001a). On the whole, districts in Jammu division lag behind the districts in Kashmir valley as far as road infrastructure is concerned.

During 1989-2000, the road network increased by 1.5 times as against 2.5 times increase in road traffic. The problem of frequent landslides alongside the road is severe. In the valley of Kashmir and the Ladakh region, the working season is also small of about six-seven months. The railroad network has been confined up to the city of Jammu and recently it has been extended up to district headquarter of Udhampur and the work is in progress to link the Valley of Kashmir with road link. Besides, the state has three civil airports at Jammu, Srinagar and Leh, which connects Jammu and Kashmir with rest of the country.

In terms of social infrastructure, the state of Jammu and Kashmir falls behind most of the developed states in India. In 1998-99, there were 10515 primary schools, 3507 middle schools and 1466 high and higher secondary schools and the literacy rate was 54.46 per cent. (GOJ&K, 2002b).

During 1981 and 2001, the number of workers registered an increase of 39 per cent. The total number of workers now stands at 36.89 lakh including 11.52 lakh marginal workers (GOJ&K, 2002a). Keeping into view the rapid population growth from 59.87 lakh in 1981 to 100.70 lakh in 2001, the increase in employment opportunities has been meager. Due to very slow industrial growth, 70 per cent of the population is directly or indirectly dependent on agriculture and allied sectors. As a result, there is acute problem of educated unemployment.

(v) Agriculture

Agriculture supports about 80 per cent of population of Jammu and Kashmir. The state is divided into three agro-climatic zones: Jammu, Kashmir and Ladakh. Each zone has its own specific geo-climatic condition, which influence the cropping pattern and productivity. In Kashmir, rice is the chief crop, followed by maize, barley and wheat, whereas Jammu region dominates both in maize and wheat production; and barley is the major cereal crop followed by wheat in Ladakh. The three important food crops, viz., rice, maize, and wheat accounts for 84 per cent of the total cropped area: the balance 16 per cent is shared by inferior cereals and pulses and contributes a significant part of the food grain in the state. Nearly 75 per cent of country's temperate fruits, mainly apples, are grown in the state.

The physiographic location of the state of Jammu and Kashmir imposes a number of constraints, particularly in development of agriculture and allied sectors. The land use pattern, which was purely agriculture, has changed over time to agri-horticulture and silvi-pastoral. Although the net area sown has remained more or less same (7.31 lakh hectare in 1990-91 to 7.33 lakh hectare in 1999-2000), the area under fruit and vegetable cultivation has increased marginally. In respect of fruit, it has increased from 176.30 thousand hectare in 1990-91 to 213.73 thousand hectare in 1998-99, whereas vegetables have shown a marginal increase, from 14,000 hectare in 1990-91 to 14,930 hectare in 1999-2000. Food grains production has shown an increase from 13664 thousand quintals in 1990-91 to 15253 quintals in 1998-99 (GOJ&K, 2002a). Many temperate fruits are also grown. Large orchards in the Valley of Kashmir produce apples, pears, peaches, walnuts, almonds and cherries. In addition, it is the largest producer of saffron in the Indian subcontinent. Artificial floating gardens on the lakes are favourable for the cultivation of flowers and vegetables. In Ladakh, there is only one cropping season-*Kharif*. Recently, strawberry cultivation has also been introduced in Ladakh. Pastoralism and cattle breeding have long been the vital features of the Ladakh economy. The Kashmir goat raised in the region provides *pashmina* for the production of fine fabrics.

(a) Land Holding

The dominant sectors of the economy of Jammu and Kashmir are agriculture and its allied activities. The land holding pattern is an important predetermining factor of social and economic development. According to the 1995 Agriculture Census, the average land holding is 0.73 hectare. The only state in India with lesser land holding than Jammu and Kashmir is Kerala (0.33 ha). Out of the total geographical area of the state, 40.94 per cent was the gross cropped area including the net sown area and area sown more than once. The net area sown was 30.47 per cent, fallow land accounted for 4.30 per cent and area under forest formed 27.23 per cent. Land not available for cultivation was 29.29 per cent (GOJ&K, 1996).

In 1995-96, marginal landholders (land holdings below 0.05 to 1.00 hectare) comprised 77.97 per cent of the total population. In the state of Jammu and Kashmir, the categorization of land holding is based on area of holding i.e. small (1.04-2.00 ha.), semi medium (2.01-4.00 ha.), medium (4.01-10.00 ha.) and large (more than 10 ha.). The small and middle farmers comprised 18.77 per cent and 2.63 per cent of the total land holdings respectively, whereas the number of farmers with high landholdings is below 1 per cent. The average size of small and marginal land holding shows a declining trend, and the number of bigger landholders is almost constant. The average landholding size for the state as a whole is 0.76 ha. According to the Agriculture Census of 1985-86, average size of the marginal and small land holdings declined by 8.33 per cent between 1970-71 and 1985-86 (GOJ&K, 1987). There is an inverse relationship between the size categories and the proportion of net sown area, with the exception of the size category of 10 hectare and above. There is a positive relationship between the size category and the land available for cultivation during both the periods.

The average size of landholding is recorded maximum for Leh (1.38 ha.) and minimum for Srinagar (0.37ha). However, the size of total arable land is not the same in different regions of the state. The size of total arable land is maximum for Jammu (159.27 thousand ha) and minimum for Kargil (12.94 thousand ha). Such a difference in size of land holding of the people and total arable land exists chiefly due to an uneven demographic distribution pattern arising out of physio- climatic conditions in Ladakh district, covering about 70 per cent of the total geographical area of the state (GOJ&K, 2001b).

(b) Land Use Pattern

The total forest area in the state is far below the area prescribed by the Forest Policy of 1952 (according to which 66 per cent of land should be under forest cover in the hilly region). However, barring Ladakh region, the state has only 50 per cent of its area under forest cover. Besides forests, the other major land use types in the state are the net sown area (30.38 per cent), land put to non-agricultural uses (12.04 per cent), barren land (12.04 per cent), permanent pastures and others grazing grounds (5.21 per cent). During 1997-98 to 1998-99, the land put to non-agricultural uses declined from 14 per cent to 12.04 per cent, and the cultivable waste declined from 5.90 per cent to 5.75 per cent, whereas the net sown area, barren land, permanent pastures and other grazing grounds increased respectively by 0.85 per cent, 2.67 per cent and 0.5 per cent (GOJ&K, 2002a).

(c) Cropping Pattern

Among the food grains, the main crops are rice (30.06 per cent), maize (29.90 per cent) and wheat (23.31 per cent) accounting for 84 per cent of the total cropped area while the balance 16 per cent is shared by inferior cereals and pulses (GOJ&K, 2002a). The commercial crops of significance grown in the state are apple and oilseeds. The consequence of such a cropping pattern is that the bulk of the cultivators have little to spares for buying other necessities of life. The small quantities of commercial crops grown in the state offer little scope for agro-based industries. The state grows nearly 75 per cent of the country's temperate fruit, mainly apples, but most of the area under fruit cultivation is concentrated in the Valley of Kashmir. The ongoing insurgency in Kashmir has destroyed the infrastructure for horticultural development. Recently, the favourable political climate and rising optimism infused a new era of growth and prosperity which are revealed by the positive trends like increase in the production and export of fruits. The new policies of the government have rejuvenated the social and economic infrastructure of the state, the outcomes of which is visible in the form of increasing trends in production and productivity of various crops.

(d) Productivity

There is regional differential in agricultural productivity in the state of Jammu and Kashmir. In Ladakh, the productivity of the land is lower as compared to other two regions (Kashmir and Jammu). As a result, the crop productivity differs from one region to other. Another important aspect of the poor agricultural development is that the climatic conditions do not allow round the year cultivation. There are limited possibilities of raising agricultural output by increasing the area of cultivation without disturbing the ecological balance. The increase in the agricultural output would, therefore, have to be achieved only through intensification, diversification and rational land use.

The productivity for sugarcane is maximum (35.82 quintal/hectare), followed by rice (21.82 quintal /hectare), maize (17.09 quintal/hectare) and wheat (15.18 quintal/hectare). The productivity of total food grains was 12.49 in 1979-80, which increased to 15.22 in 1993-94 and further, increased to 16.18 in 1998-99. The productivity of rice has shown a marginal increase from 18.03 quintal/hectares to 18.57 quintal between 1979-80 and 1993-94 and up to 21.82-quintal/ hectare in 1998-99. The productivity of wheat increased from 10.20 quintal per hectare to 14.19 quintal per hectares between 1979-80 and 1993-94 and further increased to 15.18 quintal per hectare in 1998-99. The productivity of maize went up from 13.48 quintal per hectare to 18.71 quintal per hectare between 1979-80 and 1993-94 and to 17.09 quintals per hectare in 1998-99. The productivity of pulses decreased from 5.58 quintal per hectare to 5.51 quintal per hectare between 1979-80 and 1993-94 and increased to 5.83 quintal per hectare in 1998-99 (GOJ&K, 2001c).

(e) Irrigation

Irrigation is one of the indicators for measuring agricultural development and affects agricultural productivity directly. In the state of Jammu and Kashmir, the total net area irrigated by different sources (canals, tanks, wells and others) was about 2.61 lakh hectare (41.96 per cent) in the year 1950-51, out of which the canal irrigation constitutes the largest single source of irrigation (93.75 per cent) and tanks, wells and other miscellaneous sources contribute the rest. There is a constant increase in the net irrigated area during last 50 years. In 1998-99, the area under irrigated agriculture was 3.48 lakh hectare, which is 47.19 per cent of the total area sown. However, the situation in various regions is different from the state average. In the Jammu region, the gross irrigated area is 75.14

thousand hectare, mostly irrigated by canals like Ranbir canal and Ravi lift irrigation system covering about 21.06 per cent area (GOJ&K, 2002a). The rice and maize cultivation get the maximum share of available water sources. The state offers good scope for the exploitation of ground water, as current ground water development is meager (1.33 per cent).

In sum, the production of the food crops has shown consistency in the last 20 years and there was hardly any impact on the productivity of the crop during the period of insurgency and production of the food crops shows no change during the period before and after the green revolution.

(vi) Livestock and Dairy

The animal husbandry constitutes a vital activity in Jammu and Kashmir. About 79 per cent of the population in Kashmir lives in rural areas and depends largely on the income generated by the agricultural and livestock sector. Nearly 0.13 per cent of gross state domestic product (SDP) is contributed by livestock economy, whereas agriculture contributes one third of SDP. Jammu and Kashmir has a precious wealth of livestock in the form of cattle, buffalo, sheep, goat, poultry, etc. The livestock development helps in the production of *pashmina* shawls and other animal based products like carpets, shawls and blankets and the state earns a good part of foreign exchange through their exports. The livestock industry has vast potential for the development and better economic viability.

In the state of Jammu and Kashmir, the total livestock population was 91.751-lakh and the estimated cattle population was 31.75 lakh in 1997, which constitute about 34.60 per cent of total livestock. The sheep population comes second, constituting 34 per cent of total livestock population, followed by the goat population (19.71 per cent). The Kashmir region has about 55 per cent of sheep population followed by Jammu (about 29 per cent) and Ladakh (about 8 per cent) (GOJ&K, 1997a). Yaks are chiefly confined to the Ladakh region.

Jammu and Kashmir is ideally suited for dairy development. The state has registered a steady growth in milk production. The State's milk production in 1995-96 was 3.69 lakh metric ton which stood at 6.66 lakh metric ton in 2001-02. The per capita milk consumption is 325 ml/day and national average milk consumption is 240-ml/day (GOJ&K, 2002a).

(vii) Sericulture

India is the second largest producer of silk in the world, after China. The rearing of silk worms on mulberry trees for the production of raw silk is known as sericulture. Mulberry silk is produced mainly in Karnataka, West Bengal, Jammu and Kashmir, Assam, Punjab, Tamil Nadu and Andhra Pradesh. In Jammu and

Kashmir, 25.28 thousand families were engaged in extraction of silk fibre in 1999-2000. During the same period, 2.15 thousand villages were engaged in sericulture production. The state has about 1402 thousand mulberry trees, of which 883 thousand are in Jammu division and 519 thousand in Kashmir division. About 80 thousand kg. of raw silk was produced at the cost of around Rs. 3.5 crore in 1999-2000 (GOJ&K, 2001b).

The production of raw silk showed a gradual decline during the period 1985-86 to 1995-96. For instance, the silk production was 33.70 thousand quintal in 1985-86, which declined to 9.50 thousand quintal in 1995-96. From 1996-97 onwards it shows an increasing trend. However, in terms of value of raw silk produced, there has been declining trend. Similarly, the number of household dependent on sericulture has shown a gradual decline, from 38.50 thousand in 1980-89 to 25.28 thousand in 1999-2000 (GOJ&K, 2001b), which is attributed to low return from cocoon production and climatic conditions.

In 1999-2000, about 25.28 thousand families were engaged in extraction of silk fibre. In the recent past, the performance of silk industry is declining due to inadequacy of mulberry leaves and damage caused by insects and pests. During the year 1980-81 there were 601 thousand trees, which increased to 1402 thousand in 1999-2000 (GOJ&K, 2002a). Due to the lower return from the activity and lack of proper attention of the plantation at the establishment state, growth of mulberry plantation is slow. The inconsistency in the production of cocoons due to the climatic limitation of the state and inadequate rearing equipment is another matter of concern. As a result, proper growth and development of silk worms does not take place. The production of raw silk does not have consistency due to improper disease management.

(viii) Horticulture

The post-Independence era witnessed substantial progress in respect of production and area coverage under horticulture but still needs special attention. The fruit production in the state has increased to 11.05 lakh metric tons in 1999-2000 from mere 16000 metric tons in 1953-54. Out of this, fresh fruit production accounts for 10.22 lakh metric tons. The area under cultivation of crops has increased by 17 times. It has increased up to 2.19-lakh hectare in 2000-01(GOJ&K, 2002a) from a mere 12,400 hectare in 1953-54. During the same period, per hectare yield too has gone up to 5.08 metric tons from 1.29 metric tons. Under the area expansion programme, over 44 lakh plants produced in government and private nurseries have been distributed among the prospective beneficiaries in 1999-2000 (GOJ&K, 2002a). About 4.85 lakh estimated families are involved directly in fruit cultivation and around 20 lakh persons are, directly or indirectly, being benefited by the fruit industry of the state. Apart from these achievements, this sector also faces certain challenges like small average land holding size (0.76 hectare) and the commercialization of the horticulture activity. Due to unavailability of packing and processing facilities, 30 per cent of the total fruit produced get wasted. Inadequate marketing facility is also one of the reasons for low productivity. Through certain changes in the development perspective of the department of horticulture, this sector could become one of the important sectors in the state economy. The returns from the growth in apple production should be one of the motivational factors for the growth of horticulture in the state.

(ix) Handicrafts and Handloom

The handicraft industry in Jammu and Kashmir occupies an important place in its economy. It makes significant contribution to its domestic and foreign exchange earnings besides providing employment to a large number of artisans and traders. The state enjoys a prominent position on the world map of exports with regard to handicrafts and carpets. During 1999-2000, the state exported a record value of handicrafts, which was estimated at Rs. 525 crore including carpet export to the tune of Rs. 449 crore (GOJ&K, 2002a).

The handicrafts sector provides employment to over 3.30 lakh artisans annually and the overall handicraft production has increased to Rs. 663 crore in 2000. In fact, the handicrafts sector has helped Kashmir to sustain economically during the worst ever trauma of the decade long militancy when the entire socio economic order got shattered. This is evident from the fact that the annual carpet production showed a steep increases from Rs. 293 crore in 1996 to Rs. 557 crore in March 2000. Among other crafts, papier-mache production also increased between 1998-99 and 1999-2000 (GOJ&K, 2002a); there was a seven-fold increase in papier-mache and chain stitch production. However, the production of embroidery, woodcarving and woolen shawls declined during the same period, which can be partly attributed to the increased demand for carpets both in the international and domestic markets.

The number of cooperative societies has steadily increased to support the artisans of the state. The production of the cooperatives till 1994-95 was almost at par with the 1990-91 production figures. After 1995, the production of the cooperative societies declined drastically (GOJ&K, 2002a). No satisfactory reason can be attributed to this decline, but corrective or remedial measures, which are practical and can be easily implemented, should be taken up.

(x) Tourism

The boundless beauty, snow clad mountains, large natural lakes surrounded by thickly populated pine forests with rivers flowing therein have made the state a prime tourist attraction place. Till 1989, tourism has been the major economic activity of the state. Tourism activities in the state were concentrated around

Kashmir valley, with few tourists visiting Ladakh and yet fewer interested in Jammu. But due to insurgency within the Kashmir valley since 1989 tourist inflow received a major setback. This has affected the economic stability as well as employment opportunities of its people. The government explored the possibilities of its tourism revival and concentrated on Ladakh. Further, religious traffic to Jammu went up from a few thousands to above 4 million in 1996 (GOJ&K, 1997b) and more than 5 million in 2004.

The favourable climate particularly during summer months has supplementary impact in increasing the tourist traffic to the valley. With the development of winter sports at Gulmarg and Pahalgam, the number of tourists visiting during the winter season is also increasing considerably. The main thrust since Ninth Plan is on adventure tourism. The adventure tourism offers an excellent option for undertaking a large number of activities such as mountaineering; trekking, skiing, rafting, canoeing, mountain biking, hag-gliding, para-sailing, etc. The areas developed for adventure tourism are Sonmarg, Gulmarg, Aru (Pahalgam), Suru valley (Kargil), Stock (Leh), Patnitop, Mansar. During the Eighth Plan period, tourism department was able to acquire good quality equipment of international standard for these activities. However, activity has remained at an introductory level and has not developed to the level commensurate with the scope available in the state.

Pilgrim tourism in the state has also registered considerable improvements during the last few years. Mata Vaishnodevi shrine in Jammu, famous Sufi Shrines in Kashmir and the Holy Amarnath Cave are important centres of pilgrim tourism. Ladakh has proved to be a very important tourist destination for foreigners because of the centuries old Buddhist monasteries, which are fully functional and active at present. The government has taken the initiative to combine pilgrim traffic with leisure tourism. For example, the visitors to the famous Shrine of Baba Rishi have been going to Gulmarg and using the facility of Gondola Cable Car.

(xi) Watershed Development

Numerous schemes for development of land resources are in operation. Some are watershed based while others are based on administrative boundaries. The objective of all the schemes is to put emphasis on management of soil and land resources for sustainable crop production and protection of environment (Sadhu and Sudan, 1999). Watershed development and protection is addressing the issues such as resource conservation, poverty alleviation, equity, gender issues, environmental protection, and overall improvement in livelihood conditions of the rural population. Long-term solutions to rain-fed agriculture lie in the conservation and efficient utilization of watershed resources (Jain, 1997).

In the last decade, in order to prevent and reverse the degradation process of the *Shivaliks* and *Karewas*, Integrated Watershed Development Project (IWDP), Hills-I was undertaken. Originally, the project was for a period of 7 years (1990-97), but was extended for another year up to 1998. The project was supported by the World Bank and initiated in three sub-watersheds of Devak and Ramkote in *Shivalik* hills (Jammu region) and Dudh Ganga in *Karewas* (Kashmir valley). The overwhelming evidence from natural resource management projects is that without people's involvement the benefits are not sustainable in the long run. After the funds from the government or donors dry up, conservation structures disappear, committees are disbanded or abandoned and the livelihood base of the people remains only marginally improved at all (Saxena, 1999). Fortunately, these shortcomings were taken care of, to some extent during the implementation of IWDP (Hills-I) (Sadhu and Sudan, 1999).

IWDP (Hills-I) was implemented for soil and water conservation in the watershed areas aiming at proper land use according to land potential, protection of land against all kinds of deterioration, building and maintaining soil fertility, conserving water, proper management of water for drainage, flood protection, sediment reduction and increasing productivity from all kinds of land uses. Besides, improved vegetative coverage of treated areas, increased community participation and formulation of engaged village users' group, increased crop yields and increased household incomes of marginal and small farmers, the landless and the women were included as major objectives of IWDP (Hills-I) (World Bank, 1998).

IWDP (Hills-I) has made only a modest impact and it can't be denied that as it has been the first phase of this experiment, some shortcomings were bound to remain, but, at the same time, it must have enriched the experience of the project functionaries which should equip them to carry out their role more efficiently in second phase (Sadhu and Sudan, 1999). The principal lessons learnt from IWDP (Hills-I) were:

(i) The need to develop an integrated approach to the *Shivalik* Watersheds,

(ii) The need for a coordinated approach to the use of available funds from all sources,

(iii) The need to involve stakeholders in planning, implementation and maintenance,

(iv) The need to increase stakeholder awareness of environmental and socio-economic considerations in articulating communities' needs,

(v) The need to focus on measures to arrest soil erosion and promote *in-situ* moisture conservation from ridge to valley,

(vi) The need to assess marketing prospects, especially of horticultural products,

(vii) The need to improve infrastructure within watersheds, particularly rural links to markets, water harvesting and drinking water,

(viii) The need to develop monitorable project implementation and development objectives' indicators, and

(ix) The need to involve local NGOs in the project as facilitators and trainers in the planning and implementation of the project (World Bank, 1998).

Seeing the physical targets being achieved by the participating states, the World Bank decided to further extend the programme in the form of IWDP (Hills-II), in 1999, for five years. This was aimed at providing a uniform integrated rural development platform to address the social and natural resources problems of the entire *Shivaliks* in India (World Bank, 1999). The experience gained through implementation of IWDP (Hills-I), J&K encouraged the state Government to extend the watershed development project to other rainfed areas of the state viz. Akhnoor and Ramnagar in *Shivaliks* (Jammu region) and Rajwar and Rambiyara in *Karewas* (Kashmir Valley). The main objective of the IWDP (Hills-II) is to restore the productive potential of the *Shivaliks* and *Karewas*. This would be attained by using evolving watershed development and community participation approaches. The focus is on improving *in-situ* moisture conservation, water harvesting and land management practices. An associated objective of the project is to assist with the institutional development and consolidate the progress already made under IWDP (Hills-I).

(a) Watershed Rehabilitation Interventions under IWDP (Hills-II)

Under IWDP, Hills-II, various soil and moisture conservation measures have been dovetailed with production measures. The treatment for spatial segments of watersheds: arable lands, non-arable lands and drainage lines have been designed in such a manner that they restore the ecological balance, and at the same time improve production and productivity. Diversified production measures being advocated for arable and non-arable lands.

(a) Soil Erosion Control and Water Conservation Measures: The soil and water conservation measures have been promoted using evolving participatory approach. The micro-level watershed planning was carried out using the sweeping transect and emphasis has been given on soil erosion control on hill slopes and gullies, regulation of water flow system in the watershed drainage, and rearrangement of farmlands. In the entire cultivated area, wastelands and area other than hills and hillocks which generally come under grazing lands, were fully treated with appropriate soil and water conservation measures like contour bunding, field bunding, gully plugging, field to field drainage outlet structures, etc.

In addition to this, the diversion channels were also made along all the hills and hillocks to guide the high velocity runoff from these sites on a safe and controlled way, so that the runoff with soil loads should not enter the arable land and cause further degradation. For the stabilization of bunds and gully plugs, the entire bund area was sown with pastures grass and legume. Similarly, in the hills and hillocks several of the soil conservation measures were adopted.

The adverse climatic factors of the *Shivaliks* necessitated the adoption of micro catchment techniques for run-off harvesting and conservation practices as done in similar areas elsewhere. The usefulness and scope of rainwater harvesting and conservation practices in improving tree growth in arid zones have been amply demonstrated. The staggered trenches ensured higher survival rate of out planted seedlings in the experimental plots. The contour trenches also helped in moisture retention but the most of the sub-watershed of Akhnoor being an undulated terrain without sufficient slopes–the contour interval had to be very wide. The soil and moisture conservation measures in the demonstration plots were much effective as evidenced by the enhanced survival rate of out planted seedlings.

Major efforts were made for revegetation of village common lands (VCLs) and grazing lands under hill and hillocks. As these sites were totally devoid of vegetation and barren, this cannot support and provide grazing resources to the animals of the villages of the watershed. The availability of the firewood was also negligible from these sites. The fast growing plant species like pasture grasses, legumes, shrubs and trees were planted. It is not easy to work and vegetate these highly degraded sites even without skeletal soils and also arrest runoff from rains in such steep slopes. Several of the soil conservation measures coupled with vegetational support helped in checking runoff soil loss and vegetate these sites. The trees and shrubs were planted in the pits putting earth and pebbles on the lower slopes so that these pits can hold rainwater. Small staggered trenches were also made for *in-situ* moisture conservation.

(b) VCLs, Forestland and Nursery Development: Indigenous forest practices generally ensure the protection of forests by controlling and/or restricting access to forest and its products. Indeed, in areas where the community organization is strong (homogeneous communities), various traditional systems for controlling the extraction of forest products are in use. The enclosed VCLs and forestlands were handed over to the user groups to mange and share the benefits. Through active involvement of the local community, the project has developed an understanding of the traditional farming systems. The project intends to facilitate the solutions related to the problems of low per unit productivity of different crops, soil erosion, deforestation and degradation of the overall agro-ecological system.

The poor families, who cannot afford the initial expenditure, are provided with seedling, plant and tools by the project. The works carried out by such families are inspected after one year. If seedling survival rate is satisfactory and structural measures are implemented with required quality, then more grant-in-aid is given to the farmers. The major responsibilities to carry out soil and water conservation tasks rest with field functionaries, who supervise and oversee the demonstration plots. The demonstration plots produce nursery stock and provides technical guidance to the farmers. The whole costs of nursery development and management are borne by the project. The user groups carry out the works and supervise the management under the supervision of field functionaries. The seedlings are sold to the farmers on cost-sharing basis.

Some experiments in the farm fields are performed by the local inhabitants, and not run directly by the project functionaries. In this case, mature fruit trees are planted and supervise for development of small orchards. In these cases, the field functionaries work out a comprehensive plan for controlling soil erosion and providing technical assistance. The project subsidizes the cost of nursery stock and provides some tools, whereas, the user groups takes charge of the implementation and management. However, the economic benefits in all the cases are individualized. The members of user groups, no doubt makes clear rules for nursery development and conservation measures, but they never allow any one to intervene, when comes the question of benefits.

The villagers preferred fast growing and quick yielding tree species for planting, which could generate income in a short period. They preferred grafted mango, pomegranate, pear and similar high yielding tree crops. However, the problems with the grafted varieties of mango, pear and pomegranate are their excessive water requirement for survival and the poor field establishment in the areas where the rainfall is minimum and highly erratic in nature, which require greater attention by the growers. The survival rate was reportedly high, which motivated the other farmers to go for grafting. With active participation of the executives of (village development committees) VDCs, a suitable area for the nursery development was located in each sub-watershed. The procedure of seed pre-treatments of seeds was demonstrated to the villagers and they were given an opportunity to repeat the procedure using freshly collected seeds. The germination trials with the pre-treated seeds enabled the participants to understand the advantages of pre-treating hard-coated seeds for enhancing the germination (Sudan, 2003).

(c) Livestock Development: The indigenous livestock breeds of the forested watersheds in *Shivaliks* have been exposed to natural selection for a very long time and are thus well adapted to harsh environmental conditions. IWDP (Hills-II) focus on new breeds under insemination programme at subsidized price. These changes weakened indigenous breeding system that could improve livestock hardiness. The crossbred livestock of better quality is replacing the local cattle, sheep and goat. Thus, after project intervention indigenous livestock diversity has declined precariously more in the forested sub-watersheds and

the decline is reportedly more in those of the villages where the VDCs are taking all types of decisions related to watershed development and protection. It is, thus, urgently needed to speed up the development of sustainable and long-term crossbreeding programmes (Sudan, 2003).

(d) Management of Private Lands: With project intervention, the farmer-managed nurseries are intended to produce high quality timber and fruit tree seedlings and seeds of fodder and grass. They receive technical training and support and limited financial incentives to begin with. In the second and following years, the nurseries are expected to become self-supporting. A few nurseries have survived without project support. It has been reported that non-survival of nurseries is mainly due to an unpopular choice of tree species, which is often in conflict with the current cropping systems or to emphasis on timber species when farmers prefer fruit trees. Where the species fulfill the local need, however, individually managed nurseries were successful. These nurseries appear to be more sustainable because they are easier to manage and can be operated in a self-reliant manner.

(b) Watershed Development and Protection: Achievements

The watershed development and protection component of the IWDP, Hills-II aims at promoting proven locally adopted technologies and mechanical structures through active beneficiary involvement to conserve water and reduce soil erosion. Broadly, the treatments undertaken in the project components are:

(i) Activities for arable land including contour vegetative barriers, terrace repairs and vegetative reinforcement, vegetative field boundaries, silvi-pasture, rainfed horticulture, farm forestry, on-farm fodder production, rainfed horticultural demonstrations and rainfed cropping system demonstrations.

(ii) Activities for private non-arable, common and forestland including vegetative/shrub barriers in contour trenches, pasture development, silvi-pasture, afforestation, drainage lining, gully stabilization, with wire crates with vegetative support, stream bank protection, water harvesting structures and village ponds, roadside erosion control and landslide treatment.

(iii) Other activities including livestock improvement and animal husbandry practices, rural infrastructure development (roads, buildings and marketing centre). All these activities are being promoted by using a variety of methods accomplished by strong stakeholders' participation including a number of mechanical and vegetative measures for watershed development and protection, improved livestock management, rural road rehabilitation and institutional strengthening (IWDP, Hills-II, 2001).

(a) Arable Land Treatment: The agriculture component of IWDP, Hills-II is an important aspect in consistence with the objective of the project, contributing largely in achieving the goal of poverty alleviation through ecological improvement in the selected sub-watersheds.

The technical and non-technical inputs provided under the project includes: (i) provisioning of fertilizers, seeds and pesticides for rainfed demonstrations on cost-sharing basis; (ii) training and demonstration specifically organized for women; (iii) continuous surveillance by extension staff; and (iv) supply of improved implements, seed bins and containers to the beneficiaries. Most of the farmers living in the selected sub-watersheds have received input at least once on farm rainfed demonstration. These demonstrations have successfully promoted the introduction of improved varieties, seed treatments, appropriate application of fertilizers and pesticides agriculture implements and other improved agronomic practices to ensure moisture conservation.

Likewise, horticulture plays an important role in alleviating the social and economic conditions of the people living in hilly and rainfed areas of *Shivaliks*. The horticulture sector provides better potential to increase productivity and employment and thus rural livelihood diversification is the ultimate outcome. Under IWDP, Hills-II, the activities initiated in this sector includes: rainfed horticulture demonstration; supply of plant material, which are drought resistant having versatile adaptability; introduction of new varieties and species of fruit plants; step-up of rejuvenation programme and improvement of top-working, budding and grafting of existing fruit plants of indigenous type; training and demonstration for treatment against diseases; and supply of spraying and pruning equipment on cost-sharing basis.

Prior to project intervention, the small and marginal farmers were reluctant to use improved technical know-how. Large proportions of farmers were using conventional agricultural production methods. The major impediment in the introduction of high yielding varieties (HYV) of crops was non-availability of sufficient moisture at the time of sowing. The implementation of project interventions related to soil and moisture conservation has facilitated the farmers in timely sowing and using adequate doses of chemical fertilizers. Various training camps have been organized to disseminate the scientific technology from laboratory to the farmers' fields. These training camps have been organized in the selected sub-watersheds in collaboration with agricultural university in the state. The exposure visits have also been organized and the farmers drawn from across the selected sub-watersheds were exposed to latest agricultural technologies in *Krishi Melas*, where these farmers had ample opportunities to interact with farmers from other parts of the country.

The system of agro-forestry has been implemented, where common property resources such as VCLs and other grazing and pasturelands were severely degraded before project intervention. The silvi-pasture activities have been implemented initially, but not laterally. The system of mushroom cultivation has been introduced in the sub-watershed of Akhnoor in a significant way, whereas the climate of Ramnagar is more conducive for mushroom development, where it has not been attended in desired way. Besides above, improved tools and implements have also been provided to the poor farmers on cost-sharing basis in the sub-watershed of Akhnoor, whereas the provisioning of modern agricultural tools and implements has not been made in Ramnagar. Actually the sub-watershed of Ramnagar is predominantly forested and the poor farmers mostly use self-made wooden implements in agricultural operations because of easy availability of wood from the local forests. The wooden agricultural tools and equipment are not as efficient as the factory made iron tools and equipment. At the same time, heavy dependence on forest resources for agricultural tools and equipment also add to the problem of deforestation. Thus, there is urgent need to propagate and popularize the use of factory made iron tools and implement in agricultural operations, which would help in restoring the degraded forests (Sudan, 2003).

Over the period, the sustained efforts by the project have improved the performance of agriculture. As per the crop cut experiments conducted in different sub-watersheds on standing crops during 2001-2002 in *Kharif* season, the yield of maize has increased 2.5 times. The yield of maize and wheat shows an increase from 22 quintals per hectare (maize) and 19 quintals per hectare (wheat) in the base period to 32 quintals per hectare and 27 quintal per hectare respectively, after the project intervention. In percentage terms, the increase in yield of maize and wheat respectively was recorded at 45 and 42 per cent. The area covered under HYV crops has shown remarkable progress over the period. In 1999-2000, 4201 hectares of agricultural land has been covered under HYV crops. In subsequent years 2000-2001 and 2001-2002 (ending September 2001), 5779 hectares and 2338 hectares more arable land has been covered under HYV crops. Over the period, more than 12,000 small and marginal farmers have been benefited from arable land treatment (IWDP, Hills-II, 2001).

Other important sector treated under arable land component is the horticulture. The rain fed (R.F.) demonstration has been carried out over 278 hectares of arable land in Ramnagar sub-watershed, whereas, 197 hectares of arable land has been exposed to R.F. demonstration for horticulture in sub-watershed of Akhnoor in the year 1999-2000. In the year 2001-2002 too, greater attention has been paid on R.F. horticultural demonstration. The horticultural potential is also tremendous, which has picked up after the project interventions. About 300 hectares and 244 hectares of arable land respectively have been covered under horticultural rejuvenation in Ramanagar and Akhnoor in 1999-2000. In the next year, a significant increase has taken place in hectare coverage under horticulture rejuvenation in both the sub-watersheds, which stood at 440 hectares in Ramnagar and 814 hectares in Akhnoor. In terms of percentage change, the figures stood at 46.67 in Ramnagar and 233.6 in Akhnoor (IWDP, Hills-II, 2002). The system of nursery development has also been implemented and location specific fruit plants were raised in the nurseries and supplied to the needy farmers on cost-sharing basis. A few horticultural nurseries have been created and maintained by the project with active participation of local villagers.

(b) Non-Arable Land Treatment: The non-arable lands include public lands, forestlands, community lands and private lands, which have been treated under various components of IWDP, Hills-II depending upon suitability or topography of the areas. The main component is afforestation in contour trenches besides other treatments. All the VCLs closures have been created with active participation of the people inhibiting the sub-watershed. The silvi-pasture activities have also been under taken initially, however, later, such activities have been abandoned. Besides, vegetative shrub barriers have also been created to maintain and improve the soil moisture on the degraded VCLs. Over the period, project interventions on VCLs have shown their impact and the degraded patches have been regenerated and helped improving the productivity of these lands. With the regeneration of VCLs, system of rotational grazing and equal usufruct sharing has been created with active community participation of the beneficiaries. The fodder scarcity has declined considerably and fodder demand is met from the protected VCLs. The idea of fodder bank is propagated to accumulate the surpluses for selling to the scarce households/villages.

In addition to afforestation, silvi-pasture and vegetative shrub barriers, pasture development and forest rejuvenation activities have also been carried out on non-arable forestlands. To begin with, the forest rejuvenation activities have been implemented in Ramnagar and laterally it has been extended to Akhnoor also. In 2001-2002, 409 hectares (Ramnagar) and 570 hectares (Akhnoor) of degraded forests have been enclosed for rejuvenation for which local population was actively engaged. The vegetative shrub barriers have also been created in the degraded forestlands. For instance, to begin with 203 hectares (Ramnagar) and 345 hectares (Akhnoor) of degraded forestlands have been treated with vegetative shrub barriers. In the year 2001-2002, additional 165 hectares and 345 hectares of degraded forestlands have been treated with vegetative shrub barriers respectively in Ramnagar and Akhnoor (IWDP, Hills-II, 2002).

Over the period, the interventions on non-arable VCLs and forests have resulted in increased availability of fodder, forage/grasses, fuel wood and small timber, which is reflected in increased milk production, wool production, meat production, soil moisture regime, bio-diversity and reduction in soil run-off and soil erosion. For instance, significant increase has been recorded in forage/green grass production in the project area from a yield level of 3.40 ton per hectare (base line yield) to 10.60 ton per hectare as per crop-cut experiment carried out by the field functionaries of the project. Overall, the increase in yield of forage/grasses production has been recorded at 211 per cent in the project area after the IWDP (Hills-II) intervention (IWDP, Hills-II, 2001).

The drainage line treatment interventions, which includes crate-wire structures, landslide treatment, earthen bag check dam, vegetative gully control and road drainage line have also been implemented. Besides, repair of traditional water points such as bowallis/tanks, ponds, and water harvesting structures have also been implemented to improve the water regime. More than 150 traditional water points (bowallis) have been repaired in water scarce-forested watershed of Ramnagar over the period. Similarly, 75 ponds and 60 ponds have been repaired respectively in Ramnagar and Akhnoor. A few water-harvesting structures have also been repaired in both the sub-watersheds (IWDP, Hills-II, 2001). The predominantly forested watersheds have more problem of water scarcity, especially drinking water, which have been attended on priority by rejuvenating the traditional water points and switching to gravity based water supply for drinking purposes.

The agricultural land along the *nalahs* (rainfed streams) is heavily subjected soil erosion particularly during rainy season, which have been treated with crate wire structures on priority basis. The road drainage line has also been attended. The drainage line interventions have significantly reduced the water run-off and soil erosion and rejuvenated the traditional water harvesting structures. For instance, in the year 2001 for the months of June, July, August and September, rainfall (in mm) has been recorded respectively at 228.1, 475.9, 285.1 and 201.7, whereas, the water run-off (in mm) has been recorded at 106.40, 223.8, 120.9 and 87.4. The percentage water run-off (4/3 x 100) was estimated at 46.65, 47.03, 42.41 and 43.33 per cent respectively for the months of June, July, August and September 2001. On the whole, the soil loss, which was 23.70 tons per hectare per annum in the base line period, has declined to 9.65 tons per hectare per annum after project intervention in the *Shivalik* hills (IWDP, Hills-II, 2001).

(c) Livestock Institutional Support: IWDP (Hills-II), Jammu and Kashmir has established 3 veterinary hospitals and 7 veterinary dispensaries in the project area (IWDP, Hills-II, 2002). However, all the veterinary hospitals have been established in the sub-watershed of Ramnagar. The veterinary facilities created are catering to the requirement of the cattle population. More specifically, attention have been given on (i) mass vaccination against foot-mouth diseases, haemoharrahic speticimia etc.; (ii) dosing against intestinal worms and liver fluke; (iii) artificial insemination; (iv) natural services by way of providing

breeding cow bulls and rams; (v) castration of scrub bulls; (vi) dipping of sheep against ecto parasite; (vii) distribution of cross-bred ram bouliet/marino rams; (viii) health cover for different diseases; and (ix) feed for calf rearing, pregnant eves and lambs born.

Under the component of genetic improvement of livestock, artificial insemination centres have been established. However, the impact of artificial insemination programme is modest. In order to improve the livestock health and productivity, veterinary hospitals and dispensary have been started. The dairy and poultry units have also been given assistance, however, very marginally. The problem of poverty, unemployment and underemployment is very acute and dairy and poultry rearing could be alternative viable income generating activities (IGAs) for the people inhibiting the sub-watersheds, if undertaken on group basis. The products of these micro-enterprises have ready market in the local villages and nearby townships.

The livestock development infrastructure has been created, but the maintenance of the infrastructure has not been given adequate attention. The transhumance pastoral and semi-pastoral communities depend heavily on sheep and goat rearing, for which provision has been made for migratory health cover facilities. New modified techniques have also been propagated under sheep husbandry to improve the quality of sheep and goats reared by the transhumance pastoral and semi-pastoral communities. However, the sheep husbandry has not been promoted in a desired way, keeping in view the problems being faced by transhumance and local residents.

Besides above, the project has also been providing facilities in the villages, where veterinary hospital or dispensary is not available. The veterinary camps have also been organized in each village of the selected sub-watersheds. On the whole, 2251 artificial insemination has been done, 178 veterinary camps has been organized and 104, 877 and 182 of dairy, poultry and sheep units were set up across the project area over the period ending September, 2001. The concerted efforts have resulted in a significant increase in the yield of milk and wool. For instance, the yield of cow milk has increased from 2.75 litre per day to 4.25 litre per day in case of local cow and from 6.75 litre per day to 8.60 litre per day in case of crossbred cow after project intervention. Similarly, the yield of buffalo milk has increased from 3.50 litre per day to 5.25 litre per day in case of local buffalo and from 8.60 litre per day to 10.30 litre in case of cross-bred buffaloes. Likewise, the yield of sheep wool has increased significantly from a base line yield of 2.25 Kg. per annum to 3.40 Kg. per annum (IWDP, Hills-II, 2001).

On the whole, after the intervention of IWDP, Hills-II an integrated approach has been adopted to mitigate the problem of environmental degradation and poverty alleviation, through evolving participatory approaches. The various project interventions have improved significantly the environmental resources of the project area in the shape of: (i) significant improvement in vegetal cover and bio-mass thereof; (ii) multifold increase in the production of local as well as high yielding varieties (HYV) of grasses; (iii) decrease in biotic pressure on the natural forests; (iv) revised the trend of deforestation; (v) slowing down of water run-off and increase in water regime of the catchments; and (vi) increase in yield of different crops, milk, wool and meat.

EXPERIENCES OF J&K HILL ECONOMY

J&K economy, constrained by its physiography and climatic extremes, realized that maximization of SDP should be the goal, whatever its composition might be, seeking food self sufficiency need not be a priority as the same can be imported or arranged through public distribution system (PDS) and therefore growth of overheads was not restricted even when food crop farms were converted into fruit crop farms. It made a significant contribution to SDP as also to employment generation. In fact this is what Himachal Pradesh also did in own way.

Jammu and Kashmir has also realized the importance of floricultural and medicinal herbs. Floriculture, with improved packaging and fast transportation, has become a highly remunerative enterprise internationally. The hill economies are ideally suited for the purpose and want to realize its full potential.

The Drug research laboratory at Jammu has done extensive research work on locally available medicinal herbs and developed some of these in commercially viable activities. Herbal cosmetics are an area in which hill economies have a distinct advantage. Herbal therapies are gaining international market considering the side effects of Allopathic medicines.

One of the unique things that came to be witnessed during the last three decades in the in the state of J&K, is the strip plantation and vegetable gardens all along the national highway particularly, in the Jammu region. Even though it might have resulted into some encroachment on forestland, but it has really brought about a vegetable revolution in the state and considerably enhanced the fruit production also.

Some of these things, as described above, could easily be tried in Arunachal Pradesh and other North-Eastern states with an appropriate policy package.

In a few areas where J&K failed to optimize its economic grains are as under:

(a) Hydroelectric Power: The state of J&K has an estimated power potential of 20000 MWts of which only a mere 10% has so far been harnessed. It is here that thoughtful planning has not been done and this potential not developed, as it should have been. Had the state concentrated on it, as a priority sector, it should have been supplying power to whole of Northern region of the

country and earnings through its sale should have been enough to bring a high level of affluence to the state. The hill economies in the North-East need to identify their sectors and activities where they have a comparative advantage and should develop the same as priority sector.

(b) Tourism: The state of J&K also failed in so far as.tourism diversification is concerned. Neither was tourism was diversified geographically nor was it diversified category wise. The pleasure tourism at historically known places of Pahalgam, Gulmarg and Srinagar–Mugal Gardens was the only known tourism potential of the state. It was a highly restricted perception and caused a lot of disadvantage to its economy. The state realized only very late, that the whole of state can be tourist attraction and it is required to explore newer areas of tourist destination. A good deal of work is done in this regard now.

Adventure tourism, pilgrimage tourism, business tourism and sports tourism is opening out new avenues for the state and hold a promising prospect in this regard.

(c) Industry: This is yet another area where J&K failed utterly to take timely advantage. The perception that hill economies do not suit industrialization is ill founded. Hill economies are ideally suited for precision instruments industries such as electronics, optical, and the alike. J&K realized it in late 70's and created the required environment for Hindustan Machine Tools (HMT) and other industries to expand their activities in J&K. Unfortunately, the onset of militancy did damage and not much could be done in this sector uptil now. This is however an area which needs to be focused upon.

LESSONS FOR NORTH-EAST

(a) Agriculture: The development of agriculture should be the top priority of the North-East states. In this connection, the states could adopt the following policies:

1. The states could shift its agricultural development strategy from food security mode to the value addition mode. The states should grow certain products like high-valued fruits, vegetables and some cash crops, which could give adequate monetary returns to the cultivators.

2. For optimum utilization of the productive potential of the primary sector, diversification should be the main focus. However, the states should not follow a uniform policy of diversification for all the physiographic regions. The agro-climatic crop planning for each physiographic region should be evolved with the help of the agricultural scientists and experts. This calls for in-depth studies to make a realistic assessment of the available resources, explore cost-effective means of transfer of technologies, and work out forward and backward linkages.

3. The state government should provide adequate training to farmers about the use of modern technology in agriculture. One important aspect for the increase in productivity is credit to the farmers. The states should initiate this through the nationalized bank, so that the cultivators get adequate finance on credit for agricultural development.
4. The availability of inputs should not only be insured regularly but their quality be extensively checked. There are already some provisions existing in each of the states but more needs to be done. The subsidy on the inputs should be targeted and selective. The governments should examine a suitable crop insurance scheme. These kinds of initiatives strengthen the confidence of the cultivators.
5. The respective governments should encourage a mix of supplementing crops in each state. Some regions in each state are best suited for dry farming, horticulture and fodder crops. The side valleys should be earmarked for fodder cultivation and cultivation of medicinal plants. However, these examples are illustrative and demonstrate the need for evolving the micro-region specific diversification strategies. The comprehensive cost of cultivation studies needs to be conducted in each state.
6. In the high hills, seed production of cauliflower with in one season using poly-green house technology should be attempted. This method can be extended to produce seeds of cabbage, onion, raddish, karam saag, carrot etc. This can open up a new vista for the farming community of high hills, not only towards self-sufficiency but also for export of seed outside the respective regions.
7. In Jammu and Kashmir, the farmers of the high hills of Ladakh have successfully experimented the cultivation of vegetables in the poly green houses. Three varieties of tomato SL-12, PED and AC-238 and N-13 Nasik red onion have shown a positive result in production. Among other vegetables are brinjal, capsicum, broccoli, green chili and paprika. The states in North-East could also explore the cultivation of vegetables in poly-green houses especially in high hills. This can ensure supply of vegetables to cities and towns during off-season and fetch a good price.
8. The high hill regions have great potential in the field of floriculture as well. The poly-house technology should also be attempted in development of floriculture, which can play a vital role in uplifting the socio-economic status of farmers. The governments should also encourage the production of high-value, low-volume crops like spices.
9. Apiculture is another important area with a lot of potential. The fauna and flora required for nectar collection is available in abundance through

existing orchards, field crops and wild flora. The state governments should encourage the people by way of distribution of beehives, bee-colonies and other appliances on subsidized cost with technical guidance.

10. The adaptive research output should be the answer for agricultural development. Research on multiple cropping, improved seeds, crop rotations, water management and dry land farming should take the local factors into consideration and use the results of repetitive trials as the basic input for research studies. The state governments should also provide the infrastructure to the private investor to set up agriculture and biotechnology research institutes.
11. The climate of the North-East states is ideally suited for production of exotic, high value vegetables like Broccoli and Mushrooms which can be grown profitably in the lower hills. What is needed is a planned, integrated approach, which takes care of production as well as marketing of these perishable, high-value crops.
12. The North-East states have potential for agro-based industry which needs to be tapped. The food industry has a very high multiplier affect. Besides appropriate cost-effective technology, assured supply of quality inputs and uninterrupted transport facilities are crucial for the development of agro-based industries. In this respect, the development of all weather air, rail and surface transport should be given top priority.
13. The monitoring of the various schemes physically against the target fixed by the department is an essential factor. The state governments should involve non-governmental agencies for the evaluation of the schemes and encourage participation of the village community in the monitoring of the scheme.
14. The Sisal Propagation Scheme (SPS) is beneficial for the weaker sections of the society. It shall be upgraded and the technology evolved in the past be utilized to educate the common masses in rural areas to implement it in the entire lower hill region.
15. Schemes like pasture development, soil conservation programme and soil conservation programme on forest lands should continue and spread to vast eroded chunks in new areas so that direct and indirect benefits are received by the common man.
16. The state governments should pay attention to short-term soil conservation measures aimed at stabilizing smaller slopes, preventing under-cutting of *nallahs,* and gully control measures in the initial stage of development.
17. The gap between the national average and the existing status of the state forests can be fulfilled by social forestry programme. The state governments should take certain initiatives to develop social forestry in the North-East.

18. The forest department in each of the states should prepare some project for the entire state and approach funding agencies like the World Bank, Asian Development Bank, and others for support.
19. People's participation for forest conservation is limited and has not become a people's movement. The village committee needs to be strengthened for National afforestation to be properly implemented.
20. To increase the plantation on the wasteland the state government(s) should promote the participation of voluntary and other agencies.
21. North-East India has a lot of potential for the cultivation of medicinal plants for natural health care. The state government(s) should approach the medicinal plants board to extend their support for the development of medicinal plants. Support and facilities for extraction, storage, value addition and marketing also need to be increased.
22. Opportunities for training, awareness and capacity building of the forest staff and village forest committee need to be increased.

(b) Animal Husbandry: Presently, the government's Animal Husbandry Department provides animal husbandry services in North-East states. However, due to lack of adequate funding, the department has not been able to provide these services effectively. A high proportion of its expenditure has gone towards veterinary services and animal health, while other important activities such as breed and fodder development, and extension and training, have received only small allocations. The solution lies in allowing qualified private parties to provide some of these services. At the same time, some services will have to be provided by the government. Selective privatization of animal husbandry services would be preferred approach. Services in which public interest is greater than individual interest, e.g. eradication of diseases, programmes for weaker sections, extension and education for weaker sections/areas, would continue to be provided by the government. Where the government continues its services (for example, in areas where no private investor comes forward), it will do so purely on a cost–recovery basis.

The development of the dairy sector needs to be based on the provision of specialized infrastructure such as farm bulk coolers and refrigeration systems as well as basic infrastructure like power and water. Providing a cost-effective and continual supply of power and water to procurement and processing units needs to be top priority. This will reduce costs and improve milk quality considerably. The government will also need to upgrade rural roads leading to milk collection centers (or even, as a first step, from milk collection centres to milk processing units). This will increase the frequency of collection, reduce logistical costs, and improve the quality of raw milk. Most of the specialized infrastructure required will be built by investors themselves, whether corporations or cooperatives. However, the government(s) can play an important facilitating role. For instance, it could lobby the centre to reduce duties on refrigeration and cold storage equipment. This would reduce the high capital costs that make it unviable to set up this infrastructure today.

(c) Sericulture: The following suggestions should be given due place in development of sericulture in North-East states:

1. Silkworm seed is the vital input of the sericulture industry. The local seed produced and distributed to rearers gives lower cocoon yield compared to foreign seed. The import and distribution of foreign seed needs more attention. Therefore, the first step towards boosting silk production is to evolve superior varieties of disease-resistant silkworm races, which should suit local conditions. The state government(s) should provide infrastructure to private investors in this area.
2. Profitability from sericulture largely depends on the production of mulberry leaf at an economic cost. Hence, there is an urgent need to improve mulberry leaf both qualitatively and quantitatively. Due to geographical limitations, multi-crop cultivation of mulberry is not possible. The state government(s) should encourage the farmers to plant mulberry trees on the edges of their rice fields and orchards on a large scale. These plants must also be properly maintained for ensuring higher leaf yield.
3. The department of sericulture should produce improved varieties of mulberry plants in their farms and then distribute them to the rearers. The social forestry department should be involved in the plantation programme. The department has a large number of workers on daily wages that can be replaced by motivated farmers for planting better varieties of mulberry plants on a large scale. However, these farmers should be given adequate incentives. As a consequence, there will be higher leaf production and rearers can go in for large cocoon production and receive more benefits.
4. Cocoons are the end product of a mulberry farm. The rearers should arrange proper equipment for carrying out silkworm rearing scientifically. Wooden trays must be prepared for self-rearing and traditional floor rearing should be discarded. The rearers should pay adequate attention to the artificial adjustment of environmental factors like temperature, humidity, light, air and food to create a better environment for silkworm rearing.
5. Cocoons markets need to be established in such a way that large-scale buyers from outside the state can participate. Wide publicity should be given about the sale of cocoons in these markets before starting the actual sale. Participation of purchasers from outside the state is necessary because silk reeling units in private sector have not yet started functioning in these states. Besides, arrangements should be made by the department of

sericulture for taking the cocoons of rearers to the markets at an appropriate time. This will result in higher price for cocoons for rearers.

6. Sericulture is an important agro-based industry with considerable potential for income and employment. Therefore, by integrating mulberry cultivation with farm and horticulture activity, it will provide more income and employment to the rural agricultural labour force. Marketing of the cocoon has been a neglected area, which requires proper attention. This will help the people to get cash returns at competitive rates and inculcate quality consciousness among the people.

(d) Horticulture: The North-Eastern states have high potential for development of horticulture sector. The private sector participation in development and marketing of fruits should be given high priority to exploit the huge potential in horticulture sector. The following suggestions should be taken into account while planning for horticulture development in these states.

(a) It is essential for the state governments to provide proper marketing facilities to the growers especially by promoting the private initiative in the marketing of products.

(b) APEDA should be encouraged to set up an Export Promotion Zone to promote the export of selected fruits and vegetables.

(c) There should be emphasis on the optimum use of land by using high-density fruit crops. Considering the importance of research in this field, the state governments should collaborate with agricultural research and training institutes, which has developed new technology for horticulture development.

(d) There is also need for improvement in the post harvest handling of fruits.

(e) The horticulture department should take certain initiatives for the development of area specific new variety of fruits.

(e) Handloom and Handicrafts: In order to develop the handloom and handicrafts sector, the modernization of the looms should be initiated to boost the handloom activity in the North-Eastern states. A multi-pronged strategy should be pursued to revive the handloom sector:

(a) Addition of new design and product diversification;

(b) Improvement of productivity of weavers through enhancement of skills, introduction of more efficient looms and the related equipment.

(c) Greater market access to the handloom products produced through effective marketing strategy and appropriate incentives.

For the handicraft sector, there is need to adopt a pragmatic approach to exploit the potentialities through the following steps:

(a) There is need to adopt a cluster approach by identifying and promoting various handicraft clusters in the different regions of the states of North-East India, and giving them necessary support in design development, production and marking of various handcraft items.

(b) The central silk board should provide liberal assistance to explore new potentialities and possibilities of developing the silk sector within the different states. This would help the North-East states to increase the value addition of cocoons both for yarn and converted fabrics.

(c) There should be a systematic promotion of handicrafts of North-East in international markets and developing a brand name.

(f) Tourism: In the tourism sector, there is urgent need to take drastic steps to revive the tourism activities in the North-East India:

(a) At least one of the airports in the North-East India should be declared an international airport.

(b) New airports need to be commissioned for the promotion of tourism in different states.

(c) The local residents need to be encouraged to create paying guest or houseguest accommodation, as many tourists would love to stay in local houses and experience their way of life.

(d) There is need to upgrade and refurbish the existing tourist complexes for which private participation should be encouraged. New and unexplored tourist resorts should be developed with private sector collaboration.

(e) The educated youth of the North-East India should be equipped with specialized skills in hospitality and related technical education to boost tourism.

(g) Watershed Development: The future of sustainable resource management lies more with local people though issues of non-poor domination and resource conflict may still is problematic. It is doubtful whether the few such groups that do exist can continue to do so without substantial external support. At present, resource user groups have achieved a degree of success by monitoring and enforcing resource protection and conservation activities, and thus enhancing resource productivity in environmentally and institutionally sustainable ways. However, most efforts are small scale and heavily subsidized, raising doubts about whether they can be replicated by the project.

The preconditions for success of participatory resource management should include the following:

- Clear and sustainable user rights at individual and group level;
- Compatibility between the resource potentialities, user rights and local management capacity;

- Clear responsibility and authority vested in the managing organizations;
- Adequate financial and human resources for both the maintenance of assets and the effective operation of managing organizations;
- Transparent accountability of and supporting incentives for the managing entities;
- Reorientation of the project functionaries to becoming the facilitators in supplementing the needs of the user groups; and
- A transparent system of conflict resolution mechanisms capable of settling disputes.

Under IWDP (Hills-II), Jammu and Kashmir, the policies are best geared to the improved management of enclosed VCLs, forests, grazing lands, water harvesting structures, gravity based irrigation channels, and other resource conservation and protection activities. The poor who live at the edge of subsistence necessarily place a high value on their time: if conservation of natural resources comes into conflict with meeting the immediate need for survival, then they disregard the concern for conservation. For poor to be interested in conservation, a mechanism has to be devised that incorporates it into the livelihood security of the poor. This is especially true in a differentiated society where the poor might be tempted to free ride in the hope that the non-poor would make necessary investment for conservation. Policy changes are imperative for better tradeoffs between environmental protection and poverty reduction. These are likely to arise, especially when access to a resource is restricted for a period. A strong policy response, which recognizes this tension and which is developed in consultation with local people, is essential to the resolution of conflicts. Keeping in view the resource protection and conservation needs on the one hand and meeting the livelihood needs of the rural poor on the other, the resource management policies should be supplemented by rural livelihood diversification strategy by operationalizing income generating activities (IGAs) through self help groups (SHGs). The different sources of income represent opportunities to individual or to families possessing different incomes and assets, therefore rural livelihood diversification, poverty reduction and income distribution are affected by policies that promote alternative IGAs. The operationalization of IGAs is severely constrained due to inherent institutional rigidities of formal financial institutions to give credit to the rural poor. Thus, removal of constraints to, and expansion of opportunities for, rural livelihood diversification through initiation of IGAs are desirable policy objectives because they give households more capabilities to improve their livelihood security (Sudan, 2002).

Besides above the following suggestions need special attention:

1. If the poor are to benefit from institutional arrangements for resource management, they must participate fully in setting them up. A new basis for cooperation must be created so that the appropriators can themselves devise viable institutions by mutual consent. Even in this case, however, the poor might be excluded. It is essential that the poor are encouraged and welcomed to participate in the decision making process. Outside agencies interested in institution building for the poor will need to adopt special measures to ensure that participation is genuinely all encompassing.
2. The user participation in pre-project planning such as information gathering, identification of the resources to be protected and the targeted groups to be involved, and the design of the regulations related to monitoring and enforcement has substantial bearing on the minimization of the transaction costs. Thus, it is suggested to recognize the poor villagers not only as beneficiaries of the participatory resource management, but to assign them the status of stakeholders in real practice and provide them the opportunities to participate not only in conservation and protection phase, but equally in pre-project phase also. This will help realize the goal of minimization of transaction costs.
3. It is has to be recognized that in most rural societies it would be practically impossible to ignore or bypass the traditional power structure altogether. The power base of the traditional elite may be eroding, but it still exists, and no large-scale project of watershed management can possibly be undertaken without their involvement, even if it implies agreeing to hand over portions of the community assets to the poor. Egalitarianism needs to be cast in terms of asset transfer rather than outright income transfers. While income redistribution may have no effect on productive efficiency, asset redistribution would link labour and investment with returns and income. For instance, the granting of property rights in forest resources to local communities could improve management of forest and link investment with returns. Asset redistribution can contribute to sustainable poverty reduction only if it increases the productive capacity of the poor and of the economy as a whole.
4. There is need to explore alternative ways of strengthening grass roots organizations for their empowerment and integrating them into participatory resource management. This should include user-led resource management and planning, implementation, funding and investment (through creation of rotating funds), participatory monitoring and evaluation to feedback corrections. This is to be done within the framework of commonly agreed organizations such as VDCs and user groups, which is respected by all participants. Clear rules and sanctions, and equal benefit-sharing mechanism are important for the organization building and sustainability. The conflict

resolution mechanism should be based on dominant cultural values rather than on only legal deterrents.

5. Training in farming systems improvement should be an integral part of the soil conservation effort. Considerable benefits could accrue by continuous training of the project functionaries as well as members of VDCs and user groups on such topics as: organization building; women and gender issues; participatory monitoring and evaluation techniques; viable IGAs; techniques of PRAs and use of indigenous technology. NGOs involvement in user groups/VDCs networking, watershed management professional networking, and education/training institutions networking will help update professionals in watershed management and farming systems. There is urgent need to bring all watershed management related organizations and institutions including NGOs and VDCs under one umbrella.

(h) Good Governance: The good governance is vital for accountability and transparency in decision-making and programme implementation by the various public agencies. The concept of people's participation should be operationalized in effective way to make the administrative system more accountable and transparent. Due to physical heterogeneity of the states in North-East, which consists of plains, valleys and hills, uniform pattern of development are not desirable for all the North-Eastern states. It, therefore, becomes necessary that all the regions of the North-Eastern states should be given due priority in planning and development keeping in view their own peculiar development potentialities, which will facilitate in minimizing the dissatisfaction over policies by the people concerned. There is also need to attend to the growing distrust between various communities, the increasing disparities in the regional development and the perceptible alienation and cynicism of the general public. In this context, the following measures are essential.

(a) Security concerns of officials should never become a hindrance in approaching them for the redressal of grievances by the people. Proper follow up of these complaints and grievances should be done.

(b) Geographical conditions of different states in North-East should be considered while implementing various programmes. The state governments should give importance to the hill regions as far as implementation of programmes is concerned. This will prove beneficial in minimizing the dissatisfaction over policies by the people concerned.

(c) The growing distrust among various communities the increasing disparities in regional development and the perceptible alienation and cynicism of the general public are issues that need to the addressed urgently and imaginatively.

REFERENCES

Government of India (2003), *State Development Report, Jammu and Kashmir*, Planning Commission, New Delhi.

Government of India (2002), *Census of India, 2001*, Registrar General Office, New Delhi.

Government of India (2002), *Census of India, 2001, Series 2, J&K Population Total, Paper–1 of 2001*, Registrar General Office, New Delhi.

Government of India, *Sixth Five Year Plan, 1980-85*, Planning Commission, New Delhi.

Government of Jammu and Kashmir (2003), *Digest of Statistics, 2002-2003*, Directorate of Statistics and Economics, Jammu.

Government of Jammu and Kashmir (2002a), *Digest of Statistics, 2001-2002*, Directorate of Statistics and Economics, Jammu.

Government of Jammu and Kashmir (2002b), *Annual Report, 1999-2000*, Directorate of Education, Jammu.

Government of Jammu and Kashmir (2001a), *Indicators of Economic Development, 1999-2000*, Directorate of Statistics and Economics, Jammu.

Government of Jammu and Kashmir (2001b), *Statistical Abstract, 2000-2001*, Directorate of Statistics and Economics, Jammu.

Government of Jammu and Kashmir (2001c), *Digest of Statistics, 2000-2001*, Directorate of Statistics and Economics, Jammu.

Government of Jammu and Kashmir (1997a), *Livestock Statistics, 1996*, Directorate of Animal Husbandry, Jammu.

Government of Jammu and Kashmir (1997b), *Tourism Statistics, 1996*, Directorate of Tourism, Jammu.

Government of Jammu and Kashmir (1996), *Agriculture Census, 1985-86*, Directorate of Agriculture, Jammu.

Government of Jammu and Kashmir (1987), *Agriculture Census, 1995*, Directorate of Agriculture, Jammu.

Integrated Watershed Development Project (IWDP), Hills-II (2001), *Status Report for Supervision Mission of World Bank*, IWDP (Hills-II), Jammu and Kashmir.

Integrated Watershed Development Project (IWDP), Hills-II (2002), *Physical and Financial Achievements, 1999-2000 and 2001-2002*, (IWDP), Hills-II, Jammu and Kashmir.

Jain, T.C. (1997), Watershed Management Programmes: World Bank Experience-Achievements, Constraints and Future Strategy, in Katyal, J.C. and John Farrington (eds.), *Research for Rainfed Farming*, Proceedings of the ICAR-ODA Joint Workshop, September 11-14, 1995, National Academy of Agricultural research Management (NAARM), Hyderabad.

Joshi, B.K. (1983), *Underdevelopment in Hill Areas of U.P.: A Socio-Economic Study*, Giri Institute of Development Studies, Lucknow.

Sadhu, A.N. and Falendra K. Sudan (1999), *Retrospective Study: IWDP (Hills-I)*, Integrated Watershed Development Project, Hills-II, Jammu and Kashmir, World Bank and Integrated Watershed Development Project, Hills-II, Jammu and Kashmir.

Sadhu A.N. and Falendra K. Sudan (2001), Watershed Development in Jammu and Kashmir: Recent Experience and Emerging Issues, *Indian Journal of Social Development*, Vol. 1, No. 2.

Saxena N.C. (1999), Foreword, in John Farrington, et al. (ed.) *Participatory Watershed Development*: Challenges for the Twenty first Century, University Press: Oxford.

Sudan, Falendra K. (2002), Rural Livelihood Diversification and Operationalising Income-Generating Activities through SHGs in the Watershed Context, *The Indian Journal of Labour Economics*, Vol. 45, No. 4.

Sudan, Falendra K. (2003), *Participatory Approaches and Environmental and Economic Impact: With Special Reference to Integrated Watershed Development Project (IWDP), Hills-II, Jammu and Kashmir, India*, sponsored by World Bank and Ministry of Environment and Forests (MOEF) funded EMCaB Technical Assistance Project through EERC, Indira Gandhi Institute of Development Research, Mumbai, May.

World Bank (1998), *Project Concept Document: Integrated Watershed Development (Hills-II) Project,* Rural Development Sector Unit, South Asia Region, New Delhi.

World Bank (1999), *Project Appraisal Document: Integrated Watershed Development (Hills-II) Project,* Rural Development Sector Unit, South Asia Region, New Delhi.

Website: *(http://jammukashmir.nic.in)*

8

ECONOMIC ANALYSIS OF NUTRITION PROGRAMME IN INDIA

Rajesh Jaiswal

INTRODUCTION

Increasing interest in rural poverty alleviation has resulted in a new focus on the 'nutrition dependent poor' especially women and children and the actual and potential contribution of nutrition to women and children. Nutrition-deficient areas are frequently associated with rural poverty. Remote locations, rugged terrain, low population densities, limited communication and transportation infrastructure, infertile soils, and difficult climates act as constraints that limit nutrition intake by the most vulnerable segment of the society i.e. women and children. The same factors limit economic opportunities of people living in rural areas. Development in the field of nutrition rapidly changes both the physical and the economic landscapes and the corresponding opportunities for local people. Analysis of the relationship between such development and rural development and social change is needed to better understand its impact and to target interventions aimed at improving livelihoods of rural people.

Policy makers argue that nutritional resources can be put to work to help improve the livelihoods of the poor especially women and children. Part of the discrepancy between these originates in different assumptions about the scope for creating new opportunities for rural women and children to take advantages of nutrition resources. Typically the poor rural women and children of nutrition deficient areas have not had a voice in deciding how to have adequate nutrition and lacked opportunities to transform nutrition resources into health themselves. They tend to lack money, knowledge, resources and motivation and do not have access to market-oriented technology or the information and contacts needed to take advantages of the opportunities. And there is a global focus on nutrition and health for overall human development. Decisions about nutrition are often decided by the state governments interested in the philosophy of overall human development with ultimate concern about the long-term economic impact on local people. Liberalisation and high technology and other developmental projects in rural areas tend to provide little direct benefit to nutrition deficient women and children and more commonly have a negative impact as women and children's access to resources is curtailed and the physical resource base is degraded.

On the other hand, nutrition supplement in rural areas might be expected to create new opportunities for generating employment, income and health. Poor nutrition status and market opportunities are a major constraint to poverty reduction. Nutrition development for e.g. increases peoples education level and reduces expenses on morbidity. Several studies found that nutritional development has resulted in increased local incomes and accumulation of capital for investment. Investment further increases enrolment in schools and consequently wages and self-employment through productivity and its linkages to reduce incidence of poverty. Benefits arise in the form of improved human resources, better enrolment rate, lesser drop-out rates, low IMR, low MMR, and increased productivity.

Efforts to encourage equitable and durable improvement in human well-being need to take into account of the direct and indirect livelihood impacts of the nutrition projects. In this paper, we examine these issues as they have been accorded priority by the central government as well as state government. Nutrition is the grey area which has been neglected over the years and has resulted in huge losses to the nation. The main driver of the nutrition supplement in rural areas is Integrated Child Development Services Scheme. We investigate the impact of nutrition on economic opportunities and welfare. We focus on the relationship between nutrition and productive gains. This allows an empirical test of the role of nutrition in determining productive gains. We use the government of India data as the unit of analysis. We supplement the analysis with household level data and case studies to strengthen our views.

INVESTING IN CHILD NUTRITION

Approaches to malnutrition and nutrition deficiencies are well known. The most effective programs that have grown in the recent time are community-based and deal with a range of local needs, as well as nutrition deficiency control programs, which have both local and central aspects. These methods that are estimated to have good benefits related to costs, especially in the long term, when prevention of child malnutrition leads to healthier, better-educated, and more productive adults. Current programs are seen to have too low coverage and level of resources for widespread impact, but in many cases these can be built on. Supporting policies are required to provide a favorable context.

NUTRITION PROBLEM IN INDIA

Poor diet and infectious disease interact to cause growth failure in children, physiological damage especially to the immune system, and specific clinical conditions like anaemia, leading to impaired development and death. This interaction and its biological results are called "malnutrition", or the "malnutrition-infection complex". Malnutrition is the largest risk factor in the world for disability and premature mortality, especially in India, and is entirely preventable. Eliminating malnutrition would cut child mortality by more than 50 per cent, and reduce the burden of disease about 20 per cent (Tomkins and Watson, 1989; FAO/WHO, 1992; Pelletier et.al., 1994; Murray and Lopez, 1997).

Malnutrition in early childhood retards intellectual development, through both general and specific nutrient deficiencies, notably iodine. Some of these effects are irreversible, but all are preventable with current knowledge and technology. They have serious impacts both on individuals' capabilities, and on socioeconomic development overall (Grantham-McGregor, 1995; Brown and Pollitt, 1996). Human development has emerged as a concept that focuses the overall aims and aspirations of development efforts, and "weaves development around people, not people around development". Adequate nutrition is an integral part of human development. Indeed, nutritional criteria are used to measure human development; for example the United Nations Development Program's (UNDP) "capability poverty measure" uses nutritional status as one of three components. In concrete terms, good nutrition leads to fitter and better-educated people. Malnutrition in childhood, even if later corrected, affects educational ability and eventual school achievements. Nutrition thus improves human capital. This effect extends to future generations: much child developmental failure is perpetuated because small baby girls grow up to become small mothers, in turn having low birth weight infants. Breaking this inter-generational cycle requires ensuring better growth, health, and nutrition throughout the lifecycle, particularly for women. This is urgent, especially in India, as nearly one third of babies are underweight, and more than half the adult women in rural areas weigh less than 45 Kgs, the level at which risk in utero and on delivery increases rapidly. The persistence of malnutrition is a waste of human potential, and reducing it represents a great opportunity for bringing resources to bear on people-centered development, alleviating suffering and increasing productivity—as an investment, in other words (UNDP, 1992; UNDP, 1996; Brown and Pollitt, 1996).

Both economic growth and human development must proceed together for either to be sustainable. Countries like Egypt, Mexico, and Brazil have achieved high economic growth rates in the past, but because little was done for human development, this growth was not sustainable. Some countries have achieved high levels of human development, despite poverty; but because these countries failed to grow economically, social services broke down, and the growth could not be sustained. Only those countries that have combined investment in human development through public services and investment in production have achieved high growth rates in both economic and human development; in other words, sustained development. Everyone has a right to adequate nutritional status. Nutrition is a prerequisite for human development, and therefore for development as a whole. Both the causes and the consequences of malnutrition impinge on human rights. The deprivations that directly cause malnutrition—hunger, ill health, and neglect—must be prevented in any humane society. Recognizing children's rights means that all parts of society are obligated to realize them.

Reducing malnutrition brings multiple benefits. Mortality and disability (calculated as disability affected life years [DALYs] lost) would be reduced by eliminating malnutrition by 20-30 per cent. The economic benefits from preventing lost production and ill health due to malnutrition are estimated to be substantial, certainly greater than the investment required to reduce malnutrition (the benefit-cost ratios are considerably greater than one). Improving intellectual and physical abilities—human capital—is important in its own right, and will ensure sustainability. Many of these economic benefits are long-term, being realized in adults following prevention of malnutrition in childhood. They are thus a long-term investment, analogous to other investments in people, like education (Mason et. al., 1995; Phillips and Sanghvi, 1996).

The immediate causes of malnutrition are poor diet and infectious disease, and underlying these are inadequacies of food security (Bouis, 1999), caring practices (Engle, 1999), and basic health services. Interventions can also be seen in relation to the life cycle: specific interventions are appropriate during pregnancy and lactation, for the infant and child, through adolescence, adulthood, and into old age. In India, about half the preschool children are underweight—the usual measure of general malnutrition. The distribution of malnutrition and household food security; Engle (1999) on caring practices; Haddad (1999) on women's status; Horton (1999) on opportunities for investment in nutrition; Mason et. al. (1999) on micronutrients; Mock and Mason (1999) on information systems; Tontisirin and Gillespie (1999) on community-based programs. The predominance with an estimated 62 million underweight children, is evident.

ECONOMIC DIMENSIONS

Half the population of the developing world is suffering from calorie deficient diets. Four hundred million of them are children below age ten. The economic consequences of malnourishment are very severe. Identification of policy options are to be probed. Children malnutrition is to be analysed in terms of its consequences and not in terms of food consumed by an individual. Mortality, health status and psychological achievements are a few indicators. The best indicator of measuring the malnourishment is the deficiency of calorie. The concentration of malnourished children is primarily in the lowest income groups. Malnutrition is the result of the unequal distribution of world income and not the result of an insufficient availability of food. It is clearly a poverty problem and not a food problem.

The empirical evidence shows that calorie intake is closely related to per capita income and the malnutrition attacks the poorest segments of the population. Since the poorest income groups have substantially larger family size the share of children that are malnourished becomes larger than the share of adults. It is this distributive dimension of malnourishment, the association between malnourishment and poverty that gives origin to a larger incidence of malnutrition among children.

The difference in the incidence of malnutrition between children and adults depends upon two factors. Firstly, how strong is the relation between the number of young children per household and the per capita income of the family. Secondly, how small is the size of the malnourished population as a fraction of the total population.

It has been observed that at very low levels of income, very young children experience a substantially larger deficit than adults and older children. However, the young children's consumption responds more rapidly to changes in income. The result is that young children reach their required levels of consumption at lower levels of per capita income than older children. Adults and young children reach their required levels at a similar income, while older children do so at a higher income. This shows that children tend to have a larger calorie deficit than adults. It is also likely that a particular age group of children is malnourished while the rest of the family members are consuming above requirement.

ECONOMIC JUSTIFICATION

The economic justification for improving children's nutrition is of three types. First, children's nutrition is a public good or an externality to the rest of society i.e. the rest of the society derives a consumption benefit from eliminating malnutrition. Better off members of the society should be willing to pay for the better infant nutrition. Second, resource saving effect of better children's nutrition. Better nutrition is a cheaper intervention than other intervention in achieving low infant mortality rates, reduction in the incidence of infectious diseases, increase in the minimum standard of literacy etc. There is a trade off between quality of water and sewerage against supplementary calorie intake from the public programs for undernourished children. Also there is a trade off between nutrition and the amount of school inputs in achieving a predetermined level of literacy achievement. Third, better infant nutrition can increase the future productivity of the individual. Studies have shown that a 10 per cent increase in the weight of extremely malnourished children (before age 4) could increase the future productivity of these children as manual workers by nearly five per cent. Nutrition influences the impact of later investment in human capital, particularly education. Government is already spending considerable amounts in education, improved nutrition has an important additional effect over and above the effect that it can have independently of these future investments.

(a) Economics of Intervention

Increasing their income, their preference towards consuming calorie-intensive foods and the future changes in the relative price of the cereals can only reduce calorie malnutrition in the poorest segments of the population. Calorie income elasticity is nearly 0.5 implying that a one per cent change in per capita income increases calorie consumption by half of one per cent. It may take several years for the poorest population experiencing a deficit of calories to reach the required level of calorie consumption. Simultaneously, marginally and non-deficient income groups may also increase their consumption and reach levels that can be substantially higher than requirements. Hence, malnutrition in the poorest groups may coexist with a calorie surplus. Thus, regular income growth in the poorest population and accelerated food production are unfeasible solutions. The solution may be that reshuffle food availability from the groups with calorie surplus to those in deficit. Malnutrition may be more concentrated in the poorest segment and may be more children specific given the family size and income.

Malnutrition is widely prevalent in children due to the fact that calorie-income elasticity for children is lower. Secondly, due to urbanisation women's participation in the labour force has increased resulting in the deterioration of breast-feeding. Additional food purchased for the infant, out of the additional earnings of the female participating in the labour force, does not compensate for the losses in breast milk consumption, the net effect is deterioration in the infant's nutritional status. Other factors may also adversely affect the children. Other competing expenditures like transportation, clothing, housing etc. become more important in urban areas, affecting the share of income spent on food. Relative prices of food tend to rise. New commodities become available, such as entertainment and fashion, to be consumed basically by the adults. The result is that the share of income spent on food for children can decline because expenditures other than food become necessary and new commodities, relevant basically to adults, become available.

Calorie malnutrition in young children results from the fact that the family as a whole is malnourished. Secondly, calorie-wise children are discriminated relative to adults. Thirdly, discrimination among children according to some characteristics like intelligence, sex, birth order, feeding practices etc. In case, the entire family is malnourished, increase the household overall purchasing power of food-either by increasing their disposable income or lowering the relative price of calorie intensive food. Where children are discriminated, specific food programmes that have an effect on children's consumption more than an equivalent income transfer to the household. Where there is discrimination among children, preferences of adults in allocation food to particular children can be influenced by emphasizing that it is an investment good. The rate of return to investment in education is a function of the initial level of nutrition.

But are the children in India really getting the childhood they deserve? This study is an attempt to address this concern. Based on the results that have analysed varied aspects of children's development in diverse poverty contexts, both in quantitative and qualitative terms, this report concludes that India has undoubtedly made considerable progress in the last two decades in promoting child survival and basic education. Along with a supportive policy framework, including the recent legislation to make elementary education a fundamental right, there have been in existence some major initiatives for children. More prominently, these are in the form of centrally sponsored schemes such as the Reproductive Child Health Scheme (RCH) of the Department of Health and Family Welfare. The Integrated Child Development Services (ICDS) of the Department of Women and Child Development and several primary education schemes, including the District Primary Education Program (DPEP) and the government's flagship program, the *Sarva Shiksha Abhiyan (SSA)*. As a result, noticeable progress has been made over the last fifty years, as seen in the rapid expansion of the ICDS and primary education delivery network across the country.

(b) Cost Benefit Analysis of Nutrition Program

To determine the benefits of the supplementary nutrition programmes under the ICDS for malnourished children under 6 years and pregnant and lactating mothers, we focus on benefits accruing from averting deaths of pregnant and lactating women and other 'severely' malnourished children (grades III & IV) under 6 years of age as a result of providing supplementary nutrition and the productivity gains from reduction in fertility due to improved nutrition amongst both beneficiary children under 6 years of age and pregnant and lactating women.

Changes in nutrition status are a form of investment in human capital that generates a stream of future benefits. In the assumptions made to derive benefits, improvement in weight, improvement in school performance and future productivity of infants and changes in infant mortality and morbidity are subsumed.

Also the recovery of children born with subnormal weight implies the use of medical resources. Saving those resources can be considered the lower bound estimate of improved nutrition of mothers during pregnancy. On one hand supplementary nutrition to lactating and pregnant mothers help in reducing the number of children with low weight and, on the other, increase birth weights even if they remain below the range considered normal.

Again as stated above, as far as measuring the benefits derived from better school performance as well as early school drop outs this was considered in our assumption on productivity improvements arising from improved nutrition levels. The evaluation is presented in terms of NPV, IRR and the CB ratios.

In computing the costs, we considered that both administrative and supplementary nutrition expenditure incurred on ICDS was directly and indirectly contributing to improvement of nutrition status of both beneficiary children and pregnant and lactating mothers. Since children up to 6 years of age participate in supplementary nutrition, it was assumed that over the six year period all the children would have benefited from the programme, and that total expenditures incurred during the six year period would constitute the total expenditure against which the future benefits of improved children would accrue.

The various assumptions made in the computation of benefits/cost analysis and the IRR are presented in tables. In estimating benefit streams age specific life expectancy of children when they enter labour force and of pregnant and lactating women was considered. Tables based on alternative costs and benefit stream present the evaluation of supplementary nutrition under the ICDS in terms of net present worth, IRR and the BC ratios. These computations based on three different discount rates of 3%, 6% and 10%. A perusal of the values of IRR (which is in the range of 14 to 30 at 6% discount rate) shows that, on fairly conservative and restrictive assumptions, that the supplementary nutrition programme administered under the ICDS scheme is beneficial. The benefit cost ratios (close to 2) also provide ample evidence of the benefits of the programme. It is thus concluded that SNP produced a positive net social benefit. The economic analysis of SNP clearly establishes that ICDS is a profitable investment from the social standpoint and has a significant positive impact on the nutrition status of pre-school children.

It may again be reiterated that our computations have been under very conservative assumptions, and the actual benefits may indeed be considerably larger than those indicated by our analysis.

Table 1
ICDS Programme and Its Impact

Year	*Number of beneficiaries (lakhs)*		*% children suffering from severe mal-nutrition*	*% reduction in SNP amongst Children during the Years due to ICDS*	*Number of children Saved from SMN Due to ICDS*	*Deaths averted Amongst SMN Children owing, to ICDS (lakhs)*	*Net number of childre Beneficiaries (lakhs)*
	Children 0-6 years	*Pregnant & lactating mothers*					
(1)	(2) .	(3)	(4)	(5)	(6)	(7)	(8)
1991-92	162	31	7.8*	—	—	—	162
1992-93	178	36	6.5 @	1.3	2.101	0.5265	43
1993-94	187	37	5.5 @	1.0	1.870	0.4675	41
1994-95	194	43	4.5 @	1.0	1.940	0.4850	38
1995-96	209	44	3.5 @	1.0	2.090	0.5225	47
1996-97	222	—	2.5*	1.0	2.200	0.5500	48

* Available estimates from ICDS.

@ Interpolated figures.

1. Assuming that 25% of severe grade children will die.
2. Base year children are taken as they are–for the subsequent years, net addition of beneficiary children are found on the assumption that each year 1/6th of the children will go out of ICDS scheme. For instance for 1992-93, the net addition is [{178-162}] + 162/61 = 43 lakhs.

Table 2

Worksheet for Costing Gains from SNP under ICDS

Year	*Number of beneficiaries (lakhs)*		*% children suffering from severe mal-nutrition*	*% reduction in SNP amongst Children during the Years due to ICDS*	*Number of children Saved from SMN Due to ICDS*	*Deaths averted Amongst SMN Children owing, to ICDS (lakhs)*	*Net number of childre Beneficiaries (lakhs)*
	Children 0-6 years	*Pregnant & lactating mothers*					
(1)	(2)	(3)	(4)	(5)	(6)	(7)	(8)
1991-92	162	31	7.0*	—	—	—	162
1992-93	178	36	6.5 @	1.3	2.101	0.5265	43
1993-94	187	37	5.5 @	1.0	1.870	0.4675	41
1994-95	194	43	4.5 @	1.0	1.940	0.4850	38
1995-96	209	44	3.5 @	1.0	2.090	0.5225	47
1996-97	222	—	2.5*	1.0	2.200	0.5500	48
Total		191			10.201	2.5515	379

* *Available estimates from ICDS*

@ Interpolated figures

1. Assuming that 25% of severe grade children will die.
2. Base year children are taken as they are – for the subsequent years, net addition of beneficiary children are found on the assumption that each year 1/6th of the children will go out of ICDS scheme. For instance for 1992-93, the net addition {(178-162) + 162/6} = 43 lakhs.

Table 3
Assumptions Used for Cost Analysis

	Scenario I	*Scenario II*
Productive Life Expectancy 16 years (beneficiary child)	16 years	30 years (Male) 35 years (Female)
Productive Life Expectancy of Pregnant & Lactating mothers	12 years	12 years
Average annual wage for adult	Rs. 3500	Rs. 7800 (Male) Rs. 3900 (Female)
Average rate of employment	100%	75% (Male) 100% (Female)
Male/Female Ratio	50% -50%	50% -50%
Productivity loss due to malnutrition among adults	10%	10%
Maternal mortality rate	5 per 1000	5 per 1000
Per cent maternal deaths due to malnutrition	45%	45%
Per cent deaths of children in severe grade	25%	25%
% children suffering from PEM	50%	50%

Table 4
How much the Country Benefit from Feeding Pregnant & Lactating Women under ICDS Scheme? (Analysis from 1991-92 to 1995-96)

Number of women who received SNP under ICDS during 1991-92 & 1995-96	191 lakhs	Col.3 of Table 1.1
Estimated pregnant and lactating women suffering from CED (chronic Energy Deficiency) suffer from CED	95.5 lakhs	50% of adults
Estimated maternal deaths due to malnutrition	42975	Assumption MMR=5 and 45% of deaths caused due to malnutrition
Scenario I	95.5 x 0.10 x Rs.3500	
Productivity gain due to reduction in frailty	Rs. 334.25 crores	
Discounted wage gain due to maternal deaths averted	42975 x Rs.3500 x 12 years Rs. 180.50 crores	
Scenario II	95.5 x 0.10 x Rs. 3900 = Rs.	
Productivity gain due to reduction in frailty	372.45 crores	
Discounted wage gain due to maternal deaths averted	42975 x 12 x Rs. 3900 = Rs. 201.12 crores	

Table 5
How much the Country Benefit from Supplementary Nutrition to Children (0-6 years) Under ICDS Scheme? (From 1991-92 to 1995-96)

Total number of children (under 6 years) covered by SNP during 1991-92 to 1995-96	331 lakhs	Col. 8 of Table 1.1
Estimated deaths due to severe malnutrition amongst children	2.5515 lakhs	Col.7 of Table 1.1
Estimated adults suffering from CED	165.5 lakhs	50% of adults suffer from CED

contd.

Scenario I	2.5515 x 16 years x Rs. 3500 =
Discounted wage gain on account of deaths averted amongst malnourished children in severe grade	1428.84 crores
Productivity gains due to reduction in fraility	(331/2) x 0.10 x 3500 = Rs. 579.25 crores

Scenario II
Discounted wage gain on account of deaths averted amongst malnourished children severe grade for

Set I	(a)	Male 30 x 0.75 x (1/2 x 2.5515) x Rs. 7800 = Rs. 2238.94 crores
	(b)	Female 35 x (1/2 x 2.5515) x 3900 = Rs. 1741.39 crores
Set II	(a)	Male 16 x .75 x (1/2 x 2.5515) x 7800 = Rs. 1194.10 crores
	(b)	Female 16 x (1/2 x 2.5515) x 3900 = Rs. 796.07 crores

Productivity gains due to reduction in frailty for
(a) Male (165.5 x ½) x 0.10 x 0.75 x Rs. 7800 = Rs. 484.09 crores
(b) Female (165.5 x ½) x 0.1 x 3900 = Rs. 322.73 crores

Table 6
Summary of Benefits from Supplementary Nutrition under ICDS
(Figures in Rs. crores)

Benefits	Scenario I	Scenario II	
A. Children		*Set I*	
(i) Gains due to deaths averted	1428.84	Set II	
(ii) Productivity gains from reduction in fraility	579.25	2238.94 (Males)	Rs.
		1194.10 crores	
		1741.39 (Females)	Rs.
		796.07 crores	
		484.09 (Males)	484.09
		322.73 (Females)	322.73
B. Pregnant & Lactating Women			
(iii) Productivity gains from reduction in fraility	334.25	372.45	
(iv) Gains from averting maternal deaths	180.50	201.12	201.12
Total benefits (Rs. crores)	2522.84	5360.72	3370.56

Scenario I – NPV		
3%	6%	10%
$ 8,258.97	$ 5,768.15	$ 3,485.87
IRR	22.918%	
Scenario II – NPV		
3%	6%	10%
$4,737.57	$2,915.45	$1,251.74
IRR	14.655%	
BENEFIT—COST RATIO		
SCI	3%	2.32402179
	6%	1.95165759
	10%	1.59678599
SCII	3%	1.75949728
	6%	1.48101307
	10%	1.21429214

CONCLUSION AND IMPLICATIONS

The study has put forward two complementary types of approach. Both these need support and better calculation of resource needs. Local programs through community organizations must be massively expanded, with input from facility-based resources. Micronutrient deficiency control programs, usually linked to the local programs, must be sustained and new approaches (notably multiple micro-nutrient fortification and supplementation) researched and adopted. Making the decisions to undertake these actions, and to support the steps leading to their successful planning and implementation, thus constitute the major recommendations here.

(a) Priorities for Local Programs

Nutrition programs presently cover a fraction of those in need, thus a huge expansion is a precondition for making significant inroads into the problem. It is known that programs can have this impact under the right conditions. A decision-in- principle to support an expansion of this magnitude, with appropriate intensity of resource application and concern for the most effective program content and organization, is thus an early necessary step. This must take into account the resource implications of finance and personnel and training needs, and the investment will need to be phased in over time.

(b) Policy Dialogue

Programs can be effective under the right conditions, and these tend to be related to fundamental causes of malnutrition, such as social exclusion and women's status. Policy decisions and implementation may affect these conditions. In the process of negotiating investment from international financial institutions in nutritional improvement, the basic requirements underpinning programs may prove feasible issues for modification. At the same time, the simple but crucial decisions to actually commit resources and implement the programs themselves must be taken. Beyond context, the coexistence of key programs must be fostered. Poverty alleviation facilitates nutrition improvements in two ways. First, the programs themselves provide household resources for improving nutrition. Second, poverty alleviation program organization can provide for the structure, outreach, and individual contact that nutrition activities can build on. The poverty alleviation organizations provide the best prospect of extending and supporting local programs. The direct effects of improvements such as in education, particularly for women, and in water and sanitation, have far-reaching effects on nutrition. Usually these factors are strongly associated with child growth, although the precise relations vary and need to be seen in specific circumstances (Mason et al., 1999). Nutrition considerations may help to target these. More contentious is the prospect of redirecting nutrition resources that are currently used wastefully. This refers primarily to the resources used for food subsidies and public food distribution programs. The resources spent on these are nearly enough, in some countries, to finance much of the local programs for nutrition, if they could be reallocated. Taking and implementing many of these decisions, by governments, international financial institutions, and agencies are prerequisites for reducing malnutrition.

(c) Meeting Program Needs

Implementing programs, when resources are committed will take a number of practical steps. Gaps in capacity must be filled. The needs will be:

(i) Organization: programs depend on local organisation and decentralization of resources and decision-making; including fostering community level organizations, by assigning budgets, legislation, and other means;

(ii) Training: the effort envisaged for training village level workers, and their support, is extensive, and will require multilevel structures for training, materials, incentives, and supervision;

(iii) Advocacy and social mobilization; information; education; training; and support for service delivery as defined by UNICEF; and

(iv) Mobilization of resources: direct financial inputs will be required, especially for the large numbers of village workers and their facilitators who will need incentives and remuneration, likely beyond the capacity of communities and governments; for external finance, negotiations as to type and level will be needed, in conjunction with reallocation of govern-mental resources.

(d) Issues for Program Design

A number of issues that affect all potential programs remain to be resolved. Most involve research that should be undertaken at an early stage, and represent sensible investment in terms of program effectiveness in the future. Some of the salient issues are outlined here. Resources should be applied to a problem in such a way that the population can respond and the problem is alleviated. In nutritional terms, this means identifying accurately, which population groups can respond to which type of intervention. For example, behavioral change (child feeding practices, for instance) may not be possible by some methods for some groups, and this needs to be better defined or ineffective programs will be designed. A similar issue concerns defining the contextual factors and how these can be changed by policy to improve program success. These issues can be researched and guidance provided for program design. More specifically, knowledge of the relative roles and cost-effectiveness of different community-based and facility-based activities is not yet well laid out. This could be improved from compilation and synthesis of current knowledge. Such research, although of general application, would be most useful in advance of detailed program planning. The relative effects of using resources for supplementary feeding, compared with using the same resources for behavioral change, could also be worked out as a generic issue. Population growth in India is in the cities and towns. As a result, the malnourished are increasingly in urban areas. Yet most planning for improving nutrition refers to villages and rural communities. Research is needed on the most effective means of improving nutrition in urban areas, and where these have common features and problems, this research can be generic. We need to focus on nutrition-relevant programs in cities and their evaluations, as well as understand better the parallels with rural programs, especially regarding the appropriate forms of local organization. The relationship of level of effort (for various activities) to impact needs to be better understood. This is likely to be nonlinear, which is crucial as it means that applying too low a level of resources is very wasteful. It does not mean that the problem will simply be solved more slowly; it means that it will not be solved at all until the level of effort is sufficient to cause change. This has enormous implications for planning investments, and needs to be researched. Finally, a number of technical issues need research, of which the clearest concern fortification, most urgently iron fortification of staple foods.

(e) Looking Forward

This review leads to extensive proposals for finance, and even more for recruiting and training millions of people. Better nutrition and development for children is a powerful outcome objective, with implications for society and development overall. But the process proposed is important too. What will change, what will be in place, in ten years' time if these recommendations are adopted, financed, and implemented? Most communities would have a structure of local workers and supervisors in direct contact with families in villages and urban areas, not only helping them to solve nutrition and health problems and raise healthier children, but also assisting with community development, supporting women, and providing a range of benefits. Programs would be multifaceted at the local level, and although the structure might start with nutrition as a main concern, the benefits would be wider still. In particular, problems of social exclusion, and discrimination by class and gender, would have some counteracting forces. For individuals, specific nutritional problems would be well on the way to solution. Micronutrient deficiencies would be becoming a thing of the past, with goiter and iodine deficiency vanishing, and vitamin A deficiency no longer visible and sub-clinically much reduced. Anemia would likely be in retreat, with successful fortification. Pregnant women in particular, others too, would be getting regular multiple micronutrient supplements. Low birth weight and early childhood growth failure, and associated sickness and death, would be much reduced—the next generation would be larger, healthier, benefit more from education, and be more productive. The intergenerational perpetuation of malnutrition will have been cut into, and a process of steadily improving pregnancies and child survival and development promoted. Human capital, development, and rights will all benefit. Governments have committed themselves to this scenario already. Adopting these measures will itself be a significant contribution to meeting governments' obligations.

REFERENCES

Bouis, H.E. (1999), Linking Food and Nutrition Security: Past Lessons and Future Opportunities, *Asian Development Review*, 19 (1 and 2).

Brown, J and E. Pollit (1996), Malnutrition, Poverty and Intellectual Development, *Scientific American*, 2 : 30-43.

Engle, P. (1999), The Role of Caring Practices and Resources for Care in Child Survival, Growth and Development: South and South East Asia, *Asian Development Review*, 17 (1 and 2).

FAO/WHO (1992), International Conference on Nutrition Goals, World Declaration Plan of Action, FAO, Rome and WHO, Geneva.

Grantham-McGregor, S. (1995), A Review of Studies on the Effect of Severe Malnutrition on Mental Development, *Journal of Nutrition,* 125 (85, Supplement: 2233-385).

Haddad, L. (1999), Women's Status: Levels, Consequences, Determinants, Interventions and Policy, *Asian Development Review,* 17 (1 and 2).

Horton, S. (1999), Opportunities for Investment in Nutrition in Low Income Asia, *Asian Development Review*, 17 (1 and 2).

Mason, J.B., V. Mamar and N.B. Mock (1999), Controlling Micronutrient Deficiencies in Asia, *Asian Development Review*, 17 (1 and 2).

Mason, J.U., Jonsson and J. Csete (1995), Is Malnutrition being Overcome?, Paper Presented at the Meeting on Overcoming Hunger in the 1990s, Institute of Nutrition, Mahidol University, Thailand, 7-11, November, 1994, In the World Hunger Program, Hunger Report, 1995, Brown University, Rhode Island.

Mock, N.B., and J.B. Mason (1999), Nutrition Information System for Implementing Child Nutrition Program, *Asian Development Review*, 17 (1 and 2).

Murray, C. and A. Lopez (1997), Global Mortality, Disability and the Contribution of Risk Factors: Global Burden of Diseases Study, *Lancet*, 349 (9063) 1436-42.

Pelletier. D. et. al., (1994), The Relationship Between Child Anthropometry and Mortality in Developing Countries, *Journal of Nutrition*, 124 (Supplement, 10 S).

Phillips. M., and T.G. Sanghvi (1996), *The Economic Analysis of Nutrition Projects*, Washington D.C., World Bank.

Tomkins, A.M. and F. Watson (1989), Malnutrition and Infection: A Review, ACC/SCN, State of the Art Series, Nutrition Policy Discussion paper No.5, ACC/SCN, Geneva.

Tontisirin, K., and S. Gillespie (1999), Linking Community-Based Programs and Service Delivery for Improving Maternal and Child Nutrition, *Asian Development Review*, 17(1 and 2).

UNDP (1992), *Human Development Report*, Oxford: Oxford University Press for UNDP.

UNDP (1996), *Human Development Report*, Oxford: Oxford University Press for UNDP.

9

FOOD SECURITY IN INDIA: ISSUES AND CHALLENGES

Jayasheela and Vishwanatha

INTRODUCTION

Food security has been widely defined in economic literature. The World Food Summit used the following definition: "Food Security exists when all people, at all times have physical and economic access to sufficient, safe and nutritious food to meet their dietary needs and food preferences for an active and healthy life". So the physical and economic access to food is very important. The concept of food security first emerged at the World Food Conference in 1974 held by United Nations Food and Agriculture Organization (FAO). It centered around two sub concepts (a) Food availability which refers to the supply of food available at local, national or international levels and (b) The food entitlement refers to the capability of individuals and households to obtain food.

Concept of food security is more relevant in a developing country like India where a large percentage of population lives in rural areas. They are dependant on agriculture as a source of livelihood, and spend a high share of total household income on food. The agriculture sector in India has to play twin roles in terms of providing adequate amount of food grains and also help in generating income for the rural poor. As far as food availability is concerned, India has almost reached self-sufficiency. But whether the income of the poor has also increased in a sustained manner in the rural areas is a debatable issue. Food security on a sustained basis is possible only if farm productivity can be without causing ecological harm. Otherwise it will pose a threat to future income increases of rural poor and food security.

FOOD SECURITY SCENARIO: WORLD VIEW

Modern technology and innovation have been able to overcome the Malthusian crisis at the global level. The 1980's saw a perfect achieved a near balance in the growth of population and per capita food production in most of the countries. In fact for the world as a whole, per capita food production increased during this period. Yields of major cereals have more than doubled in the past decades. As a result of this food surplus there has been a decrease in prices.

According to the World Development Report (1993) the average daily per capita dietary energy supply increased from less than 2300 cal. in 1961-63 to 2,440 in 1969-71, to 2720 in 1990-92 and is expected to reach a value of 2,900 cal. by 2010 A..D. But there are wide disparities in production across countries and millions of people are chronically hungry. The International Food Policy Research Institute estimates that by year 2020 there will be very little reduction in the number of malnourished children in the developing world as a whole. In fact it may actually increase in many of the Sub-Sahara and south Asian countries. The population with adequate access to food may decline from 21% of the population of the developing countries in the mid 1990's to 12% in 2010, but it is still likely to number 680 million people.

There it is important for food security to be made a top priority, especially by the developing countries. National level food security may not guarantee food security at the household or individual level. However, still the concept of food security is very meaningful and relevant, especially since food security is not only about availability and increased production, but also about people across to food at all times.

The 1996 and 2002 World Food Summits reached a near consensus on the concept of food security in terms of availability, stability, access and consumption by all. However, there was also a realization that food security can be s can be achieved only if there is sustainable agricultural development. Dr. M.S. Swaminathan has rightly pointed out that only ecologically sustainable agriculture can help to strengthen the livelihood security system in rural areas resulting in food security.

FOOD SECURITY IN INDIA

The key objective of India's food policy is to ensure adequate availability of food grains to the common people at an affordable price to through Public Distribution System (PDS). India's agricultural policy has been oriented to the goal of price stability. In recent years, the issue of handling the volumes of marketable surpluses of food grains has assumed importance. The surplus mobilized through procurement program has helped in creating a buffer stock, designed to cushion the country from the ravages of food security and food production shortages.

Trends in Food Availability

In India the food production has grown at a steady rate of more than 3% from 1976 to 1995. But the per capital food production and food supply has shown a declining trend in the last ten years from 1991-2000. (please see Table 1.)

Table 1
Average Annual Growth Rates (%

Period	*Population*	*Food production*	*Per capital food production*	*Cereal yield Kg/ ha*	*K-calories per capita per day.*
1971-75	2.3	2.1	-0.1	1.7	-0.5
1976-80	2.3	2.9	0.8	2.9	1.1
1981-85	2.2	4.4	2.2	4.0	1.1
1986-90	2.9	3.5	1.3	3.5	1.2
1991-95	1.9	3.0	1.0	2.5	0.6
1996-00	1.8	2.4	0.7	1.6	0.2

Source: Human Development Report, 2001.

India succeeded in increasing her food grains production from 50.8 million tones in 1950-51 to 209 million tones in 1999-2000. India had achieved self-sufficiency in food grains by the year 1976 and since then, Indian imports of cereals have remained negligible. An analysis of the food grains production indicates the following:

1. Between 1950-51 and 1999-2000, food grain production has increased from 50.8 million tones to 209.00 million tones a nearly four fold increase.
2. An analysis of cereals production indicates that while cereals accounted for 84% of the total food grains production 1950-51, their share increased to 93% in 1999-2000. Comparatively, the share of pulses declined from 16.5% to just 7.0% during the same period.
3. Within cereals, the share of rice and wheat, which was 53% in 1950-51, increased to 77% during 1999-2000. Comparatively, the share of coarse cereals has declined from 30% in 1960-51 to 17% in 1999-2000.

Food Access and Livelihood

India today has over 65 million tones of wheat and rice in government stocks; downs; yet poverty induced hunger affects over 200 million persons. Schemes like Antyodaya Anna Yojana, Annapoorna, and Sampoorna Gram Rozgar Yojana are good in concept but weak in implementation. So the future crisis on the food front is likely emanate not only from not being able to meet the increased demand; but also on the distribution front, in terms of equitable distribution of gains from economic growth.

The starvation deaths staring in some parts of India, therefore, are not entirely the outcome of the short fall in production, but more a result of inefficient distribution and inaccessibility or what Amartya Sen calls it "entitlement failure". "The state must commit itself to reducing poverty through the implementation of various target oriented poverty alleviation programs which will generate income in the hands of poor, leading to certain capabilities which in turn will give an opportunity for entitlement of food. Further, inequality on food front can also be removed by improving the distributional aspect. Therefore, one should recognize the fact that more increase in food grains at the national level just cannot ensure that benefits at the individual family level".

Poverty and Food Security

According to recent estimates, approximately 36% of the Indian population lives below the poverty line. This means their income is not sufficient to buy enough food. About 80% of these poor people live in rural areas. In this course of the years, the Government of India as well as most state governments have formulated and implemented various schemes to alleviate poverty or improve the social security of these most deprived people. These schemes aim to enhance self employment, generate wage employment, or transfer income to the poor. Among these programs, is the Public Distribution System (PDS), a large scale food rationing program meant to reduce food insecurity and improve welfare. It is one of the most important welfare programs in India and to which the government spends about Rs.90, 000 million per year. In the recent past, this amount was about 50% of government spending on anti-poverty programs and 2.5% of the overall central government expenditure.

Public Distribution System and Food Security

The Public Distribution System (PDS) was started to act as a price support program for the consumer during the periods of food shortage in the 1960's. The objective of PDS was to act as an instrument of price stabilization and become a counter veiling force against private traders who were interested in exploiting the situation of scarcity to make more and more profits. The PDS provides essential commodities such as rice, wheat, sugar, edible oil, soft cake and kerosene at subsidized prices.

In the 1990's the PDS has come under increasing criticism form various quarters. The system is deemed to be too costly as well as incapable of addressing the issue of food security. In an attempt to reform PDS, the Government of India decided in 1996-97 to introduce Targeting PDS. Under this system, the food grains for the poor become cheaper, while rich had to pay more. States with larger percentage of Below Poverty Line (BPL) population were allocated more food grains while states with lesser percentage of BPL population received less food grains. Implementation of this scheme however, proved difficult. Not only was there considerable opposition, there is no positive impact on the over all subsidy and it is also doubtful whether the poor benefit. The key objectives of the PDS since its inception in the 1960's are as follows:

1. To cope with emergency situations such as droughts,
2. To distribute food at fair price to vulnerable people, and
3. To guarantee remunerative prices to farmers.

It is believed that the effectiveness of PDS is related to the prevalent political set up in the state. Kerala, Andhra Pradesh and West Bengal are the states where PDS is functioning effectively. This is attributed to the commitment of the political leadership to the PDS.

Indian Food Projections up to 2020

The key factors that are likely to determine growth in yield up to 2020 include;

1. Rates of fertilizer and pesticide application.
2. The pace of research investment and advances in biotechnology.
3. Physical and human capital development.
4. The degradation and misuse of the natural resource base, with soil erosion and water shortages being particularly relevant.

Continued agricultural growth in India depends on a number of assumptions regarding possibility for continued yield increases, moderate levels of land degradation, and the country's ability to manage pressures from growing competition among the agricultural, urban and industrial sectors over land and water resources. Many observers believe that these assumptions are not appropriate, and India will face more severe impediments to the expansion of agricultural production. Given these uncertainties, a scenario invoking a decline of 50% in area and yield growth rate in India and a decline of 25% in livestock numbers growth and a 25% decline in GDP growth (the latter due to the economy-wide effect of the dramatic slowdown in agricultural growth), represents a plausible negative scenario for the region.

Table 2
Realized Annual Cereal Yield Growth Rates Under the Baseline and India Slow-Growth Scenario, 1997-2020

Commodity	*Base lineIndia (% year)*	*Slow Growth India*
Wheat	1.2	0.7
Maize	1.0	0.6
Other coarse grains	1.0	0.5
Rice	1.4	0.8

Source: IMPACT projections, June 2001.

As Table 2 indicates, changes in yield, growth rate etc. has resulted in an actual decline of Indian annual cereal yield growth rates from 1.2 to 0.7% for wheat, from 1.0 to 0.6% for maize, from 1.0 to 0.5% for other grains and from 1.4 to 0.8% for rice.

As expected, declining yield and area growth rates have a serious effect on total crop production in India. Indian cereal production declined by 15%, from 254 million tons under the baseline scenario to 217 million tons. As a result, India goes from near self-sufficiency in cereals in 2020 under the baseline scenario to imports of 30 million tons (a cost of $5.9 billion at projected international prices).

Moving beyond a narrow focus on cereals, India's overall agricultural trade balance under the slow-growth scenario will shift from a 1997 surplus of $1.7 billion to a deficit of $9.2 billion in 2020. In relative value terms, India's trade deficit in 2020 will represent 7% of total agricultural production. Area and yield declines in India and China affect world cereal prices by significant, though not disastrous amounts. Wheat prices under this scenario increase by 1 percent ($1 per ton) between 1997 and 2020 to $134 per ton compared with an 8% ($10 per ton) decline under the baseline scenario. Maize and rice prices increases sharply under the slow-growth scenario and decline under the baseline scenario. Other gains decline under both scenarios.

Indian Kilocalorie consumption in 2020 declines from 2,868 kilocalories per capita under the baseline scenario to 2,697 kilo caloric per capita under the slow-growth scenario. More important under the slow growth scenario, the number of malnourished children in India will increase by 2 million children over the baseline. The rate of increase in malnourished children is dependent on the ability and willingness of India and China to finance massive agricultural imports under this scenario. Measures to lower agricultural import dependency in India and China, including high import tariffs and subsidies to domestic production could considerably worsen the ultimate impact of negative shocks of these agricultural production systems.

Key Issue and Challenges in Food Security in India

Between 1990-1991 and 1991-97, the annual rate of growth of food grains was only 1.7% which is lower than the current population growth of 1.9%. The availability of food grains is only 182 kg per year as against the nutritional norm of 300 kg per year on per capita basis. Moreover, availability of pulses is only 34 grams per day against the norm of 47 grams fixed by the Indian council of Medical Research and much below the 80 grams per day fixed by the World Health Organization compounding the fragile food situation in the country.

The gains of the green revolution are limited to certain belts where irrigated farming is practiced. The crop productivity is 2.5 ton in irrigated farming areas, which is much below world standards. The crop productivity is only one ton in the dry land regions, which account for 70% of cropped area. When the production is low, it increases commodity beyond the reach of the poor people.

Out of the total geographical area of 329 million hectares, about 173.64 million hectares (53%) face degradation problems arising from water and wind erosion.

The percentage of people engaged in agriculture has come down from 74% of total work force in 1960 to 62% in 1995. The rising population pressure has resulted in increasing marginalization of land holding in India. As regards the marginal and small farmers, who constitute 78% of total farming households, the holding size is only 0.6 hectare. Yet more and more holdings are becoming economically unviable and as such unable to generate marketable surplus.

It is a matter of serious concern that agriculture is being neglected so far as public investment in farm sector is concerned. It is reported that a large portion of public expenditure on agriculture in recent years went into current expenditure in the form of increased subsidies for food, fertilizer, electricity, irrigation, credit and other agricultural inputs rather than on creation of assets.

CONCLUSION

To conclude, it can be said that even though Indian agricultural production systems have undergone dramatic changes over the last 30 years, much work remains to be completed, to ensure that the grains already achieved are extended to vast numbers who remain food insecure. Indian policy makers currently face the difficult challenge of dismantling a heavily state centered food production system that has historically involved heavy input and consumption subsidies, as well as import and export controls. Beyond the wastefulness and inefficiencies associated with such policies, a record of slow per capita consumption growth and persistent food insecurity on a massive scale speaks for itself. Given the realities of local production capacity, Indian policy makers must acknowledge the fact that food self-sufficiency is not a viable option if the nation wishes to achieve true food security in the foreseeable future. Democratic accountability renders the process of gradual liberalization inevitable over the long run, but the resistance of those who benefit from wasteful and expensive policies, as well as the reluctance among much of the leadership to return to high levels of cereal imports has rendered reforms difficult in the short run. Taking advantage of the opportunities available and working to ensure a more food-secure world in 2020 will remain the primary challenge for policy makers at all levels over the next 20 years.

It is suggested that to achieve the objective of the slogan of "Food for all-hunger free world' the conventional policies will have to be changed and modified. We must accept that the food insecurity is because of low purchasing power and poverty and therefore to fight food insecurity, poverty alleviation must be the focus. Since majority of the population lives in rural areas and depend on agriculture, more emphasis needs to be laid on agriculture. This would lead to two benefits–increased food availability and generation of additional income. Agricultural production and productivity has to be raised for food security. It will enhance supply of food, lower the prices to affordable level and improve overall access to food as well as increase the incomes of those who are most vulnerable to fluctuations relating to availability and prices. The rural non-farm economy should also be developed and more employment generated here. The government should also reallocate more funds towards development of basic infrastructure and technology in these areas. The available data on PDS shows that there is little correlation between the amount of grains distributed and the poverty across the state. PDS is not a solution to food security for the common man in the country. Increase in the area under food crops and yield rates will improve their incomes and this will provide long-term solution to the problem of food economy. Finally reduction in food insecurity also requires above all reduction in population and sustainable agricultural development.

REFERENCES

Zeba Sheereen (2004), Agriculture and Food Security in India, In Reddy Gopal and T.L.N. Swamy (Eds.), *Institutional Policy Options for Sustainable Agricultural Development*, Department of Economics, Osmania University, Hyderbad.

Arabi U. (2004), Sustainable Agriculture and Food Security Dimensions: Policy Perspectives in India, In Reddy Gopal and T.L.N. Swamy (Eds.), *Institutional Policy Options for Sustainable Agricultural Development*, Department of Economics, Osmania University, Hyderbad.

Deepak B. (2004), Recent Trends of Food Production and Issues on Food Security in India, In Reddy Gopal and T.L.N. Swamy (Eds.), *Institutional Policy Options for Sustainable Agricultural Development*, Department of Economics, Osmania University, Hyderbad.

Mark W. Rosegrant, Michael S, Paisner, Siet Meijer, and Julie W. (2001), Global Food Projections to 2020, Indian Food Policy Research Institute (IFPRI).

Darjan B. and S. Radhakrishna (2004), Food Economy in Liberalization Scenario, In Reddy Gopal and T.L.N. Swamy (Eds.), *Institutional Policy Options for Sustainable Agricultural Development*, Department of Economics, Osmania University, Hyderbad.

10

UTILIZATION OF PUBLIC HEALTH FACILITIES IN INDIA (WITH SPECIAL REFERENCE TO MATERNAL HEALTH CARE SERVICES)

Amlan Majumder

INTRODUCTION

India is a signatory to the Alma Ata Declaration and was committed to attain the goal of 'Health For All' by the Year 2000 through the universal provision of primary health care services. However, local action for achieving the goal has not been squared up with this global thinking (Singh, 2000). There has been a slippage in achieving the goal by 2000. The call at present is to achieve it by 2025. This setback is a clear indication of gradual but sure decay in the health services of the country. The fact is reflected in poor health care infrastructure, poor health status of common mass as well as very low rates of utilisation of public health facilities. Important research question at this point is that–why utilisation of public health facilities is so low? Or what are the main factors which affect choices regarding utilisation of health care across cultures and societies in India? The present study focuses on some antenatal care which one mother receives during pregnancy and investigates such research questions empirically, and also throws some light on the question of sustainability of the public health care system in sixteen major States of India utilising data from Rapid Household Survey Phase-II under the Reproductive and Child Health Project (RHS-RCH-II).

HEALTH CARE STRUCTURE IN INDIA

The public health care delivery system in India at present has a three-tier structure: primary, secondary, and tertiary. The primary tier has been developed to provide health and family welfare related services to the vast majority of rural people. It comprises three types of health care institutions: Sub-Centre (SC), Primary Health Centre (PHC) and Community Health Centre (CHC). Primary health care system is however, suffering from serious shortfall in terms of physical plants, equipments, and manpower. Table 1 shows availability and shortage of medical personnel in the primary health care system in India. It is well understood from the table that scope for utilising specialised health care is very restricted in the primary health care system.

The secondary tier, which is primary to the urban mass, includes medical care provided by the specialists at the district and sub-divisional hospitals. Tertiary health care encompasses sophisticated services provided by the super-specialists at medical colleges and specialised hospitals.

Table 1
Availability and Shortage of Manpower in Primary Health Care System in India

Resource	*Required*	*In position*	*Shortfall (%)*
Medical Specialists	11652	3731	67.98
Paediatrician	2913	448	84.62
Physicians	2913	586	79.89
Obstetrician	2913	777	73.32
Surgeons	2913	797	72.64
Doctors at PHCs	23179	25418	-

Source: Health Information 2000, Ministry of Health and Family Welfare, Government of India.

Private sources of care may be divided into two broad groups: institutional and non-institutional. Institutional sources include private hospitals, private health care research institutes, nursing homes, private clinics, etc. Non-institutional sources include doctors and medical specialists of public health care institutions who do private practice, indigenous practitioners, chemists, druggists, etc. However, private sources of care are very uneven in both quantity and quality and their presence is parallel to the public health care system.

STATUS OF HEALTH IN INDIA

Table 2 shows some crucial health indicators of India and some other selected countries according to HDR 2004. Two countries (Norway and Sweden) have been selected from the top and two other (Niger and Sierra Leone) have been selected from the bottom of the list, which have been prepared by UNDP according to HDI score. Two other transitional economies (China and Russian Federation) have also been selected to compare their results with those of India. The figures show that India is somewhat at the mid-way to the desired level of development and lagging behind other similar transitional economies.

Table 2
Some Health Indicators in India and Other Selected Countries

Country	*HDI Rank*	*IMR (2002)*	*TFR (2000-05)*	*LE (2002)*
Norway	1	4	1.8	78.9
Sweden	2	3	1.6	80
Russian Federation	57	18	1.1	66.7
China	94	31	1.8	70.9
India	127	67	3	63.7
Niger	176	156	8	46
Sierra Leone	177	165	6.5	34.3

Source: Human Development Report 2004.
IMR: Infant Mortality Rate, TFR: Total Fertility Rate, LE: Life expectancy at Birth.

Table 3 shows some computed figures on maternal health care utilisation in rural and urban areas of India form the data file of currently married women in the 15-44 age group who experienced at least one live birth since 01 January 1996 till the date of survey. The table shows very poor rate of utilisation of maternal health care services in rural and urban areas of India.

Table 3
Utilization of Maternal Health Care[Ψ] in India According to RHS-RCH-Phase II

Rural				Urban			
IFA	TT	CU	ANC	IFA	TT	CU	ANC
42.2	59.2	26.7	17.1	56.9	77.4	59.2	38.1

Source: Own elaboration on RHS-RCH-II.
Ψ: Computed % figures of eligible population in the 5-year reference period prior to survey (RHS-RCH)
IFA: Taken iron folic acid tablets/syrup during pregnancy, TT: Taken 2 tetanus toxoid injections during pregnancy.
CU: Went for at least 3 antenatal check up, ANC: Antenatal care (3 check-ups, 2 tetanus toxoid injections and iron folic acid tablets/syrup).

REVIEW OF LITERATURE

The number of factors, which affect health services utilization, can broadly be classified into three groups: characteristics of the subject (predisposing factors), characteristics of the disorder (need factors), and characteristics of the service (enabling factors) (see Andersen, 1968; Kroeger, 1983, Andersen 1995). Different factors in this category are: family characteristics (age, gender, household size, marital status), social structure (education, employment, ethnicity), culture, and assets/affordability (land, livestock, cash income). As we have considered currently married women only, we have no scope to study impact of gender and marital status towards health seeking behaviour. Also, as RHS-RCH does not provide any information on culture, employment status, land, livestock, and cash income, we cannot study impact of those factors towards preference for maternal care.

Family Characteristics

According to Feldstein (1979), though illness is a random event, it has a fair degree of predictability with respect to demographic characteristics. As age-pattern of morbidity shows a U-shaped relationship, pattern of utilisation of care is also supposed to follow likely (see Pathak et. al., 1981). Size of a family may work in both directions. In a large family per capita income may be less and so also ability to pay for health care. It may reduce chances of utilising a care from modern source. On the contrary in larger families interaction among the members or with the neighbours may be more intensive and which may increase chances of utilising a care (Feldstein, 1979; Pathak et. al., 1983; Yesudian, 1989).

Social Structure

Impact of education towards utilisation of health services is universally acceptable. Among the significant studies on this issue, Elo (1992), Gobindasamy and Ramesh (1997), Kavitha and Audinarayana (1997), Dunlop et. al., (2000), and Matsumura and Gubhaju (2001) found significant positive relationship between education and utilisation of health care or maternal and child health care services.

Trakroo (1993) examined health-seeking behaviour of scheduled caste population in rural areas of Merut district in Uttar Pradesh, India. He found that non-scheduled caste mothers utilised the maternal and child health services better than scheduled caste mothers. Gobindasamy and Ramesh (1997) also found caste or ethnicity (two categories: scheduled caste/tribe and non-scheduled caste/tribe) and religion (three categories: Hindu, Muslim and other) as significant determinants of utilisation of all types of maternal health care services.

Celik and Hotchkiss (2000) investigated how different socio-economic factors affect women's use of maternal health care services in Turkey. In their study with some other socio-economic factors educational attainment, ethnicity (three categories: Turkish, Kurdish and others), have positive and statistically significant impact on the use of prenatal care and birth delivery assistance (Kurdish women are less likely to use prenatal care).

Affordability

Celik and Hotchkiss (2000) found that household wealth (owning a car, having a flush toilet and having a modern floor) was positively associated with the use of prenatal care and birth delivery assistance but their effect was statistically significant with the acceptance of birth delivery assistance. Dunlop et.al., (2000) found that Canadians with low income are less likely to visit specialists than those with moderate and high incomes.

Characteristics of the Disorder

Severity of illness (Pathak et.al., 1981; Sauerborn et. al., 1989), and over all need (Dunlop et. al., 2000) affect utilisation of health care. The higher the severity of perceived morbidity, the higher the degree of utilization of services. Different enabling factors in this category, which may affect utilisation of health care, are: availability of health facilities, accessibility to health care, appeal (opinion and attitudes towards traditional and modern healers), quality of care, and costs.

Availability of Health Facilities

RHS-RCH does not provide any information on availability of health facilities, accessibility to health care, appeal towards traditional and modern healers, and costs. However, one may consider type of locality (rural/urban) as a proxy measure of availability of health facilities with the assumption that in the urban areas health facilities are easily available (see Elo, 1992). Among the important studies, Feldstein (1967a) found that hospital output increases with the inputs (manpower, equipments, etc.). Frost and Francis (1979) also explained variability in hospital admission for British National Health Service by availability of beds.

Quality of Care

The term quality of care has different meaning to professionals of different fields. However, the International Conference on Population and Development in Cairo in 1994 has provided with a comprehensive guideline to assess quality of reproductive health care programmes. They have recommended four factors: provider-client information exchange, provider competence, interpersonal relations, and mechanisms to encourage continuity of medical care (UNFPA, 1995). With all other UN member countries India also incorporated these aspects in the present RCH programme.

GAPS IN RESEARCH

From the above review we get a number of factors, which affect utilization of health services in general. However, the above-mentioned studies did not give any clue how different factors influence choice regarding different types (public or private) of care. In such a situation we can look forward to do an econometric analysis to know precisely how the background characteristics of the respondents, and different socio-economic and demographic factors contribute to the probability of utilizing a public or private type of care during pregnancy.

In the present study as we have focused on reproductive health care and selected women in the reproductive span with similar needs and demographic characteristics, we need a synthesis of the above review from strategic point of view. Among the enabling factors, in the family characteristics category, we may keep 'age' and 'family size' in the analysis. Adverting to the need factors, we may consider complexities or 'health problems' during pregnancy and 'birth order' to examine whether these two have any influence on utilisation of different types of care.

RHS-RCH does not provide any information on household cash income. However, the survey provides information on 'type of house', and 'type of toilet facility' which can be used as a proxy measure of affordability of a household. We intend to include another variable: 'place of residence' which is supposed to reflect cultural differences between rural and urban societies sharply and also be a good proxy measure of availability and accessibility of health care. As of quality of care, we try to put more stress on the objectivity of the programme, the scientific process by which antenatal cares are delivered. We have focussed on various components of the maternal care services, and whether one mother has received those or not. We also look forward to do a regional analysis and hence include a dummy variable 'region' to capture all other differences (which will not be captured by other variables) like dissimilarities in governance, economy, geography or climatic conditions, etc.

METHODOLOGY

Definition of the Variables

As per the scope of the study and according to the availability of data, the present study included the following set of explanatory variables, and response variable as shown in table 4. The first row shows the response variable and the remaining ones show predictor variables all of which are categorical.

Table 4
Response and Predictor Variables

Variable	*Definition*	*Value*
Utilisation	Whether the respondent visited any public health facility since 01 January 1996 till the date of survey for antenatal check up	1 if the event has occurred, 0 Otherwise.
Age	Age of the woman (15-34, 35-44)	1 if age 35-44, 0 otherwise.
Family size	Number of persons in the household	1 if size > 5 0 otherwise.
Education of the respondent	Number of completed years of education (≤ 3, 4-10, 10+)	1 if 4 ≤ years ≤ 10, 0 otherwise; 1 if years > 10, 0 otherwise.

Contd...

Variable	*Definition*	*Value*
Husband's education	Whether husband can read or write	1 if yes, 0 otherwise.
Caste	Caste of the respondent (General /SC / ST)	1 if SC, 0 otherwise; 1 if ST, 0 otherwise.
Religion	Religion of the respondent (Hindu/Muslim/Other)	1 if Muslim, 0 otherwise; 1 if other religion, 0 otherwise.
Affordability (1)	Type of house (Pucca/Semi-pucca/Kachcha) [Pucca: Concrete structure; Kachcha: Muddy floor/structure]	1 if semi-pucca, 0 otherwise; 1 if pucca, 0 otherwise.
Affordability (2)	Whether the household has any type of toilet facility	1 if yes, 0 otherwise.
Health problems	A composite index (0-1 scale) of patient's suffering on swelling of hands and feet (yes/no), paleness (yes/no), weakness or tiredness (yes/no), dizziness (yes/no), visual disturbances (yes/no), bleeding (yes/no), convulsions (yes/no), weak or no movement of foetus (yes/no), abnormal presentation (yes/no), any other problem (yes/no).	1 if high (> 0.5), 0 otherwise.
Birth order	Order of birth	1 if order > 2, 0 otherwise.
Availability of health facilities	Measured by place of residence (rural/urban) with the assumption that health facilities are easily available in urban areas	1 if urban, 0 otherwise.
Quality of care	Composite index (0-1 scale) on whether weight of a pregnant mother was taken (yes/no), blood pressure was measured (yes/no), given Iron Folic Acid tablets (yes/no), given tetanus toxoid injection (yes/no), Auxiliary Nurse Midwives visited home for check-up (yes/no), and advised for institutional delivery (yes/no)	1 if high (> 0.5), 0 otherwise
Region	Respondent's geographical region: *South* (Andhra Pradesh, Karnataka, Kerala, Maharashtra, Tamil Nadu)/*East* (Assam, Orissa, West Bengal)/*North* (Bihar, Gujarat, Haryana, Jammu and Kashmir, Madhya Pradesh, Punjab, Rajasthan, Uttar Pradesh).	1 if East, 0 otherwise; 1 if North, 0 otherwise

Source: Own Elaboration

The Model

Let P be the estimated probability of utilising public health facilities. In probability form, the model is:

$$P = \frac{1}{1 + e\,\beta_0 + \Sigma\,\beta_{1i}X_{1i} + \Sigma\,\beta_{2i}X_{2i} + \Sigma\,\beta_{3i}X_{3i}} \quad \ldots \quad \ldots \quad \text{(i)}$$

In log odds form, the model is:

$$\text{Log } \Omega = \beta_0 + \Sigma\, \beta_{1i} X_{1i} + \Sigma\, \beta_{2i} X_{2i} + \Sigma\, \beta_{3i} X_{3i} \quad \ldots \quad \ldots \quad \text{(ii)}$$

In odds form the model is:

$$\Omega = (\beta_0 + \Sigma\, \beta_{1i} X_{1i} + \Sigma\, \beta_{2i} X_{2i} + \Sigma\, \beta_{3i} X_{3i}) \quad \ldots \quad \ldots \quad \text{(iii)}$$

The equations include predisposing (X_{1i}), need (X_{2i}), and enabling (X_{3i}) factors. The variable 'region' has been accommodated in the final category. One model will be estimated taking all the 16 major States together, and 3 separate models for Southern, Eastern, and Northern regions.

RESULTS AND DISCUSSION

Descriptive Statistics

Table 5 shows descriptive statistics on pattern of utilisation of care (utilisation of public health facilities) as well on other explanatory variables. The table is self-explanatory and results can be read from it easily. For example, on an average 57 per cent of the eligible women in reproductive span in India utilised at least one public health facility. Among the regions, preference for public type of care is the highest in the Eastern region (69.5%) and lowest in the Southern region (46.7%).

Table 5
Descriptive Statistics

Variable	*Category*	*South*		*East*		*North*		*India*	
		n	*%*	*n*	*%*	*n*	*%*	*n*	*%*
Utilisation	Yes	5898	46.7	5342	69.5	14709	58.9	25950	57.3
	No	6738	53.3	2340	30.5	10250	41.1	19328	42.7
Age of the respondent	Young	12152	96.2	7222	94	22618	90.6	41993	92.7
	Old	484	3.8	460	6	2341	9.4	3284	7.3
Family size	Small	5772	45.7	3633	47.3	7246	29	28626	36.8
	Large	6864	54.3	4049	52.7	17713	71	16652	63.2
Education of the respondent	High	1870	14.8	739	9.6	2665	10.7	5274	11.6
	Medium	6065	48	3364	43.8	8668	34.7	18097	40
	Low	4701	37.2	3579	46.6	13626	54.6	21906	48.4
Husband's literacy	Literate	9665	76.5	5561	72.4	19334	80.5	34560	76.3
	Illiterate	2971	23.5	2121	27.6	5625	19.5	10717	23.7
Caste	General	9715	76.9	5377	70	18723	75	33816	74.7
	SC	2239	17.8	1497	19.5	4859	19.5	8595	20
	ST	682	5.3	808	10.5	1377	5.5	2866	6.3
Religion	Hindu	10001	79	5908	77	19224	77	35133	77.6
	Muslim	1758	14	1616	21	3774	15	7148	15.8
	Other	877	7	158	2	1961	8	2996	6.6
Affordability–House (1)	High	4248	33.6	1439	18.7	9915	39.7	15601	34.4
	Medium	5881	46.5	1518	19.8	8166	32.7	15565	34.4
	Low	2507	19.9	4725	61.5	6878	27.6	14111	31.2
Affordability–Toilet (2)	Yes	5663	44.8	3339	43.5	9238	37	18240	40.3
	No	6973	55.2	4343	56.5	15721	63	27037	59.7

Contd...

Variable	*Category*	*South*		*East*		*North*		*India*	
		n	%	*n*	%	*n*	%	*n*	%
Health problems	High	224	1.8	199	2.6	496	2	918	2
	Low	12412	98.2	7483	97.4	24463	98	44359	98
Birth order	High	5733	45.4	3709	48.3	15762	36.8	25204	55.7
	Low	6903	54.6	3973	51.7	9197	63.2	20073	44.3
Availability of health facilities	Yes	4271	66.2	1617	21.1	6016	24.1	11904	26.3
	No	8365	33.8	6065	78.9	18944	75.9	33373	73.7
Quality of care	High	11360	89.9	4600	40.1	10907	43.7	26867	59.3
	Low	1276	10.1	3082	59.9	14052	56.3	18410	40.7
Region	South	-	-	-	-	-	-	12636	27.9
	East	-	-	-	-	-	-	7682	16.9
	North	-	-	-	-	-	-	24969	55.2
Total (for each variable)*	12636	100	7682	100	24959	100	45277	100	

Source: Own elaboration;, * Except for 'Region' at regional level.

Results of Multivariate Analyses

(a) Characteristics of the Subject

Table 6 shows results of multivariate analyses. The columns display odds ratios interpretations of which are straightforward. The odds ratio of 'age of the respondent' in the Northern region is 1.133. It conveys that a change in the category of age from low (0) to high (1), holding other variables constant (henceforth we will not mention it), multiplies the odds by 0.113 (a 11.3 per cent increase). This effect is statistically significant at 0.05 level. It tells that, as compared to the younger ones, aged women in Northern India are likely to utilise public health facilities more. However, the effect of age group found to be statistically significant in the Northern region only. Impact of family size is found negative in Southern region and in India as a whole. In larger families probability of utilising a public health care is low.

Among other characteristics of the subject, respondent's education, and husband's literacy draw our special attention. Educated women and their husbands are expected to utilise private health facilities more. And this effect is well built in persons who are highly educated in all regions. Ethnic factors like caste and religion has less bearing on the preference for a particular type of care in the Eastern region. In other regions, women belong to scheduled caste and tribe groups have a strong tendency to utilise public health facilities. The Muslim and other religious communities, on the other hand, are probable to utilise private health facility more (except in the Northern region). Having a toilet facility in a household reduces the chances of using a public health care. Similarly, affordability of a household also restricts peoples' choices towards utilising public health care. Highly affordable households have, however, some preference for public type of care in the Northern region.

Table 6
Odds ratios [Exp (b)] of Utilization of Public Health Facilities in India

Predictor variables	*South*	*East*	*North*	*India*
Characteristics of the subject				
Age of the respondent (rc: young)				
Old	ns	ns	1.133**	ns
Family size (rc: small)				
Large	.898**	ns	.938*	.936**
Education of the respondent (rc: low)				
Medium education	.713***	.750***	.857***	.796***
High education	.366***	.431***	.503***	.426***
Husbands literacy (rc: illiterate)				
Literate	.801***	ns	ns	.892***
Caste (rc: general)				
Scheduled caste	1.774***	ns	1.396***	1.431***
Scheduled tribe	1.400***	ns	1.565***	1.432***
Religion (rc: Hindu)				
Muslim	ns	.706***	1.088*	.960***
Other religion	.808**	ns	ns	ns
Affordability-1 (rc: low)				
Medium	.904*	.794***	ns	.918**
High	.519***	.435***	1.125**	.795***
Affordability-2 (rc: no toilet facility)				
Have toilet facility	.839***	.809***	.753***	.789***
Characteristics of the disorder				
Health problems (rc: low)				
High	1.520**	.672*	ns	ns
Birth order (rc: low)				
High	1.280***	1.222***	1.085**	1.156***
Characteristics of the service				
Availability of health facility (rc: rural)				
Urban	1.164***	.813**	.709***	.859***
Quality of care (rc: low)				
High	ns	ns	.654***	.783***
Region (rc: South)				
Northern region	-	-	-	1.344***
Eastern region	-	-	-	2.195***

Source: Own elaboration; rc: Reference category; ns: Not significant; ***p<0.01, **p<0.05, *p <0.1.

(b) Characteristics of the Disorder

The odds ratio of high health problems in the Southern region, when it is compared with the low category, is 1.520. It conveys It conveys that pregnant women of Southern India with higher complexities or health problems are likely to utilise public health facilities more. The fact is quite reverse in the Eastern region where odds ratio decreases approximately by 33 per cent [(1–0.672)/1=0.328]. It conveys that women with complex health problems in the Eastern India are likely to utilise private health facilities more. Odds ratios of 'birth order' indicate that women with higher order of birth have a tendency to utilise public health facilities more.

(c) Characteristics of the Service

Though in the urban areas both sophisticated public and private health facilities are easily available, mere urbanism restrains people from utilising public type of care (except in the Southern region). In the Southern region urban dwellers are credible to utilise public facility for maternal health care services. The effect of quality of care has been found significant in the Northern region and in India as a whole. High quality of care sharply reduces the odds ratios of utilisation of public health facilities (in the Northern region and India as a whole). It tacitly indicates that by and large people experience higher quality of care in private health facilities. When we compare the odds ratios of the Eastern and Northern region with that of the Southern one (the final variable), we see that probability of utilising public health facilities jumps sharply. In other wards, if other things remain the same women in Eastern India strongly prefers public health care services.

CONCLUSION

We have seen that with poor health care infrastructure, and poor status of health India is on the mid-way to the desired level of development. It is well understood that public health care system which has a nation-wide network of delivering health and family welfare related services, has the crucial role to achieve that desired level of development. However, acceptability or utilisation of public health care across culture and societies in India is very poor. As the Southern region is the most demographically advanced in India, we will see whether we can take any lesson from its experience. We have seen that odds ratios of high 'health problems', high 'birth order', 'scheduled caste' and 'scheduled tribe', and 'availability of health facilities' (or place of residence) indicate chances of higher utilisation of public health facilities. On the other hand, odds ratios of large 'family size', medium and higher 'education of the respondent', 'husband's literacy', 'other religion', 'having toilet facility', and medium and high 'affordability' point towards utilisation of private health facilities. In such a situation (relaxing necessary econometric technicalities), if we assume that in the process of development health problems during pregnancy reduces, birth order comes down, and urban growth tends to stop in the upper asymptotes of its logistic pattern of growth, the credibility of the public health care system in the Southern region will be deemed to some ethnic groups only. The system may face severe crisis if the light of education touches more and more people and cultural values get worthy gradually.

A careful revision of the results would confirm that situation is almost same in other regions also and in India as whole. However, if other things remain the same, prospects of public health care system is better in the Eastern region as compared to the Southern one. If things change as above, future of the system is very uncertain in the Eastern region also. In such a situation, the only instrument in the hands of Government is to raise quality of care in the public health facilities through quantitative development in infrastructure. Failure to achieve this goal may cause serious set back of the system again in future pushing back the goal of 'Health For All' further.

REFERENCES

Andersen R.M. (1968), A Behavioral Model of Families' Use of Health Services, *Research Series No. 25*, Centre for Health Administration, University of Chicago: Chicago.

Andersen, R.M. (1995), Revisiting the Behavioural Model and Access to Medical Care: Does it Matter?, *Journal of Health and Social Behaviour,* 36: 1–10.

Celik, Y. and Hotchkiss, D.R (2000), The Socio-Economic Determinants of Maternal Health Care Utilisation in Turkey, *Social Science and Medicine*, 50 (12): 1797–1806.

Dunlop. S., P.C. Coyte and W. Mclsaac (2000), Socio-Economic Status and the Utilisation of Physicians' Services: Results from the Canadian National Population Health Survey, *Social Science and Medicine*, 51 (1): 123–133.

Elo, I.T. (1992), Utilisation of Maternal Health Care Services in Peru: The Role of Women's Education, *Health Transition Review*, 2 (1): 1–20.

Feldstein, M.S. (1967a), *Economic Analysis for Health Service Efficiency: Econometric Studies of the British National Health Service*, North-Holland: Amsterdam.

Feldstein, M.S. (1967b), An Aggregate Planning Model of the Health Care Sector, *Medical Care*, 5: 369–381.

Feldstein, P.J. (1979), *Health Care Economics,* John Wiley & Sons: New York.

Gobindasamy, P. and B.M. Ramesh (1997), *Maternal Education and the Utilisation of Maternal and Child Health Services in India, National Family Health Survey Subject Reports, Number 5*, International Institute for Population Sciences, Mumbai, Macro International Inc.: U.S.A.

Kavitha, N. and Audinarayana (1997), Utilisation and Determinants of Selected MCH Services in Rural Areas of Tamil Nadu, *Health and Population–Perspectives and Issues,* 20 (3): 112–125.

Kroeger, A. (1983), Anthropological and Socio-Medical Health Care Research in Developing Countries, *Social Science and Medicine*, 17 (3): 147–161.

Matsumura, M. and B. Gubhaju (2001), Women's Status, Household Structure and the Utilisation of Maternal Health Services in Nepal, *Asia Pacific Population Journal*, 16 (1): 23–44.

Pathak, M., Y.A. Ketkar and R.D. Majumdar (1981), Perceived Morbidity, Utilisation of Health Services and Factor Affecting It in a Rural Area, *Health and Population-Perspective and Issues*, 4 (1): 79–85.

Ramachandran, H. and G.S. Shastri (1983), Movement For Medical Treatment–A Study In Contact Patterns of a Rural Population, *Social Science and Medicine*, 17 (3): 177–187.

Sauerborn, R., A. Nougtara and H.J. Diesfeld (1989), Low Utilisation of Community Health Workers: Results from a Household Interview Survey in Burkina Faso, *Social Science and Medicine,* 29 (10): 1163–1174.

Singh P. (2000), *Health Protection in India–In the Year 2000,* Friedrich-Ebert-Stiftung: New Delhi.

Trakroo, P.L (1993), Patterns of Seeking Medical Care among Scheduled Castes and Non-Scheduled Castes in Rural Areas, *Health and Population–Perspectives and Issues*, 16 (3 & 4): 151–163.

UNFPA (1995), *The State of World Population,* UNFPA: New York.

Yesudian, C.A.K. (1989), *Health Services Utilisation in Urban India*, Mittal Publications: Delhi.

11

INDUSTRIAL SECTOR GROWTH ACCOUNTING: A DATA ENVELOPMENT ANALYSIS (EXPERIENCES OF SOME INDIAN STATES AND UNION TERRITORIES)

Somesh K. Mathur and Sahid Ahmed

INTRODUCTION

Very much in the spirit of Quah's (1993, 1996, and 1997) suggested approach (also adopted by Jones (1997), we analyze the evolution of the entire distribution of the three growth factors of net value added: technological change, technological catch-up, and capital accumulation[2]. We analyze the contribution of these three components to the growth of Indian States net value added per worker and to the shift in the states distribution of net value added per worker over time. Data envelopment analysis has been used to estimate the best production frontier .The states production frontier is constructed using deterministic methods requiring no specification of functional form for the technology nor any assumption about market structure or the absence of market imperfections. Technological catch up signifies movement towards the frontier, technical change is movement of the frontier, and capital accumulation is movement along the frontier and human capital accumulation implying changes in the efficiency of labor.

Quah (1993, 1996, and 1997) has argued compellingly that analyses based on standard regression methods focusing on first moments of the distribution cannot adequately address the convergence issue. These arguments are buttressed by the empirical analyses of Quah (1993, 1996, and 1997) posing a robust stylized fact about the international growth pattern that begs for explanation. A plot of the distribution of net value added per worker across Indian 22 states in 1997-98 and 1980 appears in Figures 1 and 2 respectively, above. Over 17-18 year period, the distribution of net value added per worker was transformed from a uni-modal distribution in 1980-81 into a multi modal distribution in 1997-98 with a higher mean. This transformation in turn means that, while in 1980-81 there were states under one single peak distribution of net value added per worker, in 1997-98 the Indian industry net value added per worker has divided, as a stylized fact, states into many categories symbolizing regional variations across Indian states in terms of net value added per worker.

Our analysis is aimed at explaining this bipolarization of the distribution of net value added per worker, as well as its growth pattern, in terms of the tripartite decomposition described below. As such, it builds upon Quah's insights about the need to examine the "dynamics of the entire cross-section distribution" (Quah, 1997, p. 29). In this study we will further identify policies, which may reduce differential levels of net value, added per worker and growth rates across Indian states and work out the reasons for the existence of multi-modal distribution. The main variable used will be net value added per worker prevailing in different Indian states included in our study.

Figure 1: Kernel Distribution, 1980-81 of the Net Value Added Per Worker for 22 Indian States

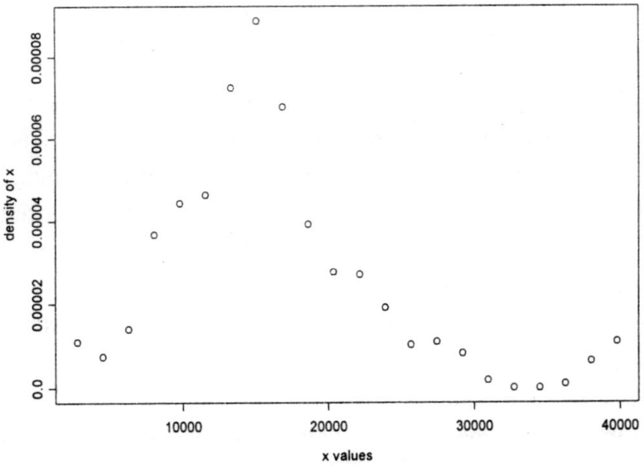

REVIEW OF LITERATURE: EMPIRICS OF GROWTH

The results of total factor productivity differ due to different assumptions made in respect of production functions and limitations of data availability on productivity of capital and labor and quality of workers. Kumar and Russell (2002) and Henderson and Russell (2003) studies are exceptions. Kumar and Russell (2002) use frontier methods to analyze international macroeconomic convergence. In particular, they decompose the labour-productivity growth of

Figure 2: Kernel Distribution, 1997-98 of the Net Value Added Per Worker for 22 Indian States

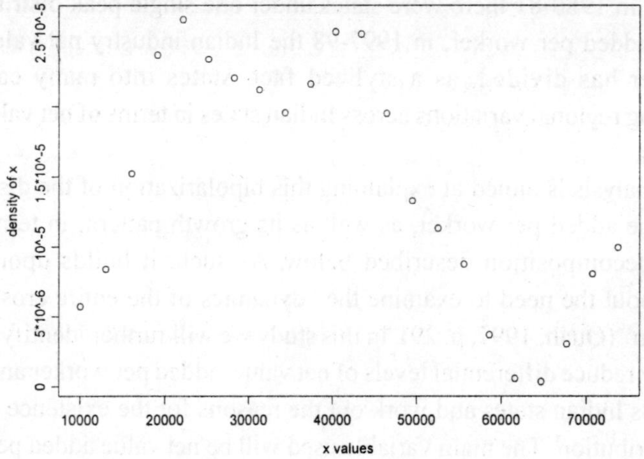

57 industrial, newly industralized, and developing countries into components attributable to (1) technological change (shifts in the world production frontier), (2) technological catch-up (movements toward or away from the frontier), and (3) capital accumulation (movement along the frontier). These calculations amount to standard growth accounting with a twist—without the need for specification of a functional form for the technology, for the assumption that technological change is neutral, or for assumptions about market structure or the absence of market imperfections. Indeed, market imperfections, as well as technical inefficiencies, are possible reasons for countries falling below the worldwide production frontier. Taking a cue from the Quah critique spelled out in the introduction of this study, Kumar and Russell (2002) go on to analyze the evolution of the entire distribution of these three growth factors.

Although the analysis of Kumar and Russell (2002) is quite simple, it yields somewhat striking results:

1. While there is substantial evidence of technological catch-up (movements toward the production frontier), with the degree of catch-up directly related to initial distance from the frontier, this factor apparently has not contributed to convergence, since the degree of catch-up appears not to be related to initial productivity.
2. Technological change is decidedly non-neutral, with no improvement—indeed, possibly some implosion—at very low capital/labour ratios, modest expansion at relatively low capital/labor ratios, and rapid expansion at high capital/labor ratios.
3. Both growth and bimodal polarization are driven primarily by capital deepening.

Henderson and Russell (2003) introduce human capital into the Kumar and Russell (2002) growth accounting analysis of international macroeconomic convergence. Henderson and Russell (2003) amend the Kumar and Russell (2002) methodology by (1) adopting the Diewert (1980) approach to dynamic frontier analysis, thus precluding implosion of the worldwide production frontier over time and (a) changes in the mean and (b) mean-preserving shifts in the distribution of productivity. Their principal conclusions were:

1. Over half of the increase in means productivity attributed to KR to the accumulation of physical capital was, in fact, the result of the accumulation of human capital.
2. In contradiction to the Kumar and Russell (2002) conclusion that capital accumulation also accounts for the shift in the distribution, primarily from unimodal to bimodal, their analysis indicates that efficiency changes account for the qualitative shift from unimodal to bimodal, whereas the accumulation of physical and human capital account for the increased worldwide dispersion of productivity.
3. There is evidence of technological progress in the developed nations only.

In this study we also do growth accounting with a twist-without the need for specification of a functional form for the technology, for the assumption that technological change is neutral, or for the assumptions about market structure or the absence of market imperfections. We use sample of 22 Indian states. The objective is to study the net value added per worker distribution across time and try to identify the reasons for its deformation across time.

OBJECTIVES AND HYPOTHESES

The main objectives of the present paper are:

1. To work out the efficiency index, technological catch up. (movement towards or away from the frontier), technical changes (shifts in the overall production frontier) and capital accumulation(movement along the frontier) indexes for the Indian Industries across states and across the years;
2. To undertake growth accounting exercise, which can decompose net value, added growth into components attributable to technological changes, technological catch up and capital accumulation; and
3. To identify reasons for the existence of multi-modal net value added distribution prevailing across Indian States by analyzing the evolution of the determinants of cross states net value added per worker over time for the 22 states included in our sample.

In consonance with the objectives of the study, the following hypotheses are proposed:

1. To test whether technological change, technological catch up and capital accumulation are primarily responsible for differential growth in net value added per worker across states and are also responsible for the existence of multi-modal net value added per worker distribution across Indian States included in our sample.
2. Efficiency across Indian states has increased over the years.
3. Smaller States tend to have higher efficiency than larger states.

METHODOLOGY

For the growth accounting exercise (net value added per worker decomposition into its three factors), we consider a sample of 22 states over the period 1980-81-1997-98,using data from the Annual Survey of Industries. Our measure of aggregate output is net value added per worker calculated at constant 1980-81 prices. Aggregate inputs used in the model are fixed capital and labour force (proxied by number of employees) Appropriate deflator was used to estimate fixed capital stock and net value added per worker at constant 1980-81 prices. The input output data is available with the authors.

We decompose labor productivity into its components, efficiency change, technological change and capital accumulation. The level of efficiency for each state has been worked out using Data Envelopment Analysis (DEA)[3] for all years in the interval period starting from 1980-81 through 1997-98.Technological change reflects shifts in the world production frontier, determined conceptually by the state-of-the-art, potentially transferable technology; while efficiency change reflects the movements toward (or away from) the frontier as countries adopt "best practice" technologies and reduce (or exacerbate) technical and allocative inefficiencies; and the third capital accumulation reflects movements along the frontier. The states production frontier at each point in time is constructed using deterministic, nonparametric (mathematical programming) methods (essentially, finding the smallest convex cone enveloping the data) and efficiency is measured as the (output-based) distance from the frontier. These data-driven methods do not require specification of any particular functional form for the technology, nor do they require any assumption about market structure or about the absence of market imperfections; market imperfections, as well as technical inefficiencies, are possible reasons for countries falling below the worldwide production frontier.

Non Parametric Construction of Technologies and Efficiency Measurement (Technological Catch Up)

Our approach to constructing the Indian States production frontier and associated efficiency levels of individual states (distances from the frontier), motivated in part by the first such effort in this direction by Fare et. al., (1994a), followed by Kumar and Russell (2002) and Henderson and Russell (2003) which in turn is based on the pioneering work of Farrell (1956) and Afriat (1972). The basic idea is to envelop the data in the "smallest", or "tightest fitting", convex cone, and the (upper) boundary of this set then represents the "best practice" production frontier. Although this data-driven approach, implemented with standard mathematical programming algorithms, requires no specification of functional form, it does require an assumption about returns to scale of the technology (as well as free input and output disposability).

In our simple case, we deal with only three macroeconomic variables: aggregate output and two aggregate inputs: labor and capital. Let (Y^j_t, L^j_t, K^j_t), $t = 1,.., T, j = 1,...J$, represent T observations on these three variables for each of the J countries. The constant-returns-to-scale reference technology (the "Farrell cone") for the world in period t is defined by

$$\tau_1 = \left\{ (Y, L, K) \in R^3_+ \mid Y \le \sum_j z^j Y^j_t, L \ge \sum_j z^j L^j_t, K \ge \sum_j z^j K^j_t, z^j \ge 0 \forall j \right\} \quad (1)$$

In this construction, each observation is interpreted as a unit operation of a linear process, zj represents the level of operation of the process and every point in the technology set a linear combination of observed output/input vectors or a point dominated by a linear combination of observed points. The constructed technology is a polyhedral cone, and isoquants are piecewise linear.[4]

Or course, typically some observed input-output combinations will be redundant in constructing the technologies, in that the observed output can be produced by some other process (generated by an alternative observed input-output vector) or by some linear combination of other processes using less of one input and no more of the other. These dominated processes are technologically inefficient. The Farrell (output-based) efficiency index for country) at time t is defined by

$$E\,(Y^j_t, L^j_t, K^j_t) = \min \left\{ \lambda \mid (Y^j_t / \lambda, L^j_t, K^j_t) \in \tau_t \right\} \quad (2)$$

This index is the inverse of the maximal proportional amount that output Y^j_t can be expanded while remaining technologically feasible given the technological τ_t and the input quantities L^j_t and K^j_t it is less than or equal to 1 and takes the value of 1 if and only if the jt observation is on of the period t production frontier. In this case of a scalar output, the output-based efficiency index is simply the ratio of actual to potential output evaluated at the actual input quantities, but in multiple-output technologies the index is a radial measure of the (proportional) distance of the actual output vector from the production frontier.

The Farrell efficiency index can be calculated by solving the following linear program for each observation:

min λ subject to

$\lambda, z^1, \ldots, z^j$

$$Y^j / \lambda \leq \sum_k z^k Y_t^k$$

$$L^j \geq \sum_k z^k L_t^k$$

$$K^j \geq \sum_k z^k K_t^k$$

$$z^k \geq 0 \forall k.$$

The solution value of λ in this problem is the value of the efficiency index for country *j* at time *t*.

Tripartite Decomposition of the Factors Affecting Labour Productivity

The decomposition of the factors affecting net value added per worker growth exploits the assumption of constant returns to scale, in which case the benchmark technology sets can be drawn in (k, y) space, where $k = K/L$ and $y = Y/L$. Very simple hypothetical (polyhedral) technologies for two periods, say a base period b and a current period c, are drawn in Figure 3 below. In this

Figure 3: Illustration of Tripartite Decomposition of Labour Productivity

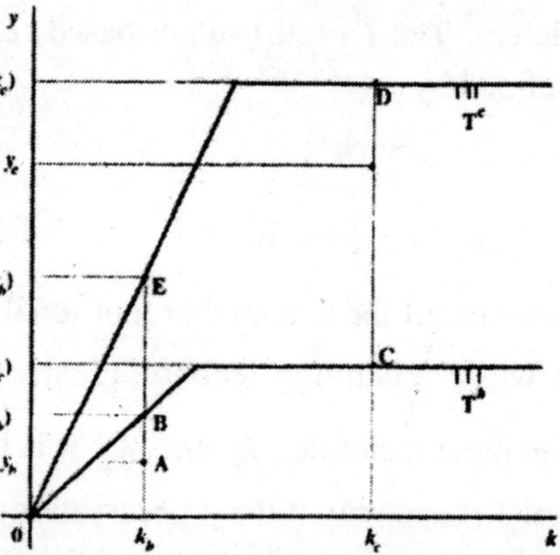

simple example, the single kink in each of the polyhedral technologies would indicate that a single state–the only efficiency state–defines the frontier.

The two points, (k_b, y_b) and (k_c, y_c), represent observed values of the two ratios in the two periods for some hypothetical states. By construction, potential outputs for this economy in the two periods are $\overline{y}_b(k_b) = y_b/e_b$ and $\overline{y}_c(k_c) = y_c/e_c$, where e_b and e_c are the values of the efficiency indexes in the two periods, calculated as in (4) above. Therefore,

$$\frac{y_c}{y_b} = \frac{e_c \times \overline{y}_c(k_c)}{e_b \times \overline{y}_b(k_b)} \tag{x}$$

Multiplying top and bottom by $\overline{y}_b(k_c)$, the potential output labor ratio at current period capital intensity using the base period technology, we obtain

$$\frac{y_c}{y_b} = \frac{e_c}{e_b} \times \frac{\overline{y}_c(k_c)}{\overline{y}_b(k_c)} \times \frac{\overline{y}_b(k_c)}{\overline{y}_b(k_b)} \tag{xi}$$

This identify decomposes the relative change in the output-labor ratio in the two periods into (i) the change in efficiency–i.e., the change in the distance from the frontier (the first term on the right); (ii) the technology change–i.e., the shift in the frontier (the second term); and (iii) the effect of the change in the capital labor ratio–i.e., movement along the frontier (the third term).

The decomposition in (xi) measures technological change by the shift in the frontier in the output direction at the current period capital labor ratio from point C to point D in Figure V and it measures the effect of capital accumulation along the base-period frontier–from point B to point C. We can alternatively measures technological change at the base-period capital-labor ratio–from point B to point E in Figure Vand capital accumulation by movements along the current period frontier from point E to point D by multiplying the top and bottom of (x) by the potential output labor ratio at base period capital intensity using the current period technology, yielding the decomposition,

$$\frac{y_c}{y_b} = \frac{e_c}{e_b} \times \frac{\overline{y}_c(k_b)}{\overline{y}_b(k_b)} \times \frac{\overline{y}_c(k_c)}{\overline{y}_c(k_b)} \tag{xii}$$

Thus, the decomposition of (discrete) net value added per worker changes (not attributable to efficiency changes) into the technological change and capital-deepening components is path dependent, and the choice between (xi) and (xii) is arbitrary. There is no avoiding this arbitrariness, unless technological change is Hicks neutral, in which case the proportional vertical shift in the frontier is independent of the value of the capital labor ratio. It is this assumption (along with constant returns to scale) that enabled Solow (1957), and the legions of growth accountants who have followed his lead, to unambiguously decompose productivity growth into components attributable to technological change and capital deepening. But without constraining technological change to be Hicks neutral, the proportional (vertical) shift in the frontier varies in unspecified ways. In fact, this arbitrariness is not, per se, attributable to the decomposition itself. It is endemic to the basic task of measuring technological change, as is evident in the necessity of normalizing on one of two technologies in the (Malmquist) productivity index proposed in the pioneering paper of Caves et al. (1982).

We follow the approach of Caves et. al. (1982) and Fare et. al. (1994b) by adopting the "Fisher ideal" decomposition, based on geometric averages of the two measures of the effects of technological change and capital accumulation, obtained by multiplying top and bottom of (x) by $(\bar{y}_b(k_c)\bar{y}_c(k_b))^{1/2}$.

$$\frac{y_c}{y_b} = \frac{e_c}{e_b}\left(\frac{\bar{y}_c(k_c)}{\bar{y}_b(k_c)} \times \frac{\bar{y}_c(k_b)}{\bar{y}_b(k_b)}\right)^{1/2}$$

$$\times \left(\frac{\bar{y}_b(k_c)}{\bar{y}_b(k_b)} \times \frac{\bar{y}_c(k_c)}{\bar{y}_c(k_b)}\right)^{1/2}$$

=: EFF × TECH × KACCUM.

Kernel Densities

We employ kernel based density functions for estimating the cross-country labor productivity distribution for various years. The density estimates are computed using the Rosenblatt-Parzen kernel density estimator. We use an optimal bandwidth parameter chosen as h=1.0592*σ*N^(-.20) where s is the standard deviation of the data and N is the number of observations. Splus software has been used to estimate the Kernel smoothers.

A conceptually simple approach to a representation of the weight sequence $\left[W_{ni}(X)_{i=1}^{n}\right]$ is to describe the shape of the weight function $W_{ni}(X)$ by a density function with a scale parameter that adjusts the size and the form of the weights near x. It is quite common to refer to this shape function as a kernel K. The kernel is continuous, bounded and symmetric real function K that integrates,

$fK(u)du = 1$.

The weight sequence for kernel smoothers (for one-dimensional x) is defined by

$$W_{ni}(x) = K_{h_n}(x - X_i) / \hat{f}_{h_n}(x) \qquad \text{(xiii)}$$

where

$$\hat{f}_{h_n}(x) = n^{-1}\sum_{i=1}^{n} K_{h_n}(x - X_i) \qquad \text{(xiv)}$$

and where

$$K_{h_n}(u) = h_n^{-1} K(u/h_n)$$

is the kernel with scale factor h_n. Suppressing the dependence of $h = h_n$ on the sample size n, the kernel weight sequence is conveniently abbreviated as $\{W_{hi}(x)\}_{i=1}^{n}$. The function $\hat{f}_h(.)$ in (xiv) is the Rosenblatt-Parzen kernel density estimator (Rosenblatt, 1956; Parzen, 1962) of the (marginal) density of X. The form of kernel weights $W_{hi}(x)$ in (xiii) has been proposed by Watson (1964) and therefore

$$\hat{m}_h(x) = \frac{n^{-1}\sum_{i=1}^{n} K_h(x - X_i)Y_i}{n^{-1}\sum_{i=1}^{n} K_h(x - X_i)}$$

is often called the Nadaraya–Watson estimator. *K* determines the shape of the kernel weights, whereas the size of the weights is parameterized by *h*, which is called the bandwidth.

DISCUSSION OF RESULTS

Technical Catch Up (Efficiency Levels)

Table 1 and 2 lists the efficiency levels of each of the 22 states for the years 1980-81 through 1997-98. Efficiency indexes are calculated from the input and output data for the 22 states included in our study.

Table 1

Efficiency Index of Indian States 1980-1 to 1984-5 to 1984-85

Indian States	*1980-81*	*1981-82*	*1982-83*	*1983-84*	*1984-85*
Andhra Pradesh	0.47	0.57	0.7	0.69	0.72
Assam	0.56	0.77	0.85	1	1
Bihar	0.37	0.67	0.66	0.83	0.55
Goa	1	0.55	1	0.59	0.9
Gujarat	0.71	0.75	0.73	0.86	0.79
Haryana	0.74	0.83	0.81	0.91	0.67
Himachal Pradesh	0.8	1	1	0.95	0.63
Karnataka	0.73	0.8	0.83	0.95	0.84
Kerala	0.73	0.78	0.76	0.67	0.85
Madhya Pradesh	0.63	0.73	0.71	0.58	0.5
Maharastra	1	1	1	1	1
Meghalaya	0.59	0.32	0.33	0.32	0.27
Orrisa	0.54	0.56	0.44	0.49	0.34
Punjab	0.59	0.58	0.5	1	0.49
Rajasthan	0.56	0.59	0.47	0.65	0.51
Tamil Nadu	0.87	0.91	1	0.85	0.94
Tripura	0.34	0.42	0.76	0.55	0.89
Uttar Pradesh	0.41	0.74	0.59	0.45	0.45

Indian States	*1980-81*	*1981-82*	*1982-83*	*1983-84*	*1984-85*
West Bengal	0.89	0.88	0.87	0.74	0.72
Andaman Nicobar Islands	0.91	0.91	0.75	1	0.36
Delhi	0.63	0.73	0.8	0.83	0.78
Pondicherry	1	1	1	0.95	1
Mean Across States	0.685	0.731364	0.752727	0.766364	0.690909

Table 2
Efficiency Indexes of Indian States: 1985-86 to 1997-98

1985-86	*1986-87*	*1987-88*	*1988-89*	*1989-90*	*1990-91*	*1991-92*	*1992-93*	*1993-94*	*1994-95*	*1995-96*	*1996-97*	*1997-98*	*Mean over the years*
0.45	0.46	0.39	0.37	0.34	0.28	0.21	0.32	0.29	0.36	0.6	0.34	0.35	0.439
1	0.88	0.95	0.41	0.82	0.72	0.43	0.54	0.57	0.6	0.72	0.42	0.3	0.697
0.56	0.63	0.81	0.7	0.65	0.65	0.57	0.62	0.9	0.61	0.6	0.76	1	0.674
1	1	0.88	1	1	1	1	1	1	1	1	1	1	0.94
0.59	0.66	0.71	0.6	0.53	0.59	0.37	0.8	0.59	0.78	0.66	0.72	0.51	0.664
0.53	0.59	0.64	0.53	0.51	0.65	0.45	0.5	0.47	0.55	0.84	0.69	0.53	0.636
0.76	0.79	0.64	0.59	0.47	0.65	0.48	0.52	0.66	0.58	0.48	0.58	0.58	0.676
0.68	0.72	0.75	0.58	0.67	0.73	0.61	0.81	0.66	0.69	0.8	0.61	0.38	0.713
0.59	0.59	0.74	0.59	0.73	0.53	0.43	0.53	0.47	0.63	0.71	0.56	0.35	0.624
0.61	0.43	0.77	0.56	0.5	0.61	0.42	0.59	0.51	0.63	0.64	0.56	0.62	0.589
0.95	0.89	1	0.81	0.79	0.91	0.6	0.93	0.87	1	0.9	0.85	0.73	0.902
0.01	1	0.51	1	0.14	0.16	0.2	0.29	0.38	0.26	0.29	0.5	0.44	0.389
0.34	0.45	0.49	0.6	0.6	0.59	0.7	0.55	0.46	0.53	0.46	0.56	0.61	0.517
0.42	0.43	0.48	0.35	0.55	0.43	0.51	0.52	0.42	0.44	0.44	0.46	0.38	0.50
0.45	0.66	0.51	0.4	0.39	0.5	0.61	0.65	0.53	0.63	0.51	0.41	0.54	0.532
0.63	0.68	0.65	0.57	0.61	0.62	0.56	0.6	0.6	0.52	0.7	0.47	0.37	0.675
0.63	0.41	0.36	0.12	0.11	0.1	0.08	0.44	0.17	0.21	0.47	0.22	0.48	0.376
0.35	0.54	0.58	0.44	0.48	0.48	0.77	0.59	0.37	0.69	0.54	0.59	0.54	0.533
0.55	0.68	0.73	0.43	0.38	0.47	0.43	0.44	0.41	0.44	0.79	0.47	0.47	0.60
0.79	0.24	1	0.08	0.17	0.53	0.76	0.22	0.17	0.59	0.3	0.31	0.24	0.518
0.86	1	1	1	1	1	1	1	1	1	1	0.62	1	0.903
0.36	0.63	0.6	0.43	0.49	0.52	0.5	0.52	0.44	0.33	0.24	1	0.79	0.656
0.596	0.65	0.69	0.55	0.54	0.57	0.53	0.59	0.54	0.59	0.62	0.57		

Goa has an efficiency of one in all years except 1981-82,1983-84,1984-85 and 1987-88.Delhi also has an efficiency score of one in all years from 1986-87 through 1997-98 except 1996-97. Pondicherry, Maharashtra, Himachal Pradesh, Punjab, Bihar, Tamil Nadu, Meghalaya, Andaman and Nichobar Islands and Assam has an efficiency score of one in at least one of the years from 1980-81 to 1997-98.

The mean efficiency index from all states over the years surprisingly shows a declining trend (see last row of Table 1 and 2) although there have been fluctuations between the years (see figure 4). The mean efficiency index which was 0.685 in 1980-81,went up to 0.76 in 1983-84 and then again came down to 0.57 in 1997-98.

Figure 4: Mean Efficiency Index for 22 Indian States Across the Years

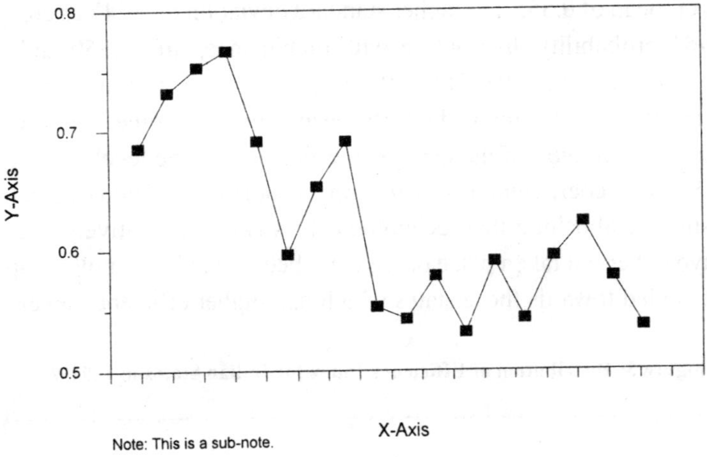

Goa has the highest mean efficiency index of 0.94 from all the years, followed by Delhi with an index of 0.903, then followed by the industrial state of Maharashtra with 0.902 (see last column of Table 2). Tripura has the lowest mean efficiency index of 0.376 among the 22 states in our country followed by that of Meghalaya with a score of 0.389.It seems that the small sizes of states has had its impact on their production efficiency. Both Delhi and Goa are small states compared to other states and are ranked first and second in terms of their efficiency scores. The North East states have not been doing well in terms of their efficiency scores. This underscores the need to transfer technological by the centre to North East states.

Assam, Meghalaya and Bihar too have scores of one in atleast one of the years from 1980-81 to 1997-98.It seems peculiar that these states are on the frontier. The interpretation of this finding is that such states have relatively low per capita state incomes because it seems that they are relatively undercapitalized and not because they make inefficient use of the relatively meager capital inputs that it has. Another (perhaps more plausible) interpretation is that the DEA method of constructing the best-practice frontier-a lower bound on the frontier under the assumption of constant returns-fails to identify the 'true' but unknown frontier, especially at low capital labour ratios[5].

It has been argued that non-convergence or slow convergence in net value added per worker across states is primarily caused by slow technological catch up. In the context of our structure, the state of Indian State wide technology is represented by a production surface in output/input space, and movement toward the frontier, reflected by increases in efficiency, represents technological catch up. Figure 5 and 6 show the distributions of the level of efficiency across states in 1980-81 and 1997-98,obtained under the assumption of constant returns to scale [6]. The 1997-98 distribution surprisingly has a probability mass with lower mean of 0.555 and higher standard deviation of .2247 as compared to 1980-81 probability distribution with higher mean of 0.6850 and lower standard deviation of .20260.The 1997-98 probability distribution shows that the probability mass has not had a shift towards one over time. Moreover, the least squares regression of the change in efficiency on the level of efficiency in 1980-81 has a coefficient of -4.768 with a t statistic of -.3906 (insignificant relationship) establishing that technological transfers to relatively backward states have either not taken place or have not been effective in pulling up their net value added towards those states which had higher efficiency levels.

Figure 5: Distribution of Efficiency Index for Indian States in 1997-98

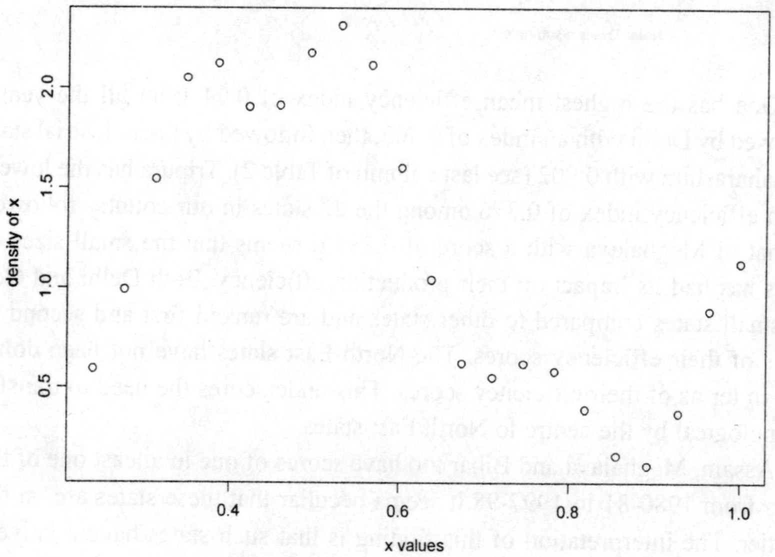

Tripartite Decomposition of the Factors Affecting Labour Productivity

We have carried out the above calculations for the years 1980-81 through 1997-98. The conceptual decomposition is discussed in the section on Methodology. Appendix Tables (available with authors) give the results for finding out the average efficiency changes, technological changes and capital accumulation from 1980-81 to 1997-98.The results of tripartite decomposition of labour productivity are summarized in Table 3.

Table 3 lists the percentage changes from 1980-81 to 1997-98 in labour productivity and each of the three components: (i) change in efficiency,(ii) technological change, and (iii) capital deepening, for all 22 states, along with the sample mean percentage changes.The overall averages provide striking evidence that none of the three factors are primarily responsible for most of

Figure 6: Distribution of Efficiency Index, 1980-81

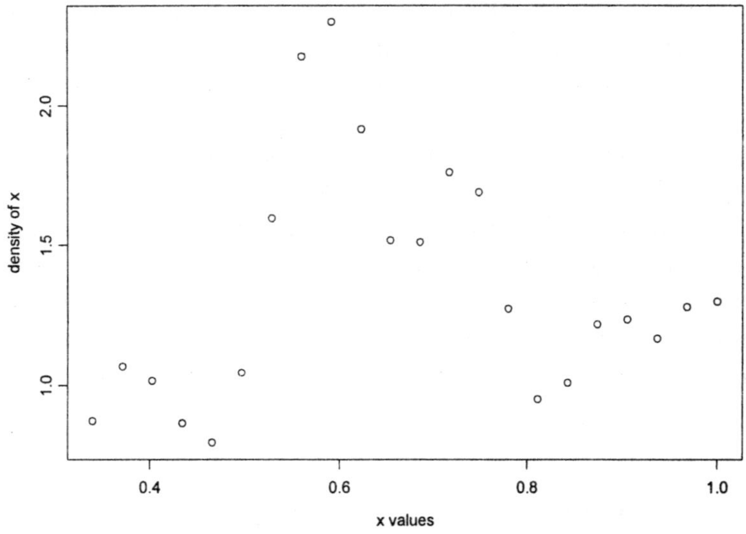

the productivity improvements of 224.2% over this period.The efficiency factor accounted for 6.56% ONLY, technological change accounted for 15.36 % while the contribution of capital deepening is realtively higher at 22.84%.The results suggest that most of the industries in different states operate along the 'best production frontier' as was found by Kumar and Russell (2002) for cross section of countries across the world.Such results,however, do convey that there are some other factors besides the ones decomposed in the growth accounting exercise which may have profound and geater affects on net value added per worker growth rates across the states included in our sample.It is this latter result where this study deviates from Kumar and Russel (2002) and Henderson and Russel (2003) results who found that capital accumulation and human capital accumulation, respectively were primarily responsible for differential levels of per capita growth across countries.

OLS regression lines are also plotted. Figure 7(a) indicates that states which had lower net value added per worker in 1980-81 grew at faster rates in terms of net value added per worker in the period 1980-81 to 1997-98.The negative slope coefficient of -.0130 with t value as -2.3729 (statistically significant at 5% level of significance) suggest that laggards grew at faster rates.

Figure 7(b), shows the relationship between the contribution of efficiency change to the initial level of net value added per worker in 1980-81.It evinces clear negative relationship. The beta coefficient has negative value of -.0007 with t value of -2.5409. States, which had lower net value, added per worker in 1980-81 were also the ones who had faster technological catching up rates (higher efficiency). Our earlier results however showed that states, which had lower efficiency levels in 1980-81, also had higher efficiency rates (although the relationship was not statistically significant).

Figure 7(c) shows that the relationship between technological changes and initial level of net value added per worker is negative (-.0007) though not significant (t value -1.88). States which had lower net value added per worker in 1980-81 did not necessarily had higher technical change.

Figure 7(d) shows that the relationship between capital accumulation and net value added per worker growth is positive but insignificant (coefficient value is .0003 with t value of .2169). The positive regression slope coefficient suggests that relatively wealthier states have benefited more from capital accumulation than have less developed states (although the evidence is not statistically significant).

Table 3
Percentage Change of Tripartite Decomposition Indexes

Indian States	*Net value added per worker, 1980-81 (Rs.) Constant 1980-81 Prices*	*Net value added per worker 1997-98 (Rs.) Constant 1980-81 Prices*	*Productivity Change (1997-98-1980-81)*	*(EFF-1) *100*	*(TECH-1) *100*	*(KACC-1) *100*
Andhra Pradesh	8762.14	20394.	132.7548	2.002513	6.159374	5.651282
Assam	9307.11	17267.	85.53378	2.25519	6.108737	10.69117
Bihar	13123.7	72890.	455.4058	9.399251	14.73762	-2.67834
Goa	39799.7	73784.	85.38995	3.59459	10.00873	3.73539
Gujarat	16280.6	37690.	131.5039	2.373045	7.2379	5.690642
Haryana	20435.4	33322.	63.06059	0.244657	4.118344	4.218503
Himachal Pradesh	27863.9	42302.	51.81788	0.154731	5.087644	4.047239
Karnataka	15218.7	22889.	50.40639	-2.00661	3.538568	5.942086
Kerala	13967.6	19307.	38.23201	-1.68312	3.281276	7.266579
Madhya Pradesh	18543.1	45266.	144.1167	3.276777	7.520385	3.222359
Maharastra	22321.5	53281.	138.7012	-0.32257	5.928066	3.371619
Meghalaya	23381.9	28899.	23.59728	-8.28338	13.59321	187.387
Orrisa	14877.6	44819.	201.2525	2.269416	9.739421	0.908728
Punjab	16418.6	24515	49.31667	2.042776	5.302551	7.222112
Rajasthan	17477.8	38289.	119.0741	2.359081	7.957927	2.683783
Tamil Nadu	15464.2	20984.	35.69719	-3.43618	2.944596	6.86422
Tripura	2735.05	29929.	994.281	32.89493	32.51594	20.6595
Uttar Pradesh	9723.26	39685.	308.1478	7.423326	14.27932	3.318002
West Bengal	14442.2	29833.	106.5728	-0.48315	5.629821	7.215262
Andaman Nicobar Islands	8031.56	10039.	25.00476	39.92834	61.25375	94.00035
Delhi	13564.3	53655.	295.5642	4.294927	11.96507	-1.15675
Pondicherry	11906.9	44895.	277.0493	13.31806	22.27353	8.051385
Mean Across States	16074.86	36542.4	224.263	6.56568	15.3636	22.8418

Figure 7: Summarizes these Calculations by Plotting the four Growth Rates (net value added per Worker and its three Components Against NVA per Worker 1980-81.

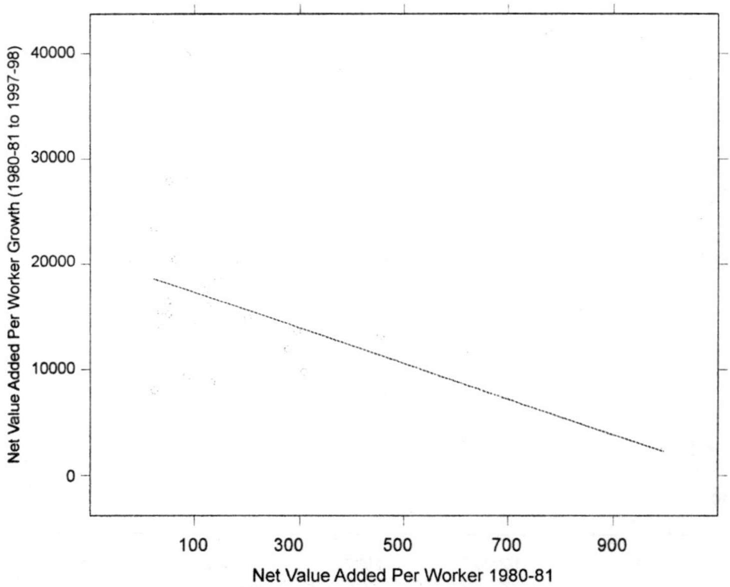

(a)

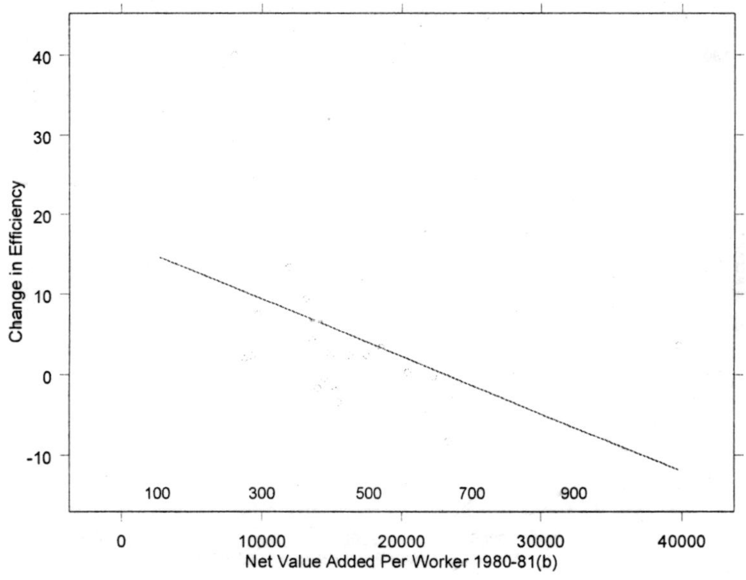

Figure 7: Percentage Changes Between 1980-81 and 1997-98 in Net Value Added Per Worker Growth and Three Decomposition Indexes Plotted Against 1980-81 Net Value Added Per Worker

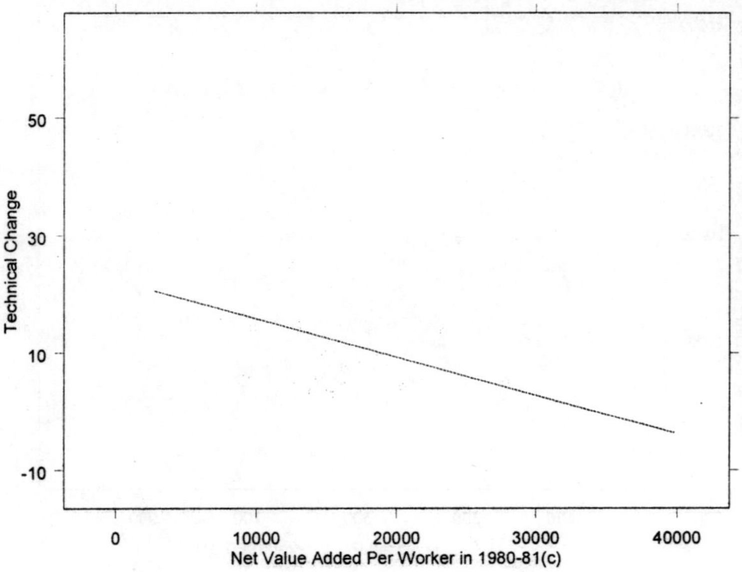

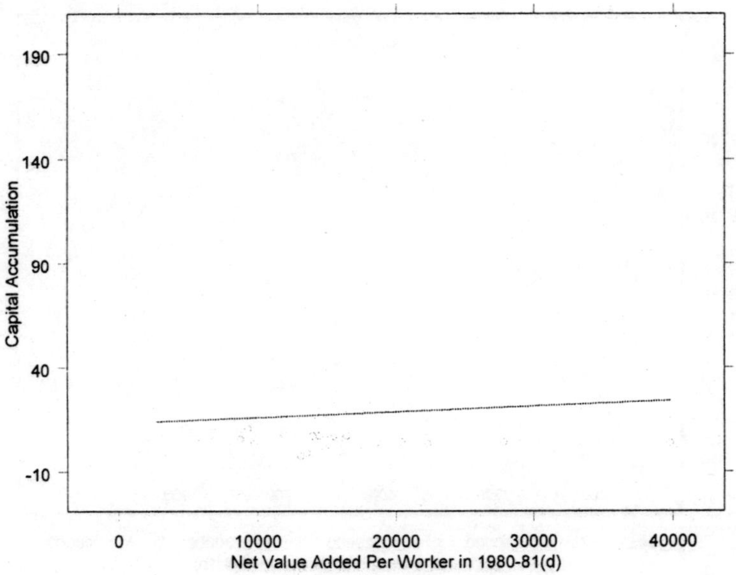

Analysis of Productivity Distributions

Our objective is to assess whether the three components can together change account for the deformation of the distribution of labour productivity from single modal distribution in 1980-81 to multi-modal distribution in 1997-98 with higher mean.

Figure 8: Counterfactual Distribution of Net VALUE Added Per Worker, 1997-98

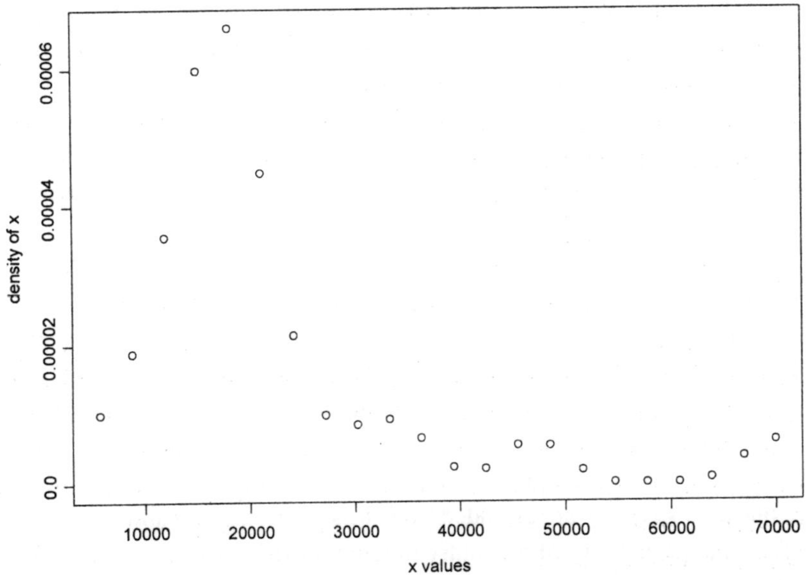

The distributions we employ are nonparametric kernel based density estimates, essentially Rosenblatt Parzen kernel density estimator.

Rewrite the quadripartite decomposition of labour productivity changes as follows:

$y_c = (EFF \times TECH \times KACC)*y_b$

Thus, the net value added per worker distribution in 1997-98 can be constructed by successively multiplying labour productivity in 1980-81 by each of the three factors. The counterfactual distribution of 1997-98 is constructed (Figure 13) by multiplying the average decomposition figures successively with the labour productivity in 1980-81.It seems from the figure that the distribution remains single modal (as the 1980-81 distribution) and therefore the three decomposition factors of labour productivity: efficiency change, technological change and capital accumulation together have not been able to transform the 1980-81 distribution and bring it at par with the actual 1997-98 multi-modal distribution of net value added per worker. This means that some other factors may have been more responsible for the transformation of single modal distribution of 1980-81 into the multi-modal distribution of 1997-98.

LIMITATIONS OF STUDY

In recent times, cross-country analysis has come under criticism from the "Twin-Peaks" literature led by Quah (1996, 1997). The researcher is interested in the evolution of the distribution of the world distribution of income and the variance is only one aspect of this distribution. Quah (1996, 1997) noticed that, in 1960, the world distribution of income was uni-modal whereas, in the 1990s, the distribution became bi-modal. He then used Markov transitional matrices & non-parametric method to estimate the probabilities that countries improve their position in the world distribution. Using these matrices, he then forecasted the evolution of this distribution overtime. His conclusion was that, in the long run, the distribution would remain bi-modal, although the lower mode will include a lot fewer countries than the upper mode.

Even though Quah (1996, 1997) triggered a large body of research, his conclusion does not appear to be very robust. Jones (1997) and Kremer et. al., (2001) have recently shown that a lot of these results depend crucially on whether the data set includes oil-producers (for example, the exclusion of Trinidad and Tobago or Venezuela from the sample changes the prediction of a bi-modal steady state distribution to a uni-modal distribution; the reason is that these are two examples of countries that were relatively rich but have become poor so if they are excluded from the sample, the probability of "failure" -that is, the probability of a country moving down in the distribution- lowers substantially).

We find that for the sample of 22 Indian State included in our study, the cross state net value added per worker distribution were single modal in 1980-81 and it is only in the 1990s that it has been transformed from single modal to multi-modal distribution. It seems that neither technological change, technological catch-up, capital accumulation nor life expectancy are primarily responsible for this transformation.

CONCLUSION

We decompose net value added per worker growth into components attributable to technological changes (shifts in the overall production frontier), technological catch up (movement towards or away from the frontier), capital accumulation (movement along the frontier) and human capital accumulation (proxied by life expectancy). The overall production frontier is constructed using deterministic methods (data envelopment analysis) requiring neither specification of functional form for the technology nor any assumption about market structure or the absence of market imperfections. We analyze the evolution of cross states net value added distribution for the 22 Indian states from 1980-81 to 1997-98 using Kernel densities. The results seems to suggest that there are other factors suggested in the literature like barriers to exit, a maze of rules and regulations, government import policies, high concentration, among others, rather than the ones that are included below for the growth accounting exercise, which are primarily responsible for the existence of multi-modal net value added per worker distribution for the 22 states. These latter factors also seem to explain reasons for the regional variations of net value added per worker across states. Also, we do find that the efficiency levels for the Indian states have gone down from what it was in 1980s to what it were in 1997-98.However, the smaller states have out performed the larger states in terms of their efficiency levels.

Generally, speaking policies that will augment technological transfers to laggard states, will help more in reducing net value added per worker differences and growth rates across states and regions and also help in achieving the basic goal of planning- i.e., reduce regional variations. We think that from policy perspective we need to work out the probabilities of states that are in the lower modal distribution reaching higher modal distribution. With time and resources we could use transitional probabilities and matrix algebra to give insights to question rose above.

NOTES

1. Senior Lecturers, Department of Economics, Jamia Millia Islamia (JMI), New Delhi-25, India.
2. This approach to Growth Accounting is not dependent on particular assumptions about the technology, market structure, technological change and other aspects of the growth process.
3. Our efficiency calculations were carried out using the Onfront software (demo version),available from Economic Measurement and Quality I Lund AB (Box 2134, S-220 Lund, Sweden (www.emq.se).
4. The non increasing-returns-to scale (NIRS) technology is constructed by restricting the process operation levels as satisfy $0 \leq z^j \leq 1$ for all j, so that observed process can be radially contracted but not expanded. The variable-returns-to-scale (VRS) technology is constructed by adding the restriction $\Sigma_j z_j \leq 1$, resulting in increasing returns as scale at low levels of input. By construction, efficiency indexes calculated under the assumption of constant returns to scale are no higher than those calculated under the assumption of NIRS, which in turn are no greater than those constructed under the assumption of VRS (see Fare et. al., 1994a for details).
5. We should note that these mathematical programming methods take no account of measurement error, sampling error and other stochastic phenomena. Recent research (Simar, 1996; Kneip et.al, 1998; Gijbels et. al., 1999; Simar, 2000) has made substantial progress on the use of bootstrapping method to construct confidence intervals around efficiency index .In this study, however, we are more concerned

about the statistical significance of changes in the distributions of efficiency indexes and the components of tripartite decomposition of net value added per worker changes.

6. Kumar and Russell (2002) in their study of 57 countries note that efficiency indexes are not perceptibly affected by recalculation of the efficiency indexes under the alternative assumptions of non-increasing returns to scale or variable returns to scale.

REFERENCES

Afriat, Sydney (1972), Efficiency Estimation of Production Functions, *International Economic Review*, 13 (3) : 568-98.

Caves, Doughas W., Christensen, Laurits R. and Diewert, W. Erwin (1982), Multilateral Comparisons of Outputs, Inputs and Productivity Using Superlative Index Number, *Economic Journal*, 92 (365): 73-86.

Diewert, E. (1980), Capital and the Theory of Productivity Measurement, *American Economic Review*, 70: 260-267.

Farrell, Michael J. (1956), The Measurement of Productive Efficiency, *Journal of the Royal Statistical Society*, Series A, General, 120 (3): 253-282.

Fare, R., S. Grosskopf, and C.A.K. Lovell (1994a), *Production Frontiers*, Cambridge University Press: New York.

Fare, R., Grosskopf, S., Norris, M. and Zhang, Z. (1994b), Productivity Growth, Technical Progress and Efficiency Change in Industrialized Countries, *American Economic Review*, 84 (1): 66-83.

Gijbels, I., Mammen, E., Park B.U., and Simar, L. (1999), On Estimation of Monotone and Concave Frontier Functions, *Journal of the American Statistical Association*, 94(445): 220-228.

Henderson, D.J. and R. Robert Russell (2003), Human Capital and Convergence: A Production-Frontier Approach, University of California, Riverside Working Paper No. 29.

Kneip, A., Park B.U., and Simar, L. (1998), A Note on the Convergence of Non-Parametric DEA Estimates for Production Efficiency Scores, *Econometric Theory*, 14(6): 783-793.

Jones, C.I. (1997), On the Evolution of the World Income Distribution, *Journal of Economic Perspectives*, Summer.

Kremer, M, A. Onatski and J. Stock (2001), Searching for Prosperity, NBER Working Paper 8250, U.S.

Kumar, Subodh and Robert Russell (2002), Technological Change, Technological Catch-up and Capital Deepening: Relative Contributions to Growth and Convergence, American Economic Review, 92(3).

Parzen, E. (1962), On Estimation of a Probability Density and Mode, *Annals of Mathematical Statistics*, 35: 1065-1076.

Quah D. (1993), Galton's Fallacy and Tests of Convergence Hypothesis, *Scandinavian Journal of Economics*, 95(4): 427-443.

Quah, D. (1996), Twin Peaks: Growth and Convergence in Models of Distribution Dynamics, *Economic Journal*, July.

Quah, D. (1997), Empirics for Growth and Distribution: Stratification, Polarization, and Convergence Clubs, *Journal of Economic Growth*, 2: 27-59.

Rosenblatt, M. (1956), Remarks on Some Nonparametric Estimates of a Density Function, *Annals of Mathematical Statistics*, 27: 642-669.

Simar, Leopold (1996), Aspects of Statistical Analysis in DEA-Type Frontier Models, *Journal of Productivity Analysis*, 7(2-3) : 177-185.

Simar, Leopold and Wilson, Paul W. (2000), A General Methodology for Bootstrapping in Non Parametric Frontier Models, *Journal of Applied Statistics*, 27 (6): 779-802.

Solow, Robert M. (1957), Technical Change and the Aggregate Production Function, *Review of Economics and Statistics*, 39(3): 312-320.

Watson,G.S. (1964), Smooth Regression Analysis, *Sankya*, Series A, 26 : 359-372.

12

ROLE OF FORESTS IN TRIBAL DEVELOPMENT IN INDIA

S. Nirmala Mary

INTRODUCTION

Forests are an important gift of nature for the well being of mankind. In India, a large population still depends on forests for their existence. Most of the non-urban people below the poverty line almost entirely depend on forests for their existence. They generally reside inside or in the vicinity of forests. Tribals are the most dominant group of communities who live inside the forest areas and depend on the forests for meeting their maximum needs. A tribe is a social group, the members of which are tribes, who collectively live in common territory, have a common dialect, uniform, social organization and possess culture homogeneity having a common political pattern. A large number of tribal communities have been identified in India. The Anthropological survey of India during 1967 recorded 314 tribal communities. According to 1991 census the tribal population of India was about 68 million, comprising 427 communities and constituting 8% of India's total population.

CONCENTRATION OF TRIBAL IN INDIA

North-Eastern Region

The North-Eastern region of India covering the status of Arunachal Pradesh, Assam, Manipur, Mehalaya, Mizoram, Nagaland and Tripura have the concentration of Manolian racial stock of tribals. This region is inhabited by Tribes such as Abor, Garo, Khasi, Kuki, Mishmi, Naga, Boro, Chakma etc.

Himalayan Region

The sub-Himalayan region covering parts of North Bengal, Uttar Pradesh, Uttaranchal and Himachal Pradesh also has concentrated tribal population in certain areas which belong to communities e.g., lepcha, Rabha, Bhoksa Bhotia, Javnsari, Raji, Tharu, Gaddi etc.

Central Indian Region

The central Indian region covering Bihar, Jharkhand, Orissa, Madhya Pradesh, Chattissgarh and west Bengal have a dense population of tribes belonging to proto-Australoid racial stock. Important tribal communities of this region are Gond, Oran, Munda, Santhal, Ho and Bhil.

Western Indian Region

This region includes Rajasthan, Maharastra, Gujarat, Goa and Dadra-Nagar Haveli where the tribal communities and Bhil, Meena, Halba, Korku, etc. These tribal groups also belong to proto-Australoid etc.

Southern Region

The region includes Karnataka, Andhra Pradesh, Tamil Nadu, and Kerala. Important tribal communities of this region are Chenchm, Irula, Kota, Kurmba and Toda.

Island Region

This region includes Andaman and Nicobar and Lakshadweep groups of islands. A number of small tribal communities such as Andamanese, Onges, Sentineless, Jarwa, Nicobarese, Shompens etc. live in this region.

FORESTRY IN INDIA

Before the advent of British raj the forest was the common property resource. So, tribal groups utilized the forest products for their traditional livelihoods following some social norms, cultural practices and religious affiliation. The sacred groves, trees, and ponds reflect such pristine culture centered round the forest resources. Hence the phase can be expressed by sustainable use with religious affiliation.

This traditional indigenous forest management system was shattered by the British policy of "Scientific Forestry" in 1855, which imposed the state management under full control in an organized department. The Silvicultural system was applied as tenting operation for coup felling of valuable timbers. The first forest policy which came in 1894 made two major enunciation-first, the cultivation are stronger than the claims of forest preservation and second, the public (material) benefit through teak extraction for the industrial purposes. Such as ship building in royal navy and railway slippers lying and bridge constructions. In 1865 forest act, an attempt was made to regulate the collection and preservation of forest products.

The commercial exploitation of forests was encouraged at the cost of forest-dwellers in the name of national interests. The colonial government issued permits to professional contractors to harvest the timbers. The Forest Department was strengthened to regulate people's rights over forestland and produces with the enactment of Indian, Forest Act 1927. That act is still followed to regulate the forest use.

The consequences of various policy, laws or acts are the depletion of forest resource, shrinkage of forest areas, loss of bio-diversity, ecological disbalances. It caused various tribal revolts and enactment of criminal tribes' act. Colonial Legacy in Forest Policy. The National Forest Policy in 1952 was just an extension of old policy followed during the colonial period. Rigid restrictions were also imposed on the forest dwellers and others to exploit the forest resources on which their cultural traditions and economy depend. The regulations were imposed on the ground that forest dwellers were the sole responsible for the destruction of forest resources.

In 1976 the National commission on Agriculture (NCA) blamed the tribal population for destruction of forests and recommended drastic reduction of people's rights on forests and stopping of free supply of forest produce to the tribals. The main thrust of the National Commission on Agriculture was to develop tree resources largely outside the recognized forest boundaries in the neighbourhood of rural areas irrespective of whether the lands earmarked for producing such resources are community, private or government. It commenced the new programmes of social forestry, which deals with (physically) sick lands and (economically) sick people, to produce goods such as fuel, fodder etc. to meet the needs of the local community. Though it was by name 'Social Forestry', but we find large scale of plantations of high-yielding varieties such as Eucalyptus, Acacia etc, in the Government lands, farms of big farmers, canal or road side etc. There was limited success of social forestry in providing forest resources to local communities, to check the continued rate of deforestation and to resolve the perpetual conflicts between people and Forest Department. Because there was least involvement of the people in decision making process, big farmers earned huge cultivating the tree crops of high fielding varieties and equity was not so much considered. During Indian Wastelands Development begun and several employment security programmes started for the social security of Indian tribals through poverty alleviation or reduction.

INTERFACE MANAGEMENT

The Government of India resolution under the heading "Joint forest Management" (JFM) was passed on 1st June, 1990 by a circular No. 6.21/89-FP from the secretary, Ministry of Environment & Forest, providing guidelines for the "Involvement of village Communities and voluntary agencies in the regeneration of degraded forests". This is a Paradigm shift from centralized, controlled custodial timber-harvesting and revenue earning forestry to the community based participatory forest management. The definition of forest management has been elaborated encompassing the totality of administrative, economic, legal, social, technical and scientific approach for the utility, conservation, and sustainability of forests.

In the Joint Forest Management programme many a number of village institutions were formed to promote partnership between the state and local communities to manage forests for the benefit of the people and state and to make livelihood strategies for the people to strengthen the economy of poor tribals. This people- centered forest management has developed a partnership business to change the existing forest conditions at the local level, pattern of forest are and to bolster collective action for bio-diversity conservation. According to some sources, so far it is seen that forest protection committees are working in 27 states covering a forest area of over 14 million Ha.

ROLE OF TRIBALS

Tribals depend upon forests for their existence in several ways. The degree of dependence of tribals on forest depends upon various factors. These factors include their socio-economic condition, distribution, cultural and religious norms, literacy, etc. The primitive tribes, who live inside the dense forests one very poor and depend entirely on forests for meeting most of their needs. However, the tribal communities, which have gained access to the modern world, have gradually started adapting to the modern ways of life.

The dwindling of forest resources has also forced them to look for alternative ways of meeting their needs. The following are the ways in which tribals are depended on forests.

Collection for Consumption Items

Tribals collect both wood and non-wood forest products in large quantities for meeting their day to day needs. The non-timber forest products include food, medicines, bamboos and canes, fibre, tans and dyes, oilseeds, etc.

Studies carried out indicate that chechm and kolam tribes of Andhra Pradesh, Abhujmarias and baigas of Madhya Pradesh, jungas and kharias of Orissa depend on forests for meeting about 50% of food requirement, 90% of health care and 100% for meeting other needs e.g. oilseeds, fibre, bamboo, cans, firewood, grasses and grazing, tanning and dyes, soaps etc. several tribes who have take to settled agriculture and being situated near means of communications, e.g. roads and rails, etc., have reduced their dependence on forest considerably.

Most of the tribals belonging to the poorest group collect non-timber forest products in large quantities. A major part of the collected produce is retained by them for meeting their own needs and only a smaller part of the produce collected is sold in the market. On the other hand tribal families, which are economically better, collect non-timber forest produce for sale.

Source of Income

Certain proportions of the collected NTFPs are sold in the market to earn some income from the sale of these forest products. The quantity of NTFPs collected by the tribals depends upon several factors. Economic status remains one of the important criteria.

In case of edible fruits, flowers, seeds etc. such as Mahua flowers, Chironji, etc are collected by the tribal people and other weaker sections of their own consumption and for sale. Relatively economically better people can afford to keep more produce for their own consumption than the lower income group people.

The NTFPs are sold in the market or local bazaars Traders and middle men generally purchase these produce from the tribals. The income generated by the sale of NTFPs is utilized by tribals for buying clothes, and other necessary items.

Source of Employment

There is an acute problem of unemployment in the country particularly in the rural and remote areas, where concentration of scheduled tribes and scheduled castes is comparatively high. There is no avenue for providing employment in forest areas, as developmental works are few as compared to other areas. The various operations in the forestry sector remain the only source for creating job opportunities for the people located inside the forest areas. There are a variety of operations such as plantation, tending, weeding, pruning, harvesting processing and marketing etc., which sufficient job opportunities for the scheduled castes and tribes population. Most of these operations are labour intensive and generate considerable labour opportunities for these people.

Dependence on Shifting Cultivation

Shifting cultivation is a transition between food gathering and food production. This practice is known as 'Jhum' in the North-east, "Kurva' in Bhiar and Jharhand, 'Dahiya' or 'podo' in Orissa, Madhya Pradesh, Chhattisgarh and Andhra Pradesh. The system consists of cutting back the forests, drying the wood and other vegetable material, burning it and cultivating the area for one or two years and moving to another place for the same purpose. Shifting cultivation is an age-old practice of cultivation. It is primitive in nature and causes damage to forests of the area the practice aims at utilizing the productivity of the forests for cultivating food grains.

Dependence for Pastoral Activity

A number of scheduled caste and scheduled tribe communities depend upon forests for grazing their cattle. Most of the tribals in India near cattle for a variety of purposes. Among the Indian tribes who depend entirely on pastoral activities are Toda, Gaddies, Gujjars, Bhotia, etc. The toda of Nilgiris in Tamil Nadu even their living by selling milk and milk products. Usually they exchange milk and milk products for other communities. Gujjars of Uttaranchal and Himachal Pradesh generally keep cows, buffaloes and sheep for commercial purpose. Similarly, bhotias are also engaged in pastoral activities. The gaddies of Himachal Pradesh near buffaloes, sheep and goats. These tribes depend on forest for grazing and leaf fodder provided by trees for maintaining their animals.

Forest Areas for Tribal Development

Due to various historical reasons, the terms, "Tribe" and "Forest" are closely associated with each other since centuries, and the bond continues equally and vigorously till the present time. Since, the relationship exists between the forest eco-system and the tribals living within that, both are interdependent to a great extend.

The problem of poverty and unemployment in dry land areas is sought to be solved within the framework of agriculture alone, including agro-forestry. Admittedly, agriculture will have a major role in this After all, it is important to make dryland agriculture absorb more man-power and also make it less vulnerable to drought. But, drylands also need diversification of their economy and reduction in the pressure of population on agriculture and agro-forestry for livelihood. Diversification can make their economy less vulnerable to uncertainties of weather, by providing alternative sources of employment.

Dryland villages and regions which have succeeded in developing rural industry and the service sector including education and health, have been able to reduce their poverty levels much better than other regions which continue to depend on agriculture alone. It should be conceded, however, that tribals will benefit mainly from sustainable development of dryland agriculture and agro-forestry. But, by dissuading non-tribals from competing with tribals in agriculture and forest sector, this sector can be increasingly reserved for tribals and employment opportunities outside agriculture be increased both for tribals and non-tribals.

India is reportedly destroying about 10,000 sq. kms of forest land-roughly 2.7 per cent of the total forestland annually. This deforestation has serious consequence on the quality of life. According to rough estimates, about 175 million hectare, i.e., 53 per cent of the total geographical area of the country-suffers from soil erosion, land degradation due to water-logging, salinity, alkalinity and other hazards. Besides, about 260 million hectare is under stress condition; 170 million hectare is subject to serve drought, 76 million hectare to moderate drought, 47 million hectare to a large drought and 20 million hectare to other hazardous conditions.

In the tribal areas, agriculture and allied activities are dependent on forest to a large measure. The agricultural implements are usually manufactured from the raw materials collected from the forest. The practice of animals husbandry is equally dependent on forestry as the forest provides rich grazing ground for the cattle and other domestically animals with its huge depository of grass and green foliage.

Forest provide the tribes with fruits, leafy vegetables succulent, shoots, honey, varieties of flowers, juice, gums, resin, jam, fish etc. to sustain life. Their knowledge of medicinal herbs and plants around them takes care of their health problems and keeps them fit to pursue their economic goals in adverse natural conditions.

Besides meeting their food demands, the forest provide the tribals with all the required raw materials for house construction. The emotional attachment of tribals with their surroundings forest has kept them secluded amidst deep forest and away from the modern 'civilized' world for generations. In spite of intense dependence on the forest, the tribals are equally great protections of the natural flora and fauna. So the economic status of the tribals has improved according to the changes in occupation and the increase in income and employment level.

CONCLUSION

The evolution of the tribal society took place within the forest and they had the birth right for their survival, livelihood, occupation, recreation, belief and act. But it is the tribals who bear the brunt of most big, industrial, mining and development projects. Due to the interference of the colonial government in their rights. They were deprived of their rights and robbed of their dignity. So, the government decided to develop tribal co-operatives societies, to prevent exploitation of tribals. Various types of tribals co-operative societies have been formed to help the cause of tribals in different stages. Still, tribals have been exploited by middlemen while purchasing the NTFPs collected by the tribals, therefore if the government wants to develop tribal economy, there is a need to protect their benefits by providing them strong marketing network. Tribal societies may also be formed to safeguard the benefits of the tribals. Thus, along with other developmental approaches the community forest management has been recognized as an effective developmental approach to alleviate the tribal people from their poverty and promote their cultural traditions of biodiversity conservation to their sustainable livelihoods.

REFERENCES

Bahuguna V.K. (2000), Forest in the Economy of Rural Poor: An Estimation of the Dependency Level, *AMBIO,* 29 (3): 126-129.

Debashis D. (2004), Tribe, Forest and Development: An Effective Combination for Promising Future, *Man and Life*, 30 (1-2): 41-52.

Dwivedi, A.P. (1993), *Non-wood Forest Products and Tribals*, International Book Distributors: Dehradun.

Roy Burman, B.K. (1982), Report of the Committee on Forest and Tribals, Ministry of Home Affairs, Government of India, New Delhi.

Soundra Pandian, M. (2003), Role of Forests in Tribal Development: A Case Study of Paliyan Tribe in Tamil Nadu, *Kurukshetra*, 51(8): 29-33.

13

ROLE OF WOMEN IN FORESTRY: AN OVERVIEW

S. Nirmala Mary

INTRODUCTION

Forests play an important role in environmental and economic sustainability. They provide numerous goods and services, and maintain life-support systems essential for life on earth. Some of these life support systems of major economic and environmental importance are: (i) Supply of timber, fuel wood, fodder, and a wide range of non-wood products; (ii) Natural habitat for bio-diversity and repository of genetic wealth; (iii) Provision of recreation and opportunity for ecotourism; (iv) Playing an integral part of the watershed to regulate the water regime, conserve soil, and control floods; and (v) Carbon sequestration and carbon sink. Despite significant resource flows and national concern, the potential of forests to reduce poverty, release economic growth, and their contribution to the local and global environment has not been fully realized. A combination of market and instructional failures has led to forests fainting to contribute as significantly to rural incomes and poverty alleviation and economic growth as would be possible under good economic and technical management.

WOMEN AND FORESTS

Women have always had a very crucial role to play in the preservation of forests because in India, since ages, women have looked after the food, fodder and water requirements of the family and they had been affected the most due to degradation of forests. For the rural women forests as common property resources provide the essential resources base for forest based livelihood strategies. Since long women folk have been actively engaged in using forest produce for their essential family needs. Collection of fuel and fodder from the forest has been the basic responsibility of rural women. However, depletion of forest cover in India over the last several decades has resulted in number of problems for women as, now they have to walk further and search harder to lop fodder for cattle and collect fuel wood. It is therefore natural that no other section of the society can be more interested in protecting, preserving and promoting forests than the women folk. It is therefore, quite befitting that the participation of women in forestry be made more meaningful through the identification of their role and planning for their maximum participation in the protection, management and development of forest resources.

Women's role in forestry in developing countries is diverse, and women take active role in a variety of non-politicized instances. Unfortunately, the information based on these various roles tends to be very poor. As a result, many recommendations for program interventions and reports on the forestry sector have over looked a number of potential avenues for involving women. Moreover, there is a worrisome tendency to over generalize women's roles in forestry based on a few location specific examples. Literature forum and agencies, environmentalist and NGO flora instances, for instance, focuses on such dramatic examples as the Chipko movement in northern India in which women become highly politicized over the issue of forest depletion.

While Chipko is an important movement, it reveals only one facet of the dynamics of women's involvement in forestry worldwide. It would be unrealistic to expect women everywhere to attempt to protect trees and forests as the Chipko women have done-because of the strong position of women in that society. Perhaps due to the poor data base on the economic role of women now play and could play in the forestry sector–in forestry on public land as well as in tree cropping within the farming system on private land- women's issues have usually been regarded as welfare and equity concerns. As a result, concrete programs have centered on easing women's fuel and fodder collecting workload in the interest of their health and welfare.

Gathering Fuelwood, Fodder and NTFPs

Apart from industrial timber, most NTFPs, such as fuel wood and fodder, come from forests and provide valuable flows for subsistence and cash income. Gathering of fuelwood, fodder and NTFPs is an important subsistence and economic activity for poor women and about 60-70 per cent of gatherers are women. Their relative status within the family is higher in well-forested villages, because their contribution to subsistence and cash incomes of households is greater in villages close to natural forests. Moreover, as their ownership of private resources is negligible, women, particularly those who are poor, depend heavily on common resources for meeting their survival needs.

Fuelwood

Between the late 1970s and early 1990s the share of fuelwood in total energy consumption increased from 55 per cent to nearly 62 per cent. Wood tends to be the main domestic fuel in poorer regions with low productivity. In Bihar, for instance, 90 per cent of the people depend on fuelwood for their energy needs. Gathering firewood, or "head loading" as it is often called, for domestic use and as a source of income is the most widespread gender-based activity for poor women. It has been estimated that two to three million people are engaged in head loading, with the majority being tribal and other poor women.

Fodder

About 30 per cent of fodder requirements are met from forests and about 25 per cent of the country's livestock graze on forestlands. A study shows that, in the absence of forest resources, 66 per cent of small and marginal farmers in Andhra Pradesh would be unable to cultivate their land, as they would not be able to maintain a pair of bullocks. According to the Forest Survey of India records, grazing takes place in over 83 per cent of forest lands in Uttar Pradesh, over 87 per cent in West Bengal, over 85 per cent in Meghalaya, over 70 per cent in Orrisa, over 75 per cent in Sikkim and over 53 per cent in Nagaland.

In Himachal Pradesh and Uttaranchal, very little fodder is grown on agricultural land and livestock graze mainly in pastures and forests. In these regions, tree fodder is predominant and it is mainly women who manage lopping and fodder collection. As many of these regions have a high degree of male migration, the responsibility of agriculture and animal husbandry lies with women.

Non-Timber Forest Products (NTFPs)

NTFPs are obtained from about 3,000 species in the country and form an important source of food and livelihood for communities, particularly tribals and rural poor living adjacent to forests. About 70 per cent of NTFPs are collected from Maharashtra, Madhya Pradesh, Bihar, Orissa and Andhra Pradesh, states that are home to 65 per cent of the country's tribal population.

Several thousand tonnes of NTFPs are removed annually from Indian forests providing earnings that run into billions of rupees each year. At the national level, 40 per cent of state revenues and 70 per cent of forest export revenues come from NTFPs mostly in unprocessed and raw forms. Some studies point out that NTFPs contribute a higher economic return than timber. About 60 per cent of NTFPs collection goes unrecorded as it is consumed or bartered by the 15 million people living in and around forests.

In Andhra Pradesh, around 58 per cent of mahua flowers and seeds and 17 per cent of tamarind fruit collected by tribals are consumed by them. In district Bastar, Chattisgarh, about 75 per cent of forest-dependent people supplement their food with tubers, flowers and fruits. In the Andaman and Nicobar Islands, several tribes subsist wholly on food derived from forests and the sea. In Maharashtra, tribal groups living near forests derive about 30 per cent of their diet from forest products.

Employment and Income

The main forest–based activities from which people derive employment and income are.

1. Sale of firewood and fodder;
2. Rearing of livestock (grazing in and/or collecting fodder from forests);
3. Collection and processing of NTFPs;
4. Forest based handicrafts and cottage industries; and
5. Employment generated in forestry can be classified broadly into direct employment, self–employment and secondary employment.

Direct Employment

The Forest Department and other departments (Rural Development, Agriculture and Cooperatives) generate direct employment under regular forestry activities in forests under their control and through special afforestation programmes. The forestry staff prefers women for forestry operations such as nursery work; transplanting and tendu leaf collection. The work is contracted either on a daily wage or piece rate basis, but women often get lower wages than men for similar work, are not paid regularly and harassed if they complain.

Self Employment

Self-employment in forestry refers to individual or family units geared towards deriving income from activities such as the sale of firewood, livestock rearing (where income is derived from the sale of milk) and collection, processing and marketing of NTFPs.

Secondary Employment

This refers to employment in wood-based and small-scale forest-based enterprises. These enterprises, many of which rely on NTFPs, provide up to 50 per cent of the income for about 25 per cent of India's rural labour force. According to a 1987 estimate, women accounted for 572 million person days (i.e., 35 per cent) of an estimated 1,623 million person days of employment in forest based enterprises. Approximately 90 per cent of this employment is generated in small scale enterprises that depend on applying local skills and village-level technology for the collection and processing of produce, where production can be pursued as a household or non-household cottage industry. Although women's participation rate in some large enterprises such as the match industry may be very high, total women's employment is less than half that of small-scale enterprises.

In addition to forest-based enterprises, secondary employment also includes employment generated through the collection and sale of NTFPs to contractors, agents of the Forest Development corporations or directly to the corporations. This is essentially for nationalized NTFPs in most states, accepts in Madhya Pradesh where select non-nationalized NTFPs can also be sold to the Minor Forest Produce Federation.

PARTICIPATION OF WOMEN IN FOREST DEPARTMENT

The employment of women as field staff and officers in forest departments helps improve interface with village women in micro-planning and forest management.

The absence of women among forestry field staff was recognized as a major constraint for promoting women's participation in social forestry projects. In response, some states have recruited a few women field staff in positions equivalent to forest guards, terming them "village forestry wormers" (Haryana, Tamil Nadu), "lady forest guards" (Himachal Pradesh) and "extension workers" (West Bengal, Madhya Pradesh, Karnataka, Maharashtra, Orissa and Bihar). Orissa is the only state to recruit women at levels equivalent to Range and Block Forest Officers.

The Indian Forest Service opened to women in 1979, but their present levels of 81 women officers constitute barely 3 per cent of the total cadre. Further, many states still do not allow women to enroll in their State Forest Services. The following table explains about the participation of women in Forestry sector.

Table 1
Women's Employment in the Forest Service

Category	*No. of Women Employed*
Indian Forest Service Officer	81
Assistant Conservator of Forests	6
Range Officer	31
Deputy Ranger	84
Forest Guard	169
Forestry Worker	34

Source: Report of the Advisory Committee to Promote the Involvement of Women in Forestry. April 1999, National Afforestation and Eco-Development Board, Ministry of Environment.

In recent years, Himachal Pradesh has issued separate notifications for all cadres to allow women applicants by specifying the required physical standards. Karnataka, West Bengal and Andhra Pradesh have taken a policy decision to reserve on-third of all government jobs, including those in forest departments, for women.

Management and Protection of Forests

Given their significant role in, and contribution to, forest-based livelihoods, women have rarely been accorded due importance in planning of forestry programmes and formal forest management and protection systems. Therefore, their role in protection and management of forests largely through informal and self-initiated women's groups (mahila mandals) remains largely invisible and consequently unrecognized, unacknowledged and poorly reported. As a result, their 'invisible' forest management systems are often destabilized when, through supervision of 'participatory' programmes, control over forests is transferred to the male elite.

Prior to 1988, the Forest Department's programmes, projects and schemes enlisted women's participation as essentially wage earners. Projects and schemes requiring participatory planning with local communities mostly involved only men. The 1988 Forest Policy mandated a shift from complete state controlled forest management to decentralized and participatory management, and to implement the new policy the Ministry of Environment and Forests initiated the Joint Forest Management Programme (in June 1990) which required state forest departments to work with local communities to regenerate degraded lands. Currently, by March 2002, there were 63,618 groups protecting and managing over 14 million hectares (18%) of state forest lands.

Several studies suggest a positive impact of both the Joint Forest Management Programme and self-initiated forest protection on the conditions of forests. Local community institutions are proving effective in protecting forests and many states have recorded increases in forest productivity often with increased flows of NTFPs.

CONCLUSION

The forest Department programmes by and large had not been planned to meet the needs of women. Though grass is available and often free of cost, it has not reduced the time women spend collecting fuel and fodder. Also closing of open grazing lands has produced additional hardships. Income generation based on forestry or non-forestry activities may stimulate women's involvement in afforestation programmes as they tend to meet their basic needs. It is essential to involve women in the micro- planning stages to obtain their constant involvement in the needs and concerns of women will have to take primary importance.

REFERENCES

Himanshu Bourai (2003), Management and Development of Forest Resources: Women's Role, *Sarvodaya*, Nov-Dec.

Narain. U. (1994), Women's Involvement in Joint Forest Management: Analysing the Issues, A Report from University of California: Berkeley.

14

GENDER AND DEVELOPMENT DEBATE IN INDIA

Vibhuti Patel

INTRODUCTION

In the post independent India, in the first quarter, important documents that expressed gender awareness were Constitution of India and Five Year Plan Documents. The former guaranteed fundamental rights (Equality, voting right and five freedoms) to all Indian women irrespective of their class, caste, religious and ethnic backgrounds but also allowed differential treatment of women on the basis of their class, caste, religious and ethnic backgrounds through religion based personal laws and thousands of customary laws. Rights, the state gave with one hand were snatched by its other hand. The Planning Commission, with its faith in "trickle down theory" and perspective of viewing "women as beneficiaries of the economy" mostly came up with welfare policies for women's upliftment. In this framework, the movement of concepts, policies, and strategies was top-down; women's agency was missing. The period soon after independence saw the earliest institutional structures for women's advancement set up by the state. The Central and State Social Welfare Boards were situated outside the bureaucratic structure. Although imbued with the idea of welfare perspective vis-à-vis women, the Boards did foster women's leadership and made the state accountable to them. This was achieved, to a large extent under the vision and leadership of Dr. Durgabai Deshmukh. However, over the years, The Boards carried out only funding and programmatic functions.

In 1972, as per the UN directive, the Committee on the Status of Women was constituted to prepare an in-depth report and within two years, *TOWARDS EQUALITY* Report[1] was tabled in the Parliament. It was a landmark contribution of an interdisciplinary team of academicians, researchers, bureaucrats and policy-makers who were influenced by "Women in Development " approach popularized by Esther Boserup in her pioneering research of the African society.[2] The report, for the first time, brought out into the open the fact that women were active producers in the house holds in the vast unorganized sectors of the economy and that their contribution had to be made visible. The declaration of 1975 as the International Women's Year and the decade 1975-1985 as International Decade of Woman also impacted on the perspective about women.

VISIBILITY OF WOMEN IN MAINSTREAM DISCOURSES

During the decade, Indian Association of Women's Studies (IAWS) and Economists Interested in Women's Issues Group (EIWIG) played a very important role in the process of policy formulations through their technical workshops, seminars, conferences and training programmes. They challenged gender-neutral and gender-biased concepts concerning 'head of the household' and provided realistic perspectives on 'Female headed house-holds'. Time allocation studies conducted by Institute for Social Studies Trust were useful in netting women's unpaid work that augmented family resources.[3] They lobbied for visibility of women in statistics and indicators for effective formulations and implementation of policies, programmes and schemes concerning women. They visualized women's issues in the mainstream developmental discourse and brought gender concerns in the development agenda. Visibility of women in statistics and indicators of Census Reports[4], National Sample Surveys[5] and Economic Surveys[6] of Government of India became 'a must' because of efforts of the scholars of IAWS and EIWIG. Original and academically rigorous papers discussed in their workshops were published in the edited volumes that were treated as major reference materials for engendering policies.[7] Scholarly contributions of women's studies and women's movement found their reflection in two extremely important policy documents SHRAM SHAKTI and National Perspective Plan for Women (1988-2000) NPPW that were widely debated in the late 1990s.[8] These policy documents are ideologically influenced by Women and Development approach that focuses on marginalization hypothesis and suggests ways of integrating women in the mainstream economic development process.

The perspective about gender equality has traversed from a welfare perspective to the current one of empowerment. The Constitution of India guaranteed women equality in all areas of life and the absence of discrimination on the basis of sex as a fundamental right. It also entrusted the State with the responsibility of realising this equality by adopting various measures including positive discrimination in favour of women. Beginning with a welfare perspective; the thrust shifted to development of women from 1974-78 onwards.

In 1974 -75, the Status of Women Committee Report, Towards Equality was published and it revealed gross inequalities and discrimination suffered by women in all areas of life.

The International Women's Conferences in Mexico, Copenhagen, Nairobi and Beijing between 1975 and 1995 were other international events that gave an increasingly radical thrust to the women's problem and provided vision on gender in the state and national policy documents. It was at Beijing that the Platform for Action to realize women's equality was announced. This, along with international convention ratified by India namely, the Convention on the Elimination of all forms of Discrimination against Women (CEDAW) in 1979, influenced very greatly the National Policy for Empowerment of Women, 2001. In the meantime, the National Commission for Women was set up in 1990 by an Act of the Indian Parliament to provide all women their legal entitlements. The 73rd and 74th amendments to the Indian Constitution gave women 33% reservation in local self-governments in rural and urban areas.

WOMEN'S COMPONENT PLAN AND GENDER BUDGETING

The planning Commission of India has always focused on women's issues as per the perceptions of their members on women's status within the economy. The five Year Plans in the pre-1975 treated women as supplementary earners, not active economic agents.

The First Five Year Plan (1951-1956) set up Central Social Welfare Board in 1953 to promote welfare work through voluntary organizations, charitable trusts and philanthropic agencies. India was the first country to introduce family planning programmes during the first five-year plan. Jawaharlal Nehru, the then prime minister of India who had only one daughter was a role model and men were encouraged to take lead in birth control practices.

The Second Five Year Plan (1956-1960) supported development of Mahila mandals for grass roots work among women. It also introduced barrier methods of contraception for both women and men.

The Third, Fourth and Interim Plans (1961-74) made provision for women's education, pre-natal and child health services, supplementary feeding for children, nursing and expectant mothers. In this plan, women's health needs were merged with their children's needs. Invasive methods of contraception and reversible (IUDs) and irreversible (sterilization for men and women) methods were promoted.

The Fifth Plan (1974-1978) marked a major shift in the approach towards women, from welfare to development. It acknowledged the fact of marginalization of women from the economy and also accepted the need for special employment generation programmes for women in the poverty groups. In terms of population policy, this period proved to be disastrous because forcible vasectomy of men during emergency rule of 18 months generated permanent erosion of faith in the top down and bureaucratically managed population policy.

The Sixth Plan (1980-85) accepted women's development as a separate economic agenda. It allotted a separate chapter to focus on women's concerns in the economic development. The Multidisciplinary approach with three-pronged thrust on health, education and employment. It introduced family welfare policy that targeted women for birth control. Promotion of male methods of contraception was found politically harmful by the ruling party. It also netted unpaid family work of women that augmented family resources due to women's efforts of collection of fuel, fodder, water, kitchen gardening, live stock rearing and work in the household enterprise.

The Seventh Plan (1985-1990) declared as its OBJECTIVE TO BRING WOMEN INTO THE MAINSTREAM OF NATIONAL DEVELOPMENT. On the front of population control, clinical trials of long acting and hormone based oral and injectable contraceptives were targeted to women from the marginalized communities.

The Eighth Plan (1992-1997) projected paradigm shift, from development to empowerment and promised to ensure flow of benefits to women in the core sectors of education, health and employment. Outlay for women rose from 4 crores in the 1st Plan to Rs. 2000 crores in the 8th Plan. Anti-pregnancy vaccines, E-P combinations, Depo-provera, Net-O-en were introduced with blessing of USAID and WHO in the form of 'Cafeteria Approach' o birth control.

The Ninth Plan (1997-2002) stated that Empowerment of women was its strategic objective. It accepted the concept of Women's Component Plan to assure at least 30% of funds/benefits from all development sectors flow to women. Gender audit of the budget during the 9th Plan period has revealed that the budgetary allocation for women specific schemes has increased only in the area of family planning. The family planning schemes got additional 700 crores in the budget.[9]

The Tenth Five Year Plan (2002-2009) has suggested specific Strategies, policies and programmes for Empowerment of women. They are as follows:

- Measurement of development has to go beyond achievement of GDP growth to indicators of distributive justice and their monitoring.
- Women headed households have to be specifically targeted, identifying added disadvantages in the rural and urban locations with reference to different parameters of deprivation.
- Formulation of Gender Development Indicators to measure Human Development and their use as a tool for monitoring development needs to be hastened.

- The Component Plan approach, which did not address compartmentalization of government functioning should be replaced with a mandated approach of convergence of services at all levels of governance, through inter-sectoral committees of all Ministries/Departments at the Centre and the States with specific responsibility given to the Panchayats and Municipalities to administer at the grassroots level."

  The United Nations India has suggested that, "To protect the gains of the past and ensure steady progress on indicators of social development and gender equality, and in order to give a fresh impetus to the process of women's empowerment, the Tenth Plan needs to take some bold policy initiatives.

- Earmarking of funds for women under all major poverty alleviation programmes and maintenance of gender disaggregated records of implementation of all poverty alleviation programmes.
- Mandatory registration of all assets provided under government programmes (land, house, animals, production units) in the joint names of husband and wife.
- Intensified focus on rights education and capacity-building interventions for women in all strategic sectors, including health and reproductive health, agriculture, natural resource management, technology (including information technology) and legal awareness.
- Revision of regulatory framework to allow women's collectives to access institutional credit, obtain medium-term leases for cultivation on wastelands and common lands, bid for contracts for collection and sale of minor forest produce and other collective activities that will ensure household food security while regenerating the natural resource base."

Women's groups have demanded allocations for women-specific programmes of strategic nature to arrive at the desired goals in a shorter time span. They should target women of different age groups in terms of strategic interventions to take specific notice of adolescent girls, older women and women in difficult circumstances. Strategic gender tools like gender audits, gender impact assessments, gender analysis and gender budgeting to monitor implementation and impacts must be developed. Gender audit of plans, policies and programmes of various Ministries with pro-women allocations has to be a part and parcel of the monitoring process.

There is a need for provisions in the composite programmes under education, health and rural development sectors to target them specifically at girls/women as the principal beneficiaries and disaggregated within the total allocation. It may also be necessary to place restrictions on their re-appropriation for other purposes.

To effectively attain population stabilization policies and plans need to empower women, promote their reproductive rights and involve men in reproductive decision-making and household responsibilities. Particular attention should be given to improve women's access to quality reproductive health services, including adolescent girls to counseling on reproductive health and sexuality issues.

The strategy of organizing women in self-help groups in the Ninth Plan period has paid good dividends for expanding micro-credit. This should be extended not only for reaching larger numbers of women but also for increasing awareness of and access to social development, apart from encouraging a process of convergence in the delivery of services in a decentralized set up.

It is important to empower women's organizations and citizens groups to monitor enforcement of equal and minimum wages legislation by State governments, and the adherence to norms in poverty alleviation programmes.

Professional Organizations including Universities should be included for undertaking monitoring, evaluation and research studies for identifying issues requiring special attention.

GENDER IMPLICATIONS OF NEW ECONOMIC POLICY

In 1991, at the behest of World Bank and International Monitory Fund, India adopted NEP that has intensified the processes pursued in the last decade and a half (mainly in the post-emergency period), as a result of a new international division of labour between the advanced capitalist economies and the post-colonial economies of Asia, Africa and Latin America. In the late 1970s, transnational and multinational corporations in the USA and Europe realized that the best way to reduce the wage-bill and to enhance profit rates was to move industrial plants to poorer countries like India, Sri Lanka, Bangladesh, etc. The cheap labour of 'docile', 'nimble fingered' and 'flexible' Asian women was found to be most attractive step to enhance profit margins. This policy was given the appealing title of 'Integration of Women in Development.' Systematic critique of this policy was made by IAWS and women economists prevailed upon the architect of NEP, Prof. Man Mohan Singh to make a provision of safety net for women and children.

(a) Gender Implications of Economic Policies in the Post-emergency Period

During the Indian emergency rule in 1975, a major policy-shift took place where the slogan of 'import-substitution' was replaced by the slogan of 'export promotion'. The 'emergency rule' provided politico-repressive instruments to push through a new economic strategy to restructure its industrial sector by introducing a higher degree of mechanisation and rationalisation on the one hand and on the other hand, the expansion of an extremely exploitative informal sector.[10]. A 14-country Alternative Asian Report on the Impact of the UN Decade for Women (1975-1985) at the Nairobi Conference stated, "The new strategy of 'Integration of Women into Development' meant in most cases getting women to work in some income-generating activities, integrating women into market oriented production and thus integrating women into the world market economy. It was not meant that women should expand their subsistence production and produces more for their consumption - for their own food and their clothes. Income-generation in this approach meant money income. Money income could be generated only if women could produce something, which could be sold. People who could buy these products live in western countries.

(b) Women in the Electoral Policy

With amendments of Constitution in 1993 to decentralize political power as per 73rd and 74th Amendments, a provision had to be made for devolution of power and decision-making in favour of women. One third of all seats in the local self-government bodies have to be reserved for women. Rural India has already elected village panchayats with one third elective seats reserved for women i.e. India has one million elected representatives. Women elected representatives are taking active interest in using budgetary allocations for promotion women's education, safe drinking water and sanitation. But,

"Neither the people's representatives at the center nor at the state level, wish to give up their powers over their constituencies and to share their power at the local level. Similarly the bureaucrats are not geared to play the role of facilitators. Giving up powers to representatives of the Panchayati Raj system is difficult for them. Voluntary organizations can play a major role in developing training programmes for all three groups- the politicians at the center and in the states and the bureaucrats in order to help develop new perspectives on their roles."[11]

Elected representatives are facing innumerable problems. Shetkari Sangathana Mahila Aghadi in Maharashtra managed to win election for their all women panels in the last Gram Panchayat elections in spite of stiff opposition from the local vested interests. In spite of threats of rape and witch-hunting by rival political parties, several women in Dhulia district contested elections in Gram Panchayat. In South Gujarat, when a woman activist working for women's rights contested election, the local vested interests tried to divide votes by putting up a 'rubberstamp' woman candidate. When Vijayatai Chowk, a courageous woman's rights activist of Dhule district applied for a Lok Sabha seat, she was refused the seat by the party bosses on the ground that while she would win votes from the brides side, she will not from the bridegroom's side because she had taken up so many cases of dowry-murders in the past 15 years. The political compromises of principles and programmes in the policy resolutions, the increasing importance of 'mafia' politics and exorbitant money power required by the electoral politics act as deterrent for women's participation in the mainstream politics.

Yet Indian women have come on the political agenda of the country through various techniques–collective actions, programmes of consciousness raising, petitioning and lobbying. In addition they have produced well-researched documents and obtained, after great effort, some media visibility for women's issues. This contradictory process must be kept in mind to evolve a proper political understanding of women's political participation in India.

(c) Recent Debate on 33% Reservation of Seats for Women in The Electoral Bodies

Last 14 years experience has revealed that the 73rd and 74th Amendment to the Constitution in 1990 has opened avenues for women's empowerment. For example, in Kerala the state government has given Panchayat bodies power, authority and finance. Out of the state budget, 40% is devolved to the Panchayat and of this 10% is mandated to be utilized for women's programmes. Other states could emulate this pattern. This would enable women to develop their capabilities, to take control of the programmes in such a way that through interaction, criticism and continuous learning, they would develop self-confidence and greater self-esteem. In this context, she cited the example of WDP from Rajasthan and Samakhya from Karnataka. For this to happen on a wider scale, she observed that the policy document ought to be a political document.

In the thirties, the women leaders of India involved in the nationalist struggles were pressing for universal adult franchise and now, sixty years later, the women leaders of the same political parties have agreed to support 33% seats for women. Is this mode one step forward or two steps backward? Those who regard it as one step forward are empowering women to do so because they think, "It will broaden the base of women's political participation and will help to strengthen women's faith in the political process which is otherwise dominated by men". (Women and Media Committee, Bombay). Those who are opposed to this move have consistently held this approach undesirable, right from pre-independence days. Moreover reservation as such is unlikely to solve the main causes of limited political participation of women in furthering women's cause, because given socio-political context where mass illiteracy prevails along with the style of politics that encourages growing violence, mafia politics, character assassination of candidates, prohibitive election expenses and opportunistic/debased politicking pursued to achieve very narrow and short term political goals. Where such influences are operative in the Indian politics in an overwhelming way, more reservation of seats has a limited value.

It is interesting, that same national level male politicians who support 33% reserved seats for women in the Panchayati Raj institutions have expressed their outrage against the reservation of 33% seats for women in the Legislative Assembly and in the Parliament.[12] They are using the same arguments as our colonial masters used against the native then, i.e. women are not be able to govern, as they are inexperienced. Many corporators of Bombay Municipal Corporation have openly expressed their discontentment over this decision of the present government.

During 1990s sharp polarization of political opinions took place around Women's Reservation Bill. It was first tabled in parliament in 1996 and was mired in the conflict over the demand for special quotas for women of the other backward classes and minorities.[13]

The autonomous women's organisations' doubts about 33% reservations have different reasons. They fear that by participating in the corrupt electoral process women's rights activists will not be able to further the broader interests of women.[14] They feel that women activists have to make compromises in their principles, programmes and practices. Moreover, the talented women will be co-opted by the system. The 33% reservation has other dangers. It prepares the ground for opponents of the women's rights movement (the mothers-in-law) to get elected in most of the places. These women are from the elite sections, mainly the kith and the kin of male politicians. Women politicians in South Asia are not different from their male counterparts.[15]

Some scholars and women's organizations do think that the entry of women in the electoral process will help the curbing of violence and corruption, in other words, female presence will moralize the system. Experiences of Karnataka and Kerala have proved the same.[16] This is the argument that women have often advanced as for example in the U.S.A.

NATIONAL COMMISSION FOR WOMEN

Through out the eighties, the National Commission for women has generated a lot of debate among the women's groups. The Committee for the Status of Women (1974) had recommended the formation of such a commission to take up women's problems. The Congress (I) government did not pay any attention to this demand. The report of the National Commission on Self-Employed Women ('Shramshakti') gave a comprehensive picture of women's status and recommended many concrete steps for women in the informal sector. This too was not officially discussed in the parliament. In this climate of official apathy to do anything concretely for women, when the bill on the National Commission for Women was tabled in Lok Sabha on May 22, 1990 many welcomed it as a forward step but these early hopes were soon belied. The content was found less than satisfactory and invited a lot of criticism from women's group as it lacks an autonomous status and has an inbuilt structure that provides far too much governmental interference. The Women's Organisations have proposed to the government that it explicitly define the clauses to protect the autonomy and independence of the commission. Moreover, the reports of the commission should go straight to parliament via the president. It should be empowered to conduct enquiries concerning women even when the government officials or agencies themselves are involved in perpetuating violation of women's rights. Alas, inspire of detailed recommendations given by the women's groups, the present government has not included all of them in the Act. Now, State level women's commissions are active in Maharashtra, Karnataka and Kerala. They are executing state policies for women, promoting advocacy work on women's problems, strengthening elected women representatives in the Panchayati Raj institutions and selectively taking up cases of violence against women. They are effective in the social sector of the economy as they take up women's problems in the areas of education, employment, welfare and health-public health and reproductive rights.

There are thirteen states that had set up women's commissions. The relation between the National Commission and State Commissions for women is not spelt out distinctly. The National Policy is silent on this, yet, a good and positive working relationship should be formalized between them for establishing a synergetic partnership for advancing the cause of women. The unique feature of the commissions is that they have two faces–one looking at the political bureaucratic constellation that is the structure of the government and the other looking at the civil society–lobbies and the other interest groups representing women of India. One advantage the commissions enjoy is that they have more flexibility to take initiative to link with women's studies centres in different states and prepare indicators for monitoring and evaluating the implementation of the Action Plan.

In this context, the National Policy for Empowerment of Women, 2001 does not contain any consistent or deep thought on the implementation mechanism. Against this background, the challenge before the National and the State Commissions would be twofold. The Action Plan must become a women's document. They must own it. It was in the process of ownership that the commissions and women's studies centre could identify meaningful roles for themselves. The constituencies of women outside the pale of states' reach must be involved in the spheres of action, support, advocacy and monitoring. States must conceptualize the plans by involving local communities of women. The resource gap is another challenge to be faced and tackled by a judicious combination of the use of the Component (resources) of the Plan mechanism and the process of gender budgeting. In this context, the example of Kerala where the Panchayat Raj bodies had been given power, authority and finance is praise-worthy. Here 40% of the State budget was devolved to the panchayats and of this 10% was mandated to be utilized for women' programmes exclusively. Other states ought to emulate this pattern. But, at the same time, we must know that several panchayats returned the funds, as they did not have capacity to spend huge funds for big developmental projects. Hence, the government policy documents are giving great emphasis to capacity building efforts to execute the agenda more effectively.

The said Policy is the first policy that the Government of India framed for women. The status of Women Committee had demanded such a policy way back in 1974. While equality between men and women was a fundamental right guaranteed by the Constitution, there were many aspects that were still not spelt out in the Constitution. There was also the question of interpretation of the concept of equality itself. Some used it to mean formal equality but it had limited application to majority of India's women. The formal equality concept did not consider the impact of culture, tradition and other inimical forces on women's capability of availing the equality provision in the Constitution. In contrast, there, was the more equitable concept of 'substantive equality' that used the test of *equality of outcomes* rather than *equality of treatment*. The concept had been enshrined in the Convention on the Elimination of All forms of Discrimination Against Women (CEDAW).

In addition to this, there had to be an affirmative action that would enable women to free themselves from the cumulative negativities of centuries. The policy document referred to these twin objectives and also spoke of changing social attitudes through active participation and community involvement so that women could enjoy all human rights-*de jure* as well as *de facto*. In the keynote address delivered at the Round Table on the National Women Empowerment Policy 2001, Dr. C.P. Sujaya[17] referred to a very important recommendation made in the policy with regard to Personal Laws pertaining to marriage, divorce, maintenance, ownership of property and inheritance etc. (Section 2.2, 2.3). This had been the most contested area in relation to the status of women in India. Yet, the State diluted the strategy of implementation by making it conditional on the initiative of the community–meaning male community leaders and male religious leaders who had all along come in the way of abolition of gender-just personal laws. What was needed was women's agency, she emphasized. Women had to wrest the initiative for legal and social change from the men who would not want to part with it.

Another prescription in the document (section 5.1) was bifurcation of the concept of empowerment into 'economic empowerment' and 'social empowerment'. The compartmentalization was artificial and weakened the process of empowerment which was an intrinsically holistic transformational process affecting all aspects of women's lives. For too long, women had been fixed in a social category. It was only from 1980s onwards (starting with the CSWI report in the mid-seventies) that women's contribution to the economy, particularly of the labouring class, came to public attention, uncovered by the Women's Studies discipline in particular. Education and heath along with nutrition, drinking water, sanitation, housing and shelter, environment, Science and Technology had been the major determinants of women's capabilities to access economic resources. The concepts of Human Development, which was being increasingly used to measure progress of nations, would be a more comprehensive category to gauge women's advancement.

Another laudable feature of the Policy document was the prominent place given to the question of female feticide. The declining sex ratio was a matter of national concern. The document condemned it severely as a violation of the rights of girl child. Drawing any action plan for woman was an enormous task because of their multiple identities and manifold needs. Therefore, no single agency could shoulder this responsibility. Many ministries, departments, agencies in civil society like women's organizations, women's movements, NGOs must be involved in conceptualizing, planning, designing and formulating a plan for advancement of women.

Keeping in view the federal nature of our polity, the diversity of state milieu and the local self-governments in rural and urban areas a national plan should harmonies the state and local level plans. Involvement and in depth consultations with state level agencies would go a long way in rendering the plan acceptable at all levels.

NATIONAL EDUCATION POLICY, 1986 AND BACKLASH AFETR SAP

The National Education policy, 1986 lamented the fact of high drop out rate from educational institutions among girls. But now, its policy imperatives of have been thrown in the dustbin of history and the General Agreement on Trade and Services (GATS) has become the source of inspiration of our policy makers. Privatization in education promoted by GATS has increased the drop out rates for girls. Mushrooming of thousands of unaided colleges and hundreds of Deemed universities charging high capitation fees have furthered gender-based segregation of girls and boys. In higher education, girls are ghettoized into traditional streams such as Humanities, Arts and Commerce. At present, women constitute 43% of the total faculty enrolment in Arts and only 6% in Engineering. Reduction of government expenditure on higher education and encouragement of private colleges have reduced women's opportunities for higher education as private sector colleges promote only the more lucrative professional and technical courses. In this context, the Department of Women and Child Development must grant special scholarships, fellowships and study finds for women and girls in universities, colleges and high schools.[18]

NATIONAL HEALTH POLICY, 2002

Women's health issues and needs have not received adequate attention in the National Health Policy, 2002. Women's groups have demanded a comprehensive policy for women encompassing all stages of women's life cycle, from womb to tomb. The Population policy should not target women of reproductive age groups, but overall physical and mental health needs of women must be addressed in the policy.[19] Gender equity must assume central role in terms of food intake, nutritious diet, right to live a life free from violence (female infanticide, selective abortion of female fetuses, domestic violence, sexual harassment, so on and so forth). The policy must clearly spell out the measure for making health delivery system more gender sensitive.[20] Occupational health and safety, gender-related health implications of environmental damage and gender related public health issues (safe drinking water, sanitation, smokeless *chulla,* pollution control) must be taken up by the National Health Policy. Mental Health Policy, 2001 of Government of India has been severely criticized for its biomedical and drug-centred approach. Resurgence of lobbying in favour of Electro Convulsive Therapy[21] (ECT) by psychiatrists by human rights and women activists. They have demanded that the policy should promote community centred rehabilitative programmes, psychotherapy and counseling of mentally disturbed women.[22] Gendering of policy on HIV-AIDS is a need of an hour. At present, Lawyers Collective is working very hard to sensitize the government departments on the legal, economic and educational rights of HIV-AIDS affected women and girls.[23]

WORLD HEALTH REPORT, 2001

The report advocates for the public health Approach to mental health. It avers "Advances in neuroscience and behavioural medicine have shown that, like many physical illnesses, mental and behavioral disorders are the result of a complex interaction between biological, psychological and social factors. The report gives special emphasis to the needs of women with mental disorder. They are summarized as:

- Medical-Early recognition, Information about illness & treatment, Medical care, Support, hospitalisation.
- Community-No stigma, No discrimination, Social participation, Human rights.
- Family-Skills for care, family cohesion, networking, crisis support, financial support, respite care.

- Rehabilitation-Social support, Education, Vocational support, day care, long-term care, spiritual needs.

WHO approach to deal with biological, psychological and social factors has components of Prevention-Treatment –Rehabilitation. WHO recommends:

- Pharmacotherapy
- Psychotherapy
- Psychosocial rehabilitation
- Vocational rehabilitation
- Housing-process of de-institutionalization & psychiatric reform

Needs of women with Mental Disorder- Women with mental disorders need support from the medical practitioners, community, family and institutions providing support to women in distress.

- Medical-Early recognition, Information about illness & treatment, Medical care, Support, hospitalization.
- Community-No stigma, No discrimination, Social participation, Human rights.
- Family-Skills for care, family cohesion, networking, crisis support, financial support, respite care.
- Rehabilitation-Social support, Education, Vocational support, day care, long term care, spiritual needs.

WHO recommendations for Mental HealthCare include the following aspects:

- Provide treatment in primary care
- Make psychotropic drugs available
- Give care in community
- Educate the public
- Involve communities, families & consumers
- Establish National policies, programmes & legislations
- Develop human resource
- Link with other sectors
- Monitor community mental health
- Support more research

SAARC POLICY ON GIRL CHILD

Declaration of SAARC has highlighted 3 main areas for strategic intervention to improve quality of life for girls. They are survival and protection of the girl child and safe motherhood, overall development of the girl child and special protection for vulnerable girl children in difficult circumstances and belonging to special groups. Government of India has taken the following measures for capacity building among girl child.

- Juvenile Justice (Care and Protection of Children) Act.
- Integrated Child Development Scheme.
- Establishment of Childline Service, a 24 hour phone service for girl children on the streets for proper counselling and information about shelter homes, NGOs, hospitals.
- Special emphasis on girl's education.
- National Commission for Children, special mandate for girls.
- National Nutrition Mission to provide supplements to adolescent girls and expectant mothers.
- Special scheme to target quality of life of adolescent girls.

Policy on HIV/AIDS keeping pace with new forms of sexual exploitation of girls, child abuse, proliferation of drugs and trafficking of children.

State governments have formulated State Plan of Action for Girl Child appropriate to the conditions prevailing in each state. Karnataka, Madhya Prudish, Thailand and Goa have taken lead in this direction.

A CASE STUDY OF STATE POLICY OF MAHARASHTRA FOR WOMEN

It was in 1994 that the Maharashtra state declared a state policy for Women. After the National Policy of empowerment of Women 2001, was declared the Maharashtra state too revised their policy in 2001 and this policy had been informed by national and international conventions ratified by the Government of India.

The policy envisaged making justice available to women in economic, political, social and legal matters by focusing on situations where they experience discrimination and iniquitous treatment. The economic empowerment was sought to be achieved through mechanisms like MAVIM, Self-Help groups and budgeting exercises. In the social sphere, emphasis has been put on improving the overall health status of women, reduction in maternal and infant mortality, nutrition and immunization programmes.

In the legal sphere, the commission's thrust had been on new legislation, rendering the approach of judges and officials dealing with legal matters gender sensitive and on having fast track courts so that justice was dispersed without delay.

Arguing that women ought to be involved in planning programmes for women in decision-making capacities, think-tank of the state government

YASHADA had published GRs issued by the government from time to time. But the machinery for implementation is weak, only 9 of 25 policies could be implemented. The rest remained only on paper and the funds allotted were also partly used. At the recently held Roundtable on Women Empowerment Policy, the Chairperson the Maharashtra State Commission for Women, Ad. Normal Savant Prabhawalkar suggested that the state government should consult the commission as well as women's organizations in planning and executing the strategies of implementation.[24]

The state government of Maharashtra took major initiative to bring gender concerns on the social and political agenda of the state by preparing a policy document, POLICY FOR WOMEN IN MAHARASHTRA. As the document declares, the policy is "an attempt to identify immediate steps that the state can take to improve the position of women." Important features of the policy are:

- Statutory provision for reserving 10 % of all income and land at the gram panchayat level under the control of women's committee.
- Government allotments and primary memberships of societies to be made in the joint names of husband and wife.
- Amendments in the Hindu Law of Inheritance (1956) for ensuring equal share of the movable and immovable property of the husband.
- Reservation of 30% of government jobs for women.
- Women would constitute 25% of the police force in the state of Maharashtra. The state should take steps to re-orient and retain police force and set up women headed police stations in metropolitan cities to safeguard women against violence and atrocities.

GENDER AUDIT OF BUDGETS

Understanding the relationship between macro economic policies and the Union Budget, state budgets and the Panchayati Raj Institutions is a MUST as it impacts women's lives in several ways. It is good economic sense to make national budgets gender-sensitive, as this will enable more effective targeting of government expenditure to women specific activities and reduce inequitable consequences of previous fiscal policies. The Gender Budget Initiative is a policy framework, methodology and set of tools to assist governments to integrate a gender perspective into the budget as the main national plan of public expenditure. It also aims to facilitate attention to gender analysis in review of macroeconomic performance, ministerial budget preparations, parliamentary debate, and mainstream media coverage. It directly promotes women's development through allocation of budgetary funds for women's programmes and reduces opportunities for empowerment of women through budgetary cuts. The process of gender budgeting has been a post-facto effort to dissect/analyze and thus offset any undesirable gender-specific consequences of the previous budget.

Structural adjustment programmes and globalization policies have directly increased women's unpaid work burden, thereby increased women- provided subsidy in the economy. Devaluation of income for the majority of masses as a result of new economic policy coupled with price rise, erosion of public distribution system and reduction of services offered by the public health system have made women bear disproportionate share of burden, because in the patriarchal families women have to shoulder responsibility of providing meals and looking after the sick family members. Hence women have high stakes in preventing an increase in the proportion of indirect taxes on essential commodities and in budgetary provisions to guarantee food security and health care. Hence, careful study of the working of PDS and local taxonomy on food security and impact on nutrition, health and health services of budgetary allocations is a must.[25]

Budgets garner resources through the taxation policies and allocate resources to different sections of the economy. The Budget is an important tool in the hands of state for affirmative action for improvement of gender relations through reduction of gender gap in the development process. It can help to reduce economic inequalities, between men and women as well as between the rich and the poor.[26] Hence, the budgetary policies need to keep into considerations the gender dynamics operating in the economy and in the civil society. There is a need to highlight participatory approaches to pro-poor budgeting, green budgeting, local and global implications of pro-poor and pro-women budgeting, alternative macro scenarios emerging out of alternative budgets and inter-linkages between gender-sensitive budgeting and women's empowerment. Serious examining of budgets calls for greater transparency at the level of international economics to local processes of empowerment. There is a need to provide training and capacity building workshops for decision-makers in the government structures, *gram sabhas*, parliamentarians and audio-visual media.

GENDER ISSUES IN ENVIRONMENTAL POLICY

In the 1980s, governments and development agencies became much more aware of the need to consider gender issues in their environmental and natural resource management programmes. This led to changes in project design and implementation. Eco-feminists have played crucial role in evolution of new gender-sensitive approach among the policy makers.[27] But in actual practice, the economic vested interests have reigned supreme.

Policy makers first came to appreciate that women 'play an essential role in the management of natural resources, including soil, water, forests and energy...and often have a profound traditional and contemporary knowledge of the natural world around them'.[28] The exclusion of women from environmental projects-through outright neglect or belief in the gender neutrality of projects-would thus be a recipe for project failure. Subsequently, donor agencies came to see women as especially vulnerable: 'their responsibilities as day-to-day environmental managers...make women both victims of and contributors to the natural environment's degradation and pollution.' On the other hand, gradually, awareness grew of many grassroots success stories of women fighting to conserve local resources-such as greening of deserts in Rajasthan, *Appiko* in Karnataka, *Chipko* in Tehri Garhwal and Junagarh in Gujarat, *Narmada BachaoAndolan* in M.P., Maharashtra and Gujarat.

GENDER BIAS AND HOUSING POLICY

The gendered construct of social and economic relations within and outside the household and deeply entrenched patriarchal attitudes in the civil society discriminate against women in virtually every aspect of housing, be it policy development, entitlement in government projects, control over household resources, right of inheritance and ownership and even the construction of housing. Important questions concerning housing policies are:

- 'Can we make policy makers and planners who are working at the state level understand the politics of built environment and gender rules?'
- 'What are our alternatives to the existing approach adopted by Sight and Service Schemes (SSS) and Slum Rehabilitation Schemes (SRS)?'
- 'What interventions can we make in the city planning which involves physical access, economic access and social access?'

Women's Right To Housing (WRH): WRH is linked with women's right in property, land and inheritance. As primary user of housing, women's stakes and requirements are the highest in housing. For women, beyond shelter, housing is a place of employment, a place for social interaction, a place for childcare and a refuge from social instability and sexual violence.

Special Needs of Women Headed Households (WHHs): In the peaceful areas of India, 1/10th of the households are headed by divorced, deserted and single women. In our country, in the conflict prone areas, over 30% households are headed by women. In WHHs women shoulder main economic responsibilities including house hunting. Even if they have money, they face hurdles while looking out for a rented place or a house on an ownership basis. Nearly one-third of households worldwide are now headed by women; in certain parts of Africa and Latin America, as many as 45 per cent are FHH. The households headed by women tend to be poorer than male-headed households. United Nations Centre For Human Settlements (UNCHS) (Habitat) estimates that at least 600 million people in the cities of developing countries live in shelters that is life-or health threatening.

Women's Rights to stay in Parental and Matrimonial Homes: In the last 20 years, many women have filed petitions in the High Courts and the Supreme Court of India demanding wife's right to live in the matrimonial home and daughter's right to stay in the ancestral home. As per Mitakshara laws applicable in the Hindu Code, only sons get coparsonary rights over ancestral property as they are considered *Karta.* Lata Mittal challenged Mitakshara laws applicable to Hindu daughters who are deprived of right to stay in the ancestral home.

Housing and Women's Identity: Women's identity is entwined with a house but housing's identity as a capital investment and the largest outlay in the household budget lies with male head of the household. Whether women are or aren't property owners, their place of sphere is considered to be within the house. Even, this cult of domesticity does not help women as it perpetuates low status of women. Market economy devalues domestic work and the mainstream planners and policy makers consider it 'non-work' and invisibles women's housing concerns.

Gender Bias and Housing Problems: The gendered construct of social and economic relations within and outside the household and deeply entrenched patriarchal attitudes in the civil society discriminate against women in virtually every aspect of housing, be it policy development, entitlement in government projects, control over household resources, right of inheritance and ownership and even the construction of housing.

Emerging Issues: There is a need to focus on housing in terms of "personal meanings" as well as affordability, women's role and the housing industry. The state must take affirmative action to empower women in exercising their housing rights because men as property owners enjoy privileged position and control housing delivery system. Moreover general subordination of women is also reflected in women's lack of representation in higher echelons political bodies. Societal restrictions reinforce women's status as second- class citizens. As a result, women professionals in the housing industry i.e. engineers, architects and agents have to sub-serve the interests of male-dominated construction industry.

Gender Aware Approach: Gender-neutral approach in housing goes against women's interest. Hence there is a need to introduce gender aware approach in housing that takes women's strategic and practical needs, concerns and rights into consideration. For that, we will have to sensitize all stake groups in the housing industry i.e. land surveyors, builders, developers, designers, financiers, mortgage bankers, lawyers, credit unions, government officers, material suppliers, real estate brokers, appraisers, contractors, interior decorators, gardeners, landscape architects and cooperative societies. In the language of economics, both, supply side-production, construction, management, maintenance, rehabilitation and the demand side community groups, consumer forum and cooperative societies should be sensitized about women's housing rights.

Gender Audit of Syllabi for Engineering, Architecture and Interior Designing: Public-private split in the syllabi of construction related academic disciplines needs to be questioned. The syllabus should emphasize that as a physical structure, the house is a site for multi-tasking- house work (cooking, cleaning, caring), home-making and wage-labour for majority of women all over the world. A house layout influences and affects gender roles among household members and therefore mirrors change in society's concept of the family. Designing of house should promote the ethos of shared housework by men and women members of the household.

International Human Rights Law on Security of Tenure: A person is said to have a secure tenure if he/she is protected from being removed arbitrarily and involuntarily from their homes and lands. Tenure is secure if it is protected by legislation rather than protected merely through customs and traditions.

Threat to Women's Security of Tenure (WST): Circumstances and conditions that threaten WST are:

- *Gender biased laws:* Preventing women from owning, inheriting, purchasing, leasing, renting, bequeathing housing, land and property.
- *Judicial Interpretation of the Law:* No explicit forbidding of WRH in gender- neutral laws, still they create obstacles for WRH because of male-chauvinistic interpretation of the gender neutral laws. General statements are considered to be applicable to only men.
- *Land and Housing Systems:* As they grant titles to private property to "Heads of Households" who are often deemed to be men.[29]
- *Customary laws, Traditions, Attitudes:* Many cultures and customs don't grant women's independent existence. In several cultures women staying alone, without male protection are punished severely due to sexist attitudes. Customary laws are not codified. In polygamous and polyandrous communities, shared community values go against individual women leading independent life.

Domestic Violence: Domestic violence challenges security of tenure of women by generating fear, tension, insecurity among women victims and their minor children. Violation of WRH can be both the cause and the consequence of violence against women, particularly in case of domestic violence.

Financial and Material Barriers: Major hurdles faced by women in the housing market are due to gender-biased policies in financing for housing, availability of services, material and infrastructure, affordability, habitability, accessibility, location and cultural adequacy to handle political economy of housing. Women face major difficulties in securing loans for purchase of good quality housing. It is not easy for single women or WHH to get rental housing. Even if they manage to get rented homes, they have to face harassment of various sorts. Unmarried single women are perceived as threat to sexual morality. In the absence of old age homes for women, the plight of women senior citizens is deplorable. Many destitute women start staying on the pavements or railway platforms.

Indian NGOs and WRH: Two decades of Debate-Two positions.

1. *WRH independent of male ownership & Control* because women's land-use priorities are different from that of men.
2. *Joint Titles*- majority of poor masses hardly manage to have one house. Hence, separate house for women is a non-issue.

The Felt Need: Need for a training manual to deal with the modalities of attaining WRH Experiences of SEWA and SPARC:

SEWA: inclusion of women's name in the title to property before granting loans for housing. As monetary benefits accrue to the family, the husband/ father and family members accept the proposal of joint titles to land/house.

SPARC: Supports Mahila Milan (MM), network of pavement dwellers, assists MM to get recognition and support from the settlements, skills & training, makes resources available for the low cost housing.

State and Civil Society Initiatives: Progressive states have empowered women by granting housing rights.e.g. Building societies in Sweden & England. Unions in Germany, Self help Groups & cooperative Enterprises in Canada, Central & Latin America, Africa and Asia. The enlightened nation states accept societal responsibility for women's housing and the rest live it to individual women to fend for themselves.

Witch-hunting of Women Exercising Right to Housing

- *Bhootali*" (Maharashtra),*Dayeen* (Bihar)-Widowed/divorcee Dalit/ tribal women.
- *In the latest Koombha Mela* 60000 women were deserted by their family members.
- *Sarpanch, Talati &Tahasildars* taking advantage of illiterate women.
- In Algeria and West African countries FFHs were burnt. International Committee of Women Living Under Muslim Laws.

Crucial Conventions for WRH:

- The Universal Declaration of Human Rights, 1948
- The Elimination of All Forms of Discrimination Against women, (CEDAW) 1979
- The housing rights of Refugees, 1951
- The Housing Rights of Indigenous People(Not yet adopted) are DIRECTED AT GOVERNMENTS.

The UN on Forced Eviction: "Women...and other vulnerable individuals and groups suffer disproportionately from the practice of forced eviction. Women in all groups are especially vulnerable given the extent of statutory and other forms of discrimination which often apply in relation to property rights (including home ownership) or rights of access to property or accommodation, and their particular vulnerability to acts of violence and sexual abuse when they are rendered homeless."

(UN Committee on Economic, Social, and Cultural Rights, Sixteenth Session, 1997).

Displaced Population due to Natural as well as man-made disasters: Women victims of natural disasters such as floods, earthquacks and social disasters such as caste, communal, ethnic conflicts and war.

There are three approaches adopted by people-oriented architects to handle the issue of shelter.

1. *Legal approach:* It deals with ownership rights and tenure, right to matrimonial property of married women, right to ancestral home for an unmarried daughter. Hema Dandekar's study of Charcop's Sight and Service Scheme reveals that in this scheme there is no bar against women owning a house. Loan facilities given for buying a flat depend upon the repaying capacity of women.
2. *Social Approach:* House as a unit is related to family structure. It gets reflected in a housing policy. Women and Shelter Group, Mumbai had done advocacy work in these regards. After 1993, some of us made interventions in changing the scenario. Feminist architect based in Mumbai shares her experiences in these words,

   "We took responsibility to reconstruct the destroyed homes in the riot-affected areas near Mahim utilizing Times of India funds. For this we had to run from pillar to post. We had to face an extremely communal attitude of the entire bureaucracy. After three-four months, we managed to get a plot of land/*pattas* in Dindoshi. We had to meet the collector a couple of times to see to it that the *pattas* given to riot-affected people are in the name of women because women use these *pattas* for subsistence while men use them as commodity in the market."

3. Physical planning of a house: Patriarchal values get reflected in the physical planning of a house. Rules and regulations, by-laws have been stipulated by the Urban Development Department. In BDD chawls, all spaces allocated for community have been used by men where women feel constrained. In slum projects and sight and service projects, kitchen and toilets are clubbed together. 'Kitchen and toilet' are treated as isolated spaces while women beneficiaries of slum development projects don't like it. Architects from MHADA don't listen to the women's point of view. Ventilation is not considered to be all that important. A small study of slums and chawls in Bombay showed that women emphasized a separate space in the community that is exclusively used for washing clothes and making *chapatis* (Collective kitchen). *Nagari Nivara* Trust headed by Mrunal Gore and Baburao Sawant is dealing with a mass housing project for five thousand people. In this, we have made a provision for a space in the community, which is exclusively used, for women's activities. Even, the ownership titles are made in the name of women. There is a need for a shelter home for women in distress and a *creche* within each plot. SPARC, Bombay has managed to get *balwadi* and community hall included in their project areas. As per the FSI regulation, while zoning and city planning, 'public' is separated from 'private' but in actual reality women's lives are not compartmentalized like this. We need to critique the existing housing policies, demystify technical language and conduct surveys to understand how women's lives are affected by the urban development. To bring changes in the by-laws that are gender sensitive and people friendly, the lawyers and architect will have to work in collaboration. We need to raise consciousness among the students of architecture, more than fifty per cent of who are women. When I ask the students of architecture the question regarding home–based professions, they identify women home-based professionals as providers of *crèche* facilities, dance-teachers or beauticians, while male home-based professionals are identified as engineers, doctors, chartered accountants and management consultants. Many women architects are going to be home-based professionals and they have to redesign the existing patterns of houses, keeping in mind both house-work and professional duties. The same applies to their women clients who are shouldering double burden. Advantages of keeping kitchen-space near drawing/living room are many:
4. Women don't feel isolated from rest of the happenings in the outside world.
5. All members of the family start taking interest in kitchen cabinet. They get encouraged to share housework.

6. It ensures cleanliness of the kitchen area, as it is visible.

Women's housing needs must be understood from the point of view of women's rights to dignified life. They should not face any discrimination in exercising their housing rights due to their caste, race, age, religion and ethnicity. State and civil society initiatives must facilitate the process of women's empowerment through exercising WHRs. The local self-government bodies should reserve 10% of all houses/flats/industrial units/shops in the market places for women. Schools of Architecture, Engineering Colleges and Institutions for Interior Designing should organize capacity building workshops and training programmes for women. Gender sensitization of the decision-makers in the housing industry and the elected representatives of the mainstream political bodies should be given top priority. For formulation of gender-sensitive policies, experts on the subject should be inducted in the apex bodies of urban, rural and tribal housing projects.

DEVELOPMENT ALTERNATIVES WITH WOMEN

During the seventies WM was highlighting marginalization of women in the economy.[30] This approach is known as 'WID'-Women in Development. Three major findings of Towards Equality (Status of Women in India) Report, 1974, which sensitized the decision-makers of our country were:

- Continuously declining sex ratio of women.
- Declining work-participation of women.
- High rate of mortality and morbidity among women.

During the eighties, women's groups made an effort to integrate women in the economy. But the means of production, exchange and distribution being controlled by men allowed women very limited space to evolve a development alternative with women (DAWN).[31] In this approach, articulate-urbane-highly educated and politically connected women got prominence as the spokespersons of women from the marginalized section. In this period, the Indian economy was most ferociously attacking the survival base of the mass of poor women in the rural, tribal and urban areas.[32] While women employees in the white-collar occupations, women professionals such as lawyers, doctors, scientists, educationists, teachers, chartered accountants, women employees in the central and state government as well as in the corporate world and financial institutions managed to get some economic gains. This decade witnessed some of the most militant mass mobilizations of women on wide range of issues–water, drought, caste riots, communal tensions, police-brutality against forest people, agricultural labourers, industrial workers, white-collar women employees problems about promotion and transfer, sexual harassment at workplace, harassment for dowry and bride price, witch hunting, widow burning, sexual violence against women, coercion in the family planning programmes, selective abortion of female foetuses, female infanticide, child-care facilities, woes of women workers in the development schemes supported by the state and central governments as well as by the international aid agencies and the voluntary organizations.[33] Several alliances and collaborative ventures of this period, engendered trust among different stake groups dealing with these issues from different positions of power. This approach is known as WAD-Women and Development. This approach focused on a patriarchal control over women's sexuality, fertility and labour. In this phase, women's groups established rapport with pro-women individuals (men and women) in the government, the state apparatus, the criminal justice system, the legal system, the political parties and the professional bodies. The decade of nineties is marked by an approach of Gender and Development (GAD). Here the focus is on the power relations determined as a result of interplay of complex class, caste, ethnicity, religion, races and gender.

This is an era of PARTNERSHIP with gender-just men with a clear-cut understanding that women constitute half of the world population, 2/3 of the world's workforce and get only 1/10th of the world's income and own only 1/100 the of the world's wealth.[34] With this resource-base the decision-makers will have to empower the mass of toiling women who are struggling to survive. Engendering state and national policy documents is an ongoing and continuous process to further the cause of women's economic and social empowerment.

GENDER MEDIA POLICY

After consistent monitoring and protests by women's rights groups against stereotypical, negative and sexist portrayal of women in the print as well as audio-visual electronic media[35], the government of India appointed P.C. Joshi Committee to recommend guidelines for the communication media. The Ministry of Information and Broadcasting has been looking at this issue from a bureaucratic perspective. The Government of India agreed to adhere to A Statement of Commitment: Forward Looking Strategies (FLS) Drawn up at the 1985 Nairobi Meet.[36] The Government of India agreed to:

- Eliminate discriminatory, stereotyped and degrading images of women in the media.
- Launch comprehensive and sustained public campaigns using media and traditional institutions of communications to challenge and abolish all discriminatory perceptions, attitudes and practices by the year 2000.
- Take steps to control pornography and portrayal of women as sex objects.
- Involve women in making decisions about all public information efforts.

- Introduce measures to ensure that women participate in council and review bodies that regulate mass media including advertising.
- Promote women's cultural projects that change traditional images of women and men.
- Mobilize mass media to ensure public consensus on the need for men to share child-rearing responsibilities.
- Support the United Nations in carrying out studies on sex stereotyping in the mass media and in advertising.

To promote women's information networks, the Government of India agreed to:

- Support groups that promote the role of women as active participants in development to set up effective information communication networks.
- Foster international co-operation related to women's sharing of experience.
- Rely on information networks to publicize the FLS document and the goals of the Decade for Women, as well as women's programmes and activities.
- Increase availability of training for women in the use of audio-visual forms of information dissemination and in use of computers.

JUDICIAL ACTIVISM FOR GENDERING STATE AND NATIONAL POLICIES

Women's groups and human rights organizations have been using Public Interest Litigations and judicial activism to engender legal system and to get new laws for women victims of violence such as rape, sexual harassment at workplace, domestic violence, trafficking of women and children, action against selective abortions of female fetuses through Pre Natal Diagnostic Techniques Act, appropriate use of government budgetary allocation and right to information. Draft bills on women related issues prepared by The Law Commission of India, the National Commission and the State Commissions for women are judiciously monitored by women's groups and gender aware legal rights groups such as Lawyers Collective, Majlis, Women's Research and Action Group, Human Rights and Law Network and India Centre for Human Rights and Law. They are making inputs from the point of view that *Women's Rights are Human Rights.*[37]

CONCLUSION

States in which women's studies and women's movement are influential and articulate in including women's needs, aspirations and demands on the decision-making agenda, we find effective engendering of state policies. The UNDP has also taken lead in evolution of Gender Equity Policy of Gujarat state. Maharashtra, Kerala, West Bengal, Madhya Pradesh, Karnataka, Andhra Pradesh and Tamil Nadu have been pro-active states with regard to engendering their policy documents. Inter-state comparison in the women empowerment discourse through Human Development Reports and in the publications of Department of Women and Child Development, Government of India have created urge among sensitive administrators, politicians and NGOs to make concerted efforts to improve women's profile in the economic, social-cultural and political spheres.

NOTES

1. *Towards Equality,* Committee on Status of Women in India, Government of India, New Delhi, 1974 and Updated Version Published in 2001.
2. Boserup, Esther *Women's Rolè in Economic Development,* London: Aberdeen George Allen and Unwin, 1970.
3. Devaki Jain, "Valuing Women's Work: Time as a Measure", *Economic and Political Weekly*, Vol. XXXI, no 43, October 26 1996, WS-46-WS 57.
4. Census Reports, 1981, 1991 and 2001 on Demographic Profile, Education and Economic Activities.
5. NSSO-Sarvekshana Reports, 38 Round Onwards.
6. Economic Survey, Government of India, 1985 Onwards.
7. Pioneering work in this regard was based on research papers presented at the I and II technical workshops of EIWIG; some of them were included in Devaki Jain and Nirmala Banerjee (ed) *Tyranny of Household*, Vikas Publishing House, Delhi, 1985.
8. **National Perspective Plan for Women (1988-2000 A.D.),* Department of Women and Child Development, Government of India, 1988.

   **Shramshakti Report,* Committee on Self-Employed Women and Women in the Unorganised Sector, Government of India, 1988.
9. See Chapter 5 "Budgetary Policies–A Gender Analysis" in Vibhuti Patel *Women's Challenges in the New Millennium*, Gyan Publications, New Delhi, 2002. Also, Vibhuti Patel "Gender Budget-A Case study of India", Centre for Advanced Study in Economics, University of Mumbai, Working Paper UDE (CAS) 7(7)/2003.
10. Desai, Neera and Patel, Vibhuti (1990), *Indian Women-Change and Challenge*, Popular Publications, Mumbai.
11. Armaity S. Desai "Challenges for the Voluntary Sector in India at the Beginning of the Twenty-first Century", Perspectives in Social Work, Vol. XVI, No. 3, Sept.-Dec., 2001, p. 11.
12 Indian Association of Women's Studies Newsletter" Indian Women in Political Process", Special Issue, Women's Studies Centre, University of Pune, January, 2002.
13. Devaki Jain *The Vocabulary of Women's Politics*, Fredrich Ebert Stiftung, Delhi, 2000. Also see, an Article by Mary John in Review of Women's Studies, *Economic and Political Weekly*, Bombay, Vol. XXXV, Numbers 43-44, pp. ws 22-ws. 60.

14. Vibhuti Patel Getting foothold in Politics, Reading in Women's Studies Series, Research Centre for Women's Studies, SNDT Women's University, Mumbai, 1993.
15. Rounaq Jahan "Women in South Asian Politics", Mainstream, Delhi, August 15, 1987, pp.35-44.
16. Uma Prachar, A resource Letter on Panchayat Raj, Vol. 8, No. 4, December, 2001.
17. C.P. Sujaya "Women Empowerment Policy, 2001", Keynote Address Delivered at Roundtable Conference on WEP, 2001, Jointly Organised by Women Development Cell and Maharashtra State Commission for Women in Mumbai, November 28-29, 2003.
18. Vibhuti Patel "Women in Economic Development' in B.L. Mungekar (ed) The Economy of Maharashtra-Changing Structure and Emerging Issues, Dr. Ambedkar Institute of Social and Economic change, Himalaya Publishing House, Mumbai, 2003.
19. Gopalan, S. and Shiva, M. (2000), *National Profile on Women*, Health and Development Country Profile-India, Voluntary Health Association of India and World Health Organization.
20. V. Mohanan Nair "Draft National Health Policy, 2001: A Leap Forward in Assessment but Limping in Strategies", The National Medical Journal of India, Vol. 15, No. 4, 2002, pp. 216-221.
21. Pathare, Soumitra "Beyond ECT: Priorities in Mental Health Care in India", Issues in Medical Ethics, Vol. XI, No. 1, January-March, 2003, pp. 11-12.
22. Davar, Bhargavi "Women-centred Mental Health: Issues and Concerns", Vikalpa-Alternatives, Special Issue, Gender and Transformation, Vikas Adhyayan Kendra, Mumbai, Vol. IX, No. 1 & 2, 2001. pp. 117-130.
23. POSITIVE Dialogue, Lawyers Collective HIV/AIDS Unit, Mumbai, Newsletter # 6; August 2000, p. 4.
24. Sharayu Anantram and Vibhuti Patel "National Policy for Empowerment of Women", Urdhva Mula, An Interdisciplinary Journal focusing on Women and related Issues, Mumbai, Sophia Centre for Women's Studies and Development, Vol. 2, No. 2, December, 2003, pp. 103-139.
25. Vibhuti Patel "Gendering the Budget at State and National Level and Gender Audit of the Union Budget-A critical Approach", Urdhva Mula, Mumbai, Vol. 1, No. 1, 2002, pp. 30-57.
26. National Centre for Advocacy Studies *Parliament Digest For the People*, Pune, 2003.
27. Vandana Shiva *Staying Alive-Women, Ecology and Development*, Zed Books, London, U.K., 1988.
28. World Development Report, World Bank, Oxford University Press, N.Y., 1991.
29. Jeemol Unni (1999) "Property Rights of Women: Case for Joint Titles to Agricultural Land and Urban Housing", Economic and Political Weekly, Mumbai, May 22-28.
30. Pioneering work in these regards has been by Esther Boserup (1970), *Women's Role in Economic Development*, Aberdeen George Allen and Unwin, London.

31. Geeta Sen and Caren Grown (1985), *Development Alternative with Women*, DAWN Network, Monthly Review Press, 1987.
32. Shirin Kudchetkar and Sabiha Al-Issa (eds.), *Violence Against Women*, Pencraft International, Delhi, 1998.
33. Documentary evidences of the mass mobilisations of women are available in the issues (1985 onwards) of Economic and Political Weekly (Bombay), Social Action (Delhi), Mainstream (Delhi), Seminar (Delhi), Manushi (Delhi) and Samya Shakti(Delhi), Lokayan Bulletin (Delhi).
34. This data is culled out from the country reports submitted during Women's Decade (1975-1985) to The United Nations, INSTRAW and UNIFEM, New York, 1990. Conceptual basis of the same lies in the debate around paid and unpaid work, wage-work and housework (cooking, cleaning and caring), unpaid family labour of rural women which augments family resources such as collection of fuel, fodder and water, invisibles work of women and girls who are working for family\ households businesses among the artisan classes such as potters, weavers, handloom and power loom owners, lace makers, brass workers, carpet industry, owner cultivators.
35. Vimal Balasubramanyan *Mirror Image*, A CED Publications, Bombay, 1988.
36. International Women's Tribunal Centre, New York, 37/38, 1986-87.
37. See The Lawyers Collective and Combat Law from Delhi & Mumbai, Majlis and WRAG publications from Mumbai.

REFERENCES

Balasubramanyan Vimal (1988), *Mirror Image*, A CED Publications: Bombay.

Boserup, Ester (1970), *Women's Role in Economic Development,* Aberdeen George Allen and Unwin: London.

Davar, Bhargavi (2001), Women-centred Mental Health: Issues and Concerns, *Vikalpa-Alternatives*, Special Issue, Gender and Transformation, Vikas Adhyayan Kendra, Mumbai, IX(1& 2): 117-130.

Desai, Armaity S. (2001), Challenges for the Voluntary Sector in India at the Beginning of the Twenty-first Century, *Perspectives in Social Work*, Vol. XVI, No. 3, Sept.-Dec., p. 11.

Desai, Neera and Patel, Vibhuti (1990), *Indian Women-Change and Challenge*, Popular Publications: Mumbai.

Devaki Jain (1996), Valuing Women's Work: Time as a Measure, *Economic and Political Weekly*, XXXI(43) : WS-46-WS 57.

Devaki Jain and Nirmala Banerjee (ed.) (1985), *Tyranny of Household*, Vikas Publishing House, Delhi.

Gopalan, S. and Shiva, M. (2000), *National Profile on Women*, Health and Development Country Profile-India, Voluntary Health Association of India and World Health Organization, New Delhi.

Government of India (1974, 2001), *Towards Equality,* Committee on Status of Women in India, New Delhi.

Government of India (1981, 1991, 2001), *Census Reports*, New Delhi.

Government of India (Various Years), *Sarvekshana Reports*, NSSO, New Delhi.

Government of India (Various Years), Economic Survey, New Delhi.

Government of India (1988), *National Perspective Plan for Women (1988-2000 A.D.)*, Department of Women and Child Development, New Delhi.

Government of India (1988), *Shramshakti Report,* Committee on Self-Employed Women and Women in the Unorganised Sector, New Delhi.

Indian Association of Women's Studies Newsletter (2002), Indian Women in Political Process, Special Issue, Women's Studies Centre, University of Pune, January.

Jahan, Rounaq (1987), Women in South Asian Politics, *Mainstream*, August 15, pp. 35-44.

Jain, Devaki (2000), *The Vocabulary of Women's Politics*, Fredrich Ebert Stiftung, Delhi.

John, Mary (2000), Review of Women's Studies, *Economic and Political Weekly*, XXXV (43-44): ws22-ws 60.

Kudchetkar, Shirin and Sabiha Al-Issa (eds.) (1998), *Violence Against Women*, Pencraft International: Delhi.

Nair, Mohanan (2002), Draft National Health Policy, 2001: A Leap Forward in Assessment but Limping in Strategies, *The National Medical Journal of India*, 15(4): 216-221.

National Centre for Advocacy Studies (2003), *Parliament Digest For the People*, Pune.

Patel, Vibhuti (2002), Gendering the Budget at State and National Level and Gender Audit of The Union Budget-A Critical Approach, *Urdhva Mula,* 1 (1): 30-57.

Patel, Vibhuti (2002), Budgetary Policies- A Gender Analysis, in Patel, Vibhuti (Ed.) *Women's Challenges in the New Millennium*, Gyan Publications: New Delhi.

Patel, Vibhuti (2003), Gender Budget-A Case Study of India, Working Paper UDE (CAS) 7(7)/2003, Centre for Advanced Study in Economics, University of Mumbai, Mumbai.

Patel, Vibhuti (2003), Women in Economic Development, in B.L. Mungekar (ed.) The Economy of Maharashtra-Changing Structure and Emerging Issues, Dr. Ambedkar Institute of Social and Economic Change, Himalaya Publishing House, Mumbai.

Patel, Vibhuti (1993), Getting Foothold in Politics, *Reading in Women's Studies Series*, Research Centre for Women's Studies, SNDT Women's University, Mumbai.

Pathare, Soumitra (2003), Beyond ECT: Priorities in Mental Health Care in India, *Issues in Medical Ethics*, XI(1): 11-12.

POSITIVE Dialogue (2000), Lawyers Collective HIV/AIDS Unit, Mumbai, Newsletter #6, August, p. 4.

Prachar, Uma (2001), A Resource Letter on Panchayat Raj, Vol. 8, No. 4, December.

Sen, Geeta and Caren Grown (1985*),* Development Alternative with Women, *DAWN* Network, Monthly Review Press, 1987.

Sharayu Anantram and Vibhuti Patel (2003), National Policy for Empowerment of Women, Urdhva Mula, *An Interdisciplinary Journal Focusing on Women and Related Issues*, Mumbai, Sophia Centre for Women's Studies and Development, 2 (2): 103-139.

Shiva, Vandana (1988), *Staying Alive-Women, Ecology and Development*, Zed Books, London, U.K.

Sujaya, C.P. (2001), Women Empowerment Policy, 2001, Keynote Address Delivered at Roundtable Conference on WEP, 2001, Jointly Organised by Women Development Cell and Maharashtra State Commission for Women in Mumbai, November 28-29.

Unni, Jeemol (1999), Property Rights of Women: Case for Joint Titles to Agricultural Land and Urban Housing, *Economic and Political Weekly*, May 22-28.

World Bank (1991), *World Development Report*, Oxford University Press: New York.

15

AGRICULTURAL ENVIRONMENT AND ITS IMPACT ON NUTRIENT SUPPLY IN RURAL ANDHRA PRADESH

K. Dasaratha Ramaiah, Y.V. Ramanaiah and N. Sreedhara Naidu[3]

INTRODUCTION

The burning problem of the developing and under-developed nations facing today is the population explosion and scarcity of resources especially the food resource. The chaotic growth of population certainly creates an intense economic strain on the country and in such a situation if food supply becomes inadequate will lead people to suffer from both under-nutrition and malnutrition. In our country at present more than two-thirds of population is directly depending upon agriculture for their livelihood. It is of the general opinion that the people who were below poverty line are suffering from under-nutrition and mal-nutrition, in one way or other. Therefore, the study of nutritional problems with reference to quality and quantity of agricultural production available is of paramount importance. It is true that agriculture and nutrition become more important in our country because most of the rural population depends upon agriculture for their livelihood. The total availability of food i.e., 565 grams per head is the lowest in India as against the developing countries (779 grams/head) and the world average (681 grams/head) (Dubey and Mishra, 1984). It is a fact that the progress and welfare of the country depend upon the food availability.

Hence a factual knowledge on existing use of agricultural lands, their yielding rates, potential production units, standard nutrition units for production, consumption and in consequence, a picture of per head per day intake of nutritional factors is essential for agri-nutritional planning at micro-scale. A micro-level study on such perspectives helps to understand the nutritional standards as well as problems of rural population. Further, this would help to evolve curative measures for improvement of agricultural performance and nutritional standards of rural areas.

OBJECTIVES AND HYPOTHESES OF THE STUDY

The main objectives of the study are:

1. To analyze the environmental setting of sample villages,
2. To focus upon the demographic structure and occupational pattern
3. To examine the ground realities of agriculture in terms of land use pattern, irrigation development, cropping pattern and yield levels, and
4. To assess the nutrients supply from different food crops and the per capita nutrients availability.

The main hypotheses of the study are:

1. The environment and socio-economic conditions decide the cropping pattern and performance of the crops, and
2. The cropping pattern decides the status of nutrient supply and nutrient availability.

DATA AND METHODOLOGY

To achieve the set objectives and hypotheses of the study, the secondary data is collected on various parameters of the sample villages concerned. For the purpose of analysis 16 sample villages were chosen from all over the state. The selection of sample villages is based upon multi-stage stratified random sampling method.

There are two methods of computation of nutrients supply and availability in an area: (i) food balance sheet method, and (ii) household food consumption survey. The present study is based on food balance sheet method which was suggested by Shafi (1960) and Sukhatme (1962), and adopted in many number of studies made by the geographers. On the basis of food balance sheet method (FBS), the final tables are prepared about (i) nutrient supply from different crops, and (ii) nutrients availability per head per day for all the sample villages. The village-wise disparities are compared in terms of the contribution of different food materials towards nutrients supply and per capita nutrients availability as well as compared with the standard requirements. In order to examine the spatial variations and geographic relationships in the distribution of nutrients, statistical methods like averages, standard deviation, co-efficient of variation and coefficient of correlation are employed in the analysis.

LOCATIONAL AND ENVIRONMENTAL SETTING

The sample villages, which are taken for the purpose of analysis are possessing, varied terrain, isohyetal, edaphic and vegetative conditions (Table 1). These diversified physical conditions of sample villages certainly have had a bearing effect on demographic structure, land resource utilization, cropping pattern and crop productivity levels.

Table 1
Location and Environment of Sample Villages in Andhra Pradesh

Name of the Sample Village	*Location*	*Geographical Area (Hect)*	*Topography*	*Rainfall (cm) (Rainy days)*	*Soil*	*Natural Vegetation*
Kondavalasa	Srikakulam	159	Peneplain	172 (64)	Light block	Dense
Chinthalaveedi	Visakhapatnam	315	Hilly terrain With steep slopes	118 (70)	Red loamy	Dense
Ramanaiahpet	East Godavari	1265	Plain terrain	128 (59)	Light block clay loamy sandy	Sparse
Singarayapalem	Krishna	207	Plain	92 (56)	Alluvium delta	—
Ballipalli	Prakasam	38788	Peneplain	80 (52)	Red sandy	Sparse
Millampalli	Prakasam	3099	Highly undulating with moderate slopes	60 (51)	Red loamy	Dense
Kanalapalli	Kurnool	569	Plain	114 (47)	Black regur	Sparse
Narasapuram	Anantapur	4644	Plain	47 (36)	Red sandy	Sparse
Thippepalli	Anantapur	1308	Undulating terrain	36 (36)	Red sandy	Sparse
Ramapuram	Chittoor	281	Plain	96 (64)	Red sandy, loamy	Sparse
Ankole	Nizamabad	554	Peniplain	131 (49)	Light block	Dense
Nidigurthi	Mahabubnagar	1860	Undulating terrain medium slopes	54 (39)	Red sandy Light block	Sparse
Jonnalabogada	Mahabubnagar	775	Undulating raggude Terrain rocky exposures	77 (41)	Light red sandy	Sparse
Mutharam	Karimnagar	517	Highly undulating rocky exposures	77 (40)	Red sandy	Dense
Pochavaram	Khammam	384	Largely undulating deep Valley and steep slops	184 (75)	Block	Dense
Dhanura	Adilabad	808	Undulating terrain	111 (58)	Block	Sparse

In terms of geographical area of the sample villages, Narasapuram (Anantapur district) is the largest village followed by Ballipalli, Millampalli

(Prakasam), Nidigurthi (Mahabubnagar). In contrast, smallest village is Kondavalasa (Srikakulam) followed by Singarayapalem (Krishna). It reveals that the size of the village is quite large in drought prone districts while small in the high rainfall, irrigated, and river valley regions.

Demographic Structure of Sample Villages

The demographic structure of sample villages consists of population distribution, density of population, age structure, religion, social status, literacy and agricultural population.

Population Distribution

The size of population distribution ranges between a maximum of 4041 persons in Narasapuram (Anantapur) village to a minimum of 944 in Pochavaram (Khammam) village. The former one is geographically a large in size while the later one is a tribal village. If we examine the geographical size of sample villages, and their population size, a close positive correlation is found out with the co-efficient 0.77. Thus, it is very clear to say that the size of population of sample villages is more or less in true accordance with geographical size. The total population of all sample villages consists of 50.8 per cent male population and 49.2 per cent female population. The sex ratio of the sample villages consists of 968 females per 1000 male population.

Population Density

The average density of population of all sample villages consists of 1.5 persons per hectare. Among the 16 sample villages, the highest density of population of 7.2 persons per hectare is found in Singarayapalem (Krishna) while the lowest 0.5 persons/hectare in Ballipalli (Prakasam). It is interesting to state that both the villages are located in Coastal Andhra region but they have contrast physico-socio-economic conditions. The village consists of maximum density of population is hailed from Krishna delta system, where the high potentiality of agriculture and high carrying capacity of land have been supporting for high density of population. The village with minimum density of population is hailed from drought prone region where the potentiality of agricultural land is very low and carries low carrying capacity of land. It is also proved through correlation analysis explaining that the size of population of the village is not matching with the volume of density of population i.e., greater the size of population of a village with higher the density of population. Here, there is an inverse relationship (coefficient of correlation is–0.55) between the size of absolute population and the volume of the density of population. In other words it can be explained as the areas which are very potential besides being smaller in size in terms of geographical area could support more number of population. In contrast, the areas, which are very poor in potential status especially, located in drought areas besides being their large in size in geographical area, could support sparse population.

Age Structure

Out of the total sample population, children account for (<12 years) 25.85 per cent, adults (12–60 years) 54.65 per cent and aged people (>60 years) 19.5 per cent. It shows that adults are found with dominant size in all the sample villages.

Religion

It is needless to emphasize that the rural population is overwhelmingly dominant by Hindu population. The total sample population consists of 99.1 per cent of Hindu population, 0.77 per cent of Muslim population, and 0.13 per cent of Christian population.

Social Status

The composition of caste certainly places an explanatory variable in the process of agriculture production system. The distributional pattern of social status in terms of caste groups described as 38.91 per cent of backward classes (B.C.) considered being the highest proportion followed by scheduled tribes (S.T.) with 23.1 per cent, scheduled castes (S.C.) with 20.38 per cent and other castes / upper castes (O.C.) with 17.61 per cent.

Literacy

Education is considered to be the most facilitating factor for socio-economic development. Obviously, the rural areas have been still lagging behind urban areas in achieving higher literacy. In the present study, the average literacy of the total sample population consists of 36 per cent. But it varies from a maximum of 66.9 per cent of Singarayapalem (Krishna) to a minimum of 16 per cent of Millampalli (Prakasam).

Agricultural Population

Cultivators and agricultural labourers are to be considered as two important components of agricultural population. Out of the total sample population of all the villages, cultivators accounted for 17.8 per cent and agriculture labourers 27.2 per cent.. Generally, the agricultural labourers account higher proportion of agricultural population in any part of the state. Here, the proportion of agricultural labourers varies from a maximum of 48.6 per cent in Ramapuram (Chittoor) to a minimum of 12 per cent in Thippepalli (Anantapur). It is obvious that most of the agricultural labour force rises from S.C., S.T. and backward communities in which the landless people ought to prefer agriculture labour as the main occupation of their livelihood. Female agricultural labourers (54.7%) are out numbered the male labourers, which is also a unique feature of agricultural labour force in the state, because females are more suitable in many operations of agriculture.

AGRICULTURAL LAND HOLDINGS

There are 5,246 agricultural land holdings with different sizes noticed in all the sample villages. The largest share of agricultural land holdings confined to small size possessing with 2 hectares of land. The small size of land holds accounted for three-fourth of total number of agriculture land holdings. Here also, there is a direct relationship between size of small holdings and strength of backward population. It means wherever S.C. and S.T. as well as backward community population is prominent, the land holdings are generally small in size because the small and marginal farmers are largely confined to weaker sections. Medium size of land holdings (2-5 hectares) accounted 19.2 per cent of the total land holdings. Here, it is observed that the large size of land holdings is found more in the villages of drought prone areas.

Land Utilization

Rural land use pattern generally preponderance with agricultural land resource since it is the main source of livelihood of the rural people. On an aggregate, the net sown area accounts for 39.7 per cent of the total geographical area of all the sample villages. The second important land use type is barren land with 17.3 per cent and it is fallowed by fallow land (14.2%), forest land (11.8%), non- agricultural land (9.5%),cultural land(4.9%) and land under groves(2.1%).

Intensity of Cropping

Intensity of cropping refers to double or tripple cropping system i.e., area sown more than once of the cultivated land. It is measured and expressed as the percentage of gross sown area to net sown area. Average intensity of cropping of all the sample villages accounts for 112.7 per cent. It varies from a maximum of 200 per cent in Singarayapalem village (Krishna delta) to a bare minimum of 100 per cent in Jonnalabogada and Pochavaram villages drought.

Intensity of Irrigation

Irrigation plays an important catalytical role in the development of agriculture. Irrigation by wells is the major source which accounts for 43.7 per cent of the total irrigated area. it is followed by canal irrigation (22.1%), tank irrigation (20.7%) and other sources of irrigation (13.5%).Intensity of irrigation means the extent of gross sown area brought under irrigation facility. On an average, 20.71 per cent of gross sown area has been provided by irrigation facility, but it varies from one village to another village ranging between a maximum of 100 per cent in Singarayapalem (Krishna district) to a minimum of 2.1 per cent in Thippepalli (Anantapur). It is found that the intensity of irrigation is insignificant in drought prone villages.

Cropping Pattern

The cropping pattern is highly diversified due to diversity in physico-socio-economic conditions of the sample villages. However, there are few crops which are very significant in terms of areal concentration. Among all the crops, groundnut is the first rank crop accounting 44.5 per cent of the total cultivated area of all the sample villages. It is mostly cultivated as rainfed crop and its cultivation is confined to 12 sample villages with varied proportions. The villages situated in the low rainfall areas particularly Rayalaseema region are predominant for the cultivation of groundnut.

The second important crop is paddy. With 19.3 per cent of the total cultivated area of all the sample villages. The interesting feature observed here that the paddy cultivation is confined to all the sample villages in varied proportions. The third important crop is pulses and grams accounting for 12.3 per cent of the total cultivated area of all the sample villages. The cultivation of pulses is also confined too much number of sample (13) villages, but in varied concentrations. The fourth important crop is jowar which accounts for 5.9 per cent of the total cultivated area of all the sample villages. Its cultivation is not as wide-spread as in the case of first three crops. It is cultivating in seven villages situated in the drought prone areas of Mahabubnagar and Prakasam districts where low rainfall and black soil conditions are conducive for its cultivation.

Crop Yield Levels

The performance of the crops in terms of per hectare yield levels is generally dependent upon the nature of inputs as well as quantity of inputs and other technologies employed. Generally, the per hectare yield levels of crops differ between irrigated and unirrigated crops. In the case of irrigated crops the necessary technological inputs will be sufficiently applied and thus yielding better performance with high per hectare returns. In contrast, in the case of unirrigated crops, low rainfalls, frequent occurrences of drought, meager application of technological inputs combinedly has had a shattering effect on yield levels. The above theoretical account is quite vivid in the present sample study is found that the irrigated crops like paddy, maize, sugarcane, fruits, vegetables and species and condiments have registered high per hectare yield levels than the other crops which are rain fed. Obviously, it is quite fascinating that the fruits of Green Revolution have benefited the only few cereal crops namely, paddy and maize and taking them into pride of place in the productivity levels and relegating all other food grain crops into poor secondary importance.

NUTRIENT SUPPLY

Obviously, for balanced diet, sufficient quantity and quality of nutrient intake is very essential. In the countryside, consciously or unconsciously people can give priority to the quantity of diet for intake rather than quality of food. The quality of food intake should consist of all nutritional factors with certain proportionate supply of all the food items in the diet. Therefore there should be no satisfaction on the contribution of only a few food items in the diet and in the intake if any element is higher than the standard requirement. This aspect of nutrient intake is generally lacking due to non-production of all the food materials at the local level. In the semi-subsistence and semi-commercial agricultural systems, people of the concerned region consume more in their diet what they produce more rather than going for import of all the required food materials for their balanced diet. This is a common phenomenon quite happening in rural India. Hence, in the study of nutrition geography it is necessary and important to describe and delineate that what kind of nutrients supply and intake pattern is there in the sample villages.

Nutrient Supply from Different Food Materials

It is very clear that the nutrient supply of all the sample villages has indicated that the contribution of paddy, millets and pulses is great. The contribution of other food items like spices, fruits and vegetables are insignificant and displayed significant disparity among the sample villages.

Calories

Taking the total sample villages as one unit, then the highest caloric supply i.e., 68.3 per cent is from paddy. It shows that paddy is the chief source of food in the common diet of the people of Andhra Pradesh. Caloric supply from millets is found next in importance and accounting 16.2 per cent share of the nutrients available. But the share of millets is high in drought prone villages .It is interesting to state that the millets especially jowar is one of the principle food items of the poorer strata of Telangana region. The supply from pulses and grams towards calories is found the third largest food item with 10.8 per cent. The supply of calories from fruits (2.3%), spices and condiments (2.1%) and vegetables (0.4%) is less important.

Proteins

In protein supply, the contribution of cereals is rather low as compared to that of calorie. However, paddy is the largest supplier of protein with 50.1 per cent. The second important food stuff which supplies protein in sizeable proportion is pulses with 27 per cent of the total proteins available per head per day.

Fats

The position of fat supply is different from other nutrients. On an average, the largest supply of fat is obtained from millets (38.5%) followed by cereals (31.9%), pulses (13.9%), spices (12%), fruits (2.8%), and vegetables (0.8%).

Carbohydrates

In carbohydrate supply, the situation is like that of calorie. Its supply from cereals, on an average, is 72 per cent, followed by millets (15.3%) and pulses (8.5%).

Calcium

The highest calcium supply is from pulses which accounts for 36.2 per cent of the total calcium supply from all the food crops.. Cereals and millets have the second and third place in the calcium supply with 20.6 per cent and 18.5 per cent respectively. Calcium supply from spices and condiments is also considerable with 13 per cent.

Iron

Cereals, millets, pulses and vegetables are the important food items available in the sample villages for the supply of iron to the nutrient intake. The highest proportion of iron supply is made from cereals (45%) followed by millets (19.9%), pulses (16.1%) and vegetables (14.3%). These four food stuffs together accounted for 95.3 per cent of the total iron supply per head per day.

Vitamin –A

Vitamin-A supply is very high from millets (47.4%). followed by pulses (18.2%), spices (13.1%), fruits (10.9%) and vegetables (10.3%). Though fruits and vegetables are important for the supply of vitamin-A, but their production and net availability from the local places is very low.

Thiamine

Since thiamine is foodgrain based nutrient, its supply from cereals (29.9%), pulses (23.6%), and millets (21.9%) is great which together accounted for 75.4 per cent of the total nutrient available for intake per head per day.

Riboflavin

Among the food crops pulses supply a higher share of riboflavin with 41.7 per cent and it followed by cereals (18.7%) and millets (17.6%). All these foodgrains together accounted for 78 per cent of riboflavin supply.

Niacin

Maximum supply of niacin is from foodgrains in the sample villages. Cereals (50.3%), millets (31.3%), and pulses (9.1%) together accounted for 90.7 per cent of the total niacin supply.

Vitamin-C

Fruits supply the largest share of vitamin-C with 71.8 per cent of the total vitamin-C supply vegetables (15.8%) and millets (9.9%).

NUTRIENTS AVAILABILITY

The study of nutrients availability based on local food cropping systems and food production patterns is necessary to bring out the relationship between the status of nutrition and the level of agricultural development of the area concerned. It is based on the assumption that in the subsistence economy if the entire local food production whatsoever it may be consumed for the local people then what is the real situation of nutrient intake per head per day. Such a hypothetical study based on 'Food Balance Sheet' method provides information pertaining to surplus or deficit of per capita availability of nutrients. The measurement of nutritional availability rests on the determination of the quantity of food that may fetch human consumption locally (Dubey, 1984). This type of analysis relating the agriculture with nutrition becomes more important in our country because most of the rural population directly depends upon agriculture for livelihood. The present study of nutrients availability at sample village level reveals the actual food available for human consumption in the village concerned at a given point of time. It needs distinction from the food intake or food consumption.

Calorie

Considering all the 16 sample villages in the state as one unit, the average per capita per day calorie availability is 3025 which is considerably higher (i.e., 26%) than the standard requirement. The calorie availability in about half of the villages is lower than the standard requirement of 2400 calories. These villages are located in drought prone and backward areas of Rayalaseema and Telangana regions.

Proteins

The average per capita protein availability is found to be 80.4 grams per day which is also considerably higher than the (i.e., 68 grams per head per day) standard requirement.

Fats

The average daily per capita availability of fats in the sample villages is about 9.8 gms which are far lesser (i.e., deficit of 83.7%) than the standard requirement of 60 gms per head per day. This large deficit of fats availability is due to the fact that the fats oriented milk and animal products are not taken into the analysis. Here the present availability of fats is computed from the food crop items and as a result, the deficit of fat availability is very large.

Carbohydrates

The daily per capita carbohydrates availability is 651.4 mg., which specifies surplus (i.e., surplus of 7.7%) over the standard requirement (i.e., 605 mg). The pattern of availability of carbohydrates is as similar as in the case of protein availability.

Calcium

Average calcium availability per capita per day is 283.9 mg as against the standard requirement of 900 mg. It shows that there is a deficit of 68.5 per cent which is a significant deficit indeed.

Iron

Daily per capita iron availability in all the sample villages is 40.1 mg. as against the standard requirement of 17 mg. It shows that the iron availability is found in surplus situation which is to the tune of 135.9 per cent over the standard requirement. It is interesting to reveal that out of all nutrients availability, iron availability situation is very much better with large surplus.

Vitamin-A

Average per capita availability of vitamin-A is 790.7 I.U.mg which is very much lesser (i.e. deficit of 84.2%) than the standard requirement 5000 I.U.mg. The deficit of vitamin-A availability is found in all sample villages.

Thiamine

Thiamine availability per head per day is 1.9 mg which is higher than the (i.e., surplus of 45.7%) standard requirement (1.2 mg).

Riboflavin

Per capita per day riboflavin availability is 0.9 mg which villages. is lower (deficit of -33.8%) than the standard requirement of 1.4 mg.

Niacin

Niacin availability is found to be surplus to the tune of 75.9 per cent. The per capita per head niacin availability in the sample villages is 22.2 mg as against to the standard requirement of 12.6 mg.

Vitamin-C

Per capita per head vitamin-C availability is 31 mg which is lower (i.e., deficit of 36.7%) than the standard requirement of 49 mg,

CONCLUSION

From the above descriptive account on nutrients supply from different food stuffs it is found that the main source of supply of nearly all the nutrients is from cereals followed by millets and pulses in almost all the sample villages. It is perplexing to note that the supply of different nutrients from fruits and vegetables is far less which hinders the balanced diet in rural Andhra Pradesh. It is of paramount importance to focus keen attention on fruit and vegetable production in each and every village for easy accessible and available for free consumption and for maintenance of balanced diet. From the analysis it is also found that (i) the production of different food stuffs in the sample villages is not providing all the nutrient factors and satisfying the balanced diet, (ii) some of the important nutrients are found in better situation because of being based on foodgrain diet, (iii) the surplus condition in nutrient factors is found in calories, proteins, carbohydrates, iron, thiamine and niacin, (iv) the deficit in the nutrient factors is found in fats, calcium, vitamin-A, riboflavin, and vitamin-C, (v) significant disparities both in surplus and deficit nutrients availability is recorded village to village which is due to variation in the cropping pattern and crop production, (vi) in some of the villages especially situated in backward areas and drought prone areas, the nutrients availability is found to the deplorable condition, and (vii) the nutrients available from fruits and vegetable production is deplorably poor.

REFERENCES

Dubey, R.S. and Misra, R.P. (1984), Nutritional Availability Patterns in Madhya Pradesh, *Trans, Inst. of Indian Geographers*, 6(2): 79-89.

Shafi, M. (1960), Land Utilization in Eastern Uttar Pradesh, Aligarh Muslim University: Aligarh.

Sukatme, P.V. (1962), The Food and Nutrition in India, *Journal of the Indian Society of Agricultural Statistics*, 19: 49-87.

16

MAGNITUDE OF WASTE MANAGEMENT PROBLEM IN INDIA: A REVIEW

Md. Abdus Salam

INTRODUCTION

The application of new techniques and technology created environmental hazards not only for the developing countries but developed countries also. India has achieved significant progress in the field of agriculture as well as industries. India's Green Revolution rescued the nation from famines. But the adoption of modern agricultural technologies has culminated into serious problems of crop losses, pesticide resistance in major pests, and elimination of populations of natural parasites, environmental pollution and health hazards. Along with above environmental problems in India the additional problems are pressures on eco-systems and the consequent loss of bio-diversity, air pollution, water pollution, coastal and marine pollution and pollution caused by inadequate collection and disposal of solid waste. Solid Wastes are in the form of *Garbage* (fruits, meat, vegetables etc.), *Rubbish* (paper, glass, ceramics, wood etc), *Industrial wastes* (chemicals, paints, sand, metal use, fly ash, sewage treatment sludge etc.), *Agricultural wastes* (animal manure, crop residue etc.), *Miscellaneous* (Medical wastes & warfare wastes). These wastes both solid and liquid forms (which pollute the land, soil, water & air etc.) arise out of human activities, agricultural processes, mining, industries, medical fields etc. Waste disposal is one of the major problems being faced by all nations of the world.

India policy document, which examines waste as part of a cycle of production-consumption-recovery or perceives waste through a prism of overall sustainability. Until now, the problem of waste has been seen as one of cleaning and disposing as rubbish. But a closer look at the current and future scenario reveals that waste needs to be treated holistically, recognizing its natural resource roots as well as health impacts. In India, over a million people find livelihood opportunities in the area of waste; they are engaged in waste collection (popularly known as rag picking) and recycling through well-organized systems. Waste can be wealth, which has tremendous potential not only for generating livelihoods for the urban poor but can also enrich the earth through composting and recycling rather than spreading pollution as has been the case. Increasing urban migration and a high density of population will make waste management a difficult issue to handle in the near future. The wastes generated by various sectors need to be assessed and evaluated for their energy potential or reuse in any other form.

WASTE MANAGEMENT

Waste Management generally refers to the collection, transfer, recycling, and the ultimate disposal of waste. With the changing consumption patterns among urban/rural populations of India, waste management is becoming a serious environmental issue. The concept of Waste Management is still in its very early stage in India but awareness and pressures from public opinion and the judiciary has seen a lot of activity in this field in the recent years. Waste is also generated at different stages of construction activity. Construction activity leads to generation of solid wastes, which include sand, gravel, concrete, stone, bricks, wood, metal, glass, plastic, paper etc.

Despite knowing the facts that Indian Construction Industry is highly employment intensive and accounts for a significant proportion of the population of the country the management of construction and demolition waste is a major concern due to the increasing quantum of demolition's rubble, continuing shortage of dumping sites, increase in transportation and disposal cost and above all growing concern about pollution and environmental deterioration. Wastes which are available in liquid, solid or gas forms they are all dangerous for human health and the environment of the country. During the last few years India has witnessed a major rise in industrial output and consequent rise in hazardous wastes release. Presence of various chemicals in these wastes makes them toxic, poisonous, corrosive, flammable, explosive and infectious in nature.

Studies revealed that (http://www.indianngos.com/issue/wastemgmt/overview.htm) the daily hazardous wastes generated by different sources take a long time for the disposal from the time of its generation. According to one estimate India will probably see a rise in waste generation from less than 40,000 metric tonnes per year to over 125,000 metric tonnes by the year 2030. Due to lack of waste management system like inadequate capacity for collection and transportation of MSW (municipal solid waste) result in the uncollected waste in sewers eaten by the cattle, or left to rot in the open, or burnt on roadsides. Estimated quantity of waste generated in India (*http://www.indianngos.com/issue/wastemgmt/overview.htm*) is as follows:

Statistical Dimension of Waste Management

27.4 million tonnes/year Municipal solid waste.

12145 million litres/day Municipal liquid waste (121 class I and II cities).

8057 kilo litres/day; 243 Distilleries.

9 million tonnes/year-Press mud.

4.5 million tonnes/year Food and fruit processing waste.

30000 tonnes/year-Willow dust.

50–60 million litres/day-Dairy industry waste (COD level 2 kg/m3).

1600 m3 waste water/day-Paper and pulp industry waste (300 mills).

52500 m3 waste water/day; 2000 Tanneries.

About 13% to 20%-recyclable content of waste.

There are different categories of waste generated, each take their own time to degenerate:

Organic wastes - vegetable and fruit peels, leftover foodstuff, etc.-a week or two

Paper-10-30 days

Cotton cloth-2-5 months

Wood 10-15-years

Woolen items-1 year

Tin, aluminum, and other metal items such as cans-100–500 years.

Plastic bags-one million years or more Glass bottles undetermined

Central Pollution Control Board (CPCB) has also carried out an inventory of municipal solid wastes generation, collection, transportation and disposal in the country and published status reports (http://www.cpcb.delhi.nic.in/pamsweb/statusmsw.htm) under Control of Urban Pollution Series (CUPS). The reports revealed the following facts:

1. The major mode of disposal of solid waste is by land dumping and composting.
2. With concentration of industrial and commercial activities around the city nodes, rapid urbanization attracted by large-scale migration of rural population. The Industrial Development Areas created in and around the urban centres do not cater to the needs of basic civic amenities for the migratory population.
3. The migrated rural Population has not been able to easily adapt to the social change and to urban living conditions. This has to a great extent

contributed to the deteriorating sanitary, conditions and solid waste generation problems.

4. The other aspect, which contributed to the generation of solid waste, is the economic growth in the urban pockets and the consequent increase in consumerism and package disposals.
5. The collection, transportation and disposal of loose garbage in bulk quantities by manual methods are unhygienic for the carriers.
6. The dumping areas have become serious health hazards to the people living the neighborhood. The ground water in the area is also liable for contamination.
7. Basic care and precautions are not being taken in handling and safe disposal bio-medical waste, which is being treated as domestic garbage in majority of the cases.
8. Enough care and attention are not being paid for the safe disposal of Industrial Hazardous wastes.
9. Local Governments are legally bound to provide efficient and effective solid waste services. With increased population and economic activities and changing urban lifestyles, local Governments are unable to cope with the mounting solid wastes in cities.
10. As we witnessed after the plague scare at Surat in the year 1994, local communities and people themselves were involved in cleaning up the city. The awareness generated during the plague scare and the motivation of the people, however, could not be sustained for long.
11. In large cities, the composition of wastes is changing with rapid increase in Paper, Plastic, Metal and Hazardous materials components.
12. Many cities in India have turned to private contractors for transportation of garbage to disposal sites.

Cheap labour, poor environmental standards and growing market for cheap raw materials are all attributable to place India as a dumping ground for hazardous waste. Thousands of tonnes of toxic waste are being illegally shipped to India for recycling or dumping, despite the ban on imports of toxic materials. During Post economic reforms, the gross national product (GNP) improved from an average of about 5.7 per cent in the 1980s to an average of about 6.5 per cent in the Eighth and Ninth Plan periods, making India one of the ten fastest growing developing countries, where the dismantling of the industrial licensing system, free investments by foreign companies, lowering of import tariffs on capital goods all contributed. Encouraging progress was also made in other sectors. The percentage of the population in poverty continued to decline, even if not as much as was targeted. Population growth decelerated below 2 per cent for the first time in four decades. Literacy increased from 52 per cent in 1991 to 65 per cent in 2001 with improvement evident in all states. Software services, entertainment and information technology-enabled services emerged as new sources of strength, creating confidence about India's potential to be competitive in the world economy. However all these development has come at a higher price. Rapid population growth coupled with rapid Industrialization has caused severe environmental degradation and pollution with local, national, regional and global impacts.

Government has recognized that mere economic growth is not enough and that development must be environmental friendly. Therefore the basic objective of the Tenth Plan is to bring about all round enhancement of human well being by eradicating poverty through adopting well-conceived development strategies in which environmental concerns are treated as the vital aspects. Environmental management and economic development are mutually supportive aspects of the same agenda. A poor environment undermines development, while inadequate development result in a lack of resources for environmental protection. In order to promote 'sustainable development' air pollution, soil degradation, deforestation, shrinking wetlands. Inadequate public health and sanitation, indoor pollution in rural areas, growing water scarcity, falling ground water tables, the lack of minimum flow in the rivers and over extraction of water for irrigation purposes are some of the environmental problems that need to be given top priority.

Some of the other goals set for the Tenth Plan include effective implementation of the Public Liability Insurance Act; preparation of database on risk-prone areas; setting up of hard hazardous-based disposal facilities in all states where significant quantities of hazardous waste are being generated; establishment of sub-regional training centres for implementation of the Basel Convention, setting up of custom laboratories and capacity building of custom officers for checking contraband trade in hazardous chemicals/waste; implementation of environmentally sound practices in ship dismantling and proper management of biomedical wastes; municipal solid waste; plastic waste; and, chemical waste etc.

POLICIES FOR WASTE MANAGEMENT

India has adopted a series of environmental protection Acts and rules in conformity with the global environment pact following the Rio summit. Yet it continues to witness environmental degradation in various forms. This clearly indicates a gap between principles and practice. The rapid increase in greenhouse gases, degradation of land, pollution of air and water, deforestation, loss of bio-diversity and the fragile ecosystem have put a challenge to the country's policy makers and planners to ensure economic growth along with sustainability. Responding to the challenge, the Ministry of Environment and Forests has recently formulated a holistic environment policy for the nation (Draft National Environment Policy 2004 (NEP-2004)).

The Hazardous Wastes (Management and Handling) Rules 1989 were introduced under Sections 6, 8, and 25 of the Environment (Protection) Act of1986 (referred to as HWM Rules, 1989). The HWM Rules, 1989 provide for the control of generation, collection, treatment, transport, import, storage and disposal of wastes listed in the schedule annexed to these rules. The rules are implemented through the SPCBs and pollution control committees in the states and union territories. India is also a signatory to the Basel Convention, 1989 on the Control of Trans boundary Movement of Hazardous Wastes and their Disposal. There were a few inherent limitations to the implementation of the HWM Rules, 1989, and amendments to this Rule were introduced in 2000 and2002, widening the definition of hazardous waste and harmonizing the hazardous waste list with that of the Basel Convention.

Besides these rules, in 1991, the MoEF issued Guidelines for Management and Handling of Hazardous Wastes for (a) generators of waste, (b) transport of hazardous waste, and (c) owners/operators of hazardous waste storage, treatment and disposal facilities. These guidelines also established mechanisms for the development of a reporting system for the movement of hazardous waste. In 1995, these were followed by the publication of Guidelines for Safe Road Transport of Hazardous Chemicals that established basic rules for Hazardous Goods Transport and provided for the establishment of a Transport Emergency Plan and for provisions on Identification and Assessment of Hazards.

In addition to these direct rules dealing with issues of hazardous waste management, the Government has moved to enact legislation and additional incentives for industries to comply with environmental provisions and bring out market forces into the business of environment. The Public Liability Act 1991 was adopted to require industries dealing with hazards to ensure against accidents or damages caused by release of pollutants. The National Environmental Tribunal Act, 1995, provides for expeditious remedies to parties injured by environmental crimes. Legislation on the Community's Right to Know has been adopted to provide more access to information regarding potential hazards from industrial operations.

Emerging policy directions in the field of hazardous waste management emphasize the need for scientific disposal of waste and policies to encourage Hazardous waste management in India. It has been observed that the amendment rules promulgated by the MoEF in the year's 2000 and 2002 dealing with hazardous waste management fail to provide any incentive for waste reduction/ minimization efforts. The main laws dealing with the hazardous waste in the country are unable to tackle the alarming situation of hazardous waste because of the negligence shown on the part of officials of the government, lack of concern on the part of industry, as Industries are reluctant to adopt such measures and lack of awareness of the people. Further despite the ban on import of hazardous waste in the country, hazardous waste is coming to our shores in a regular phenomenon. Although India has lack of environment friendly technology to reuse and recycle hazardous waste but in the name of reuse and recycling, India invites import of such waste.

CONCLUSION

Studies revealed that due importance has not been given to the subject of waste management in the country. Lack of National policy, lack of interest by the State Govt., inability of the local bodies to provide efficient services, lack of awareness and apathy of the community towards waste management, unenthusiastic involvement of NGOs and use of inappropriate technology for collection of transportation and disposal of waste, institutional weakness, inadequate trained manpower, shortage of committed financial resources, marginal legislative support and ineffective implementation of laws and regulations are responsible for ineffective management services in the country. The lack of a preventive approach to waste management has led to generation of more and more hazardous wastes. The need of the hour is that there should be environmental friendly hazardous waste management in the country and it needs participation of all the people of the country. The strategy required ensuring scientific management of hazardous waste whose generation is expected to increase due to our liberalized economic policies. Therefore it is essential to organize Seminars, Conferences and Workshops in different parts of the Country to create general awareness among the people regarding all aspects of waste management cycles starting from its generation to its handling, segregation, transportation, treatment, and disposal.

REFERENCES

Bakthavatsalam V. (1999), The Indian Market for Sustainable Energy, *IREDA News*, 10 (3): 11–19.

Bhattacharya A., and Shrivastava R. (1994), The Night Air Turned Poisonous, *Down to Earth*, December.

Government of India (2002), *Tenth Five-Year Plan 2002-2007*, Planning Commission, New Delhi.

Government of India (2000), *Draft on Status of Implementation of the Hazardous Waste Rules*, Ministry of Environment and Forests, New Delhi.

Government of India (2000), Municipal Solid Waste (Management & Handling) Rules 2000, Ministry of Environment and Forests, New Delhi.

Pachauri R.K. and Sridharan P. V. (eds.) (1998), Solid Wastes, In *Looking Back To Think Ahead*, Tata Energy Research Institute: New Delhi.

Shankar V., Martin M., Bhatt A. and Erkman S. (1994), Who Cares Where It's Dumped?, Down to Earth, June.

Sharma A and Bannerji R. (1996), The Blind Court, *Down to Earth*, April.

Singh K.K. (ed.) (1996), Potential for Energy Generation from Waste in India, *Bioenergy News,* 1 (1): 8–13.

Tripathy, K.K. (2004), Integrated Environment Management, *The Hindu,* December 28.

17

ENVIRONMENTAL ACCOUNTING AND REPORTING FOR SUSTAINABLE DEVELOPMENT

Siddhartha Sarkar

INTRODUCTION

Environmental accounting is relatively a recent entrant in the domain of accounting. It is the process of identification, measurement and communication of information on the environmental responsibility performance of an entity to permit economic decision-making by the users of information. Environmental accounting is essential for an organization implementing the concept of sustainable development as it facilitates to take into account ecological activities of an organization in economic measurement (Sarkar, 2004). However, strong sustainability recommends a greater emphasis on the conservation of natural assets within the broader goal of prudently managing a portfolio of assets overtime. With a view to advocating strong sustainability, it is the physical protection of absolute levels of natural assets, which is a prerequisite for sustainability. The rationale underlying this is that natural assets provide complex ecological functions, crucial to the maintenance of life and further more that these critical functions can not be substituted for other assets (Norton and Toman, 1997). Natural assets that exhibit these characteristics are termed as critical natural assets (Pearce et. al., 1989). It has been argued that allowing the stock size of these critical assets fall below a threshold level could result in serious, if not catastrophic consequences for well being. However, identifying critical assets and determining thresholds are far from trivial and are at the frontier of interdisciplinary research (Hamilton, 1997).

Much debate has taken place in recent years concerning the demand for development in environmental accounting and reporting, which comprises economic assets (produced and non produced) and environmental assets exhibited both in quantity and amount (Annexure I). There has been a particular emphasis on need for accountants to become more proactive in encouraging and enriching such practices (Gray *et al.*, 1993). In particular, accounting experts should make a significant contribution to the debate on environmental issues and its protective in the following areas (Owen, 1992).

- Agreed definitions of what is to be measured and why.
- The technology to measure and capture the required data.
- Systems to record it and controls to ensure that corrective actions are taken when required.
- Reporting systems to convey performance measurement data to those requiring it.
- An audit, which can arrest to the reliability of the data reported.

A willingness to accept estimates when precise cost apportionment is not possible. Senghe (1993) has stated that progress in environmental accounting depends on re-examination of the target audience, the expansion of information reported and the ability to account for completely new activities. The following is comprised in the environmental accounting (Gray et. al., 1993):

- Recognizing and seeking to mitigate the negative environmental effects of conventional accounting practice.
- Separately identifying environmentally related costs and revenues within the conventional accounting systems.
- Taking active steps to set up initiatives in order to ameliorate existing environmental effects of conventional accounting practice.
- Developing new forms of performance measurement, reporting and appraisal for both internal and external purpose.

Gray et. al. (1993) have suggested practical approach towards both financial and non-financial environmental accounting and reporting as under:

United Nation's recommendations

- Disclosure of accounting policies
- Cost of current environmental expenditure
- Environmental expenditure capitalized in the period
- Liabilities, provisions and reserves
- Contingent liabilities
- Tax effects
- Grand received

Develop disclosure with auditor in mind

- Reconsider provisions for remediation and abandonment
- Provisions for inventory, accelerated depreciation, new investment and
- Actual and provided for legal costs

Make the environment more visible

- Disclose energy (including transport) cost
- Disclose waste handling and disposal costs
- Disclose legal compliance costs
- Consider packaging costs and
- Consider the disclosure of environmental fines

Rubenstein (1990) has pointed out that current accounting practices suffer from two major problems in relation to environmental accountability. These include unaccounted for the full costs of production including costs of consuming natural resources and penalizing by accounting rules rather than encouraging the environmentally responsible organization. Chadick et. al. (1993) have shown the appropriate tests applicable to accounting for environmental contamination costs as expenditures extend the useful life or improve the efficiency or safety of the property, expenditure mitigate future environmental contamination or expenditures relate to preparation of property designated for sale.

The treatment of environmental expenses, liabilities and investment has been examined by Senghe (1993). Proper treatment begins with objectives for environmental accounting as ability to match revenues and expenses, alert managers and other stakeholders and support ethical management behaviour. This involves accruing environmental expenses as an end of period adjustment. This accrual alerts stakeholder to the environmental risks associated with firm activities through both income statement and balance sheet disclosure. The accrual and subsequent recognitions also promotes ethical management behaviour by not rewarding unethical management behaviour. He recognized the use of these practices as part of the existing accounting framework that should provide the most immediate guidance. New transactions and new focus on existing transactions both require a new outlook at existing practice in the environmental spotlight.

Schoemaker and Schoemaker (1995) observe that information about organizational potential future environmental liability can be used as encouraging defensive and prudent operations and waste reduction, improving manufacturing, waste disposal and shipping practices, negotiating and setting with insurance carriers, influencing regulations and public policy makers, reassessing corporate strategy and management practices, articulating a comprehensive risk management programme, improving public citizenship and assessing hidden risks in takeovers and acquisitions.

Johnson (1993) has argued that as for an environmental liability to be evaluated independently from any potential claim for recovery and the loss arising from the recognition of an environmental liability to be reduced only when a claim for recovery is probable of realization. In addition, discounting environmental liabilities for a specific clean up site is allowed, but not required, only if the aggregate amount of the obligation and the amount and timing of the cash payments for that site are fixed or reliably determinable.

The United Nations has also initiated in preparing International Accounting Standards in the area of protection and restitution of the environment. The United Nations Inter-governmental Working Group for International Standards and Reporting has issued two reports on environmental accounting. The group followed research on legal requirements and practice in the area of recording and disclosing expenses and liabilities arising as a result of environmental protection and restitution in ten participating countries. The results of the research indicate that although the definition of the issues may vary, the recording of environmental expenses is possible. It is argued that the expenses for minimizing the emission of pollution should be termed as environmental expenses.

CONCEPT OF ENVIRONMENTAL ACCOUNTING

According to Federation des Experts Compatibles Europeans (1995) "environmental accounting concerns the treatment of environmental issues within the financial statements and within environmental evaluations". Sefcik, Soderstrom and Stinson (1997) defined "environmental accounting is a course (or subject) that investigates how environmental issues affect traditional accounting sub-disciplines". Gray, Bebbington and Walter (1993) observed "environmental accounting can be taken as covering all areas of accounting that may be affected by the business response to environmental issues, including new areas of eco-accounting". According to Das Gupta (1997) "environmental accounting, one of the methods, takes into account environmental resources and services and changes therein and measures their effects on gross national product and net national product to reveal true maximum income (true net capital formation which a nation can consume while maintaining a sustainable development and growth without jeopardizing the interest of the present and future generations as well as of our neighbours". Thus, environmental accounting is a process of identifying and measuring data about natural resources and communicating the information to permit economic decision making by the users of it. The fundamental objectives underlying environmental accounting is to facilitate effective and efficient management of natural resources.

Environmental accounting has inkling of the following objectives:

- Firstly, segregating and collaborating of all environmental related flows and stocks of assets or resources.
- Secondly, assessing deterioration of environment in terms of cost and benefits.
- Thirdly, minimizing environmental impacts through improved design of product or process.
- Fourthly, reducing costs through resource conservation.
- Fifthly, releasing organizational accountability and increasing environmental transparency.
- Sixthly, ensuring effective and efficient management of natural resources.
- Seventhly, aiding strategic decision process regarding continuing or abandoning a particular product or process.
- Finally, linking physical resource accounting with monetary accounting.

The following have been identified as potential elements of environmental accounting (Gray et. al., 1993).

General

- Involvement with the environmental policy
- Involvement with environmental audit preview
- Involvement with the development and monitoring of environmental management systems.
- Involvement with environmental impact assessments, and
- Assessment of sustainability

Management Accounting and Costing

- Accounting for energy usage and costs
- Accounting for waste, pollution and disposal
- Accounting for recycling, packaging and containers
- Budgets and performance appraisal
- Research and development, forecasting and design

External Reporting and Audit

- Lending, insurance and shareholders
- Environmental spending and commitment

- Statutory audit implications
- Environmental reporting in financial statements

The following stages are involved in environmental accounting:

- The organization potential environmental problems and possible modes of remedy should be identified through effective communication within the organization and outside.
- Environmental costs must be projected and future costs, if any, must be forecasted after due consultation with environmental project engineering.
- Full disclosures should be made of all uncertainties and liability recognition may be required.
- Environmental budget should be prepared by the organization with a view to ascertaining the amount to be allocated for environmental activities. It involves comparing the environmental costs with the budgeted amount and to find out variances if any.
- The organization should report for the environmental activities, the cost imposed by the organization on environment, benefits rendered by the organization, social responsibilities will be fulfilled by the reporting.

Generally, information on the following environmental accounting aspects is needed by different categories of users:

- To determine the extent of resource protectiveness and expected regular return on investment.
- To determine environmental taxation policies.
- To be able to decide whether to provide resource to the organization or not.
- To assess the production efficiency, cost effectiveness and effect on overall profitability of the organization for being an environmental friendly.
- To regulate the activities of the organization.
- To assess the ability of the organization to pay and provide environmental benefits.
- To assess the stability and profitability of the organization.

Environmental accounting has *inter alia* some limitations and obstacles. These are as under:

(a) The methods of estimating the social value of environmental goods and services are still imperfect, misleading and controversial.

(b) Estimated values for environmental goods and services are often only partly or poorly quantified or qualified in terms, which have no fixed conversion into money.

(c) Social values placed on environmental goods and services are changing so fast that the estimates are likely to be obsolete before they are available for use.

(d) The reason for estimating economic values for environmental goods and services is to include those values in cost benefit, cost effectiveness, input-out or other economic analyses. Such techniques however are based on assumptions and if these do not apply in particular cases, conclusions based on them may be vague. Hence, every analysis should make its assumptions explicit and examine the sensitivity of its conclusions to failures in these assumptions.

(e) On account of unrecorded environmental costs and difficulty in extracting and separating environmental cost, the industry data is usually unreliable. The industry's concern to maintain confidentiality and widely differing accounting systems also makes the job very difficult.

AN INSIGHT INTO GREEN BALANCE SHEET

The preparation of green or environmental balance sheet has become an integral part of financial accounting. It is merely a statement, which summarizes environmental performance and net environmental capital of an organization. It reveals investment of the organization in the form of environmental friendly assets, environmental liabilities and environmental capital.

The environmental assets can be categorized as water pollution treatment plants, sewage treatment plants, air pollution preventive systems, investment in social forestry, human training and development cost, capital work-in-progress of aforesaid assets, renewable energy sources, eco-friendly production machines, packaging materials, aquifers etc. Besides, environmental liabilities include amount of compensation payable according to court rulings, non-government organizations rulings, pending lawsuits in occurs against environmental hazards and amount of damages yet to be assessed. As far as the environmental capital is concerned it is the excess of environmental investment made over environmental liabilities. A schematic presentation of environmental balance sheet can be put forth as follows:

Liabilities	*Amount (Rs.)*	*Assets*	*Amount (Rs.)*
Green/Environmental CapitalEco-Liabilities Compensation payable Pending lawsuitsDamages yet to be assessed		Eco-AssetsWater pollution treatment plantsSewage treatment plants Air pollution preventive systemsInvestment in social forestryHuman training and development cost Capital work-in-progress of above assetsRenewable energy sources Eco-friendly production machinesPackaging materials Aquifers etc.	

ENVIRONMENTAL REPORTING AND DISOURSE

Environmental reporting requires incorporation of environmental related matters into the corporate annual reporting. It is carried out mandatory or voluntary basis. It includes the quantities of environmental and natural resources consumed and of the pollution and other effects of the organization on the environment. Environmental reporting involves both recognition and disclosure. It may be descriptive or quantitative. Descriptive reporting means enumeration of the environmental activities of the organization without any quantification, but quantitative reporting requires quantification of environmental activities in terms of money and incorporating the same into financial statement. Environmental reporting may be negative or positive. Negative reporting implies disclosure of harms done to the environment by the organization's activity and positive reporting means disclosure of the fact that organization's operation is made in an environmental friendly manner.

The flowing framework of environmental reporting has been suggested as:

- A statement of environmental policy and program on issues relating to the organization.
- A statement of how environmental policies is being implemented.
- Provision of realistically measurable environmental targets.
- Monitoring of achievements towards targets.
- Environmental improvement achievements achieved during the year.
- Any legal proceedings being instigated against the firm for environmental misdemeanors.
- Amount charged to profit during the year and amount capitalized in relation to environmental initiatives, with appropriate description there of.

The environmental reporting practices normally fall into following categories.

- Statements of policy and selected elements of hard quantitative data.
- Descriptive and performance approach to environmental reporting includes description of environmental policies and corporate activities plus data on performance in such areas as emissions, control and energy savings.
- Financial disclosure of environmental information includes amount spent on environmental matters, environmental contingent liabilities and anticipated pattern of future environmental expenditure.

OBJECTIVES AND METHODOLOGY

Research studies have examined the extent to which organizations produce social information of which environmental information would be a part. Since environmental reporting practices in India has been dismal and a few corporate houses pay attention and space to environmental issues in their annual report, there is an immediate need to study the perception of corporate executives on environmental reporting practices. The present study is based on the primary data collection from a sample of 120 executives from different corporate houses through face-to-face interview. A stratified random sampling method has been undertaken to select the individual respondents.

FINDINGS

An analysis of the perceptions of corporate executives presented in table 1 reveals that 66.67 per cent of the respondents agreed strongly for disclosure of policy for the environmental protection. Most of the respondents either strongly agree or agree that environmental management system, environmental audit report, research and development on environment, and environmental impact assessment should be disclosed in the annual report. All respondents agreed for reporting on environmental spending. Most of the respondents also agreed for reporting liabilities for accumulated pollution and allocation of external environmental cost. The study shows that 80 per cent or more respondents either strongly agreed or simply agreed for the reporting of awareness program of environmental issues, community development program undertake and global environmental issues and standards.

Table 1

Perception on Environmental Disclosure Practices (%)

Information to be Disclosed in Corporate Environmental Reporting	*Strongly Agree*	*Agree*	*Strongly Disagree*
• Policy, program and initiatives for environmental protection	66.67	33.33	0
• Environmental management system	46.67	42.50	10.83
• Environmental audit report	81.67	12.50	5.83
• Legal compliance with environmental issues	55.00	35.00	10.00
• Research and development on environment	50.84	38.33	10.83
• Health and safety issues in work environment	59.17	33.33	7.5
• Environmental impact assessment and risk management	35.00	58.33	6.67
• Energy consumption and its environmental effects	53.33	36.67	10.00
• Environmental capital and operating expenditure	78.33	21.67	0
• Liabilities for accumulated pollution	68.34	23.33	8.33
• Pollution charges and tax paid	52.50	31.67	15.83
• Allocation of external environmental cost	41.67	49.17	9.16
• Awareness program on environmental issues	35.00	45.83	19.16
• Community development activity undertaken	25.83	63.34	10.83
• Global environmental issues and standard	14.17	67.50	18.33

CONCLUSION

The term environmental accounting is the compilation of data on environmental resources within an accounting framework. It also covers the interpretation of data and reporting. The challenge of environmental accounting is to deliver meaningful disclosure within accounting practices and standards. Further challenge of environmental accounting is to extend practices to include new accounting procedures for costing out and investigating possible recycling alternatives. Introducing environmental accounting and reporting the organization need to ascertain all environmental impacts from a cost benefit point of view and to measure eco-assets and liabilities for the organization. An accounting standard devoted for the purpose of measurement and reporting of environment must be pronounced. Although a global environmental accounting standard is under consideration by the International Accounting Standards Committee, there is an urgent necessity of a generally accepted environmental accounting standard to keep pace with the sustainability.

REFERENCES

Chadick, B., Rouse, R.W. and Surma, J. (1993), Perspective on Environmental Accounting, *The CPA Journal*, January, 18-24.

Federation des Experts Compatibles Europeans (1995), *Environmental Accounting, Reporting and Auditing: Survey of Current Activities and Developments within the Accounting Professionals*, Bruxells.

Gray, R.H., Bebbington, K.J. and Walter, D. (1993), *Accounting for the Environment*, Paul Chapman Publishing: London.

Gupta, N.D. (1997), *Environmental Accounting*, Wheeler Publishing: New Delhi.

Hamilton, K. (1997), Preservation and Strong Sustainability, *Environment and Development Economics*, 2 (1): 72-76.

Johnson, L.T. (1993), Research on Environmental Reporting, *Accounting Horizons*, 7 (3): 118-123.

Norton, B.G. and Toman, M.A. (1997), Sustainability: Economic and Ecological Perspectives, *Land Economics*, 73(4): 663-668.

Owen, D. (ed.) (1992), *Green Reporting: The Challenge of the Nineties*, Chapman and Hill: London.

Pearce, D.W., Markandya, A. and Barbier, E. (1989), *Blueprint for a Green Economy*, Earthscan Publications: London.

Rubenstein, D.B. (1990), There's No Accounting for the Exxon Valdez, *The CPA Journal*, July, 40-45.

Sarkar, S. (2004), Valuation of Natural Resources, *The Indian Journal of Commerce*, 57 (1): 106-111.

Sefcik, S.E., Soderstrom, N.S., and Stinson, C.H. (1997), Accounting through Green Coloured Glasses: Teaching

Environmental Accounting, *Accounting Education*, l.12 (1): 129-140.

Senghe, S.V. (1993), Accounting for the Environment: An Analysis of Issues, *The Ohio CPA Journal*, February, 33-41.

Shoemaker, P.J., and Shoemaker, J.A. (1995), Estimating Environmental Liability: Quantifying the Unknown, *California Management Review*, 37 (3): 29-61.

United Nations (1997), *Environmental Financial Accounting Guidelines, Reports Prepared for the UNCTAD*

Inter-governmental Working Group of Experts on International Standards of Accounting and Reporting, New York.

ANNEXURE-I

Schematic Environmental Accounts

Produced Assets — *Amount Rs.*

Opening stock of produced assets

Add:

- Gross capital formation of all other produced assets for environmental protection
- Gross capital formation of produced assets for environmental protection
- Other accumulation of produced economic assets

Gross capital accumulation

Less:

- Consumption of fixed capital of other than produced assets for environmental protection
- Consumption of fixed capital of produced assets for environmental protection
- Degradation of produced assets not reflected in market value of assets

Net capital accumulation

Add:

- Holding gains on produced assets

Less:

- Other charges in volume of produced assets other than degradation
- Holding loses on produced assets

Closing stock of produced assets

Non-Produced Economic Assets

Opening stock of non-produced economic assets

Add:

- Gross capital formation of all other non-produced economic assets
- All other increases in non-produced economic assets

Gross capital accumulation

Less:

- Depletion (consumption) of non-produced economic assets
- Degradation of non-produced assets reflected in market value of assets
- Degradation of non-produced assets not reflected in market value of assets

Net capital accumulation

Add:

- Holding gains on non-produced economic assets

Contd....

Produced Assets	*Amount Rs.*
Less:	
• Other charges in volume of produced economic assets other than depletion, degradation and other accumulation	
• Holding loses on non-produced economic assets	
Closing stock of non-produced economic assets	
Other Non-Produced Environmental Assets	
Opening stock of other non-produced environmental assets	
Add:	
• Gross capital formation of all other non-produced environmental assets	
• Other accumulation of other non-produced environmental assets	
Gross capital accumulation	
Less:	
• Depletion of other non-produced environmental assets	
• Degradation of other non-produced environmental assets	
Net capital accumulation	
Less:	
• Other charges in volume of other non-produced environmental assets other than depletion, degradation and other accumulation	
Closing stock of non-produced environmental assets.	

18

BAMBOO CULTIVATION FOR LIVELIHOOD SECURITY

S. Vaidehi and K. Raja Mohan Rao

INTRODUCTION

Bamboo is an important resource in the Indian socio– economic, cultural, ecological, climatic and functional context with more than 1,500 recorded uses. It has multiple economic possibilities, important ecological value and enormous potential to meet the needs of the people. However, bamboo has always been considered as the poor man's timber. Even the forest departments, which control about 9.6 million hectares of bamboo forests both, natural and planted, consider bamboo as minor forest produce. Bamboos have played a significant role in human societies since time immemorial. It contributes significantly to the subsistence needs of over two billion people living in the tropical and sub-tropical belts of Asia Latin America, and Africa.

BAMBOO CULTIVATION IN INDIA

India is blessed by rich bamboo resources. With about 22 genera and 136 species, it has one of the largest resources of bamboos, next only to China with 26 genera and 300 species. The areas particularly rich in bamboo are the North Eastern states, the Western Ghats, Chattisgarh, Madhya Pradesh and Andaman & Nicobar Islands. Bamboo is one of the fastest growing plant an earth gaining approximately 75 to 400 mm growth per day. In Japan, Phyllostachy Edulus, has recorded a growth of 1.2 mts in 24 hours. It grows three times faster than most of Eucalyptus species. A story goes that one a forest officer kept his hat on a new growing bamboo culm and forgot to retrieve it. The next day when he went to collect his hat, it was beyond his reach, for the culm had grown beyond his hand's reach in 24 hours.

Bamboo belongs to the grass species and hence forms part viz. Gramineae, which also includes important staple food plants like rice and wheat. Various estimates limit bamboos to about 1,250 species under 75 genera, which are thought to have made its first appearance about 200 million years ago. The plant now occurs in the tropical subtropical and temperate zones of all regions except Europe and Western Asia. Recent findings have revealed that bamboo was prevalent in Europe some three million years ago but vanished sometime during the last ice age. Bamboo finds a mention in Rigveda, which indicates that it must be in use for at least 4,000 years.

Bamboo is a group of fast growing woody perennial grasses represented by 23 genera and 125 species in India. It grows abundantly almost all over India, expect in Kashmir valley represented by 23 genera and 125 species. Several exotic bamboos also grow very well in many art of India. Bamboo constitutes 12.8 per cent the total forest area. The total annual production of bamboo is estimated to be 4.5 million tones, second only to china. Bamboo forms rich belt of vegetation in well-drained parts of tropical and subtropical habituates and rise up to 3700 m of altitude in the Himalayas. About 50 per cent of the bamboo produced in India grows in north- eastern region and West Bengal. Area of natural distribution of bamboo in the country is given in the tables 1 and 2.

Table 1
Distribution of Bamboo in India

State/Region	*Area %*	*Growing Stock %*
North–East	28.0	66
Madhya Pradesh	20.3	12
Maharastra	9.9	5
Orissa	8.7	7
Andhra Pradesh	7.4	2
Karnataka	5.5	3
Others	20.2	5

Source: Planning Commission Report, Government of India, July 2001.

Use of Bamboo

Traditional uses of bamboo are varied fuel wood, food, house construction, tools, musical instruments, house hold vessels, fish traps, furniture etc. bamboo is now belts known as a "wonder plant" "emperor of all grasses" or "green gold". Bamboos are aptly called the poor man's timber and are found in greatest abundance. Asian forests also call it the Timber for Twenty First century. Their strength, straightness, lightness combined with extra–extra-ordinary hardness, range in size, abundance, easy propagation and the short period in which they attain maturity, make them suitable for a variety of purposes. This fascinating plant bio diversity has to be conserved, not just for financial to my access to our biogenetic raw materials but more importantly to engage creatively in the revitalization of traditional sciences and technologies, and to use their fruits for the benefit of our own people and share them on fair terms with the rest of world.

Table 2
State Wise Bamboo Growing Stock and Potential Yield

States /UTs	*Tree Crop in Bamboo ('000Cum)*	*Bamboos (No.)*	
		1994-95	*1995-96*
Andhra Pradesh	652	143573.00	83732.00
Assam	6558	409877.00	N.A
Bihar*	1621	6691.00	8125.00
Goa**	-	21000.00	10000.00
Gujarat	-	50006.00	12636.59
Haryana	-	678125.00	1423590.00
Karnataka	49	33618.00	59504.00
Kerala	-	15962967.00	1339741.00
Madhya pradesh	-	28413.00	-
Maharastra	5156	300989.00	245910.00
Manipur	3081	810950.00	900865.00
Meghalaya	11795	-	-
Nagaland	1077	-	-
Mizoram	2452	1097344.00	1277525.00
Orissa	6574	-	217802.00
Punjab	-	165743.00	151357.00
Rajasthan	-	165743.00	151357.00
Tamil Nadu		1410.18	1154.00
Tripura	510	544.09	695.55
Uttar Pradesh	579	208675.00	185851.00
West Bengal		9950	10550.00
A&N Islands		1661665.00	2068352.00

* Bamboo in metric tone
** Bamboo in Numbers
Source: State Forest Department, 1995, 1996.

1. Bamboo can substitute wood products to mitigate the pressure on trees in natural forests and contribute to conservation of biodiversity.
2. Bamboo is most suited for rehabilitation of degraded lands with good biomass yields.
3. Bamboo with its extensive root system can conserve soil and water in catchments areas, minimize salutation and control floods in the valleys and plains.
4. Watershed management can be taken up effectively by planting bamboo where other trees fail.
5. Bamboo is most effective in controlling landslides.

6. Bamboo is effective in protection of sea banks, river banks, dam sites and canal banks.
7. Bamboo as a carbon sequestration agent can play a major role in offsetting the continued emission of CO_2 in the atmosphere and also retards the pace of climatic change.

All discussions about bamboo will remain incomplete if China is not mentioned. The maximum number of species occurs only China and they have utilized Bamboo as a major input for industrial use. Bamboo production has been streamlined right from adopting improved nursery technology, modern cultivation and management practices, integrated into processing and utilization including exports. At present bamboo in China has three billion in China has three billion US$ 600 million is from exports. The latest development in China has been the extensive use of bamboo as a viable replacement for wood. Bamboo mat boards have been acknowledged as excellent substitutes for plastics, steel and cement in new application for construction of houses, manufacturing of furniture and agricultural tools with application of sophisticated design, knowledge and use of improved composite technologies.

NATIONAL MISSION ON BAMBOO

Realizing the importance of bamboo in poverty alleviation and employment generation, planning Commission set up National Mission on Bamboo Technology and Trade Development, the report of which was submitted in April 2003. The major objective of the mission was to implement an action plan for placing bamboo as key component in the national scene to generate employment and mitigate environment degradation and strengthen the process of bamboo-based industrial development including handicrafts. Some of the major recommendations of the mission are:

8. The mission has proposed to bring an additional 6 million ha area under bamboo plantation, 2 mha during 10th Plan and 4 mha during 11th Plan. Together these are expected to fulfill the existing and emerging demands and provide the right types of raw material for making new generation value added products.
9. The requirement of fund of development of bamboo plantation in 2 mha, technology development and transfer for generation quality planting material, technology intervention for process and products including standards and codes, handicrafts, trade and market development has been estimated at Rs.2,608.00 crore.

It is recommended that under the aegis of the Planning Commission, workshops be organized at different locations to orient and seek necessary support from various stakeholders in implementation of the Mission's activity in the right perspective.

It is hoped that the integrated bamboo development programme under the National Mission, will create gainful employment for 8.6 million persons and enable 5.01 million families to escape poverty on a sustainable basis.

The current estimated demand of bamboo for various purposes is 26.69 million MTs as against a supply of 13.47 million MTs. In order to meet the existing gap of 13.22 million MTs and also meeting future demand, it is essential to raise large scale plantation in various agro-ecological regions of the country. However, care should be taken so that such plantations are raised around utilization centers so that transport costs are kept at minimum.

Bamboo cab substitute wood products. New generation bamboo products such as mat boards, mat veneer composite, mat corrugated sheet, mat overlaid particle board, mat moulded article and laminates/composites can develop bamboo based industry of about Rs. 26,000 crore annually by the end of the 11th plan.

Bamboo development has to be marketed and technology driven. It has been estimated that the combined value of internal and commercial consumption of bamboo in the world is to the tune of US$ 10 billion (approximately Rs. 50,000 cr.), which is expected to reach about US$ 20 billion by 2015. The size of the domestic bamboo economy as of now is Rs. 2,043 crore, while the market potential is estimated at Rs. 4,463 cr. with a projected annual average growth rate of 15-20%. The bamboo industry could grow to Rs.26, 000 crore by 2015, which is close to the current size of the bamboo industry in China.

Bamboo is being used in various industries. Recent research in China has resulted in production of an excellent alcoholic beverage from bamboo leaves. Research in Japan has shown that bamboo based charcoal may be a major source for chemical substances for exotic application of very high value. Recognizing the urgent need for an appropriate and cost-effective roofing technology for disaster prone areas, a technology for manufacture of laminated bamboo mat corrugated roofing technology for manufacture of laminated bamboo mat corrugated roofing sheets has been development at the Indian Plywood Industries Research and Training Institute. Bangalore, in collaboration with the Building Materials and Technology Promotion Council, New Delhi.

REFERENCES

Karmakar K.G. and Haque, M.S. (2004), Bamboo and Rural Employment, *Yojana*, July, 48.

Murthy, C. (2004), Forest Resources in India, *Kisan World*, 81(7).

Government of India (2001), Report of the Task Force on Greening India for Livelihood Security and Sustainable Development, Planning Commission , New Delhi.

19

EXPORT OF NTFPS: WITH SPECIAL REFERENCE TO MEDICINAL PLANTS FROM INDIA

S. Vaidehi and K. Raja Mohan Rao

INTRODUCTION

Forests are an important for the mankind not because they provide timber and a variety of non-wood forest products but because they influence various environmental factors. Forests are also popularly known as earth's blanket and world's air conditioner. They are crucial to survival of mankind because they constitute the life-supporting system in the earth. The total geographical area of the country constitutes 328.8 million-hectare. Out of it, approximately 63 million hectares. This is about 19.27 per cent of the geographical area of the country. Forests in India are generally under the government ownership. These forest products or forest produces may be broadly classified into two main groups: (i) wood produce and (ii) non-wood produce. The wood produce includes timber and firewood and non-wood produce include all produces other than timber and firewood. Non-wood produce is commonly referred to as Minor Forest Produce (MFP) or Non-Timber Forest Products (NTFPs).

ROLE OF NTFPS IN INDIA

The NTFPs act as a linking agent between development and environment. For instance, most of the ecology and environment related problem area owing to heavy exploitation of timber and firewood. The important Non-timber forest products are Edible products, grasses and grazing, Fodder trees and shrubs, bamboo and canes, Medicines, Oilseeds, Essential Oils, Tans and dyes, Cum and resins, Fibers and flosses, special and flavorings, Animal products, Tendu leaves and other leaves, and miscellaneous products etc… these products will supplement the household income in rural areas through which it reduces unemployment and poverty. The NTFPs activities have a higher scope in future, since the employment generation in agriculture is declining year after year.

The Collection processing and trade of NTFPs may encourage rural poor communities to live within forest stands, which won't allow the rural poor to migrate to towns.

The NTFPs provide raw materials for large number of industries processing, cater employment, to 40 per cent of poor artisans and contribute 54 per cent of forest revenue to state. A systematized mechanism for sustainable management, harvest and marketing of NTFPs form the grass roots level to the level of export to international markets does not exist. Looking at the magnitude of the NTFPs resource and its potential for international trade there is a huge scope for strengthening and streamlining the existing market channels for profitable trade and export of these NTFPs to the international markets. In order to make these products internationally competitive it is mandatory to ensure that these products are responsibly extracted from sustainable managed and certified forest area.

TRENDS IN EXPORTS OF NTFPS IN INDIA

NTFPs in India are derived from over 3,000 species. According to the Centre of Minor Forest Products, 325 species producing NTFPs are very common, commercial and have a base in major industry–they are exported or imported; 879 species are used locally; 677 species are potentially useful only locally; and 1,343 species can be described as "others lesser known". India exports a large number of NTFPs to other countries after meeting internal requirements. Foreign exchange earnings total about Rs.10 billion (US$384 million) annually (Shiva, 1995). NTFPs are primarily exported as raw materials (Gupta, 1994) (See annexure Table 1 & 2).

Table 1
Value of NTFPs Exported from India

	In values					
	1991–92	*1992–93*	*1993–94*	*1994–95*	*1995–96*	*1996-97*
Value of NTFPs exported from India (in million US$)	510.96	505.47	786.8	1 033.28	1 248.25	1 311.39

Source: Shiva and Pandey (1998).

A number of tree species provide edible plant products. Important fruits come from Buchanania lanzan (chironji, achaar or char), Anacardium occidentale (cashew nut or kaju), Pinus gerardiana (chilgoza or neoza), Emblica officinalis (aonla), Tamarindus indica (tamarind), Aegle marmelos (bel), Feronia elephantum (kaitha), Artocarpus lakoocha (barhal), Syzygium cuminii (jamun), Annona squamosa (custard apple) Carissa opaca (karaunda), Juglans regia (akhrot), Moringa oleifera (drum stick) and Zizyphus jujuba (ber). Edible flowers come from Madhuca indica and M. longifolia (mahua). Roots and tubers of Amorphophalus campanulatum, Dioscorca belophylla, D. oppositifolia and Ipomoea aquatica are also important. See annexure (Table-3).

Table 2
Percentage Contribution of Different NTFPs Groups to the Total Export Value of NTFPs

NTFPs groups	1991–92	1992–93	1993–94	1994–95	1995–96	1996–97
Edible products	53.5	58.6	52.5	56.4	54.1	48.74
Medicinal products	9.1	9.4	6.8	6.5	6.0	7.4
Spices	6.5	7.0	8.0	7.0	5.2	9.3
Essential oils	3.4	3.1	2.2	1.9	2.0	3.2
Oil seeds/fatty oils	8.3	8.7	10.5	10.1	14.9	11.1
Gums/resins	7.6	9.4	7.4	6.2	7.6	9.2
Tans/dyes	0.7	0.9	0.64	0.4	0.4	0.5
Fibres/flosses	0.4	0.4	0.3	0.25	0.29	0.33
Bamboos/canes	0.01	0.01	0.0004	0.003	0.001	0.007
Miscellaneous	1.25	1.13	1.0	0.9	1.0	0.95
Animal origin including lac and shellac	0.02	0.02	0.03	0.05	0.12	0.08
Mineral origin	9.32	1.36	10.63	10.3	8.4	9.2

Source: Shiva and Pandey (1998).

MEDICINAL PLANTS IN INDIA

Medicinal plants are one of the important products of the non-timber forest products. In India, medicinal plants are widely used by all sections of the population, and over 7,500 species of plants are alone estimated to be used by the Eco-system people" that belong to some of ethnic communities. Presently 75 different plant derived secondary metabolites are in use and the medicines made from them represent a fraction of slightly more than 5% of the total. Substances most frequently used in medical preparations are cardiac glycosides, theophylline, vincamine, atropine, pilocarpine codeine and scopolarnine. Additionally lot of important steroid compounds and harmonies are derived semi synthetically from plant precursors. India probably has the oldest, richest and most diverse, cultural traditions in the use of medicinal plants in all systems of health care.

Exploring of forest based plant products for new pharmaceutical and ever increasing demand for medicinal plants is increasing in both developing and developed countries (WHO) especially among youth and surprisingly the bulk of the material traded is still from wild harvested sources on forest lands and very small number of species are cultivated. The expanding trade in medicinal

Table 3
NTFPs Exports from India

NTFPs	*1991–92*		*1992–93*		*1993–94*		*1994–95*		*1995–96*		*1996–97*	
	Quantity (in MT)	*Value (in Rs.)*	*Quantity (in MT)*	*Value (in Rs.)*	*Quantity (in MT)*	*Value (in Rs.)*	*Quantity (in MT)*	*Value (in Rs.)*	*Quantity (in MT)*	*Value (in Rs.)*	*Quantity (in MT)*	*Value (in Rs.)*
Edible products	22 842 5.25	114 864.25	264 419.93	124 472.42	291 531.17	173 616.20	312 942.42	244 735.02	374 742.24	283 416.41	348 541.67	268 392.66
Medicinal products	387 44.43	19 485.66	37 405.18	20 030.82	32 948.78	22 391.03	35 953.07	28 280.73	35 493.85	31 301.50	42 592.97	40 814.00
Spices	43 244.27	13 877.38	48 006.14	146 52.73	484 168.75	26 376.91	58 080.28	30 309.44	47 297.81	27 124.31	73 046.25	51 499.04
Essential oils	4 864.78	7 196.62	2 918.71	6 577.77	2 630.69	7 161.31	2 491.78	8 201.50	3 020.33	10 612.59	3 554.43	17 663.80
Oil seeds/fatty oils	89 735.87	17 787.60	295 277.30	18 490.95	379 424.28	34 729.03	168 758.98	43 901.89	374 275.48	78 085.01	264 139.51	61 173.81
Gums/resins	72 626.39	16 294.87	76 088.16	19 880.28	84 179.32	24 521.46	78 590.48	26 829.40	94 220.88	40 042.52	107 158.43	50 493.67
Tans/dyes	10 101.91	1 472.73	9 332.50	1 816.03	10 297.68	2 131.73	5 369.71	1 635.43	6 415.73	2 009.07	8 193.01	2 765.57
Fibres/flosses	4 838.87	869.27	5 283.16	953.26	4 283.92	894.35	5 512.36	1 096.56	5 593.31	1 512.73	5 908.42	1 797.86
Bamboos/canes	91.34	12.42	120.01	31.27	5.55	1.45	113.03	14.45	103.98	7.77	867.71	39.96
Miscellaneous	6 630.36	2 681.81	4 270.87	2 455.56	10 157.08	3 289.88	16 263.56	3 873.13	9 303.04	5 433.17	83 914.60	5 257.18
Animal origin including lac and shellac	98.63	36.82	9.22	38.85	237.94	119.85	205.17	203.77	549.28	677.08	651.22	435.84
Mineral origin	617 698.53	262 977.11	2 893.88	10 05433.32	35 221.34	12 34036.01	44 898.07	11 838 99.92	50 450.3	20 026.47	44 044.02	938 083.01
Grand total value of MFPs (in Rs.)	11 171 00.63	2 146 05.90	10 061 08.29	2 122 95.82	2 305 298.48	3 304 54.54	19 183 16.85	4 339 79.39	21 349 15.85	5 242 66.18	18 766 51.23	5 507 83.70
Grand total value of MFPs (in US$ million)		510.97		505.47		786.80		1 033.28		1 248.25		1 311.39

Source: Shiva and Pandey (1998).

Table 4
Export Data of Some NTFPs with a Monopoly in World Trade

NTFPs	*1991–92*		*1992–93*		*1993–94*		*1994–95*		*1995–96*		*1996–97*	
	Quantity (in MT)	*Value (in Rs.)*	*Quantity (in MT)*	*Value (in Rs.)*	*Quantity (in MT)*	*Value (in Rs.)*	*Quantity (in MT)*	*Value (in Rs.)*	*Quantity (in MT)*	*Value (in Rs.)*	*Quantity (in MT)*	*Value (in Rs.)*
Sterculia urens (karaya gum) (Indian tragacanth)	573.55	489.45	843.33	724.48	1 443.06	1 110.24	1 467.13	1 074.97	1 224.42	1 159.43	941.11	893.87
Myrobalan fruit extract Terminalia chebula (harra)	540.62	122.02	975.52	242.05	867.91	218.22	1 371.39	324.08	1 110.05	283.90	1 127.59	249.39
Myrobalan amla used in tanning Emblica officinalis (amla)	7.0	0.77	107.2	12.62	102.69	27.34	330.83	73.66	467.02	73.92	248.98	53.44
Myrobalan other (whole or cut) used in tanning	43.4	4.4	370.85	32.51	221.84	32.9	140.79	20.58	121.26	26.72	235.97	51.96
General myrobalans	613.4	134.00	1 453.66	287.44	1 196.44	279.40	1 875.01	425.07	1 745.83	392.05	1 705.25	427.42
(Annatto dye) Bixa orellana	18.94	12.73 (1990–91)	-	-	-	-	-	-	-	-	109.24	97.34
Sandalwood chips and dust, (Santalum album)			0.77	1.04	-	-	-	-	-	-	-	-
Sandalwood oil (Santalum album)	-	-	2.00	4.65	0.03	0.16	0.16	0.86	0.003	0.02	0.50	1.45

Sources: Shiva and Pandey (1998).

plants has serious implications on the survival of several plant species, with many under threat to become extinct. Today this rich biodiversity of medicinal plants are facing serious resource threat because of the rapid loss of natural habitats, and overexploitation of medicinal plants from the wild. To meet the demands of the Indian herbal industry which has annual turnover of about US $300 million, tons of medicinal plants are being harvested every year from some of 165,000 ha. of forests.

EXPORTS OF MEDICINAL PLANTS IN INDIA

India and other most of the countries have little or no regulations controlling the collection of material for the wild. India is one exception and has banned export of several threatened wild species in the form of raw materials although the export of finished products containing the material is selectively allowed. A legal instrument known as Bio-diversity conservation Bill is under the process of legislation in the parliament. An estimated into Germany is wild harvested and very few species among these are currently propagated on a large scale by in-site or ex-site cultivation. The following table examines the export of medicinal plants among the 12 countries during the year of 1992-1995 and also the next table is the lists of the medicinal plants in India. *(See annexure* Table 5 & 6).

Table 5
Leading Countries Exports of Medicinal Plants
(Average Volume in 1992-1995)

Country of export	*Volume (tonnes)*	*Value (USD1, 000)*
China	121,900	264,500
India	32,600	45,950
Germany	14,400	68,500
Singapore	13,200	54,000
Egypt	11,250	12,350
Chile	11,200	23,500
USA	10,150	35,700
Bulgaria	7,800	11,000
Morocco	6,800	12,850
Mexico	6,300	9,300
Pakistan	4,800	3,300
France	4,700	26,300

CONSERVATION IMPLICATIONS OF MEDICINAL PLANTS

It is evident that trade in medicinal plant has serious implications on the survival of species. If one considers the material exported to developed countries and the material collected or indigenous use certainly the survival of many species may well be under threat, given the increasing demand fir medicinal plants. There are number of reasons as to why the trade in wild harvested material has been left to reach such a critical point is that the legislation that exists to control harvesting and trade of medicinal plants is inadequate and ineffective in its current form; new policies and easier mechanisms to control the trade are needed. Lack of awareness among many of the end users, as to the extent to has become a subject of concern. In an attempt to control the market, the traders will give virtually no information on the extent of wild harvesting. It has become absolutely essential to apply process of sustainable harvesting immediately to these species.

Table 6
Lists of Medicinal Plants

No	*Plants*	*Parts*
1.	Plantago ovata	Seed & husk
2.	Cassia angustifolia	Leaf & pod
3.	Rheum emodi	Rhizome
4.	Inula acemosa	Rhizome
5.	Rauwolfia serpentina	Roots
6.	Hedychium Spicatum	Rhizome
7.	Zingiber officinale	Rhizome
8.	Colchicum luteum	Rhizome & seed
9.	Valeriana wallichii	Rhizome
10.	Acorus calamus	Rhizome
11.	Adhatoda vasica	Whole plant
12.	Juglan regia	Bark
13.	Punica granatum	Flower, root, bark
14.	Berberis aristata	Root
15.	Juniperus communis	Fruit
16.	J. macropoda	Fruit
17.	Heracleum candicans	Rhizome
18.	Picrorhiza kurroa	Root
19.	Aconitum species	Root
20.	Saussurea lappa	Rhizome
21.	Swertia chiraita	Whole plant
22.	Podophyllum emodi	Rhizome

The bio-diversity loss is not only a threat to ecology of the planer but also a more immediate threat to the livelihood security of rural communities. Thus the developing countries are put under tremendous pressure to adopt Intellectual Property Rights (IPR) regimes that accord with the standards which now prevail in North America, Europe, and Japan.

It is well under stood that bio-technology cannot replace the present need but endangered plant species can be protected in their natural environment, and establishment of botanical garden, gene-bank to conserve the genes and techniques of sustainable harvesting will certainly help to conserve the natural resources. Since the beginning of this century more than half of the worlds tropical forest area has been destroyed and today more than 11 ha of tropical forest are lost every day, and the experts estimate that only 5-10% of all plants in the world have been systematically investigated for their pharmacological activity and many of them are uninvestigated and are threatened in the tropical forest. Strong strategies in terms of conservation through biotechnology and legal support need to be evolved.

CONCLUSION

Medicinal plants are one of the important products of the non-timber forest products. In India, medicinal plants are widely used by all sections of the population, and over 7,500 species of plants are alone estimated to be used by the Eco-system people" that belong to some of ethnic communities. Today this rich biodiversity of medicinal plants are facing serious resource threat because of the rapid loss of natural habitats, and overexploitation of medicinal plants from the wild. To meet the demands of the Indian herbal industry which has annual turnover of about US $300 million, tons of medicinal plants are being harvested every year from some of 165,000 ha of forests. India is one exception and has banned export of several threatened wild species in the form of raw materials although the export of finished products containing the material is selectively allowed.

REFERENCES

Gupta, B.N. (1994), India, *In Non-Wood Forest Products in Asia,* Food and Agriculture Organization of the United Nations: Rome.

Ojha Hemat R. (2001), Commercial Use of Non-Timber Forest Products: Can the Poor Really Get Benefit, *Journal of Forestry & Livelihoods*, Nepal.

Prasad, R.X. and Saxena, N.C. (1996), *Role of the State in NTFPs Marketing Exchanges*, Action Aid: Bangalore.

Shiva, M.P. and Pandey, B.C. (1998), A Potential Indicator to Augment Production of on Timber Forest Products (NWFP) for Export and Import Substitution, Centre of Minor Forest Products: Dehra Dun.

Shiva, M.P. (1995), Collection, Utilization and Marketing of Medicinal Plants from the Forests of India with An Overview on NWFPs in Asia Pacific Region, Paper presented at the Regional Expert Consultation on Non-Wood Forest Products: Social, Economic and Cultural Dimensions, 28 Nov. to 2 Dec., 1994, Bangkok. (Thailand).

20

AGRICULTURAL POLICY AND LAND REFORMS IN INDIA

S.N. Yogesh

INTRODUCTION

The National Agricultural Policy was presented in the parliament on July 28, 2000. The policy has been necessitated due to the relatively poor growth of agriculture during the 90s. The policy document stated: "capital inadequacy, lack of infrastructural support and demand-side constraints such as controls on movement, storage, and sale of agricultural products etc., have continued to affect the economic viability of agricultural sector, consequently growth has also tended to slacken during 90s." The establishment of an agrarian economy which ensures food and nutrition to India's billion people, raw-materials for its expanding industrial base and surplus for exports and a fast and equitable reward system for the farming community for the services they provide to the society will be the mainstay of reforms in the agricultural sector.

Thus, the National Agricultural Policy aims to attain the following objectives:

1. A growth take of over 4 per cent per annum in the agricultural sector.
2. Growth that is based on efficient use of resources and conserves our soil, water and biodiversity.
3. Growth with equity i.e., growth which is wide-spread across-regions and farmers.
4. Growth that is demand-driven and caters to domestic markets and maximises benefits from exports of agricultural products in the face of challenges from economic liberalization and globalization.

5. Growth that is sustainable technologically, environmentally and economically.

HIGHLIGHTS OF THE POLICY

The main highlights of agricultural policy of India are given as under:

1. The growth of agricultural sector is to be achieved through combination of measures including structural, institutional, agro-economics and tax reforms.
2. The focus of the new policy is on efficient use of resources and technology.
3. The focus of the new policy is on adequate availability of credit to the farmers.
4. Protecting the farmers from seasonal and price fluctuations.
5. Privatization of agricultural sector would be encouraged and promoted through contract farming and land leasing arrangements.
6. Private sector investment would be encouraged particularly in areas like research, human resource development, post-harvest management and marketing.
7. Commodity-wise strategies would be evolved to protect farmers from adverse impact of under-price fluctuations in the world market.
8. Dismantling of quantitative restrictions on imports as per WTO agreements.
9. In order to fulfill the requirement of milk, eggs and livestock products, the policy envisages a 'National Livestock Breeding Strategy'.
10. Plant varieties would be protected through registration.
11. High priority would be accorded to evolve new location specific and economically viable improved varieties of crops.
12. The restrictions on the movement of agricultural commodities throughout the country would be dismantled.
13. The structure of taxes on foodgrains and other commercial crops would be reviewed and correct accordingly.
14. Rural electrification would be given high priority.
15. Steps would be taken to provide comprehensive insurance policy to the farmers which would cover all these farming operations.

ASSESSMENT OF THE POLICY

The new agricultural policy promises Green Revolution, while revolution–(pertaining to milk and dairy products) and Blue Revolution (pertaining to aqua/fish culture). It has been described as a policy of promising 'Rainbow Revolution':

1. Over 4% annual growth rate in aggregate
2. Greater private sector participation through contract farming
3. Price protection for farmers
4. National Agricultural Insurance Scheme to be launched for all farmers and all crops.
5. Dismantling of restrictions on movement of age commodities throughout the country.

CRITICAL REVIEW OF THE POLICY

1. There has been virtual stagnation in Indian agriculture during the later half of the nineties.
2. The speak of 4% growth during the next two decades appears to be wishful thinking, but the fact that the new policies under economic reforms have neglected agriculture completely.
3. During the 90s, the growth of agricultural production averaged 2.1%, which was just equal to the growth rate of population. It is equally true that the goal of food security for all still appears to be a distance dream.
4. The new agricultural policy does talk of growth with equity, but fails to identify the states, which have lagged behind in the utilisation of their agricultural potential.
5. The policy speaks of encouraging private investment in agriculture. There is no doubt that private investment does help big-farmers to improve these levels of productivity. But the small farmers unable to undertake private investment effectively to boost their productivity.
6. New agricultural policy intends to seek private sector participation through contract farming by land leasing arrangements. The adoption of contract farming will result in contraction of employment.
7. The government after making comprehensive recommendations in all areas of agricultural development has not outlined any machinery of implementation.

LAND REFORMS

The agrarian structure in pre-independence period was woven around the vested interests of intermediaries. These intermediaries created a parasitic class which did not work on land, but snatched away whatever surplus over and above the minimum subsistence the cultivators produced. The rather were forced to lead a wretched life of slavery and depravation. It was basically to stop the exploitation of the actual tillers of the soil and pass on the ownership of land to them that land reforms were introduced in the post-independence period of India.

The purpose of land reforms is, therefore, twofold. On the one hand, it aims to make more rational use of the scarce land-resources by affecting the conditions of holdings, imposing ceilings and floors on holdings, so that cultivation can be done in the most economical manner i.e., without any waste of labour and capital. On the other, it is a means of redistributing agricultural land in favour of the less privileged classes, and of improving the terms and conditions on which land is held for cultivation by the actual tillers with a view to ending exploitation.

Basically, land reform measures are aimed at alleviating rural poverty in the following manner. The government has defined the objectives of land reforms as:

1. To remove such impediments to increase the agricultural production as arise from the agrarian structure inherited from the past.
2. To eliminate all forms of exploitation and social security for the tiller of soil and assure equality of status and opportunity to all sections of the rural population.
3. By distributing land among the landless by taking possession of surplus land from large land holders.
4. By providing security of tenure and ownership lights to tenants and share croppers and by regulating rent payable by them to the landholders.
5. By protecting the interests of tribals in land preventing non-tribals to encroach upon tribals land.
6. By promoting consolidation of holding to improve the size of operational holdings thereby paving the way to raise productivity.
7. By development of public lands thereby providing better access to the rural poor to obtain full wood and fodder.
8. By providing access to women to land and their productive assets.
9. By protecting homestead lights of the rural poor on lands owned by them.

The scope of land reforms entails:

1. Abolition of Intermediaries.
2. Tenancy Reforms.
3. Ceilings and floors on land holdings.
4. Agrarian Reorganization.
5. Organization of co-operative farms.

The measures contemplated to achieve these objectives all as follows.

Abolition of Intermediaries

Before Independence, there were '3' types of land tenure systems prevailing in the country: (a) The Zamindari System; (b) The Mahalwari System; and (c) The Ryotwari System. Under Zamindari System, the ownership of land vested with landlords. These landlords were entrusted with the task of collecting rent from the tenants and passing it on to the government. A big portion of the rent was kept by the Zamindars as their remuneration. Under Mahalwari System, the whole village was treated as one unit. The responsibility of collecting the land revenue and depositing it with the government rested with the village headman. Under Ryotwari System, the responsibility of paying land revenue to the government was the cultivated himself and there was no intermediary between him and the state. Under Zamindari system, farmers were exploited in the hands of intermediaries under Mahalwari and Ryotwari system also. The practice of cultivation by tenants became widely prevalent. Also, the existence of intermediaries was the most important impediment to agricultural development in the later half of 19th and the first half of 20th century. It was on account of these reasons that legislations were passed to abolish all types of intermediaries and to pass the land to actual tiller of land.

The general pattern of abolition of intermediaries was as follows:

1. Common lands such as waste lands forests etc., which belonged to the intermediaries were vested in the state government for the purposes of management and development.
2. Home farms and lands under personal cultivation of the intermediaries were left with them and lesses of home farms lands continued as tenants of them in some states and brought in direct contact with government in other states.
3. The abolition of intermediaries was done with compensation to intermediaries. The basis of land the rate of compensation varied from state to state.

The abolition of statutory landlordism covering a variety of intermediary tenures has now mare or less accomplished bringing nearly 2 crores cultivators into direct contact with the states. It has been estimated that in all 173 intermediaries and distributed among landless agriculturists.

Tenancy Reforms

Under this heading, 3 measures are discussed. (a) Regulation of Rent (b) Security of tenure & (c) Conferment of ownership lights on tenants.

(a) Regulation of Rent: In the pre-Independence, the rent charged by Zamindars from the tenants was exorbitant. The rate varied between 40% to 80% of the produce in different states. These highly exploitative tales spelt

misery on the tenants who could hardly make both the ends meet. As a consequence, legislations were enacted after independence to regulate the limits of rents and reduce the burden on tenants. Different states fixed different rents ranging between 25% to 40%. However, legislations fixing maximum limits of rents have been often violated. Back of the strong socio-economic and political hold of landowners: they have been able to extract considerably more rent from the peasants them the rent fixed by the legislations.

(b) Security to Tenure: To provide security to tenure, and to protect tenants from ejectments legislations have been passed in most of the states. Legislation for security of tenure had three essential aims:

1. Ejectments do not take place except in accordance with provision of the law.
2. Land may be resumed by an owner, if at all, for personal cultivation only, and
3. In the event of resumption, the tenant is assured of a prescribed minimum area.

However, the light of resumption combined with flaws in the definition of personal cultivation rendered all tenancies insecure. The landlord could eject any tenant on the plea of personal cultivation. It was on account of this fact that IV five year plan recommended that all tenancies should be declared non-resumable and penalty should be imposed on wrongful eviction.

(c) Ownership Rights for Tenants: Legislations provide for bringing tenants of non-resumable lands into direct relationship with the states in the following three ways:

(i) By declaring tenants as owners and requiring them to pay compensation to owners in suitable installmetns.

(ii) Through the acquisition of light of ownership by the state on payment of compensation and transfer of ownership to tenants.

(iii) Through the acquisition by the state of landlord rights and bringing tenants into direct relationship with the state, option being given to tenants to continue as such on payment of fare rent to the government or to acquire full ownership on payment of the prescribed (manner) minimum.

It has been estimated that as a result of laws conferring ownership rights on tenants in various states, approximately 124.2 lakh tenants have acquired ownership rights on 6.32 million hectare of land.

Re-organization of Agriculture: Re-organization of agriculture included the following policies : (a) Redistribution of land (b) Consolidation of holdings and (c) Co-operative farming.

(i) *Re-distribution of Land:* Re-distribution of land was to be undertaken by imposing ceilings on amount of land which an individual could hold and distributing the surplus land among the landless farmers. A ceiling on land holding means statutory absolute limit on the amount of land which an individual may hold. A ceiling of 18 acres on wet land and 54 acres on dry land has been fixed. It has been estimated that 3.04 million hectares of land has been declared surplus and 2.15 million hectares has been distributed among 5.54 million people.

(ii) *Consolidation of Holdings:* This measure aims to solve the problem of fragmentation of holdings. The method adopted is to grant one consolidated holding to the farmer equal to the total of the land in different scattered plots under his possession. The programme of consolidation faces a number of difficulties.

(iii) *Co-operative Farming:* This measure also aims to solve the problem of fragmentation of holdings. The idea is that farmers having very small holdings should join hands and poor their resources for the purpose of cultivation. This will enable them to reap the benefits of large scale farming. However, reviewing the working of the co-operative farming societies it has been found that they have failed to make any significant contribution.

Evaluation of Land Reforms

The land reforms which raised so many hopes when they were initiated, have been subjected to criticism on the following grounds:

Lack of Political will

Implementation of land reforms calls for hard political decisions and effective political support, direction and control. No tangible progress is expected in the absence of the requisite political will. Land reforms have failed back of the lack of political will.

Flaws in Legislations

(a) Definition of personal cultivation: The definition of personal cultivation was highly unsatisfactory.

(b) Substantial limits for personal cultivation.

(c) Malafide transfers: To escape the laws relating to land ceilings, the Zamindars indulged in large-scale transfer of land to their family members.

(d) Inadequate definition of tenants.

(e) The problem of voluntary surrender.

(f) Inadequacies of ceiling laws.

CONCLUSION

Thus we find that land reforms in India have failed miserably. The process of implementation of land reforms was wrought with serious defects. The speedy and successful implementation of land reforms requires not only strong political will on the part of government but also awareness of lights on the parts of peasants.

REFERENCES

Nagarjuna, Boppana (2004), *Economic Reforms and Perspectives*, Serials Publications: New Delhi.

Rajapurohit, A.R. (1984), Land Reforms and Changing Agrarian Structure in India, in A.R. Rajapurohit (ed.) *Land Reforms in India*, Ashish Publishing House: New Delhi.

21

GLOBALIZATION AND INDIAN AGRICULTURE

S.N. Yogesh

INTRODUCTION

The last decade has witnessed much talk about globalisation, economic liberalization and economic integration of the Indian Economy with the world economy. Specially, after the completion of Uruguay Round of Trade Negotiations in April 1994 and the establishment of the World Trade Organisation in January 1995, many issues have been raised regarding India's participation in World Trade in future, its integration with the world economy and the likely costs and benefits from the integration.

Globalization is a process of increasing economic integration and growing interdependence between countries in the world economy. It is a relative softening up of economic and trade barriers across the countries so as to facilitate a free-interflow of capital, technology, people, goods and services. Eventually, Globalization would mean being able to manufacture in the most cost-effective way anywhere in the world. It means being able to procure raw materials and labour and drawing management resources from the cheapest source anywhere in the world.

Globalization intends to integrate the Indian economy with the world economy. Globalization is considered to be an important element in the reforms package. It has 'four' parameters:

1. Reduction of trade barriers to permit free-flow of goods and services across national boundaries.
2. Creation of an environment in which free flow of capital can take place.
3. Creation of an environment permitting free-flow of technology among nation-states.

4. Creation of an environment in which free movement of labour can take place in different countries if the world, it is most important from the point of view of the developing countries.

The advocates of Globalization, more especially from developed countries, limit the definition of Globalization to only three components, namely, unhindered trade flows, capital flows and technology flows. And conduct the debate on Globalization within the boundaries set-by them. But several economists and social thinkers in developing countries believe that this definition is incomplete. If the ultimate aim of the Globalization movement is to integrate the world into 'One Global Village', then the fourth component of unrestricted movement of labour cannot be left-out. But whether the debate about Globalization is carried out at the World Trade Organization or at any other international forum, there is a deliberate effort to black-out 'labour flows' as an essential component of Globalization.

Globalization, indicating the desire to integrate nation-states within the overall framework of the WTO is nothing but a 'Modern version of the Theory of Comparative cost Advantage'. It was argued that international specialization benefits both the countries which enter into the trade relations. The same argument has been brought forth by the advocates of Globalization now. They want an 'Export–led pattern of growth' to replace the 'import–substitution trade policies'.

During the last two decades, the developed nations more especially U.S.A. and the European union countries have emphasized 'Globalization as the new Mantra for the World Development', the developing countries would be able to improve their competitive strength and usher in a period of raid economic development consequently, the developing countries are cajoled and through various kinds of soft and hard pressures are persuaded to fall in line.

As a result, as it happened in India, the process of dismantling trade barriers was started in 1991 and subsequently, every year the Govt. has been announcing reduction in custom duties and removing quantitative restriction. It is argued that, this shall enable free flow of goods, capital, technology and services and thus Globalization becomes a motivating factor for nations to develop themselves at a faster rate. For a developing countries like India, it opens access to new markets and new technology. Thus, import-substitution strategy has been replaced by Export-led growth during 1991.

The following factors facilitated and accelerated the pace of Globalization.

1. The recent developments in information and communication technology.
2. International financial markets.
3. Trans-border production networks.
4. Acceleration of capital flows across national frontiers.

"The Report on Human Development in South Asia (2001) rightly mentioned: "Global integration of the economies is no longer an option it is a fact".

GLOBALIZATION AND AGRICULTURE

India followed the policy of globalization for over a decade. It is need of the now to study empirically the impact of these policies on various sectors of economy, especially on agricultural sector. Agriculture forms the backbone of the Indian Economy. The country is predominantly agricultural with 65% of work force depending directly on agriculture. It contributes about one-third (1/3) of gross value added in India. Its role in economic development apart, it is a way of life and therefore in its development lies the general well-being of the people. It has a big role in the development of industries especially the agro based industries such as textiles, sugar, tea, paper. The country's foreign trade specially in the export of traditional commodities like jute, tea, tobacco, coffee depends a great deal on the supplies of the agricultural sector. Its important lies in the fact that it has low capital output ratio. Last, but not the least, agricultural prosperity reflects directly upon the budgetary resources of the Government.

CASE FOR GLOBALIZATION IN AGRICULTURAL SECTOR

1. It is argued that Globalization of agricultural sector will improve the allocative efficiency of resources.
2. It is argued that, it will reduce the capital-output ratio in agricultural sector.
3. It will increase the labour productivity.
4. It will help to develop the export spheres and export culture.
5. It will increase the inflow of up-dated technology into the country.
6. It will increase the degree of competition.
7. It will give boost to the average growth rate of the economy.
8. It will help to restructure the production and trade pattern in a capital scarce, labour abundant economy in favour of labour intensive goods and techniques.
9. With the entry of foreign competition and the removal of import tariff barriers, domestic production will be subjected to price reducing and quality improving effects.
10. Employment opportunities would go up.

GLOBALIZATION AND ITS IMPACT ON AGRICULTURE

The significance impact of Globalization on agricultural sector can be best explained in the following contexts.

Table 1
Share of Agriculture in the National Income

Year	*GDP (1) at Factor Cost*	*Agriculture (2)*	*(2) as a % of (1)*
1990-91	6,92,870	2,42,010	30.9%
2001-02	12,65,429	3,30,272	26.1%

Figures provided by the central statistical organization reveal that between 1990-91 to 2001-02. The share of agriculture in GDP has been declined and reached the level of 26% as a consequence of globalization.

Increase in Agricultural Production

Agricultural production in India, apart from which is determined by area, productivity per hectare and total output, it is also determined by the level of technology and foreign capital. It has increased from 176 million tonnes to 276 million tonnes during 1990-91 to 2003-04.

Table 2
Total Agricultural Production (Million tonnes)

Year	*Production*
1990-91	176
1995-96	180
1990-2000	209
2000-2001	195
2002-2003	265
2003-2004	276

Changes in Cropping Pattern

By cropping pattern we meant the proportion of area under different crops at a point of time. After 1991, i.e. implementation of Globalization, the ratio of food grains to non-food grains was 75:25. It was 80:20 in 1980-81. Because the prices of non-food grains has increased in the international market.

Implementation of Land Reforms

In order to increase production and productivity of age, land reforms has been implemented very effectively after 1991.

Institutional Audit

In order to release the farmers from the clutches of money-lenders and also increase the production and productivity of age.

Procurement of Support Prices

The policy measure initiated is the announcement of procurement and support prices to ensure fall prices to farmers so that they do not suffer losses.

National Agricultural (Prices) Policy

A national agricultural policy aimed at achieving 4% per annum growth was announced in July 2000 in the form of structural, institutional, agronomics and tax reforms.

Food-Security

The issue of food-security has gained greater importance to ensure that the threat of famine no longer stalks the country.

Increased Exports

Agricultural products–tea, sugar, oilseeds, tobacco, spices etc., constituted the main items of exports of India. The proportion of agricultural gods which were exported came to 50%.

Specific Programmes

Special Rice Production Programme and National Watershed Development for Rainfed agriculture were initiated during 7th plan.

MEASURES TOWARDS GLOBALIZATION

To achieve the objective of Globalization, the following measures have been taken:

Convertibility of Rupee

The most important measure for integrating the economy of any country is to make its currency fully convertible i.e., allow it to determine its own exchange take in the international market without any official intervention. As a measure toward fully convertibility of rupee, rupee was devalued against major currencies in 1991. This was followed by introduction of dual exchange rate system in 1992-93 and fully convertibility of the rupee on trade account in 1993-94. Certain steps towards fully convertibility on capital account have also been taken.

Import Liberalization

As per the recommendations of the World Bank, free trade of all items excepts negative list of imports and exports have been allowed. The peak rate of custom duty has been brought down from 150% in early 90's to just 30% in 2001-02.

In addition to the phased reduction of import duties, India, as a member of World Trade Organization had also committed itself to the phasing out of quantitative restrictions over a six year period beginning 1997, according to an appeal made by U.S.A. against India in Dispute Settlement Body of the WTO. The QRs have been totally removed. Moreover, as a pact of the agreement on Trade Related Intellectual Property Rights, the patents Act 1999 was passed in 1999 to provide for 'Exclusive Marketing Rights'.

CASE AGAINST GLOBALIZATION

1. The Globalization process is in essence a tremendous redistribution of economic power at the world level which will increasingly translate into a redistribution of political power.
2. One study reveals that in the globalizing world, the economies of the world are ironically moving away from one another more than coming together.
3. With the lightening speed at which Globalization is taking place, it is increasing the pressure on economies for structural and conceptual readjustments to a breaking point.
4. It is becoming hard for the countries to ask their public to go through the pains and uncertainties of structural adjustment for the sake of benefits yet to come.
5. Slowing-down of the process of poverty reduction in the post- globalization period.
6. Higher GDP growth accompanied with a decline in employment growth.
7. India's ancient use of Haldi was sought to be patented under the American Law in 1995. Luckily for India, Dr. B.A. Mashelkar challenged the U.S. Patent office acknowledged.
8. An American company has been granted a patent light for Neem as a pesticide. Basmati rice, which was a universal variety in India has been patented as Kasmati and Texmati.
9. Danger lucks with regard to Tulsi plant.
10. There is a lot of divergence between what the Government says and what it is doing in this regard.

CONCLUSION

From a (view) review of decade of performance after the introduction of Globalization, it became evident that Globalization policies related to agricultural sector had not been able to deliver the intended benefits.

REFERENCES

Gaston Gaudard (1999), A Certain Regulation for Globalisation, *International Journal of Development of Planning Literature*, 14 (2).

Jalan Bimal (2002), *India and Globalisation*, Reserve Bank of India Bulletin, February.

Government of India (1995), Economic Survey 1994-95, Planning Commission, New Delhi.

Tendulkar, Suresh D. and L.R. Jain (1995), Economic Reforms and Poverty, Economic and Political Weekly, June 10.

22

DYNAMICS OF DEMOGRAPHY: AN EMPIRICAL STUDY FROM UTTAR PRADESH

Manju K. Johri and Anjani Koomar

INTRODUCTION

The population–development linkage has always been viewed as a mutually interacting relationship that is, fertility affects development and development affects fertility. The impact of high fertility and population growth on development goals has been the focus of a lot of investigations lately. The "thresholds" levels of various indices of socio economic development at which fertility could be expected to decline based on the experiences of developed countries are very well published. To calculate per cent change in development that could be expressed as the expected percentage changes in fertility, where the data is not reliable, is a complicated process. United Nations has suggested a very comprehensive framework for analyzing population variables including fertility; 15 development variables (per capita income etc.), 14 economic variables (capital stock etc), 15 socio cultural and exogenous variables. Instrument variables such as Family Planning Programmes etc. are also included (Warren, et. al., 1988). Some evaluations of programmes, which have direct health and family planning inputs, either organized by an NGO or by the government, do exist (Jain, 1984, 1985; Das et. al., 1991; Gandotra et. al., 1996), but they are mostly limited to quantitative studies in advanced states like Gujarat and Tamil Nadu. This research is limited to socio–economic variables related to the psychological affect on demography of a developing state of India.

In the Indian context, the fertility behaviour of women varies from urban to rural areas, depending on the availability of family planning devices. In rural and tribal areas people have their own traditional system of controlling fertility, which are not reported. Women of different caste and religions follow their own social and cultural taboos, which interrupt cohabitation, making the task of measuring the exact risk of conception impossible for developing accurate fertility models. Infrastructural facilities vary in different districts and villages affecting the general health and demographic rates. The scenario is ever changing making impact assessment of any development difficult. Hence, the aim of this research is to explore beyond the questionnaire level and quantitative studies and focus on finding solutions for women, which would be suitable for their existing conditions and would also be acceptable to them psychologically. It has to be recognized that women do comprise half the population and they are ultimately responsible for high fertility rates so they need to be brought into the main stream of any development. The work participation rates for women in India including advanced states, has remained very low in last three decades (See Table 1)

Table 1
Work Participation Rates of females in India

Year/ Female Workers	*1971*	*1981*	*1991*	*2001*
1. Female workers as % of Female Population	14.22	20.85	22.69	25.6
2. Female workers per 1000 male workers	215	367	408	-

Source: Various Census Reports.

The importance of this study is can be gauged from the data in Table 2. It points to the fact that in U.P. 53 per cent of mothers of two children who are in the age group 25-34, which is half the population, don't want more children. 74.4 per cent women, which is more than three fourth of the women population, in the age group 35-39 don't want to have any more children after the first two. 82.4 per cent women would prefer not to have more children after the age of 35; still the average number of children born to women aged 44-49 is 5.8 (NFHS1998-99). Apart from low contraception practices it directs our attention towards deep psychological factor, which may be affecting fertility levels of women in U.P.

Table 2
Currently Married Women Who Desire to Have No More Children

Ages	*Number of living children*				
of women	0	1	2	3	4
15-24	0.5	4.3	27.5	51.2	74.9
25-34	2	15.6	53	67.7	78.8
35-39	9.5	51.3	74.4	84.1	82.4

Source: NFHS (National Family Health Survey) 1998-99.

The premise of this research is built upon finding the realities and solutions to population problems from the grass root levels hence; the research is carried out with following objectives:

1. To develop a conceptual framework linking social and economic development in influencing the fertility behaviour through identifying appropriate variables.
2. To dig out the problems which women are facing in fertility matters by in-depth personal interviews with the respondents
3. To analyze the characteristics of the women with a view to understand what policies could be formulated to bring about a change in their fertility behaviour

REVIEW OF LITERATURE

Fertility has been linked to several variables, which may have a causal relationship with each other or may affect fertility independently or collectively. A review of literatures explores the determinants of fertility and links between such variables, which have already been established.

(a) Modernization, Urbanization and Fertility: Some researchers examined the determinants of fertility in India linking the census of 1981 and 1991. They have observed that modernization and development such as urbanization, poverty reduction and male literacy bear no significant association with fertility decline (Dreze and Murthy, 2001). An analysis of the relationship to fertility of various modernization variables such as urbanization and enhanced economic status failed to show any consistent correlation of such variables with reduced fertility (Freed and Freed, 1985) The experience of prosperous nations prove that the fertility increasing effects of modernization can be expected to last a limited time until maximum natural fertility levels occur (Srinivas, 1986). It was also found that the strength of the relationship between literacy and child population ratio increased with increased level of development (Pandey et. al., 1997).

(b) Poverty and fertility: Child labour problems in many regions bear testimony to the fact that poor produce more children without thinking and poverty forces them into menial jobs. Teenage marriages and fertility are also related to issues of poverty and employment (Sharma, 1994, 1995). It has been found that the per cent population above the poverty line was correlated with high fertility (Rao and Balakrishna, 1988) though fertility tends to decline as income increases up to a point (Mukhopadhyay and Savitri 2001). In a study from U.P. it is stated that poverty and illiteracy hamper the use and knowledge of contraception (Mukherjee, 1997).

(c) Socio-economic development and fertility: The fertility pattern in a developing country like India is quite different from the western pattern of fertility. It has been demonstrated that the slow pace of social development appears to be responsible for the slow pace of fertility decline (Jain, 1984; Prasad, 1994). It has been recognized that the social, economic and infrastructural development is the only way of reducing the incidence of child marriages due to poverty (Srivastava, 1990; Srivastava et. al., 1991) and decline in desired family size (Srinivas, 1986; Rajaram, 2000).

(d) Religion and fertility: Some studies from developing countries have revealed that the low levels of social development more than socio economic development are related to high fertility (Sharma, 1997). Religious differential in fertility are known to persist even after controlling for the effect of several major indices of social and economic development (Das and Pandey, 1985). From another study it is learnt that Muslims have higher fertility due to their relatively low status and high rates of illiteracy (Sharma, 1994).

(e) Women's Education and Fertility: Researches in many developing countries have highlighted that education is a crucial determinant of fertility behaviour, including contraception use (Chaudhry, 1978; JeJeebhoy, 1980; Jain, 1981; Nag, 1983; Jain and Nag, 1985; 1986; Kurup, 1986; Bhargava, and Saxena, 1987; Sunder, 1990; Chaudhry, 1990; Sharma, 1992). Rajan (1987) supports the slogan that education is the best contraceptive. Increasing education is seen to result in decline in number of son's desired (Ware, 1981) and increasing job opportunities through education is known to affect family size negatively (Parthsarthy, 1976; Jejeebhoy, 1980; Gulati, 1988; Vaidyanathan, 1989).

(f) Child Mortality and Fertility: A strong positive correlation between infant mortality and fertility has been found in many studies, (Jain, 1985; Pathak, and Murthy, 1985; Gurumurthy, 1985; Seal, 1988; Arora, and Singh, 1989). Due to lack of adequate health facilities in developing countries, realized or expected children's death is also known to affect fertility decisions (Jeffery et. al., 1989; Atella, and Rosati, 2000; Easterlin and Crimmins, 1985; Pathak, 1997).

(g) Autonomy and Fertility: Women's autonomy and decision making power also seem to affect their attitudes towards number of children desired, use of birth control measures as well as communication (Das et. al., 1998). Jejeeboy (1980) has documented a positive effect of women's involvement in domestic decision-making and the length and use of contraceptive in Tamil Nadu. However, women's powerlessness in the matter of contraceptive use in South Asia and India has been sufficiently evidenced by Koenig and Foo in their study in 1985. It has also been recognized that education helps to bring about a change in self-images, fostering independent aspirations among women.

Such an impact can be seen in their performance, decision-making and behavior pattern (Jolly, 1976; Khan and Singh, 1987; Raju, 1987; Vaidyanathan, 1989).

The review of literature suggests that it is quite natural and expected that pregnancy is profoundly influenced by circumstances of a woman's life, by the economic and environmental conditions in which she lives, as well as by her social status. The path through which the dynamics of changes occur is outlined in the following framework (Page 10).

Conceptual Framework

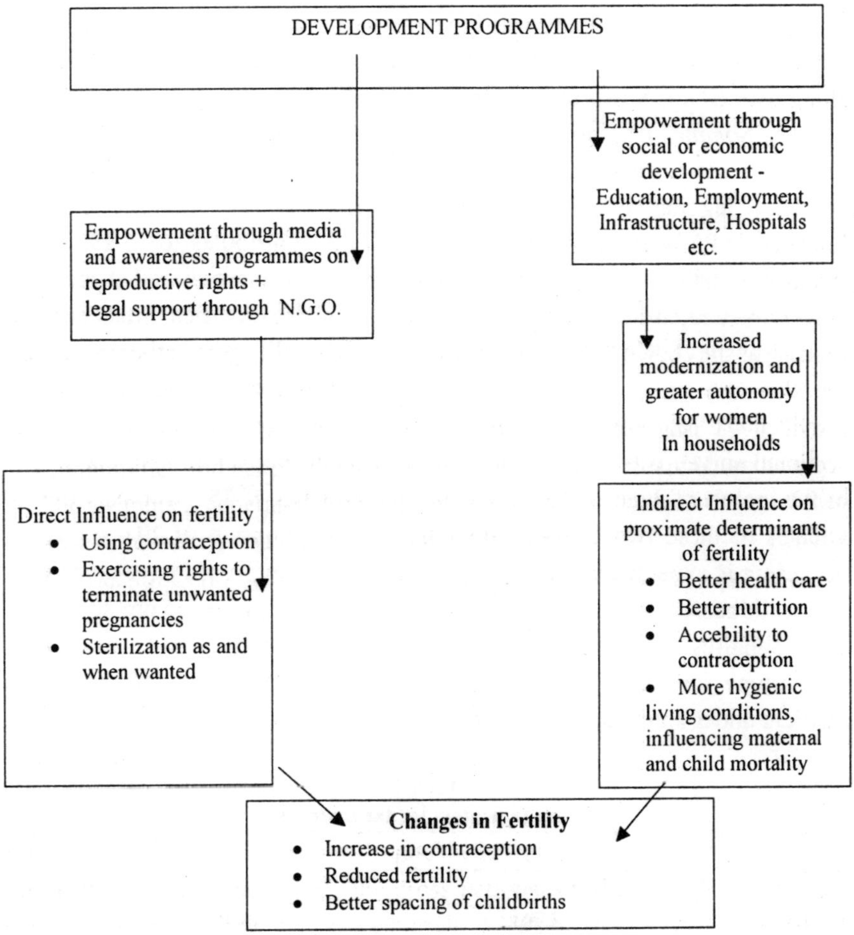

The conceptual framework linking the hypothesized relationship between development through socio economic empowerment and women's fertility behavior has been designed to take the research for selection of variables and further data analysis The aim is to explore how much variability exists among the variables and what are the factors, which affect the fertility significantly.

Selection of Variables: The exploratory research of the existing fertility variables, as outlined in the review of literature, provided the base for the selection of variables for this research. Demographic variables that directly affect fertility are taken as, present age of women (at the time of survey, June 1999), age at marriage (age at first stable cohabitation), number of children born and surviving, contraception practices, infant deaths etc. However, the socio economic variables that have an indirect impact on fertility are as important to a population where contraception is not the only fertility-reducing factor. Socio cultural variables like religion, caste, educational levels of women and their husband's are included. Type of house, water source etc. are included as indicators of economic status of the women. A brief summary of the variables along with CODES is presented in Annexure 1.

The Sample: It is pointed out that India's population problem is due to four large states, which are demographically, economically, socially, and politically lagging behind most other states (Bose, 2001), among which Uttar Pradesh (U.P.) is at the bottom of the list. U.P. contributes to 16.2% to the Indian population. The concern for the Indian Government as well as the State Government regarding the population problem is quite justified. Study of Uttar Pradesh as the choice for research area is not only challenging to the researchers but also very much needed. The Population Research Centre of Lucknow provided the required data of the sample for the present research. A cross sectional survey was carried out in Firozabad and Rai Bareli districts of U.P. in the month of June in 1999. The sample consists of 751 women from 18 villages of these two districts, who are in the age group of 29 - 49 years, because it is expected that due to early marriages they would have completed their childbearing period. The research is based on responses to pre-structured questionnaires conducted by PRC Lucknow, sponsored by Aid's Awareness Programme for Rapid House Hold Survey. The population structure of the districts under study is presented in Table 3

Table 3
Key Indicators for the Districts

State/District	*Persons*	*Males*	*Females*
U.P.	166,052,859	87,466,301	78,586,558
Firozabad	2,045,737	1,105,203	940,534
Rae Bareli	2,872,204	1,473,690	1,398,514

Source: Rapid Household Survey, 2001.

The frequency distribution curve for number of children born to 751 women, who are included in the sample, was plotted to confirm the accuracy of the data (figure 1). The mean of total number of children born to women was found to be 4.109, excluding women with no children, which falls between the total fertility rate for eastern U. P. at 4.02 and total fertility rate for illiterate population of U. .P. at 4.54 (NFHS, 1998- 1999).

Table 4
Frequency Distribution of Women According to Total Number of Children Born in Firozabad and Raibareli Districts of U.P. (June 1999)

No. of Children	*No. of Women*	*No. of Children*	*No. of Women*
0	21	6	82
1	32	7	40
2	104	8	17
3	159	9	10
4	162	10	2
5	121	12	1

Source: Population Research Centre, Lucknow University, Lucknow.

Figure 1: Frequency Distribution Graph for Total Number of Children Born to Women

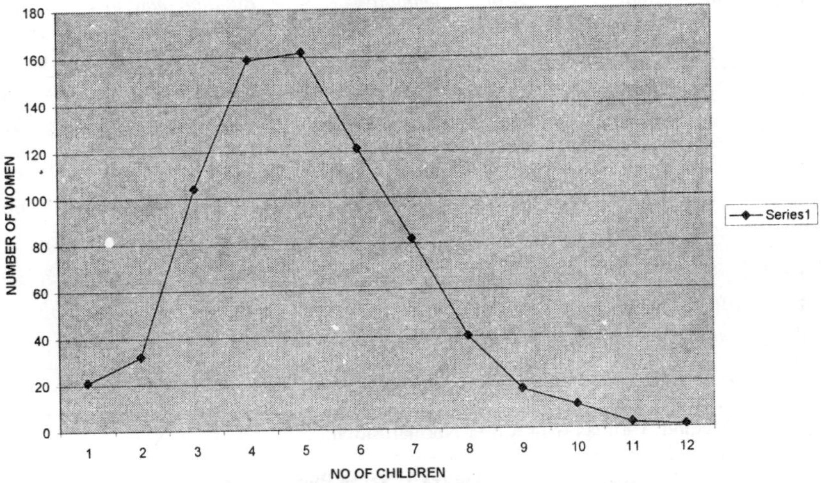

X-Axis represents the total number of children born to each woman
Y- Axis represents the number of women. (Frequency)

Data analysis: The data analysis was carried out in three stages:

1. An exploratory research of the variation in data using Principal Component Analysis.
2. Estimating the criterion variable through a set of predictor variables using correlation analysis and Kendall Tau b.
3. Dividing the data in two groups comprising of mothers who have more than two children and those who have two or less children. A comparison of the characteristics of the women in each group was followed by discussions.

An analysis of the correlation matrix was carried out because the variables were measured on different scales (See Annexure 2). Principal Component extraction method was used to form uncorrelated linear combinations of the observed variables. Initial factor solutions were found using principal component analysis. Factors with eigen values greater than 1 were extracted. The first component has maximum variance. Successive components explain progressively smaller portions of the variance and all are uncorrelated with each other. Varimax rotation with Keiser normalisation was used to control the number of factors to be extracted. Initial 12 variables collapsed into five factors, which were able to explain 60.788 per cent of the variance in the data (See Table 6)

Table 5
Factor Analysis and Total Variance Explained
(Extraction Method: Principal Component Analysis)

Component	*Total*	*% of Variance*	*Cumulative %*	*Rotation Sums of Squared Total % of Variance %*		*Loadings Cumulative*
1.	2.571	21.423	21.423	2.360	19.667	19.667
2.	1.461	12.173	33.596	1.450	12.087	31.754
3.	1.189	9.911	43.507	1.360	11.329	43.083
4.	1.063	8.857	52.364	1.081	9.008	52.091
5.	1.011	8.425	60.788	1.044	8.698	**60.788**
6.	.946	7.882	68.670			
7.	.844	7.031	75.701			
8.	.728	6.065	81.765			
9.	.635	5.292	87.057			
10.	.593	4.942	91.999			
11.	.554	4.616	96.615			
12.	.406	3.385	100.000			

Rotation Method: Varimax with Kaiser Normalization.

Figure 2: Scree Plot

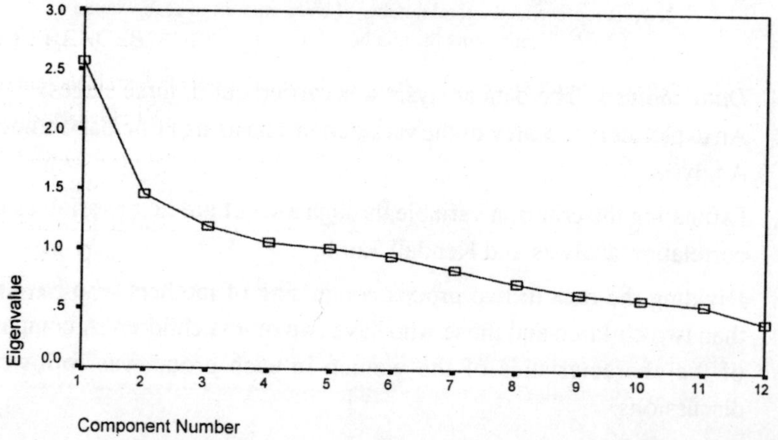

The Scree plot shows a distinct break between the steep slope of the large factors and the gradual trailing of the rest (See figure 2). Variance can be associated with only five 5 main factors.

Table 6
Component Score Coefficient Matrix

Component		*1*	*2*	*3*	*4*	*5*
V1	Religion	-.057	.547	-.115	.140	.027
V2	Caste	.041	.521	.097	-.136	-.020
V3	Water Source	-.020	.057	.010	.769	.110
V4	House Type	-.210	-.148	-.013	.214	.124
V5	Present Age	.172	-.004	.687	-.036	.095
V6.	Women's years of schooling	.379	-.051	.115	-.012	.032
V7	Husband's years of Schooling	.339	-.129	.025	.079	.040
V8	Age at Cohabitation	.292	.105	-.007	.062	.125
V9	Total No. of children ever born	-.061	.175	.288	.138	-.116
V10	Total Infant Deaths	-.033	-.102	.443	.000	-.028
V11	Still Birth or abortion	.075	-.038	.021	.085	.868
V12	Use of Family Planning methods	-.170	.169	-.036	-.466	.377

Factor Analysis (Table 6): The first factor loads heavily on couple's education, which seems to have a positive relationship with age at marriage (stable cohabitation). Religion and caste contribute to some variation, (12%) which is revealed in the second factor. Third factor loading is on present age of women, which is positively related to number of children born. This points to the fact that longer reproductive span is responsible for more number of children to some extent. Infant deaths are positively related to total number of children born, which supports the evidences, provided in the review of literature, that uncertainty of child survival forces couples to have more children. The fourth factor loads on source of water and type of house, which are indicators of economic status or poverty levels. There is an indication of a negative relationship with accessibility or adoption of family Planning methods. It could be concluded that there is very little acceptance for family planning at the grass root levels. The fifth factor supports the fact that numbers of stillbirths or abortions as well as family planning reduce the number of children born, because these variables show a – ve correlation (Table 6). The new combination of variables that represent independent factors can be summarized as:

1. Education
2. Social factors (Religion and Caste)
3. Demographic Factors (Age of women and Infant Deaths)
4. Infrastructural facilities (Type of house, water source and accessibility to health care)

5. Fertility reducing factors (Stillbirths / abortions and Family Planning).

It is concluded that 60.788 per cent of the total variation in the data can be captured by five of these independent factors in the order of importance.

Correlations: The basic measurement required for any fertility data is the knowledge of birth rate. Hence, the dependent variable selected for this study (Y), is the total number of children born to each respondent. For the selection of independent variables (X's), which have an impact on Y, the correlation pattern was studied (Annexure 2). Since the data for most of the variables was categorical, the measure of association between the variables had to be decided. A nonparametric measure of association for categorical variables that take ties into account was found to be Kendall's tau b. The sign of the coefficient indicates the direction of the relationship, and its absolute value indicates the strength, with larger absolute values indicating stronger relationships. The correlation coefficients are presented in Table 7

Table 7
Correlations: Kendall's tau b Dependent Variable Y

Independent Variables	*N*	*Correlation Coefficient*	*Sig. (2-tailed)*
X1 Religion	737	.084**	.009
X2 Caste	737	-.019	.534
X3 Water Source	737	.066 *	.032
X 4 House Type	737	.046	.134
X 5 Present Age	751	.143**	.000
X 6 Women's years of schooling	751	-.177**	.000
X 7. Husband's years of Schooling	751	-.151**	.000
X 8 Age at Cohabitation	751	-.146**	.000
X 9 Infant deaths	751	-.141**	.000
X10 No. of Still Birth or abortion	751	.002	.947
X11 Are you using any (Family Planning) devices	751	.023	.469

** Correlation is significant at the .01 level (2-tailed)
* Correlation is significant at the .05 level (2-tailed).

Variables, which have significant correlation with the dependent variable Y (Total No. of children born) were identified as, X1, Religion, X3, Water Source, X 5, Present age (Age in June 1999), X 6, Women's years of schooling, X 7 Husband's years of Schooling, X 8 Age at Cohabitation, X 9 Total infant deaths (See Table 7).

In the third stage of the analysis, the total number of respondents was divided in two groups. Group I is the group of women who had less than two children, and group II comprises of women who have more than two children. A comparison of the socio- demographic characteristics of the two groups is presented in Table 8.

GROUP 1-Total Number of Women with 2 or less children is 157=20.90 %
GROUP 2-Total Number of Women with more than 2 Children is 594=79.09 %

Table 8
Comparative Study of Group 1 and Group II

GROUP 1	*Infant deaths*	*Religion*	*Water source*	*Present age (Years)*	*Women's years of schooling*	*Husband's years of schooling*	*Age at Marriage (Years)*
Group 1							
Mean	1.1324			34.8750	4.2426	7.7574	17.3015
Median		Hindu	Hand Pump	34.0000			17.0000
Mode		Hindu	Hand Pump	29.00			15.00
Std. Deviation	1.8250			4.5255	6.0437	5.9784	3.5367
Group 2							
Mean	1.1077			35.8064	2.4579	6.3384	16.1330
Median		Hindu	Hand Pump	35.0000			16.0000
Mode		Hindu	Hand Pump	34.00			15.00
Std. Deviation	1.3676			4.4184	4.2707	5.3411	2.4648

A comparison of the characteristics revealed that the infrastructural facilities like type of house, water source are similar for both the groups which is expected, because the data is from rural areas of the two districts where people are mostly below poverty line and there is no piped water supply in the villages. Hindus dominate the population in this cross section of society. The data does not provide any significant difference in the number of infant deaths, which speaks for overall lack of health services across the villages (See Table 8).

However, a difference in the educational levels of the two groups provides results of vital importance. In the first group the average number of years women had gone to school was 4.2. In the second group the average school education was only 2.4 years for women. Similarly the husband's school education in the first group was for eight years on the average and in the second group it was found to be around six years. The link between higher education and lower fertility is well supported by the present research.

As far as age at marriage is concerned there is a gap of one year, (median) 17 years, for first group and (median) 16 years for the second group. This reveals the extent of social progress, because, those who married one year later in life generally had two or less children. There is also a gap of one year in the present age (at the time of survey) of women, which implies that longer reproductive span is responsible for more number of children to some extent. The average age structure of 34 years in the first age group and 35 years for second age group also points to the fact that child bearing time duration is completed earlier by women who have two or less than two children than those who have more than two children. In the first group the fertility is controlled in spite of the long marriage duration (34 years–17 years), because the women have two or less children in seventeen years, which speaks for effective family planning this group.

CONCLUSION AND POLICY RECOMMENDATIONS

Empirical evidence provided by this research supports all the theories, which are outlined in the review of literature. However, the variation captured is only 60.788 per cent (Factor Analysis. The correlations or the strength of relationship between the predictor variables and the dependent variables (Y, total number of children born) are too weak to be fully convincing. The explanation needs to go beyond these variables to theories that are less explored so far and more conclusive.

As seen from Table 8, there are 21% women who have been able to control their fertility in spite of all the existing infrastructure and low education levels. It is evident that some women do find their own solutions to control the number children born to them. In depth interviews with the respondents have revealed that most of the newly married brides are too scared and inexperienced to make their own fertility decisions. The out dated ideas of the mother in laws and other important family members are thrust on them. The role of autonomy of women in fertility decisions is a subject, which is less explored though it has been included in the NFHS 1998-99 (page 47) in terms of decision-making at household levels.

The present research suggests that women can control their own fertility by traditional methods, by family planning or simply by abstaining, if only they could decide for themselves. According to NFHS 1998-99, per cent of women involved in decisions about their own health is only 44.8% in U.P. The mean number of children ever born to women in U.P. (age 40-49) is 5.76 where, most of the women go through unwanted pregnancies after 2 children. Development programmes that include infrastructural facilities, education and hospitals etc. are long-term goals and require a lot of political will. The need of the hour is to find quick and effective solutions for the masses who are mostly illiterate. In some households the male members and older women in the houses did not even allow the young daughter in laws to come out and talk to the interviewers. Purdah system was being followed in most of the households, which is an indicator of subversive status being given to the daughter in laws. To bring such women to join the development process psychological support at local levels is required which is only possible by N.G.O s. in the absence of family support. Women in low economic strata are not aware that reproduction is their human right. They also do not know that they are not to be compelled to go through unwanted pregnancies. If this simple fact is advertised and they are provided with legal support through NGO's, so that they are empowered to make their own fertility decisions, the population goals could be attainable. It is possible through media and T.V. interventions. Hence, it can be concluded from this research that "Autonomy" could become the main fertility-reducing factor in future; especially for developing countries where family planning has not been so effective and socio economic condition continues to be at low levels.

Acknowledgements

The researchers are grateful to Dr. R.K. Singh, Head of Department (Statistics) Lucknow University, for his valuable guidance. Thanks are also due to Dr. Prdeep Misra for providing the data from Population Research Centre, Lucknow. Related literature was made available by Dr. Prakasam from International Population Research Center, (Mumbai) and Ms. Mandy Brown, John Hopkins Research Institute, U.S.A. Without their help, this research would not have been possible.

REFERENCES

Arora, Y. L., P. Singh (1989), Analysis of Fertility Decline in India Through Weighted Path Analysis, *Demograpgy India,* Jan-Dec; 18(1-2): 21-26.

Atella, V. and F.C Rosati (2000), Uncertainty About Children's Survival and Fertility: A Test Using Indian Microdata, *Journal of Population Economics,* 13 (2): 263-278.

Bhargava, P.K. and P.C. Saxena (1987), Determinants of Status of Women and Fertility in Greater Bombay, *The Indian journal of Social Work,* 48 (1).

Bose Ashish, (2001), *India's Billion Plus People,* B.R. Publications: New Delhi.

Chaudhary, R.H. (1978), Female Status and Fertility Behaviour in a Metropolitan Urban Area of Bangladesh, *Population Studies,* July, 32 (2).

Chaudhry, M. (1990), Role of the Social and Cultural Factors in Human Fertility in India, *Population and Environment,* Winter, 12 (2): 117-137.

Das, N.P., Gita Patel, Urvi Shah and Nitin Bhatt (1991), Evaluation of Mini Family Welfare Centre Scheme, (Saheli Project), Mimeographed, Population Research Centre, M.S. University, Baroda.

Das, N. and D. Pandey (1985), Fertility Differentials by Religion in India: An Analysis of 1971 Census Fertility Data, *Canadian Studies in Population,* 12(2): 119-135.

Das, N.P., M. M. Gandotra, Divya Pandey, Urvi Shah (1998), *Status of Women and Reproductive Behaviour among Urban Indian Women: Understanding the Linkages,* A Project Report of a Collaborative Study, W.H.O., Geneva; Population Research Centre, M.S. University, Baroda and Research Centre for Women's Studies, S.N.D.T., Mumbai.

Dreze, J. and M. Murthi, (2001), Fertility, Education, and Development: Evidence from India, *Population and Development Review,* 27(1): 33-63.

Easterlin R.A., and E.M. Crimmins (1985), *The Fertility Revolution: A Supply-Demand Analysis,* University of Chicago Press, p. 209.

Freed, S.A. and R.S. Freed (1985), Fertility, Sterilization, and Population Growth in Shanti Nagar, India: A Longitudinal Ethnographic Approach, *Anthropological Papers of the American Museum of Natural History,* 60 (Pt 3): 229-286.

Gandotra, M.M., N.P. Das, Urvi Shah, Saroj Bhavsar (1996), Women's Development and Family Planning Project at Bhivandi-An Evaluation, A Project Report, Population Research Centre, Baroda.

Gulati, S.C. (1988), *Fertility in India: An Econometric Analysis of a Metropolis,* Sage Publications: New Delhi.

Gurumurthy, G. (1985), The Study of Mortality in Relation to Fertility among Yanadis-A Tribal Community of Andhra, *Population Council, Center for Policy Studies* Working Paper No. 114.

Jain A.K. (1981), The Effect of Female Education on Fertility, A Simple Explanation, *Demography,* 18.

Jain A.K. (1984), Development Impacts on Fertility in India [tables] Presented at the Annual Meeting of the Population Association of America, Minneapolis, Minnesota, May 3-5.

Jain, A.K. (1985), The Impact of Development and Population Policies on Fertility in India, *Studies in Family Planning,* 16(4): 181-198.

Jain A.K. and J. Stoeckel (1986), Methodological Issues in Assessing the Fertility Impact of Development Projects, In: *Fertility in Asia: Assessing the Impact of Development Projects*, edited by John Stoeckel and Anrudh K. Jain, St. Martin's Press: New York, 35-70.

Jain, A.K. and M. Nag (1985), Female Primary Education and Fertility Reduction in India, Population Council, Center for Policy Studies Working Paper No. 114, New York.

Jeffery P., R. Jeffery and A. Lyon (1989), *Labour Pains and Labour Power: Women and Childbearing in India* Zed Books: London.

Jejeebhoy, S.J. (1980), *Women's Status and Fertility in Tamil Nadu,* Family Planning Association of India, New Delhi.

Jolly, S.K.G. (1976), Impact of Inter-Spouse Communication on Family Planning Adoption, *Journal of Family Welfare*, 23.

Koenig, M.A. and G.H.C. Foo (1985), Patriarchy and High Fertility in Rural North India, Paper prepared for the Rockefeller Foundation's Workshop on *Women's Status and Fertility*, June, 25–29, New York.

Khan, M.E. and R. Singh (1987), Woman and Her Role in the Family Decision Making Process: A Case of Uttar Pradesh , *Journal of family Welfare, June* 33 (4).

Kurup, R.S. (1986), *Demographic Transition in Kerala, In: Fertility and Mortality: Theory Methodology and Empirical Issues*, ed. K. Mahadevan with P.J. Reddy and D.A. Naidu, Sage Publications: New Delhi.

Mukherji, S. (1997), Poverty and Fertility in Uttar Pradesh: Strategies for Poverty Alleviation and Better Health Services, In: *Population and Development in Uttar Pradesh*, edited by Kamla Gupta and Arvind Pandey, B.R. Publishing Corporation New Delhi : 389-401.

Mukhopadhyay, S. and R. Savithri, (2001), Poverty, Gender and Reproductive Choice: An Analysis of Linkages, Manohar: New Delhi.

Nag, M. (1983), Impact of Social and Economic Development on Mortality: Comparative Study on Kerala and West Bengal, *Economic and Political Weekly*, 18(19, 20 and 21).

Pandey, A., D. Sahu and S. Rajaram (1997), Determinants of Child Spacing in Uttar Pradesh: Findings from the National Family Health Survey, In: *Population and Development in Uttar Pradesh*, edited by Kamla Gupta and Arvind Pandey, B.R. Publishing Corporation, New Delhi : 235-246.

Parthasarthy N.R. (1976), Status of Women and Family Planning in India, *TheJjournal of Family Welfare*, 22 (4).

Pathak, K.B. and P.K. Murty (1985), Socio-Economic Determinants of Fertility and Mortality Decline in India, *Demography India,* 14(1): 17-33.

Pathak, K.B. (1997), Population Dynamics of Uttar Pradesh, In: *Population and Development in Uttar Pradesh* ed. Kamla Gupta and Arvind Pandey, B.R. Publishing Corporation: New Delhi.

Prasad R. (1994), Fertility in Bihar: An Appraisal of Situation, In: *Population and Development in Bihar,* ed. U.P. Sinha and R. K. Sinha, B.R. Publishing Corporation: New Delhi.

Raju, S.S. (1987), Husband Wife Communication and Contraceptive Behaviour', *The Journal of Family Welfare,* 33 (4).

Rajan, S.I., Sudha, S., Mohanachandran, P. (2000), Fertility Decline and Worsening Gender Bias in India: Is Kerala No Longer an Exception?, *Development and Change,* 31(5): 1085-1092.

Rajan S.I. (1987), Educating the Rural Masses, *Population Education News,* 14 (5): 2-4.

Rajaram, S. (2000), Fertility and Child Mortality in India: A District Level Analysis Using Simultaneous Equations, *Demography India,* 29(1): 53-74.

Rao, K.V. and Balakrishna, N. (1988), Some Correlates of Fertility, *Health and population: Perspective and Issues,* 11 (2): 64-82.

Seal, K.C. (1988), Economic Development and Population Growth, In: *Socio-Economic Development and Population Control*, eds. M.E. Khan and D.V.N. Sarma, Manohar: New Delhi.

Sharma, A.K. (1994), Muslim Fertility in Urban U.P.: A Qualitative Study, *Demography India,* 23(1-2): 41-49.

Sharma, A.K. (1995), Teenage Reproductive Behaviour in Rural Uttar Pradesh: Some Observations and Analysis, In: Workshop on Strategy Formulation to Reduce Teenage Fertility in Uttar Pradesh, India. Final Report. Organized by UP Academy of Administration, Nainital, 15-16 May, ed. R.B. Gupta, Suresh Joshi, Nainital.

Sharma, A.K. (1997), Social Development and Prospects of Demographic Transition in Uttar Pradesh, In: *Population and Development in Uttar Pradesh*, eds. Kamla Gupta and Arvind Pandey, B.R. Publishing Corporation: New Delhi.

Sharma, H.L. (1992), A Study of Relationship Between Migration and Fertility, *Demography India*, 21 (1): 51-57.

Srinivasan K., (1986), Modernisation and Fertility Change: A Review of Theoretical Developments, In: *Fertility and Mortality: Theory, Methodology and Empirical Issues*, eds. K. Mahadevan with P.J. Reddy and D.A. Naidu, Sage Publications: New Delhi.

Srivastava, J.N., D. N. Saxena, and Mathur, R.S. (1991), Demographic Evaluation of a Development Programme in Rural Uttar Pradesh, A Field Study sponsored by the Rockefeller Foundation, U.S.A. Yash Publishers: Lucknow.

Srivastava, J.N. (1990), Inter-District and Inter-Regional Variations in Incidence of Child Marriage Among Females and its Inter-Censal Changes in Uttar Pradesh, *Journal of Family Welfare,* 36(4): 20- 31.

Sunder, R. (1990), The Status of Women and Family Planning Acceptance - Some Field Results, *Journal of Family Welfare,* 36 (2).

Vaidyanathan, K.E. (1989), Status of Women and Family Planning: The Indian Case, *Asia Pacific Population Journal, ESCAPE:* Bangkok, 4 (2): 3-18.

Ware, H. (1981), *Women Demography and Development*, The Australian National University: Canberra.

Warren, C. Robinson and John, F. Kantner (1988), The Impact of Development Programmes on Fertility: A Framework of Analysis, Asia *Pacific Population Journal*, 13 (3).

ANNEXURE 1
Summary of the Variables

Variables	*Code*	*Frequency*	*Valid %*	*Variables*	*Code*	*Frequency*	*Valid %*
X1 Religion				X3. Water Source			
Hindu	1	584	79.2	Tap	1	119	16.1
Muslim	2	149	20.2	Hand Pump	2	498	67.6
Jain	6	4	0.5	Well	3	86	11.7
X2 Caste				Other	6	34	4.6
SC	1	244	33.1	X 4 House Type			
ST	2	13	1.8	Pucca	1	314	42.6
OBC	3	223	30.3	Semi-Pucca	2	204	27.7
Other caste	4	227	30.8	Kachcha	3	219	29.7
Do not know	9	30	4.1	X 7. Husband's Years of Schooling			
X 5 Present Age					0	233	31
In Years	29	58	7.7		1	2	0.3
	30	55	7.3		2	8	1.1
	31	56	7.5		3	14	1.9
	32	57	7.6		4	17	2.3
	33	56	7.5		5	75	10
	34	66	8.8		6	23	3.1
	35	49	6.5		7	17	2.3
	36	47	6.3		8	78	10.4
	37	40	5.3		9	25	3.3
	38	49	6.5		10	85	11.3
	39	40	5.3		11	1	0.1

Contd....

Variables	*Code*	*Fre-quency*	*Valid %*	*Variables*	*Code*	*Fre-quency*	*Valid %*
	40	40	5.3		12	65	8.7
	41	40	5.3		13	1	0.1
	42	37	4.9		14	18	2.4
	43	30	4		15	19	2.5
	44	31	4.1		16	70	9.3
X 6. Women's Years of schooling				X11 Any Still Birtl or Abortion			
	0	521	69.4	Yes	1	238	31.7
	1	1	0.1	No	2	513	68.3
	2	1	0.1	X12 (Family Planning) ever used			
	3	6	0.8	Never used	0	45	6
	4	10	1.3	Currently using	1	297	39.5
	5	53	7.1	Not using	2	409	54.5
	6	8	1.1	X 9 Total No. of children			
	7	4	0.5	In Numbers	0	21	2.8
	8	45	6		1	32	4.3
	9	8	1.1		2	104	13.8
	10	27	3.6		3	159	21.2
	11	1	0.1		4	162	21.6
	12	21	2.8		5	121	16.1
	14	9	1.2		6	82	10.9
	15	14	1.9		7	40	5.3
	16	22	2.9		8	17	2.3
X 8. Age at Cohabitation					9	10	1.3
	13	98	13		10	2	0.3
	14	101	13.4		12	1	0.1
	15	149	19.8	X10 Total Infant Deaths			
	16	101	13.4	In Numbers	0	349	46.5
	17	77	10.3		1	189	25.2
	18	100	13.3		2	113	15
	19	31	4.1		3	54	7.2
	20	51	6.8		4	20	2.7
	21	9	1.2		5	13	1.7
	22	13	1.7		6	6	0.8
	23	4	0.5		7	3	0.4
	24	7	0.9		8	2	0.3
	25	2	0.3		9	1	0.1
	26	4	0.5		11	1	0.1
	27	1	0.1	Total		751	

ANNEXURE 2

Correlation Matrix	*V1*	*V2*	*V3*	*V4*	*V5*	*V6*	*V7*	*V8*	*V9*	*V10*	*V11*	*V12*
V1 Religion	1.000											
V2 Caste	.337	1.000										
V3 Water Source	.146	-.010	1.000									
V4 House Type	-.094	-.156	.131	1.000								
V5 Present Age	-.025	.048	.011	.068	1.000							
V6 Women's years of schooling	-.005	.110	-.089	-.360	-.011	1.000						
V7 Husband's years of Schooling	-.035	.015	-.059	-.308	-.071	.540	1.000					
V8 Age at Cohabitation	.140	.161	-.042	-.270	-.050	.478	.343	1.000				
V9 Total No. of children ever born	.066	.080	.073	.041	.187	-.220	-.186	-.188	1.000			
V10 Total Infant Deaths	-.093	-.018	.041	.192	.255	-.213	-.274	-.270	.079	1.000		
V11 Still Birth or abortion	-.025	-.037	.013	.045	-.028	-.038	.002	.015	.003	-.009	1.000	
V12 Use of Family Planning methods	.024	.010	-.027	.116	.090	-.186	-.207	-.173	.009	.060	.063	1.000

INDEX